Lecture Notes in Computer Science 12001

More information about this series at http://www.springer.com/series/7410

Emil Simion · Rémi Géraud-Stewart (Eds.)

Innovative Security Solutions for Information Technology and Communications

12th International Conference, SecITC 2019
Bucharest, Romania, November 14–15, 2019
Revised Selected Papers

Springer

Editors
Emil Simion
Polytechnic University of Bucharest
Bucharest, Romania

Rémi Géraud-Stewart
École Normale Supérieure
Paris, France

ISSN 0302-9743 ISSN 1611-3349 (electronic)
Lecture Notes in Computer Science
ISBN 978-3-030-41024-7 ISBN 978-3-030-41025-4 (eBook)
https://doi.org/10.1007/978-3-030-41025-4

LNCS Sublibrary: SL4 – Security and Cryptology

This Springer imprint is published by the registered company Springer Nature Switzerland AG
The registered company address is: Gewerbestrasse 11, 6330 Cham, Switzerland

Foreword

This volume is devoted to the proceedings of SecITC 2019, the 12th International Conference on Innovative Security Solutions for Information Technology and Communications, held in Bucharest, Romania, during November 14–15. This session was organized under the auspices of the following academic and research institutions: Academy of Economic Studies (Faculty of Economic Cybernetics, Statistics and Informatics, Department of Economic Informatics and Cybernetics), Military Technical Academy (Faculty of Information Systems and Cyber Security), Politehnica University of Bucharest (Faculty of Applied Sciences-Department of Mathematical Methods and Models), and Advanced Technologies Institute Bucharest.

The conference covered the following topics:

- Security Technologies for ICT
- Cryptographic Algorithms and Protocols
- Information Security Management

These topics include a broad range of recent and ongoing work in areas featuring: cryptology, algorithmic tools for security and cryptography, authentication biometry and watermarking, blockchain and security aspects of alternative currencies, attacks and countermeasures, cloud and web security, distributed and embedded systems security, hardware security, Internet of Things (IoT) security, mobile security, network security, privacy and anonymity, reverse-engineering and code obfuscation, surveillance and anti-surveillance, trust management, etc.

These topics involve considerable interaction between various theoretical disciplines and real application requirements in the era of communicating data systems and future critical inter-networking applications.

SecITC 2019 had 4 invited keynotes and 14 accepted papers, out of 34 submissions evaluated by a highly exigent Program Committee of almost 40 experts from 15 countries, which were presented to more than 100 attendees at the conference.

For 12 years SecITC has been bringing together computer security researchers, cryptographers, industry representatives, and PhD students serving as an exchange forum between established and young researchers as well as industry players. For the last five years, the conference proceedings have been published in Springer's *Lecture Notes in Computer Science* series, and articles published in SecITC are indexed in most science databases.

We thank all authors for having submitted high-quality papers.

The sponsors of SecITC 2019 are also gratefully acknowledged for their support, allowing for an excellent organization of the conference. I would like to particularly thank the Program Committee and its chairs as well as the conference's local

Organizing Committee for their efforts in setting up and managing this successful edition of SecITC together with two associated workshops.

November 2019   Traian Muntean

Preface

This volume contains the papers presented at the 12th International Conference on Information Technology and Communications Security (SecITC 2019) held during November 14–15, 2019, in Bucharest.

There were 35 submissions. Each submission was reviewed by at least two, and on the average 3.9, Program Committee (PC) members. The committee decided to accept 14 papers, and the program also included 6 invited talks.

The SecITC conference started 11 years ago, in a small room from the Bucharest University of Economics Studies, which hosted the first edition of the conference. At that time the auditorium was made up of 15 students and professors. Since then the conference has grown, accomplished by the excellent quality of PC members, a yearly improvement of conference paper quality, and valuable keynote speakers at each edition. Our conference is now indexed in several data bases and probably the most notable one is in the cryptologic events calendar from IACR and Springer accepted for publication as a post-proceedings (since 2015). The conference covers topics from cryptographic algorithms, to digital forensic, and cybersecurity. If this conference was created today, probably a better name for the conference would have been CyberSecurity Conference, but for now SecITC is already a brand and it is not yet the time for rebranding.

The conference was organized by the master programs for information security within the Military Technical Academy and the Bucharest University of Economic Studies, as well as by the Institute for Advanced Technologies. At the same time, partners of the conference included the master's program Coding Theory and Information Storage within the Faculty of Applied Sciences, Polytechnic University of Bucharest and the Center for Research and Training in Innovative Techniques of Applied Mathematics in Engineering from the same university.

Thank you to all PC members for reviewing the papers, Organizing and Technical Committees for their efforts, and sponsors for their support.

A special word of gratitude to invited keynote speakers Traian Muntean, Marc Joye, Peter Roenne, Valentina Banciu, and Natacha Laniado who came to support and improve the quality of SecITC 2019.

November 2019

Emil Simion
Rémi Géraud-Stewart

Organization

Program Committee

Ludovic Apvrille	Télécom ParisTech, France
Lasse Berntzen	University of South-Eastern Norway, Norway
Ion Bica	Military Technical Academy, Romania
Catalin Boja	Bucharest Academy of Economic Studies, Romania
Guillaume Bouffard	Cybersecurity Agency of France (ANSSI), France
Christophe Clavier	Université de Limoges, France
Paolo D'Arco	University di Salerno, Italy
Eric Diehl	Sony Pictures, USA
Pooya Farshim	ENS, France
Eric Freyssinet	LORIA, France
Rémi Géraud-Stewart	ENS, France
Helena Handschuh	Independent, USA
Shoichi Hirose	University of Fukui, Japan
Miroslaw Kutylowski	Wroclaw University of Science and Technology, Poland
Jean-Francois Lalande	CentraleSupélec, France
Jean-Louis Lanet	Inria-RBA, France
Giovanni Livraga	University of Milan, Italy
Diana Maimut	Advanced Technologies Institute, University of Bucharest, Romania, and ENS, France
Florian Mendel	TU Graz, Austria
Kazuhiko Minematsu	NEC Corporation, Japan
David Naccache	ENS, France
Svetla Nikova	KU Leuven, iMinds, Belgium
Ruxandra F. Olimid	Norwegian University of Science and Technology, Poland, and University of Bucharest, Romania
Victor Patriciu	Military Technical Academy, Romania
Reza Reyhanitabar	Elektrobit Automotive GmbH, Germany
P. Y. A. Ryan	University of Luxembourg, Luxembourg
Emil Simion	Politehnica University of Bucharest, Romania
Daniel Smith-Tone	NIST, USA
Agusti Solanas	Smart Health Research Group, Rovira i Virgili University, Spain
Pantelimon Stanica	Naval Postgraduate School, USA
Rainer Steinwandt	Florida Atlantic University, USA
Willy Susilo	University of Wollongong, Australia
Ferucio Laurentiu Tiplea	Alexandru Ioan Cuza University of Iaşi, Romania
Mihai Togan	Military Technical Academy, Romania

Cristian Toma	Bucharest University of Economic Studies, Romania
Damien Vergnaud	Université Pierre et Marie Curie, Institut Universitaire de France, France
Qianhong Wu	Beihang University, China
Sule Yildirim-Yayilgan	Norwegian University of Science and Technology, Norway
Lei Zhang	East China Normal University, China

Additional Reviewers

Barcau, Mugurel
Blaskiewicz, Przemyslaw
Catak, Ferhat Ozgur
Catuogno, Luigi
Connolly, Aisling
Elezaj, Ogerta
Feng, Hanen
Gao, Qiyuan
Graux, Pierre
Hristea, Cristian
Kang, Burong
Karmakar, Angshuman
Li, Na
Marghescu, Andrei
Meng, Xinyu

Mogage, Andrei-Catalin
Pasol, Vicentiu
Perez Del Pozo, Angel L.
Petrovic, Slobodan
Pura, Mihai Lica
Reynaud, Léo
Slowik, Marcin
Słowik, Marta
Teseleanu, George
Velciu, Alexandru
Wang, Lulu
Wilke, Pierre
Wu, Lei
Zhang, Yan

Short Papers

Trends and Future Challenges for Security and Privacy of Autonomous and Mobile Critical Communicating Systems

Traian Muntean

Honorary professor of Computer Science, Aix-Marseille University, France
muntean.traian@gmail.com

Abstract. Autonomy and mobility are keystones technologies for the design of future highly adaptive communicating systems. Deploying existing data security solutions to the autonomous mobile communicating systems is not straightforward because of systems heterogeneity, highly evolving and possibly unprotected or hostile environments, and required large scale deployment. Communication protocols used, data security, availability, and quality are other critical areas fore such applications. Developing comprehensive security and privacy solutions for autonomous mobile objects requires revisiting almost all security techniques we may think of. Encryption protocols need to be engineered so to be efficient and scalable for deployment on large-scale systems and devices with limited computational resources. In addition, scalability of such protocols is critical, in that in many safety-sensitive applications encryption operations must be kept very efficient. Addressing such problems may require new techniques based, for instance, on embedded security mechanisms and integrated and proved co-design in the deployment of secure applications.

In this talk, after outlining key challenges in data security and privacy for mobility, we summarize research directions for securing data in various fine-grained devices (IoT, mobile terrestrial and space vehicles, etc.), including efficient and scalable encryption protocols, software protection techniques for small devices, efficient generic embedded security protocols, provable security protocols, etc.

As a case study of critical communicating systems, IoT has become in the last few years a very widely emerging spread concept for secure applications. The reason for this is mainly the need to control most of the surrounding objects and have access to data required for environment understanding in real time.

As stated for instance in [12–14], IoT systems are often highly dynamic, and continuously change because of their mobility or networking reconfigurability. They are also highly heterogeneous with respect to communication medium and protocols, platforms, and devices involved. IoT systems, or parts of them, may be physically unprotected and attacks, against which there are established defense techniques in the context of conventional information systems and mobile environments, are thus much more difficult to protect against in the IoT.

The OWASP Internet of Things Project [10, 11] has identified the most common IoT vulnerabilities and has shown that many such vulnerabilities arise because of the lack of adoption of well-known security techniques, such as encryption, authentication, access control,... Therefore, developing comprehensive security and privacy solutions for IoT requires revisiting almost all security techniques we may think of.

The EU's CyPhERS (Cyber-physical European Roadmap and Strategy; www.cyphers.eu/project) project has been investigating the relationship between cyber-physical and IoT systems. Some techniques developed for cyber-physical systems can be the source of good practices for software engineering for the IoT. However, some factors, such as mobility, reconfigurability and safety/reliability, still require attention. In this sense, IoT systems tend to be extremely dynamic, where different devices can be added or removed in a specific IoT ecosystem during runtime while maintaining reliable communications. Finally privacy introduces new challenges, including how to prevent personal devices from acquiring and/or transmitting information depending on the user location and other personal context information, and how to allow users to understand risks and advantages in sharing their personal data!

Software running on such devices must be secured by design. Major challenges here arise from the fact that many devices are based on dedicated heterogeneous processors which have differences in the instruction sets with respect to support for security. Such diversity has an implication for example on the techniques for protecting software from attacks (e.g. run-time software to be secured from memory vulnerabilities). Cybersecurity techniques using provable effects are therefore required.

Availability requires among other things to make sure that relevant data is not lost. Addressing such requirement entails designing protocols for data acquisition and transmission that have data loss minimization as a key security goal.

Finally privacy and anonymity introduce new challenges, including how to prevent personal devices from acquiring and/or transmitting information depending on the user location and other context information, and how to allow users to understand risks and advantages in sharing unprotected personal data. This remain also an ethical, deontological, critical requirement for the existing mass-products (f-booking!, googling!, binging!...) and their possible disastrous effects on society and fundamental human rights.

References

1. Atighehchi, K., Muntean, T.: Generic parallel cryptography for hashing schemes. In: ISPDC (2013). https://www.academia.edu/13606746
2. Atighehchi, K., Muntean, T., Rolland, R.: A cryptographic key transfer protocol for secure communicating systems. https://www.academia.edu/8312871
3. Muntean, T., et al.: An Efficient Parallel Algorithm for SKEIN Hash Functions, Best paper award PDCS'10 & IACR-ePrint. http://eprint.iacr.org/2010/432
4. Risteruci, G., Mugwaneza, L., Muntean, T.: A new secure virtual connector approach for end-to-end communication within large heterogeneous distributed systems. In: ISPDC2015 https://www.academia.edu/11845209
5. Atighehchi, K., Muntean, T.: Towards fully incremental cryptographic schemes. In: ASIACCS (2013). https://www.academia.edu/9498639
6. Ene, C., Muntean, T.: A broadcast-based calculus for communicating systems. In: FMPPTA (2001). https://www.academia.edu/8062016

7. Faurax, O., Muntean, T.: Security analysis and fault injection experiment on AES. In: 2ème Conférence sur la Sécurité des Architectures Réseaux et des Systèmes d'Information, (SAR-SSI 2007)
8. NIST: Cyber-physical Systems. www.nist.gov/cps
9. Gupta, J., Nayyar, A., Gupta, P.: Security and privacy issues in Internet of Things (IoT). Int. J. Res. Comp. Sci. **2** (2015)
10. https://www.owasp.org/index.php/OWASP_Internet_of_Things_Project
11. https://www.owasp.org/images/7/71/Internet_of_Things_Top_Ten_2014-OWASP.pdf
12. Won, J., Seo, A., Bertino, E.: Efficient key management schemes for mobile devices, CSD-Purdue Univ, Cyber2SLab, and CERIAS
13. Bertino, E.: Security and Privacy in the Internet of Things, CS Purdue University, Cyber2SLab & CERIAS
14. Shebaro, B., Oluwatimi, O., Midi, D., Bertino, E.: Identidroid: Android can finally wear its anonymous suit. Trans. Data Priv. **7**(1), 27–50 (2014)
15. Singla, A., Mudgerikar, A., Papapanagiotou, I., Yavuz, A.A.: Hardware-accelerated authentication for IoT in mission critical vehicular networks. In: IEEE Military Communications Conference (2015)
16. Baldini, G., Peirce, T., Tallachini, M.C.: Internet of Things: IoT Governance European Research Cluster on the Internet of Things (2014). http://www.internet-of-things-research.eu/pdf/IERC_Position_Paper_IoT_Governance_Privacy_
17. Whitehouse, O.: Security of Things: An implementers guide to cyber-security for IoT. NCC Group (2014). https://www.nccgroup.trust/globalassets/our-research/uk/whitepapers/2014-04-09_-_security_of_an_implementers_guide_to_cyber_security_for_internet_of_things_devices_and_beyond-2.pdf
18. Oltsik, J.: The Internet of Things: A CISCO and Network Security Perspective, ESG White Paper (2014). https://www.cisco.com/web/strategy/docs/energy/network-security-perspective.pdf
19. http://www.isaca.org/Knowledge-Center/Research/ResearchDeliverables/Pages/internet-of-things-risk-and-value-considerations.aspx
20. http://www.business.att.com/content/article/IoT-worldwide_regional_2014-2020-forecast.pdf
21. http://blog.talosintel.com/2016/02/trane-iot.html
22. http://krebsonsecurity.com/2016/02/iot-reality-smart-devices-dumb-defaults/
23. http://www.gsma.com/connectedliving/gsma-iot-security-guidelines-complete-document-set/
24. https://www.iot-now.com/news/reports/

Post-quantum Cryptography in Bitdefender

Miruna Rosca[1,2]

[1] ENS de Lyon, Laboratoire LIP (U. Lyon, CNRS, ENSL, Inria, UCBL), France
[2] Bitdefender, Romania

Abstract. Existing public-key cryptography is mainly based on the hardness of two problems: factoring and solving discrete logarithms. In the eventuality of building large scale quantum computers, these two problems become easy to solve [Sho97]. Post-quantum cryptography refers to cryptographic algorithms that are thought to be secure against attacks which can be implemented on a quantum computer. Lattices, multivariate systems of equations, codes, isogenies and hash functions provide problems which are conjectured to remain hard to solve even using a quantum computer and which can be used as security foundations for post-quantum cryptographic schemes.

At Bitdefender, we are interested in post-quantum cryptography with a focus on lattice-based solutions. One of the most well known lattice problems is the Approximate Shortest Vector Problem (ApproxSVP). Still, there are few cryptographic schemes built directly on the conjectured hardness of ApproxSVP. Instead, most of the schemes in the literature are built either on the hardness of an intermediate problem, the Learning With Errors Problem (LWE), which has been proved to be as hard as ApproxSVP ([Reg05]), or on one of its algebraic variants ([SSTX09], [LPR10], [LS15]).

In this invited talk, I will give a general overview of our recent results. In the past few years, at Bitdefender, we built advanced primitives from LWE ([LST18], [LT19]) and studied the hardness of (new) algebraic variants of LWE ([RSSS17], [RSW18], [Bol18], [BBPS19]).

References

[BBPS19] Bolboceanu, M., Brakerski, Z., Perlman, R., Sharma, D.: Order-LWE and the hardness of ring-LWE with entropic secrets. In: Galbraith, S.D., Moriai, S. (eds.) ASIACRYPT 2019. LNCS, vol. 11922, pp. 91–120. Springer, Cham (2019). https://doi.org/10.1007/978-3-030-34621-8_4

[Bol18] Bolboceanu, M.: Relating different polynomial-LWE problems. In: Lanet, J.-L., Toma, C. (eds.) SecITC 2018. LNCS, vol. 11359, pp. 492–503. Springer, Cham (2018). https://doi.org/10.1007/978-3-030-12942-2_36

[LPR10] Lyubashevsky, V., Peikert, C., Regev, O.: On ideal lattices and learning with errors over rings. In: Gilbert, H. (ed.) EUROCRYPT 2010. LNCS, vol. 6110, pp. 1–23. Springer, Heidelberg (2010). https://doi.org/10.1007/978-3-642-13190-5_1

[LS15] Langlois, A., Stehlé, D.: Worst-case to average-case reductions for module lattices. Des. Codes Crypt. **75**(3), 565–599 (2015)

[LST18]   Libert, B., Stehlé, D., Titiu, R.: Adaptively secure distributed PRFs from LWE. In: Beimel, A., Dziembowski, S. (eds.) TCC 2018. LNCS, vol. 11240, pp. 391–421. Springer, Cham (2018). https://doi.org/10.1007/978-3-030-03810-6_15

[LT19]   Libert, B., Titiu, R.: Multi-client functional encryption for linear functions in the standard model from LWE. In: Galbraith, S., Moriai, S. (eds.) ASIACRYPT 2019. LNCS, vol. 11923, pp. 520–551. Springer, Cham (2019). https://doi.org/10.1007/978-3-030-34618-8_18

[Reg05]   Regev, O.: On lattices, learning with errors, random linear codes, and cryptography. In: Proceedings of STOC, pp. 84–93 (2005)

[RSSS17] Rosca, M., Sakzad, A., Stehlé, D., Steinfeld, R.: Middle-product learning with errors. In: Katz, J., Shacham, H. (eds.) CRYPTO 2017. LNCS, vol. 10403, pp. 283–297. Springer, Cham (2017). https://doi.org/10.1007/978-3-319-63697-9_10

[RSW18]   Rosca, M., Stehlé, D., Wallet, A.: On the ring-LWE and polynomial-LWE problems. In: Nielsen, J., Rijmen, V. (eds.) EUROCRYPT 2019. LNCS, vol. 10820, pp. 146–173, Springer, Cham (2018). https://doi.org/10.1007/978-3-319-78381-9_6

[Sho97]   Shor, P.: Polynomial-time algorithms for prime factorization and discrete logarithms on a quantum computer. SIAM J. Comput. 26(5), 1484–1509 (1997)

[SSTX09] Stehlé, D., Steinfeld, R., Tanaka, K., Xagawa, K.: Efficient public key encryption based on ideal lattices. In: Matsui, M. (ed.) ASIACRYPT 2009. LNCS, vol. 5912, pp. 617–635. Springer, Heidelberg (2009). https://doi.org/10.1007/978-3-642-10366-7_36

Privacy... Please! (Extended Abstract)

Fari Assaderaghi[1] and Marc Joye[2]

[1] NXP Semiconductors, San Jose, USA
fari.assaderaghi@nxp.com
[2] OneSpan, Brussels, Belgium
marc.joye@onespan.com

Abstract. The Internet-of-Things does not only refer to a wide variety of inter-connected devices but also to the data generated by these devices. This large amount of data is an opportunity but is also a threat: for example, information collected about the physical health or behavior of the consumer can be very detailed and poses a real privacy risk. This paper discusses privacy-preserving approaches which might play a differentiating role in the success and deployment of IoT solutions.

With the growing Internet-of-Things and its billions of connected devices, one of the main challenges the industry is facing is how to make sense of the enormous amount of data generated by the IoT devices. This is where machine learning techniques come into play. The basic premise of learning from data is to uncover a process from a set of observations. In that sense, machine learning is different from traditional statistics. Although applying traditional statistical methods is very efficient at extracting information from a huge amount of information it needs a built-in model. Machine learning, on the other hand, can dynamically adapt to a certain task given the data and the desired goal. Hence, it learns the important impact factors of the model from the data itself. Machine learning enables the development of a multitude of new applications: regression, classification, recommender systems, clustering, personal assistants, monitoring systems, and more [1, 6].

The EU General Data Protection Regulation (GDPR) [9] that took effect in all EU countries in May 2018, aims at giving users control over their data. Companies need to comply to a set of rules, including the requirements of (i) obtaining the clear consent of users for processing their personal data; (ii) offering means to users for accessing, rectifying and erasing their personal data. Likewise, in the US, California has passed the California Consumer Privacy Act (CCPA) [8] that will take effect in January 2020. It grants users the right to know what personal information a business has collected and with whom it is shared. It also provides more control by granting users the right to opt-out to have their personal data sold or made available to third parties.

The combination of increasing public awareness of privacy threats and the ongoing implementation of compliance rules are creating momentum in the development of privacy technologies. This is the right time for IoT companies to properly address privacy issues in the design of their products and solutions. Two different approaches are available: differential privacy and data encryption.

Differential privacy As famously exemplified by the Netflix competition [10], it is well known that anonymizing a dataset is insufficient to conceal the users' identity. Differential privacy [3] is a technique that guarantees that the distribution of the system's output is insensitive to any individual's record, preventing the inference of any single user's data from the output. But this comes at a price. Differential privacy works by incorporating noise to the data. More noise injected in the data implies better privacy guarantees but also less precision in the system's output. Differential privacy is therefore essentially a trade-off between privacy and accuracy.

Working over encrypted data Data encryption is an alternative way to enable privacy. However, one limitation and fundamental property of traditional encryption schemes is that data first needs to be decrypted prior to being processed. The privacy control therefore lies in the hands of the recipient of the encrypted data. A fundamentally different approach is to rely on (fully) homomorphic encryption [5]. This allows the recipient to directly operate over encrypted data.

Other useful cryptographic tools to work on encrypted data include functional encryption [2], garbled circuits [7] and secure multi-party computation techniques [4].

We note that most known practical implementations for machine learning over encrypted data require two non-colluding entities (this is known as the two-server model). It is also important to stress to that, although significant progresses have been made, working over encrypted data remains a topic of intense development in the research community. Known techniques in general involve heavy computing resources and do not offer a one-solution-fits-all breakthrough solution. Only certain use-cases can be shown to be practical. The current situation can be compared to the 1980's, when at the start of the era of public-key cryptography the algorithms were also too slow for general purposes. New advances made public-key cryptography one of the foundational building blocks in modern computer security and the same is expected for these privacy-preserving techniques.

References

1. Abu-Mostafa, Y.S., Magdon-Ismail, M., Lin, H.T.: Learning From Data: A Short Course. AMLbook.com (2012). http://amlbook.com
2. Boneh, D., Sahai, A., Waters, B.: Functional encryption: definitions and challenges. In: Ishai, Y. (ed.) TCC 2011. LNCS, vol. 6597, pp. 253–273. Springer, Heidelberg (2011). https://doi.org/10.1007/978-3-642-19571-6_16
3. Dwork, C., McSherry, F., Nissim, K., Smith, A.: Calibrating noise to sensitivity in private data analysis. In: Halevi, S., Rabin, T. (eds.) TCC 2006. LNCS, vol. 3876, pp. 265–284. Springer, Heidelberg (2006). https://doi.org/10.1007/11681878_14
4. Evans, D., Kolesnikov, V., Rosulek, M.: A Pragmatic Introduction to Secure Multi-Party Computation. Now Publishers (2019). https://doi.org/10.1561/3300000019
5. Gentry, C.: Fully homomorphic encryption using ideal lattices. In: Mitzenmacher, M. (ed.) 41st Annual ACM Symposium on Theory of Computing (STOC), pp. 169–178. ACM (2009). https://doi.org/10.1145/1536414.1536440

6. Hastie, T., Tibshirani, R., Friedman, J.: The Elements of Statistical Learning, 2nd edn. Springer Series in Statistics. Springer, New York, (2009). https://doi.org/10.1007/978-0-387-84858-7
7. Yao, A.C.C.: How to generate and exchange secrets. In: 27th Annual Symposium on Foundations of Computer Science (FOCS), pp. 162–167. IEEE (1986). https://doi.org/10.1109/SFCS.1986.25
8. The California consumer privacy act of 2018. https://leginfo.legislature.ca.gov/faces/billTextClient.xhtml?bill_id=201720180AB375
9. The EU general data protection regulation (GDPR). https://eur-lex.europa.eu/legal-content/EN/TXT/HTML/?uri=CELEX:32016R0679&from=EN
10. The Netflix prize. https://www.netflixprize.com

Contents

Authenticated Key Distribution: When the Coupon Collector is Your Enemy

Marc Beunardeau[1], Fatima-Ezzahra El Orche[2,4], Diana Maimuţ[3(✉)],
David Naccache[2,4], Peter B. Rønne[4], and Peter Y. A. Ryan[4]

[1] Nomadic Labs, Paris, France
marc.beunardeau@nomadic-labs.com
[2] ENS, CNRS, PSL Research University, Paris, France
{fatimaezzahra.elorche,david.naccache}@ens.fr
[3] Advanced Technologies Institute, Bucharest, Romania
diana.maimut@dcti.ro
[4] SnT, FSTC, University of Luxembourg, Esch-sur-Alzette, Luxembourg
{fatima.elorche,peter.roenne,peter.ryan}@uni.lu

Abstract. We introduce new authenticated key exchange protocols which on one hand do not resort to standard public key setups with corresponding assumptions of computationally hard problems, but on the other hand are more efficient than distributing symmetric keys among the participants. To this end, we rely on a trusted central authority distributing key material which size is independent of the total number of users, and which allows the users to obtain shared secret keys. We analyze the security of our construction taking into account various attack models. Importantly, only symmetric primitives are needed in the protocol making it an alternative to quantum-safe key exchange protocols which rely on hardness assumptions.

Keywords: Symmetric cryptography · Key exchange protocol · Authentication · Provable security · Post-quantum cryptography

1 Introduction

Symmetric key primitives are the preferred choice for fast encryption applications. On the other hand, public-key cryptography is widely adopted for ensuring (authenticated) key exchange functionalities. Many currently deployed applications take the best of both worlds and use key encapsulation mechanisms where keys are exchanged using public key protocols and are subsequently used as input to efficient symmetric primitives.

This paper proposes an intermediate construction. We introduce a cryptographic protocol approaching some of the functionalities of public-key encryption while relying entirely on *symmetric* primitives. Before we proceed, we stress that our models are very different from those of classical public key cryptography, and so are their security and efficiency metrics. However, it appears that *in many*

© Springer Nature Switzerland AG 2020
E. Simion and R. Géraud-Stewart (Eds.): SecITC 2019, LNCS 12001, pp. 1–20, 2020.
https://doi.org/10.1007/978-3-030-41025-4_1

practical settings, the proposed constructions can successfully replace classical public-key encryption.

Given that our techniques do not resort to number-theoretic cryptography, the construction is naturally resistant against attacks from quantum computers.

Prior Work. Key exchange protocols play an important role in protecting end-to-end communications. Initially introduced in [5], the previously mentioned notion revolutionized cryptology. These protocols allow two parties to generate securely a common secret key, which will be used later for different cryptographic purposes such as sending authenticated and encrypted messages. Another closely related flavour of such protocols may be defined as authenticated key exchange protocols. The first basic understandings of this category of schemes were presented in [2,4]. Considering that such constructions could lead to practical and efficient protocols, the authors focused on formalizing the security notions related to entity authentication and key distribution.

Note that contrary to the Needham-Schroeder symmetric key protocol [8], the central authority is only active in the enrolment phase in our protocol, not during the actual key establishment.

ID-based secret key cryptography was first presented in [7]. While the paradigm similarity between this paper and [7] is obvious (*i.e.* mimicking public key cryptography with symmetric primitives), the technical details are of different nature and granularity. We stress that even though [7] introduces applications like a challenge-response authentication protocol and an ID-based MAC algorithm, it does not provide an in-depth security analysis. Moreover, our key exchange protocol can use more than one key per user which, as we will see, allows us to non-trivially optimise security.

Structure of the Paper. We present our authenticated key distribution protocol in Sect. 2, describing particular and general cases. In Sect. 3 we discuss the adversarial advantage in various attack scenarios, computing probabilities and expectation values. We provide a security analysis of our scheme in Sect. 4. Finally, we conclude in Sect. 5 and discuss future work ideas. We introduce notations, definitions and security assumptions used throughout the paper in Appendix A. Appendix B presents the proofs of the lemmas from Sect. 3. Appendix C tackles parameter choices and discusses the efficiency of our protocol.

2   The Protocol

Participants. Let n be the number of the users in the system (n can be very large, for instance a billion), each having a unique identity ID_i, where $i \in [1, n]$. In the following, ID_i will designate both the (alphanumeric) name of user i and the user itself as a physical entity. The proposed protocol relies on a central authority (CA) which creates r key tables (called "racks") each containing ℓ random κ-bit keys. CA distributes to each user u distinct keys chosen randomly from each rack, *i.e.* $u \times r$ keys per user. CA also provides each user with supplementary key material that will be described later.

Building-Blocks. Let $f(k, m)$ be a MAC function, where k is the key and m is the message. The protocol also uses a hash function h.

For the sake of clarity, we describe the protocol in steps. We first consider and analyze a basic one-rack case ($r = 1$) and one key per user ($u = 1$).

2.1 Basic Scheme ($r = 1$ and $u = 1$)

Key Generation. CA generates one rack of ℓ secret keys: $\{k_1, \ldots, k_\ell\}$.

User Enrolment. CA then gives to ID_i:

- A secret key $k_{I(i)}$, where $I(i) \in_R [1, \ell]$;
- A table T_i containing the ℓ derived keys: $T_i = \{t_{i,1}, \ldots, t_{i,\ell}\}$ where $t_{i,j} = f(k_{I(j)}, \mathrm{ID}_i)$.

Remark 1. Two users, ID_i and ID_j may get (and in reality are actually expected to get) from CA the same $k_{I(i)} = k_{I(j)}$. Note however that $T_i \neq T_j$ as key tables are derived from identities (Fig. 1).

Key Exchange. Assume now that users i and j want to establish a secure communication channel (Fig. 2). They proceed as follows:

1. Exchange $I(i)$ and $I(j)$;
2. User j generates $t_{i,I(j)} = f(k_{I(j)}, \mathrm{ID}_i)$;
3. User i generates $t_{j,I(i)} = f(k_{I(i)}, \mathrm{ID}_j)$;
4. Both users generate the common key $\mathsf{sk} = h(t_{i,I(j)}, t_{j,I(i)})$ and use sk to protect their communications.

Remark 2. To avoid ambiguities in the order of parameters of h, we assume that $\mathrm{ID}_i > \mathrm{ID}_j$.

Informally, here is the intuition behind this protocol: We first note that to gain the capacity to listen into all communications, an opponent would need to set his hands on all the k_is. This assumes compromising at least ℓ *chosen* devices.

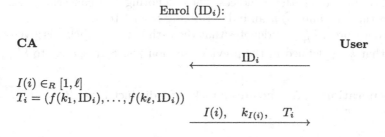

Fig. 1. User enrolment

ID_i knows $I(i), k_{I(i)}$ and T_i ID_j knows $I(j), k_{I(j)}$ and T_j

$$\xrightarrow{\quad I(i) \quad}$$

$$\xleftarrow{\quad I(j) \quad}$$

$t_{j,I(i)} \leftarrow f(k_{I(i)}, ID_j)$ $t_{i,I(j)} \leftarrow f(k_{I(j)}, ID_i)$

Read $t_{i,I(j)} = f(k_{I(j)}, ID_i)$ from T_i Read $t_{j,I(i)} = f(k_{I(i)}, ID_j)$ from T_j

sk $\leftarrow h(t_{i,I(j)}, t_{j,I(i)})$ **sk** $\leftarrow h(t_{i,I(j)}, t_{j,I(i)})$

Fig. 2. Key exchange

Indeed, if at least $t_{i,I(j)}$ or $t_{j,I(i)}$ is unknown, sk is still safe. Evidently, this is not as satisfactory as classical public-key cryptography. Nonetheless, the achieved protection is still useful in many practical scenarios where choosing the target ID_i is impossible[1]. The number of compromised devices required for learning all the ℓ keys with a given probability p is known as the coupon collector's problem (cf. *infra*).

The coupon collector's problem is a famous question introduced at graduate probability lectures. If each box of cookies contains a coupon, and there are ℓ different coupons, what is the probability that more than t boxes need to be bought to collect all ℓ coupons? An alternative statement is: Given ℓ coupons, how many coupons do you expect you need to draw with replacement before having drawn each coupon at least once? The mathematical analysis of the problem reveals that the expected number of trials needed grows as

$$\ell \log(\ell) + \gamma\ell + \frac{1}{2} + O(\frac{1}{\ell}) \text{ where } \gamma = 0.57721\ldots$$

For example, when $\ell = 50$ it takes about 225 trials on average to collect all 50 coupons. We hence see that the defender enjoys a *little advantage* over the attacker. Can this advantage be amplified by engaging in several draws? This is the goal of the next sections.

2.2 General Case: $r \geq 1$ and $u \geq 1$

In this scenario each user gets u distinct keys per rack. The function I is hence generalized by taking three indices: ① i denoting the concerned user, ② ρ denoting the rack and ③ μ an index running from 1 to u.

In other words, $k^{\rho}_{I(i,\mu,\rho)}$ denotes that the μ-th key from rack ρ is given to user i. Note that $k_{I(i)}$ defined in the previous section just corresponds to $k^1_{I(i,1,1)}$.

Key Generation: CA generates r racks of ℓ distinct keys: $R_{\rho} = \{k^{\rho}_1, \ldots, k^{\rho}_{\ell}\}$, where $\rho \in [1, r]$.

---

[1] For instance, if the ID_is are identity cards, the attacker needs to collect and compromise enough cards hoping to complete his collection of k_is.

User Enrolment. CA gives to user ID_i:

- $u \times r$ secret keys:

$$
\begin{array}{cccc}
k^1_{I(i,1,1)} & k^2_{I(i,1,2)} & \cdots & k^r_{I(i,1,r)} \\
k^1_{I(i,2,1)} & k^2_{I(i,2,2)} & \cdots & k^r_{I(i,2,r)} \\
\vdots & \vdots & & \vdots \\
k^1_{I(i,u,1)} & k^2_{I(i,u,2)} & & k^r_{I(i,u,r)}
\end{array}
$$

where $\forall \rho \in [1, r], \forall \mu \in [1, u], I(i, \mu, \rho) \in_R [1, \ell]$
- A table T_i of $\ell \times r$ derived keys:

$$
T_i = \begin{bmatrix}
t^1_{i,1} & t^2_{i,1} & \cdots & t^r_{i,1} \\
t^1_{i,2} & t^2_{i,2} & \cdots & t^r_{i,2} \\
\vdots & \vdots & & \vdots \\
t^1_{i,\ell} & t^2_{i,\ell} & \cdots & t^r_{i,\ell}
\end{bmatrix}
$$

where $\forall \rho \in [1, r], \forall j \in [1, \ell], t^\rho_{i,j} = f(k^\rho_j, ID_i)$

Remark 3. Note that the user can derive the table values for his own keys and in principle does not need to store these. In this way memory can be saved at the cost of computational efficiency during key derivation.

Key Exchange: Assume now that users ID_i and ID_j want to establish a secure communication channel. To generate their common secret key they do the following:

1. Exchange their indices $I(i, \mu, \rho)$ and $I(j, \mu, \rho)$ for $\mu \in [1, u], \rho \in [1, r]$;
2. User ID_i:
   - generates $u \times r$ derived keys:

$$
t^\rho_{j,I(i,\mu,\rho)} = f(k^\rho_{I(i,\mu,\rho)}, ID_j), \quad \forall \mu \in [1, u], \quad \forall \rho \in [1, r]
$$

   - reads $u \times r$ derived keys from his table T_i:

$$
t^\rho_{i,I(j,\mu,\rho)} = f(k^\rho_{I(j,\mu,\rho)}, ID_i), \quad \forall \mu \in [1, u], \quad \forall \rho \in [1, r]
$$

3. User ID_j:
   - generates $u \times r$ derived keys:

$$
t^\rho_{i,I(j,\mu,\rho)} = f(k^\rho_{I(j,\mu,\rho)}, ID_i) \quad \forall \mu \in [1, u], \quad \forall \rho \in [1, r]
$$

   - reads $u \times r$ derived keys from his table T_j:

$$
t^\rho_{j,I(i,\mu,\rho)} = f(k^\rho_{I(i,\mu,\rho)}, ID_j) \quad \forall \mu \in [1, u], \quad \forall \rho \in [1, r]
$$

4. Both users ID_i and ID_j generate a common session keys by using h to combine the $2u \times r$ derived keys (Fig. 3):

$$\mathsf{sk} = h\big(t^\rho_{i,I(j,1,1)}, \ldots, t^\rho_{i,I(j,u,r)}, t^\rho_{j,I(i,1,1)}, \ldots, t^\rho_{j,I(i,u,r)}\big).$$

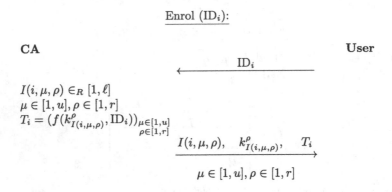

$$\text{Enrol } (\mathrm{ID}_i):$$

CA **User**

$$\overset{\mathrm{ID}_i}{\longleftarrow}$$

$I(i, \mu, \rho) \in_R [1, \ell]$
$\mu \in [1, u], \rho \in [1, r]$
$T_i = (f(k^\rho_{I(i,\mu,\rho)}, \mathrm{ID}_i))_{\substack{\mu \in [1,u] \\ \rho \in [1,r]}}$

$$\overset{I(i, \mu, \rho), \quad k^\rho_{I(i,\mu,\rho)}, \quad T_i}{\longrightarrow}$$

$$\mu \in [1, u], \rho \in [1, r]$$

Fig. 3. User enrolment for the General Case: $u > 1$ and $r > 1$

Remark 4. For clarity, in Fig. 4, we reduce the writing of sk and we write $\mathsf{sk} = h\big(t^\rho_{i,I(j,1,1)}, \ldots, t^\rho_{j,I(i,u,r)}\big)$ instead of writing: $\mathsf{sk} = h\big(t^\rho_{i,I(j,1,1)}, \ldots, t^\rho_{i,I(j,u,r)}, t^\rho_{j,I(i,1,1)}, \ldots, t^\rho_{j,I(i,u,r)}\big).$

ID_i knows: ID_j knows:
$I(i, \mu, \rho), k^\rho_{I(i,\mu,\rho)}$ and T_i $I(j, \mu, \rho), k^\rho_{I(j,\mu,\rho)}$ and T_j
$\mu \in [1, u], \rho \in [1, r]$ $\mu \in [1, u], \rho \in [1, r]$

$$\overset{I(i,\mu,\rho)}{\underset{\mu \in [1,u], \rho \in [1,r]}{\longrightarrow}}$$

$$\overset{I(j,\mu,\rho)}{\underset{\mu \in [1,u], \rho \in [1,r]}{\longleftarrow}}$$

$t_{j,I(i,\mu,\rho)} \leftarrow f(k^\rho_{I(i,\mu,\rho)}, \mathrm{ID}_j)$ $t_{i,I(j,\mu,\rho)} \leftarrow f(k^\rho_{I(j,\mu,\rho)}, \mathrm{ID}_i)$
$\mu \in [1, u], \rho \in [1, r]$ $\mu \in [1, u], \rho \in [1, r]$
Read $t_{i,I(j,\mu,\rho)} = f(k^\rho_{I(j,\mu,\rho)}, \mathrm{ID}_i)$ Read $t_{j,I(i,\mu,\rho)} = f(k^\rho_{I(i,\mu,\rho)}, \mathrm{ID}_j)$
from T_i s.t. $\mu \in [1, u], \rho \in [1, r]$ from T_j s.t. $\mu \in [1, u], \rho \in [1, r]$
$\mathsf{sk} \leftarrow h\big(t^\rho_{i,I(j,1,1)}, \ldots, t^\rho_{j,I(i,u,r)}\big)$ $\mathsf{sk} \leftarrow h\big(t^\rho_{i,I(j,1,1)}, \ldots, t^\rho_{j,I(i,u,r)}\big)$

Fig. 4. Key exchange for the general case: $u > 1$ and $r > 1$

3 Adversarial Advantage

In this section we consider an adversary who has corrupted n_c out of the n users and obtained their key material, *e.g.* by physically attacking the IoT devices containing those keys. The corruption can happen before the user gets the key material or afterwards, however, the main assumption of this section is that the indices of the stolen keys are random. We will consider targeted attacks in Sect. 4.3.

We compute probabilities and expectation values for the adversarial advantage as well as the optimal selection of security parameters in Sect. C for fixed memory.

3.1 Expected Number of Collected Keys

Let N_{key} be the number of distinct keys that the adversary gets on average after corrupting n_c users. Since two users may share keys, we get less than $u \times n_c$ keys per rack. The precise calculation is given below:

Lemma 1 (The expected number of keys obtained by the adversary).
Assuming that the adversary corrupts n_c users, the expected total number of distinct keys that the adversary holds is

$$N_{\text{key}} = \ell \times \left(1 - \left(1 - \frac{u}{\ell}\right)^{n_c}\right).$$

The proof of Lemma 1 can be found in Appendix B.

3.2 Probabilities

We now consider the probability for the adversary to get a non-corrupted user's keys, *i.e.* that the targeted user's key indices are all among the key indices obtained from the corrupted users.

In the following, we denote by K a random variable taking values from 1 to ℓ. We let $K_a^i, i \in [1, n]$ and $a \in [1, u]$ be the random variables defining the key indices for user i (considering only one rack, *i.e.* $r = 1$). Note that these variables are not independent since we assume each user gets u distinct indices. Let $\mathcal{C}$ be the set of corrupted users and $\mathcal{H}$ the set of non-corrupted ones. We define $n_c := \text{card}(\mathcal{C})$ and $n_h := \text{card}(\mathcal{H})$, *i.e.* $n = n_c + n_h$.

Lemma 2 (The probability to get a targeted user's key). *With the above notations, for some given $i_0 \in \mathcal{H}$, the attacker's probability to get a specified user's keys is denoted by $P_1 = P(\forall \mu \in [1, u] : K_\mu^{i_0} \in \{K_b^j\}_{j \in \mathcal{C}, b \in [1, u]})$, and the value is:*

$$P_1 = 1 - \sum_{i=1}^{u} (-1)^{i+1} \binom{u}{i} \prod_{j=1}^{i} a_j^{n_c}, \quad \text{with} \quad a_j = \frac{\ell - j + 1 - u}{\ell - j + 1}.$$

For $r > 1$ we have

$$P_1 = \left(1 - \sum_{i=1}^{u} (-1)^{i+1} \binom{u}{i} \prod_{j=1}^{i} a_j^{n_c} \right)^r .$$

The proof of Lemma 2 is given in Appendix B. Based on the probability P_1 we can also find the probability of getting an arbitrary user's keys:

Lemma 3 (The probability to get an arbitrary user's key). *The probability of an attacker to get an arbitrary user's key, $P_2 = P(\exists i \in \mathcal{H} \ \forall a = 1, \ldots, u : K_a^i \in \{K_b^j\}_{j \in \mathcal{C}, b \in [1,u]})$, is given by (also valid for $r > 1$):*

$$P_2 = 1 - (1 - P_1)^{n - n_c}.$$

The proof can be found in Appendix B.

Finally, we can consider the probability of getting the keys for two users which will allow the attacker to break a session keys.

Lemma 4 (The probability of getting two targeted users' keys). *The probability of the attacker to get two targeted users' keys and hence to break a shared key between them is $P_3 = (P_1)^2$.*

Lemma 5 (The probability to break an arbitrary session key). *The probability of an attacker to get two arbitrary users' keys and thus to break a session key is $P_4 = (P_2)^2$.*

Both Lemmas 4 and 5 follow directly from the independence of the allocated keys between users.

3.3   Optimising u

Given the probability P_1 defined in the last subsection, we can pose the question whether there exists a non-trivial optimal value for u. To be specific, we fix a risk-level p and determine the maximal number of users that can be corrupted, n_c, while satisfying $P_1 \leq p$. The optimal value of u is the one allowing the largest amount of corrupted users, n_c. The problem is non-trivial since increasing u makes it harder for the adversary to get all keys from the targeted user, but on the other hand the attacker gets more keys per corrupted user. Figure 5 shows that we indeed have non-trivial optimal values.

To make a precise analysis, we consider a large ℓ limit. A power expansion of P_1 gives

$$P_1 = \left(1 - \left(1 - \frac{u}{\ell} \right)^{n_c} \right)^u + \mathcal{O}\left(\frac{1}{\ell^2} \right).$$

We then observe that $n_c \sim \log(1 - P_1^{\frac{1}{u}}) / \log(1 - \frac{u}{\ell})$, *i.e.*

$$n_c/\ell \sim -u^{-1} \cdot \log(1 - P_1^{\frac{1}{u}}) ,$$

see Fig. 5. We can use this expression to find the optimal value for u, forcing the adversary to corrupt as many possible users. By differentiation, we find the optimal u-value as

$$u = -\frac{\log P_1}{\log 2}.$$

To be able to have a risk level $P_1 = 2^{-m}$, the optimal u-value is $u = m$ and the adversary needs to corrupt approximately

$$n_c \sim -\ell \frac{\log^2 2}{\log P_1} = \ell \frac{\log 2}{m}$$

users. If we naively used $u = 1$, the attacker needs to corrupt

$$n_c \sim -\ell \log(1 - P_1) \sim \ell P_1 = \ell 2^{-m}$$

users to breach the risk level, where in the last approximation we assumed P_1 small. That is choosing the optimal u gives a significant advantage, actually logarithmic in the desired risk level. However, the flip side of increasing u is that the adversary has to corrupt fewer users to fully break the system.

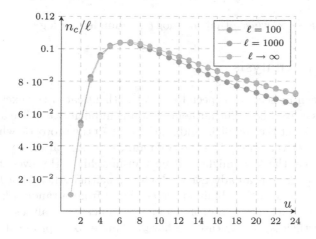

Fig. 5. The relationship between u and n_c/ℓ for different values of ℓ ($\ell = 100, 1000, \infty$) and $P_1 = 1\%$; $\ell = 100, 1000$ have been found directly via the formula for P_1 in Lemma 2, whereas the curve for infinite ℓ plotted using the approximation above.

3.4   Expected Number of Corrupted Users to Full Breach – the Coupon Collector Problem

We now consider the expected number of users that the adversary needs to corrupt to reveal all keys, *i.e.* fully break the system. As discussed above, for

$u = r = 1$ we have the classical coupon collector problem, where $n_c = \ell H(\ell)$ with H being the harmonic series.

For $u > 1, r = 1$ we clearly have $n_c \leq \ell H(\ell)/u$. The problem was analysed in the context of data package scheduling in [9] and the solution is $n_c = \sum_{i=0}^{\ell-1} \left(1 - \binom{i}{u}/\binom{\ell}{u}\right)^{-1}$. For large ℓ the speed-up is actually close to u: $\lim_{\ell \to \infty} \frac{n_c}{\ell \log \ell} = \frac{1}{u}$.

In the case $u = 1, r > 1$ we have only obtained an upper bound on n_c. Let n_i^ρ be the number of users needed to corrupt to get the ith new key in rack ρ. Each n_i^r is geometrically distributed with probability parameter $p_i = (\ell - i + 1)/\ell$. Denoting the expectation value by E, for $r = 1$ we have that $n_c = E(\sum_{i=1}^{\ell} n_i) = \sum_{i=1}^{\ell} E(n_i) = \sum_{i=1}^{\ell} 1/p_i = \ell H(\ell)$ as mentioned above. For general r we have $n_c = E\left(\max_{\rho \in [1,r]}(\sum_{i=1}^{\ell} n_i^\rho)\right)$. However, even for the average of the maximum of geometric random variables, we do not have an explicit large r limit [6], only a closed sum formula. Nevertheless, using the bound for the maximum of geometric variables given in [6], we can get the following rough upper bound

$$n_c \leq \sum_{i=1}^{\ell} E\left(\max_{\rho \in [1,r]}(n_i^\rho)\right) \leq \sum_{i=1}^{\ell} \left(1 - \frac{H(r)}{\log(1 - p_i)}\right) \leq \ell + \sum_{i=1}^{\ell} \frac{H(r)}{p_i} \leq \ell + H(r)\ell H(\ell)$$

Thus in limit $r \to \infty$ we see that $n_c/\ell \log \ell$ is bounded by $\log r$.

4   Security Analysis

The protocol can be seen as a special form of authenticated key exchange where the outcome is a fixed key. The authentication is implicit, *i.e.* Alice and Bob will hold the same key at the end of an undisturbed run of the protocol, whereas for an adversary who actively interrupts the communication and alters the transmitted indices, can make the keys might end up non-matching. However, the security guarantee we can give is an adversary who holds neither Alice's nor Bob's secret keys cannot distinguish the obtained secret key(s) from a random key.

Standard key-exchange protocols require complicated analyses of concurrent sessions. Nevertheless, in our case we have a simple fixed protocol and we can split our analysis into three cases: ① a passive attacker only monitoring the communication, ② a man-in-the-middle attacker changing the information of the indices exchanged and, finally, ③ an active attacker trying to impersonate Alice or Bob.

Remark 5 (Explicit Authentication). To achieve a protocol with explicit authentication, an extra key-confirmation round can be added. One way to do this is by Alice sending $h_2(\mathsf{sid}, \mathsf{sk})$ and Bob sending $h_3(\mathsf{sid}, \mathsf{sk})$, where h_2 and h_3 are independent hash functions and the session identity sid contains Alice and Bob's ID and the indices exchanged. This is for one time use only, otherwise we need to include nonces in the protocol to ensure freshness.

General Assumptions. Security in general relies on an honest setup ensured by a CA without information leakage (see, however, Sect. 4.4 on how to distribute the trust in CA). We also assume that the identities ID_i are publicly known and that they uniquely identify the users.

4.1 Passive Attacker

We start our analysis with the weakest attacker model, where the attacker can only observe the communication (*i.e.* see the indices $I(i)$ and $I(j)$ exchanged between participants ID_i and ID_j). Clearly, if the adversary holds the secret keys of both participants (*i.e.* $k^\rho_{I(i,\mu,\rho)}$ and $k^\rho_{I(j,\mu,\rho)}$ for all $\rho, \mu,$), then he will be able to reconstruct their secret key. We will now show that the obtained key is indeed indistinguishable from a random key for the adversary if he doesn't have all keys.

We consider two cases. First where the combiner function h is modelled in the ROM and f is EUF-CMA-secure.

Theorem 1. *Let the combining function h be modelled in the ROM and assume that f is an EUF-CMA-secure MAC. Then, a passive attacker can not distinguish the secret key sk obtained by ID_i and ID_j from a random key with a non-negligible probability unless he has obtained all of their keys* $k^\rho_{I(i,\mu,\rho)}, k^\rho_{I(j,\mu,\rho)}$ *for all* $\mu \in [1,u], \rho \in [1,r]$.

Proof. The secret key is $\mathsf{sk} = h\big(t^\rho_{i,I(j,1,1)}, \ldots, t^\rho_{i,I(j,u,r)}, t^\rho_{j,I(i,1,1)}, \ldots, t^\rho_{j,I(i,u,r)}\big)$. In the ROM this key can only be distinguished from random if the input value has been computed. This is only possible if all the MACs are either computed or already known by the adversary. Regarding the latter, the known tabulated MACs from the corrupted users are not useful since they contain the wrong ID. Thus the adversary has to compute the MACs which, by the EUF-CMA assumption, is only possible using the corresponding keys. If even a single key is unknown by the adversary, the probability of distinguishing sk from random is, thus, bounded by the advantage in the EUF-CMA game. Note that the space of possible keys is reduced by the adversary's known keys since the keys in each rack are distinct, but for ℓ maximally polynomial in the key size, this is a negligible advantage.

Remark 6. The probability of breaking some session key for a static passive adversary or an adversary corrupting random users is given by P_4 and the probability to break an sk between two specific users is P_3.

Remark 7. Note that if the two users have the same index, the theorem still holds, but it is simply easier for the adversary to obtain all the keys.

Remark 8. The EUF-CMA assumption is too strong in the sense that we only need the adversary to be unable to compute the MAC of the identities. Even choosing f as a hash function of the ID and the key is safe in the ROM following the same proof structure.

Remark 9. It is also possible to relax the ROM and only consider h and f to be randomness extractors. This ensures that the adversary does not learn anything useful from the T_i tables of the corrupted users. Further, if just a single key is unknown, the obtained sk will still be indistiguishable from random.

4.2   Man-in-the-Middle and Authentication Attacks

We now consider an attacker who alters the sent messages, or even tries to pose as someone else to break authenticity. Note that in this case we do not have any sk-security in the Canetti-Krawczyk model since the attacked users will not end up with the same key, but a key confirmation would help.

We also note that if the adversary gets all of Alice's keys, he can pretend to be any ID_j to Alice. The adversary simply sends an index, $I(j')$, from one of the corrupted users. Note that Alice is not supposed to keep a record of indices, so Alice will probably not detect that the wrong index is being sent. The adversary can now calculate sk using that all keys are known and hence the MACs can be constructed.

Nevertheless, if the adversary is missing one of Alice's keys he cannot distinguish the key computed by Alice from random.

Theorem 2. *Let the combining function h be modelled in the ROM and assume that f is* EUF-CMA-*secure MAC. Consider a user ID_i wanting to establish a key with ID_j. Even if the adversary alters the sent indices, he cannot distinguish the secret key sk obtained by ID_i from random with a non-negligible probability unless he has obtained all of the keys $k^\rho_{I(i,\mu,\rho)}$ for all $\mu \in [1, u], \rho \in [1, r]$.*

The proof follows as before, and all remarks about relaxing the assumption given in Sect. 4.1 also hold here.

Remark 10. An active adversary can thus successfully attack a specified user with probability P_1 and some arbitrary user with probability P_2.

4.3   Adaptive Corruption

In the protocol the key indices are sent in clear. However, this is problematic in the case of adaptive attackers. If the adversary wants to target a specific user, he can then observe any key establishment to learn the index of that particular user. The adversary can then look for other users with the same index who might be easier to corrupt.

One possible countermeasure would be to use hybrid security techniques to make the indices private. Nonetheless, a more interesting approach would be to use the fact that both users entering into a key establishment already know that the resulting key will be one of ℓ different possible keys (here we take $r = u = 1$). As an example, ID_i wanting to talk to ID_j knows that the key is going to be $\mathsf{sk} = h(t_{i,I(j)}, t_{j,I(i)})$ and she can then simply compute all possibilities for $I(j) = 1, \ldots, \ell$. The two users could hash their corresponding possibilities – the correct key will yield the same hash on both sides. They could now exchange these hashes in random order, and thus determine the shared key without revealing the indices. This could be done even with logarithmic efficiency.

4.4 The Central Authority

As our proposed protocol relies on a trusted third party (TTP), for analyzing security we assume that the CA is not malicious. However, in real life applications this is not always the case. For example, due to the distributed nature of IoT devices, various dedicated authenticated key exchange protocols appeared in the literature. We are particularly interested in the results of [1] in terms of cryptographic layer separation and, more precisely, role distribution. Building on the model proposed in [1, Section 2.1] involving different roles for achieving different goals, we believe that distributing the power that a single CA normally has in a classical architecture can be useful especially in the context of our coupon-collector security-based protocol. As we introduced the idea of having r racks of keys, we may naturally distribute a rack per CA to minimize the security impact of a malicious third party. Nonetheless, other more exotic secret sharing schemes may be used to distribute the power between several CAs.

On another note, the idea presented in [7] bases its security on a TTP which *"also serves as an arbitrator when disputes arise due to a user denying certain actions"*. Besides relying on various CAs as previously mentioned, we stress that there are various methods of circumventing issues like trusting TTPs.

4.5 Post-quantum Security

The primitives used in our proposed protocol (such as MACs and hash functions) seem to be good quantum-safe candidates. The main (optimal) quantum algorithm to break these is Grover's algorithm, which only gives a quadratic speed-up.

5 Conclusion and Further Development

We presented a new authenticated key exchange protocol entirely based on symmetric primitives and analyzed its security. We also discussed parameter choices and efficiency, especially we found interesting ways of improving the security by handing out more keys per user while keeping memory usage constant.

Future Work. A natural research direction would be to formally analyze both the similarities of our proposed construction with standard public key cryptography schemes and the post-quantum nature of our key distribution protocol. For a more precise security assessment it is important to achieve better bounds for the expected number of corrupted users required to get a full breach in the case of general r, u – a problem which is an interesting coupon collector problem in its own right. It would also be interesting to understand in detail the u and r duality phenomenon seen in Appendix C when dealing with constrained memory and a large ℓ.

Another possible venue of future research is to consider hybrids of the current protocol, *e.g.* by achieving forward secrecy relying on a computational assumption.

Acknowledgements. PBR and PYAR acknowledge support from the Luxembourg National Research Fund (FNR) under the FNR CORE project Q-CoDe, and the European Union's Horizon 2020 research and innovation programme under grant agreement No. 779391 (FutureTPM), in particular Fatima-Ezzahra El Orche was supported by the Luxembourg National Research Fund through grant PRIDE15/10621687/ SPsquared.

The authors would like to thank Natacha Laniado for her useful comments.

A   Preliminaries

Notations. Throughout the paper, κ denotes a security parameter. We use the notation $x \in_R X$ when selecting a random element x from a sample space X. We denote by PPT a Probabilistic Polynomial-Time algorithm.

Random Oracles. Let RO represent the notion of a *random oracle*. Also, we denote by ROM the *random oracle model*. The widely adopted ROM was introduced in [3]. The model is characterized by either considering perfectly random functions or ROs (*i.e.* ① each new query is returned a random answer and ② if a given query is repeated it receives the same answer). Practical instantiations are usually done by means of hash functions.

Security of Message Authentication Codes. The experiment *existential unforgeability under chosen message attack* will further be denoted by EUF-CMA when referring to the security of message authentication codes (MACs). A MAC consists of three PPT algorithms $\mathsf{Setup}(1^\kappa), \mathsf{MAC}_k(m)$ and $\mathsf{Verify}_k(m, \mathrm{tag})$.

We define the experiment $\mathsf{Exp}(n)_{\mathcal{A},\mathrm{MAC}}^{\mathrm{EUF\text{-}CMA}}$ by:

1. $k \leftarrow \mathsf{Setup}(1^\kappa)$;
2. $(m, \mathrm{tag}) \leftarrow \mathcal{A}(1^\kappa)$. Let $\{m_i\}_1^q$ denote $\mathcal{A}$'s queries to MAC_k;
3. If $\mathsf{Verify}(m, \mathrm{tag}) = 1$ and $m \notin \{m_i\}_1^q$ return Valid;
4. Otherwise return $\mathsf{Invalid}$.

Definition 1 (EUF-CMA). *A MAC consisting of the three algorithms* Setup, MAC *and* Verify *is* EUF-CMA *(or simply secure) if for all PPT adversaries* $\mathcal{A}$ *there exists a negligible function* negl *such that:*

$$\Pr[\mathsf{Exp}(n)_{\mathcal{A},\mathrm{MAC}}^{\mathrm{EUF\text{-}CMA}} = 1] \leq \mathsf{negl}(n).$$

Definition 2. *A MAC is considered* (t, ε)-secure *(*EUF-CMA*) if for all t-time adversaries* $\mathcal{A}$

$$\Pr[\mathsf{Exp}(n)_{\mathcal{A},\mathrm{MAC}}^{\mathrm{EUF\text{-}CMA}} = 1] \leq \varepsilon.$$

B   Proofs from Sect. 3

B.1   Proof of Lemma 1

Proof. From the first user the adversary gets u keys. The second gives on average $u \times \left(1 - \frac{u}{\ell}\right)$ new keys since u keys are already taken. In general let N_i be the number of new keys gotten from the ith user. We then have the average number of keys with n_c corrupted users

$$N_{\text{key}}(n_c) = E(\sum_i N_i) = \sum_i E(N_i).$$

We note that we have a recursion

$$E(N_i) = u \times \left(1 - \frac{\sum_{j=1}^{i-1} E(N_j)}{\ell}\right).$$

To see this let $p(k)$ be the probability of having k different keys just before the ith corrupted users, that is $\sum_{j=1}^{i-1} E(N_j) = \sum_k k \cdot p(k)$. Given k keys the probability of getting m new keys is $\binom{u}{m} \left(\frac{l-k}{l}\right)^m \left(\frac{k}{l}\right)^{u-m}$. Thus

$$E(N_i) = \sum_{m=0}^{u} \sum_k m \binom{u}{m} \left(\frac{l-k}{l}\right)^m \left(\frac{k}{l}\right)^{u-m} p(k).$$

Using standard differentiation methods, rewriting and solving we find that $\sum_{m=0}^{u} m \binom{u}{m} \left(\frac{l-k}{l}\right)^m \left(\frac{k}{l}\right)^{u-m} = u(1 - \frac{k}{l})$, from which the relation follows.
  We can rewrite the recursion as:

$$N_{\text{key}}(n_c) = N_{\text{key}}(n_c - 1) + u \times \left(1 - \frac{N_{\text{key}}(n_c - 1)}{\ell}\right),$$

with the solution

$$N_{\text{key}}(n_c) = \ell \times \left(1 - \left(1 - \frac{u}{\ell}\right)^{n_c}\right).$$

□

B.2   Proof of Lemma 2

Proof. For a given $i_0 \in \mathcal{H}$, we have:

$$
\begin{aligned}
P_1 &= P(\forall \mu \in [1, u] : K_\mu^{i_0} \in \{K_\mu^j\}_{j \in \mathcal{C}, \mu \in [1,u]}) \\
&= 1 - P(\exists \mu \in [1, u] : K_\mu^{i_0} \notin \{K_\mu^j\}_{j \in \mathcal{C}, \mu \in [1,u]}) \\
&= 1 - P(K_1^{i_0} \notin \{K_\mu^j\}_{j \in \mathcal{C}, \mu \in [1,u]} \text{ or } \cdots \text{ or } K_u^{i_0} \notin \{K_\mu^j\}_{j \in \mathcal{C}, \mu \in [1,u]}) \\
&= 1 - P_1'
\end{aligned}
$$

Let $A_i = \{K_i^{i_0} \notin \{K_\mu^j\}_{j \in \mathcal{C}, \mu \in [1,u]}\}$ for all $i \in [1, u]$.

Since $P_1' = P(A_1 \cup A_2 \cup \ldots \cup A_u) = \sum_{i=1}^{u}(-1)^{i+1}\binom{u}{i}P(A_1 \cap \ldots \cap A_i)$, it only remains to compute $P(A_1 \cap \ldots \cap A_i)$ for all $i \in [1, u]$ to complete the calculation of P_1:

$$P(A_1 \cap \ldots \cap A_i) = P(K_1^{i_0} \notin \{K_\mu^j\}_{j \in \mathcal{C}, \mu \in [1,u]} \text{ and } \ldots \text{ and } K_i^{i_0} \notin \{K_\mu^j\}_{j \in \mathcal{C}, \mu \in [1,u]})$$

$$= \prod_{j=1}^{n_c} P(K_1^{i_0} \notin \{K_\mu^j\}_{\mu \in [1,u]} \text{ and } \ldots \text{ and } K_i^{i_0} \notin \{K_\mu^j\}_{\mu \in [1,u]})$$

$$= P(K_1^{i_0} \notin \{K_\mu^1\}_{\mu \in [1,u]} \text{ and } \ldots \text{ and } K_i^{i_0} \notin \{K_\mu^1\}_{\mu \in [1,u]})^{n_c}$$

$$= \left(\frac{\ell-u}{\ell} \cdot \frac{\ell-u+1}{\ell-1} \cdots \frac{\ell-i+1-u}{\ell-i+1}\right)^{n_c}$$

$$= \prod_{j=1}^{i}\left(\frac{\ell-j+1-u}{\ell-j+1}\right)^{n_c}$$

The value for $r > 1$ follows from independence between the racks.   □

B.3   Proof of Lemma 3

Proof. We have:

$$P_2 = P(\exists i \in H, \forall \mu \in [1, u] : K_\mu^i \in \{K_b^j\}_{j \in \mathcal{C}, b \in [1,u]})$$

$$= 1 - P(\forall i \in H, \exists \mu \in [1, u] : K_\mu^i \notin \{K_b^j\}_{j \in \mathcal{C}, b \in [1,u]})$$

$$= 1 - P(\bigcap_{i \in H}\{\{K_1^i, \ldots, K_\mu^i\} \notin \{K_b^j\}_{j \in \mathcal{C}, b \in [1,u]}\})$$

$$= 1 - P(\{K_1^i, \ldots, K_\mu^i\} \notin \{K_b^j\}_{j \in \mathcal{C}, b \in [1,u]})^{n-n_c}$$

$$= 1 - (1 - P_1)^{n-n_c}$$

□

C   Parameter Choice and Efficiency Analysis

In this section, we analyze the efficiency of our protocols based on the consideration of two types of attacks: small scale attacks and full breach attacks that we define in the next sections.

The user's global memory usage is determined by r and ℓ (as $r \times \ell$). Hence it is natural to fix $r \times \ell$ to some reasonable constant (*e.g.*, 1Mb) and assume that keys are 128 bits long (as in NIST's PQ-cryptography standardization). This implies that $r \times \ell = 2^{13}$. Thus the question boils down to finding the optimal u, r (and by implication the corresponding $\ell = 2^{13}/r$) maximizing n_c (the expected number of corrupted users) for a given n.

C.1   Low-Threat Scenario

Definition 3. *A low-threat scenario happens when the adversary succeeds to break the $u \times r$ keys of a (targeted or random) user with probability greater than or equal to ϵ, which we call later the risk-level.*

This section provides numerical values for lowering the adversary's success probability below ϵ. In the following, we consider the two different values of $\epsilon = 1\%_0$, $0.01\%_0$ and we evaluate the attack probabilities found in Sect. 3.

Attack 1: Breaking the Keys of a Targeted User. This attack happens with probability P_1 which does not depend on n. Therefore, we are interested in finding the optimal u and r allowing maximizing n_c under the constraint:

$$P_1(\frac{2^{13}}{r}, u, n_c, r) \leq 1\%_0, 0.01\%_0$$

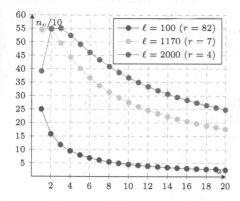

Fig. 6. u and n_c for (ℓ, r) values s.t. $\ell r = 2^{13}$ and $P_1 = 1\%_0$.

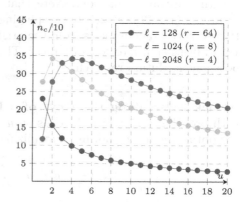

Fig. 7. u and n_c for (ℓ, r) values s.t. $\ell r = 2^{13}$ and $P_1 = 0.01\%_0$.

Repeating the analysis from Sect. 3.3 for general u, r with a fixed memory size $\ell r = 2^{13}$, we find for large ℓ that the optimal parameter choice is reached for $ur = -\frac{\log P_1}{\log 2}$. We see clearly in Figs. 6 and 7 the presence of an optimum in some curves ($r = 4, 7$ in Fig. 6 and $r = 4, 8$ in Fig. 7). This optimum corresponds to a non-trivial optimal ur and it is increasing when P_1 is decreasing ($ur \sim 10$ for $P_1 = 1\%_0$ and $ur \sim 16$ for $P_1 = 0.01\%_0$). No optimum is noticed when $r > -\frac{\log P_1}{\log 2}$. Moreover, n_c reaches the highest values when the probability risk-level is large ($n_c^{\max} \sim 569$ for $P_1 = 1\%_0$ and $n_c^{\max} \sim 341$ for $P_1 = 0.01\%_0$).

To see whether we can differentiate the the parameters satisfying $ur = -\log P_1/\log 2$, we further compute the expected number of corrupted users n_c needed for a full breach for the corresponding parameters (r, u, ℓ). We take $(r, u, \ell) = (r, -\frac{1}{r}\frac{\log P_1}{\log 2}, \frac{2^{13}}{r})$. Tables 1 and 2 show the numerical values.

Table 1. $n_c^{\max}$ to fully breach the system with $P_1 = 1\%_0$ and $\ell \times r = 2^{13}$

(r, u, ℓ)	$(1, 10, 2^{13})$	$(2, 5, 2^{12})$	$(5, 2, 1638)$	$(10, 1, 819)$
$n_c^{\max}$	7343	7885	7859	7853

Table 2. $n_c^{\max}$ to fully breach the system with $P_1 = 0.01\%_0$ and $\ell \times r = 2^{13}$

(r, u, ℓ)	$(1, 16, 2^{13})$	$(2, 8, 2^{12})$	$(4, 4, 2^{11})$	$(8, 2, 2^{10})$	$(16, 1, 2^9)$
$n_c^{\max}$	4929	4919	5065	4732	4928

We notice from Tables 1 and 2 that for all the possible optimal (r, u, ℓ) combinations, $n_c^{\max}$ always takes approximately the same value (well within the standard deviation of the Monte Carlo simulations used to obtain the tables) and only depending on the chosen P_1 level. Hence, the optimal combination (r, u, ℓ) is not *unique*. We conjecture that there is a duality between u and r with constrained memory. Note that we could try to explain this *e.g.* for $(r, u, \ell) = (1, 2, 2\ell) \mapsto (2, 1, \ell)$ by splitting a rack of size $2 \times \ell$ into two of size ℓ. However, two random keys from the original rack only have probability around $1/2$ of being split into separate racks. Thus, further analysis is needed, which we postpone for future research.

Attack 2: Breaking the Keys of a Random User. This attack happens with probability P_2 which depends on n. Therefore, we are interested in finding the optimal u and r allowing maximizing n_c for a given n under the constraint:

$$P_2(\frac{2^{13}}{r}, u, n, n_c, r) \leq 0.1\%_0, 0.01\%_0$$

Tables 3 and 4 investigate this for $n' = \log_{10}(n) = 1, \ldots, 6$. Values were obtained using a Python code.

Table 3. $(r^{\mathrm{opt}}, n_c^{\max})$ for $P_2 = 1\%_0$

	$u = 1$	$u = 2$	$u = 3$	$u = 4$	$u = 5$
$n' = 2$	$(9, 7)$	$(2, 57)$	$(1, 60)$	$(1, 67)$	$(1, 69)$
$n' = 3$	$(1, 1)$	$(3, 15)$	$(2, 46)$	$(2, 83)$	$(2, 114)$
$n' = 4$	$(1, 1)$	$(3, 5)$	$(2, 21)$	$(2, 45)$	$(2, 69)$
$n' = 5$	$(1, 1)$	$(2, 2)$	$(2, 10)$	$(2, 26)$	$(1, 43)$
$n' = 6$	$(1, 1)$	$(1, 1)$	$(2, 5)$	$(2, 15)$	$(1, 27)$

Table 4. $(r^{\mathrm{opt}}, n_c^{\max})$ for $P_2 = 0.01\%_0$

	$u = 1$	$u = 2$	$u = 3$	$u = 4$	$u = 5$
$n' = 2$	$(9, 4)$	$(6, 35)$	$(3, 66)$	$(2, 65)$	$(1, 72)$
$n' = 3$	$(1, 1)$	$(4, 9)$	$(4, 28)$	$(3, 50)$	$(2, 70)$
$n' = 4$	$(1, 1)$	$(3, 3)$	$(3, 13)$	$(3, 28)$	$(2, 43)$
$n' = 5$	$(1, 1)$	$(4, 2)$	$(4, 7)$	$(3, 16)$	$(2, 27)$
$n' = 6$	$(1, 1)$	$(1, 1)$	$(2, 3)$	$(2, 9)$	$(2, 17)$

From Tables 3 and 4 we see that the highest value of n_c is reached when $(u, r, n) = (5, 2, 1000)$ ($n_c^{\max} = 114$) for $P_2 = 1\%_0$ and when $(u, r, n) = (5, 1, 100)$ ($n_c^{\max} = 72$) for $P_2 = 0.01\%_0$.

Remark 11. We notice that the value of $n_c^{\max}$ for Attack 1 is about 5 times bigger than the one for Attack 2 ($n_c^{\max}(P_1 = 1\text{‰}) = 569 > n_c^{\max}(P_2 = 1\text{‰}) = 114$ and $n_c^{\max}(P_1 = 0.01\text{‰}) = 341 > n_c^{\max}(P_2 = 0.01\text{‰}) = 72$).

C.2   Full Breach

Definition 4. *A* full system breach *happens when the adversary succeeds to recover all the $\ell \times r$ secret keys given by the CA.*

In the following, we are interested in finding the maximal value of n_c needed to fully breach the system and the corresponding r and u for a fixed memory size $M = \ell \times r = 2^{13}$. Table 5 shows the numerical values obtained after running Monte Carlo simulation in Python and taking $N = 1000$.

Table 5. Values of $n_c^{\max}$ to fully breach the system ($\ell \times r = 2^{13}$ and $N = 1000$). In all cases $r^{\text{opt}} = 1$.

u	1	2	3	4	5	6	7
$n_c^{\max}$	40159	39270	25430	18323	15544	13283	10606
u	8	9	10	11	12	13	14
$n_c^{\max}$	10219	8413	7361	6884	6645	6326	5636

$n_c^{\max}$ is strictly decreasing when u is increasing and reaches the highest value when $u = r = 1$.

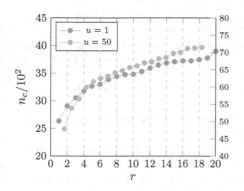

Fig. 8. r and n_c for $\ell = 400$ and $u = 1, 50$ to recover all secret keys.

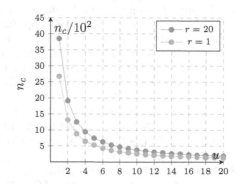

Fig. 9. u and n_c for $\ell = 400$ and $r = 1, 20$ to recover all secret keys.

C.3   Expected Number of Corrupted Users to Fully Breach the System

This section gives numerical values of n_c to fully breach the system. The following values are obtained using Monte Carlo simulation in Python and taking $N = 10000$.

Table 6. n_c values from Monte Carlo simulation and theoretical formulas

Cases	$u = r = 1$	$u > 1, r = 1$	$u = 1, r > 1$
$(n_c^{\text{simu}}, n_c^{\text{theo}})$	$(2627, 2630)$	$(47, 47)$	$(3850 < 9854)$

From Figs. 8 and Fig. 9 we see clearly that n_c is increasing when r is increasing and decreasing when u is increasing. The values obtained through this simulation are very close to the theoretical results of Sect. 3.4. We consider the main cases $(u = r = 1, u > 1, r = 1$ and $u = 1, r > 1)$ and refer the reader to Table 6 for precise values.

References

1. Avoine, G., Canard, S., Ferreira, L.: IoT-Friendly AKE: forward secrecy and session resumption meet symmetric-key cryptography. In: Sako, K., Schneider, S., Ryan, P.Y.A. (eds.) ESORICS 2019. LNCS, vol. 11736, pp. 463–483. Springer, Cham (2019). https://doi.org/10.1007/978-3-030-29962-0_22
2. Bellare, M., Rogaway, P.: Entity Authentication and Key Distribution (1993). http://cseweb.ucsd.edu/~mihir/papers/eakd.pdf, full version
3. Bellare, M., Rogaway, P.: Random oracles are practical: a paradigm for designing efficient protocols. In: CCS 1993, pp. 62–73. ACM (1993)
4. Bellare, M., Rogaway, P.: Entity authentication and key distribution. In: Stinson, D.R. (ed.) CRYPTO 1993. LNCS, vol. 773, pp. 232–249. Springer, Heidelberg (1994). https://doi.org/10.1007/3-540-48329-2_21
5. Diffie, W., Hellman, M.: New directions in cryptography. IEEE Trans. Inf. Theory **22**(6), 644–654 (1976)
6. Eisenberg, B.: On the expectation of the maximum of IID geometric random variables. Stat. Probab. Lett. **78**(2), 135–143 (2008)
7. Joye, M., Yen, S.M.: ID-based secret-key cryptography. SIGOPS Oper. Syst. Rev. **32**(4), 33–39 (1998)
8. Needham, R.M., Schroeder, M.D.: Using encryption for authentication in large networks of computers. Commun. ACM **21**(12), 993–999 (1978)
9. Sharif, M., Hassibi, B.: Delay considerations for opportunistic scheduling in broadcast fading channels. IEEE Trans. Wirel. Commun. **6**(9), 3353–3363 (2007)

The Ups and Downs of Technology in Society

Natacha Sylvie Laniado[✉]

Research Coordinator at ENS, Paris, France
natacha.laniado@ens-paris.fr

1 Introduction

New technologies in culture have generated a revolution in the way people observe, understand and relate to the world. However, Georjes J. Bruel, Head of Content at TD - TransformacaoDigital.com believes that *"cultural transformations and technological progress are disassociated issues. Both the influence of new technologies on culture and the interference of the cultural context in technological advances show how these two strands are fully immersed in each other."* But is it?

Since the beginning of times to where we are today, men/women have been coming up with inventions, and these have been developing as time goes by. In this new technological era that we find ourselves now, the pace has quadrupled, and every day something new arises, putting our minds to work at a 24/7 pace to be able to create something better, something that will bring us glory, something that will revolutionise the world. But has anyone ever stopped to think about the impact that technology has on society?

Many creators, innovators, scientists, etc., come up with new ideas every day, believing that their idea is the answer to all the problems we may be confronting due to the development of technology. It is believed that both the influence of new technologies on culture and the interference of the cultural context in technological advances show how these two strands are fully immersed in each other. But how many people consider this, when coming up with an innovative idea that they believe will revolutionise the world, how this new technology will impact on cultures, societies and people. This paper's aim is to show how the technological context has interfered in the development of human relations, mental health and also show how our culture has an influence on the formulation of these technologies.

2 How Did Technologies Change Society

In recent decades, the way people relate to each other has changed. Also, the expectations concerning the labour market, the mode of consumption and the performance of companies have undergone a revolution. Today, we realize that technologies have had (and still have) the potential to transform the cultural context and, as a consequence, to change ourselves. Technologies have had a positive impact on cultures and societies, but how many people are conscientious of the negative impact it had on our society in

© Springer Nature Switzerland AG 2020
E. Simion and R. Géraud-Stewart (Eds.): SecITC 2019, LNCS 12001, pp. 21–33, 2020.
https://doi.org/10.1007/978-3-030-41025-4_2

the last few years? How many creators, innovators, Engineers, scientists stop to think of the effects it will cause on society. How many of them stop to think of the mental impact that technology has on children and young people.

Below, we can see a list of these impacts.

3 ART

Musicians, writers, music and book shops, most cultural businesses were threatened by technological innovations. Like the big names in the music industry who felt the strong impact of the Internet and the availability of free or paid content, but without the intermediation of a record company.

Other cultural businesses were also affected. Newspapers and bookstores, for example, also felt the changes generated by the development of cheaper tools and technologies, which altered the relationship between the content producer and the reader.

With the internet, subscription-based media platforms, such as YouTube, Spotify and others, have eliminated intermediaries, enabling the artist's direct contact with his/her audience and even modifying future works, where the fan gains a voice.

The free content available on the Internet has formulated, in an entire generation, the idea that it was possible to access cultural content without having to pay for it. It was the ads that banked these productions, such as Putlocker, 123 movies, etc., and people always like a freebie, why pay to see a movie when it can be seen online in the comfort of our own home. The negative side to this would be the adverts, the bad quality and sometimes not in the expected language, and due to these negatives, the relationship with culture is currently changing once again. People are again paying for online content. Subscription-based platforms are growing, and audiences are paying to access more specific productions and also for personalized services such as Netflix, Prime, Spotify, which offer good quality and advert free programs and music that cater for each individual's taste.

The financing of cultural products is beginning to drive a digital economy that tends to change this relationship between the public and the artist once again.

4 Dating Apps

Relationship sites appeared in the 1990s, which changed the way people met. However, in 2012, with the creation of Tinder, the way to start a relationship was revolutionized once again. According to the Technology Review article, in the U.S., more than one-third of the weddings only took place through a first virtual meeting.

These dating sites and platforms have changed the way people meet. In the past, people knew their possible partners through friends, at work, in bars, in the educational process, in church or even through their families. Today, that's changed. A person can find affinities with strangers who have no ties to the people or places they frequent; this breaks a cultural barrier, as online dating is currently the second most common place for heterosexual - couples to meet. You can meet people from any background, religion, status, culture. These online dating apps have become popular to the point that we have so many it has made it very easy to meet people but, as well, suffer quite a bit of heartache, as trust has become something a bit difficult to have once these apps are so easy to access, and many are free, as Juliet Marateck, in Online dating lowers self-esteem and increases depression, studies say CNN May 29, 2018, states. We can mention as examples of free dating apps, OkCupid, Tinder, Badoo, etc., for same-sex couples, online sites and platforms such as Grinder are the first choices for dating.

However, the question here is how did this transition, from meeting through people, face to face to online impacted on society?

It had a tremendous impact, the number of people who meet their other half online to the number of people that end up in dangerous liaisons or who lose money, are duped has been higher than people who have found love. According to a recent article in the Los Angeles Times, **David Lazarus**, a Business columnist on the 25th of September 2019 "Match.com conned people into paying for subscriptions via messages the company knew were from scammers", which means that women and men who were looking for love were duped by scammers and lost their money.

According to an article in the Mail Online on the 4th of August 2017 by **Shivali Best**, Researchers from the University of Bath and mathematicians "have found that the chance of finding love on a given day is 1 in 562 if you leave down to fate". The researches from Bath have calculated the odds of finding love online. The studies based their calculation on 18 key factors, including location, desired age, physical attractiveness and relationship status.

The researchers of the University of Bath alongside **Professor Andrea Kyprianou,** a researcher in Probability Theory at the University of Bath said: "This is a fascinating piece of research which takes into account the many different variables that can contribute to the odds of finding love."

But their results showed that just 84,440 people in the UK fit the average person's romantic requirements from an adult population of over 47 million.

The odds of finding love decrease based on your criteria		
Factor	Percentage of population matching preference	Number of compatible people in the UK remaining
Suitable age range	17%	8,131,275
Mutual attraction	18%	1,467,195
Gender and sexuality	39%	576,994
Compatibility rate	40%	230,798
Relationship status	48%	110,200
Spiritual and religious views	77%	84,440

(*continued*)

(*continued*)

The odds of finding love decrease based on your criteria

Factor	Percentage of population matching preference	Number of compatible people in the UK remaining
Total percentage odds	0.18%	84,440
The mail online source		

But is love down to an equation? How do these applications impact on your life, how much money do you have to spend to find love? What is the impact for those who try and are taken advantage of? Do the creators of these apps and their company believe in what they are selling or is it another way to make easy money? Do they check the veracity of each profile? Unfortunately, these websites are not all they seem to be, and it is hard for you to trust that who the person saying he/she is are genuine. Many people as well base their choices on elements of attraction, and hence the non-attractive people do not have a chance. In the end, meeting online is a gamble, you may meet your other half, or come out of it heartbroken, scarred and traumatised.

5 Consumption

Consumption and consumer demands have been significantly modified by the intervention of new technologies in culture. Previously, purchases were made in physical stores and, most of the time, the seller's opinion was the only basis of information to make the product choice. Moreover, the variety of brands of an article was limited, and price comparison was only possible through inserts or going from establishment to establishment. Today, online sales have entirely changed the way we shop. Price research in online stores has become much easier, as well as discovering the product's specifications and functionality. Virtual sales have changed consumer demands. Currently, issues of information security, ease of payment, fast delivery, good service, if the customer contacts the company to clarify any doubts, are factors that make all the difference to the success of an establishment.

Once again, however, the relationship between consumers and businesses is changing. A few years ago, shopping meant going to the shop, facing the crowds, walking around window shopping until you found what you liked, it was a day out, and by the end of the day, you were shattered. Today, shopping has become more complex, due to online shopping the buyer checks the qualifications of the article and the store on the complaint's sites, reads the opinions of people who have already bought the product or used the service of an establishment and also seeks the advice of social media influencers to make the purchase.

Moreover, the consumer consults comparison sites and price history to ensure the purchase of the product for the lowest amount.

We can also say that our society has become lazier due to all the applications that facilitate our lives. As people become busier and busier, more applications are created to cater for our busy lives, making us in a way lose contact with reality as they can access anything and everything by a simple click on an app.

Apps such as Amazon that began as a simple application to buy books online, and now offers 24/7 service from alcohol to technology with same-day delivery, because we have become a society that cannot wait, we want it all now.

Buying things online has made the human being to become a big spender, buying items that are not always necessary, nonetheless, the amount of product advertisements that we receive on a daily basis instigates us to look and promotions makes us want to desire the product, and we end up buying things that we do not always need.

Online shopping has become almost an addiction; if you are on any social platform, you will notice how advertisements are continuously appearing on your page, emails. Once you have searched anything on Google, Amazon, eBay, Ali Baba, supermarkets, etc., immediately your information is saved, and you are bombarded with unwanted emails. This information is like brainwashing people to consume more and more, creating a great portal for easy spending and an easy way to get into debt.

However, it is not only the technological aspects that have changed our way of acting in society. Culture also has an influence on technological forms and developments, it has helped societies become a materialistic society always wanting the next best thing, as Technical revolutions have also turned out to be cultural revolutions, as witnessed by the changes wrought by inventions such as the wheel, the steam engine etc., and also by the passage from an oral culture to a written one (Combi 2006).

6 The Interference of Culture Intechnological Development

Technology expresses all the issues and problems of culture. Artificial intelligence (AI), for example, was developed from human aspects. AI, as well as robotics and other technologies, seek to solve critical issues of our time. With development, environmental and social issues are increasingly in the focus of these digital tools. Of course, AI is being seen more and more like the future of technology and people have been praising it for years, the next big thing. Many young students are immersing themselves in the study and research of AI, but once more are they questioning the pros and cons of what AI has to offer and how will this affect society, cultures and the future generations. Many articles published come to the same conclusion of the pros and cons of AI.

The Pros and Cons of AI, according to an article in vittana.org by Natalie Regoli, shows us to these pros and cons, which were also highlighted in many other articles, this list is as follows:

Pros:

1. AI gives a business more opportunities to be productive – Humans need to rest, AI does not

2. Repetitive tasks – AI can do repetitive tasks allowing people to focus on other tasks, that need human comprehension.
3. It improves life – People can control their heating, music, doorbell, etc., from their phone.
4. New opportunities to explore – AI can put together pictures and show researchers what a city would have looked like; it helps us to find jobs.
5. Fewer errors with AI – the chances of a mistake happening with AI is unlikely.
6. AI can work in risky situations - you can send it to the ocean floor, to unknown planets, not putting human life at risk, or when doing repetitive jobs where employees have been known to get hurt.
7. AI in medicine – enables better x-ray and MRI machines, CT scanners, 4D ultrasound scanners, improving diagnosis, creates artificial limbs, enable deaf people to hear and those who are blind to see.
8. 3d learning – It helps schools' access smart boards, project the human body where students do not need to imagine what it would look like but actually can see it.

Cons:

1. It can be a dangerous technology – Concerning weapons, spying, elections, wars, terrorism, more and more weapons are being developed, and if they fall into the wrong hands the result can be fatal.
2. Risk of overtaking humanity – it is still early days and AI for now has straightforward tasks, but as it develops in the near future it is expected to take care of more intuitive and crucial processes
3. AI struggles to learn on its own - It does not have the capability of being proactive – It cannot analyse situations to create proactive responses.
4. AI applications are not creative – modern AI cannot recognise creativity on its own, it is programmed, and it sticks to that.
5. AI doesn't understand complexity, emotions, humans – It a machine, as some human beings sometimes have difficulties reading people because their brains are wired differently, AI is a machine, hence no emotions or social skills. You can see that in Google translate vs Deepl.com
6. Job loss causing economic difficulties and generating more poverty – The more machines take over human jobs, more people will be unemployed and relying on the State, causing controversy and affecting their mental health, increasing alcohol and drug intake, suicide rates and theft.
7. Expensive to be implemented – although in the long term it will become cheaper for companies to use it in the short term it can be very expensive for some businesses as it requires a significant amount of investments.
8. AI can impact on society – As time goes by society and cultures are changing radically. Many people have begun to have robots in their homes, and some people are even using them as physical partners and marrying them. In 2017 the engineer Zheng Jiajia had a wedding ceremony with a robot he created in the form of a young woman.

Concerning communication with digital devices, the machine imitates human relationships. To this end, social robots use both technical and linguistic issues to communicate.

Jason Borenstein and Ronald C Arkin, Robots, Ethics and Intimacy, in their paper: The need for scientific research says that " Many types of robots are in the process of being developed, but the discussion here is largely focused on "human-like" robots designed to serve as companions for people, and at least some of these robots may eventually have intimate relationship with a human being".

It is worth mentioning that forming a vision about the social impact of digital transformation is fundamental; this is because no business or person exists in isolation from society.

Companies have become experts in getting us hooked on the next great discovery, the next great phone, the next Alexa, the future driverless car. Humans have become conditioned to wanting the next best thing, queuing for days in front of a flag shop to be the first to acquire the new device.

Scientists, Engineers, Mathematicians, etc., are being hired at full speed to come up with the next greatest invention and how to make the human being desire it. Teenagers cannot wait for the next best thing; they have their names on waiting lists. Having a child nowadays has become very expensive, due to all the gadgets that are continually being launched. But, how does this impact on people, people who cannot afford it?

According to an article in the Independent newspaper by Lizzie Dearden - Home Affairs Correspondent - Friday the 27th of April 2018 - on the Children as young as 13 are being stabbed in a tide of violence sweeping Britain, but the reason for the spike is the subject of fierce argument.

Children as young as 4 years old are walking into school with knives, The Independent newspaper 23rd of August 2019, technology, unfortunately, have an impact on this increase.

A report by the government cited drug dealing and social media as key drivers, but police have called for more funding to turn around the loss of thousands of officers and voluntary groups are attacking cuts to youth services.

7   The Individual's Transformation

We do and build on our relationship with others and the way we consume. We are social individuals and not isolated hermits in the world.

Moreover, we affirm our social position based on what we have, the places we go, the relationships we establish, the lifestyle we choose and the reliability of our opinions - our reputation. Thus, the evident change in the way we interact with each other and with brands is transforming the human being, who is much more exposed to the opinion of others.

We also have more means to influence people. In a few clicks, we can all share experiences, speak ill of an advertising campaign, engage large groups against corporate policy, denounce actions, evaluate products and provide opinions on a wide range of topics.

Thus, the choices we make are influenced by groups of people with whom we interact; this is because we are more confident when we see that, in addition to our own, there is approval from a greater number of people for our choice, which can be a travel destination, for example.

But that influence goes far beyond that.

Nowadays, the number of young people wanting to be influencers is vast. People as young as 5 have become known on YouTube and now have followers as young as them. Parents show these videos to their kids and tell them, "if he or she can, so can you". Adolescents are hooked on reality celebrities. According to an article on the Newport Academy website on the 28th of August 2018, they found that many teenagers have eating disorders because they want to be just like the celebrities they have put on a pedestal.

8   Examples of Social Impact

Nowadays, many people spend their life posting on Facebook, Snapchat, Instagram, Twitter, etc.; our young generation is so influenced by these social media platforms that their lives depend on it. Ever since the creation of these social platforms, there has been a considerable increase in anxiety and depression in teenagers, leading as well to the rise in teenage suicide and bullying. It seems that the young generation has lost the meaning of what being a human being is and relying on how many likes they can get seems to have become primordial to them.

According to a study from Duke University: "More use of technology is linked to later increases in attention, behaviour and self-regulation problems for adolescents already at risk for mental health issues, a new study from Duke University finds.", this doesn't mean that only children or adolescents with prior issues or at risk are the only ones who will develop mental health issues. There is great competition amongst youngsters nowadays to be an influencer, to compete with their peers, to be sure that they are one step ahead, from posting their food to posting photographs that are not always appropriate and can put them into risky situations.

Social Impact has caused many issues for young ones, but parents are also at fault here. Due to their busy lifestyles, children are left to their own devices, and they are not getting the necessary attention. Parents many times are not aware of what their child is up to and many times acknowledging that their child may have a mental issue is taboo within their culture, which does not help the child who is suffering from anxiety, depression, panic attacks, suicidal thoughts.

According to research, Social Media and suicide is a new phenomenon, which influences suicide- related behaviour. Suicide is a leading cause of death worldwide. According to the World Health Organization, in the year 2019, approximately 1.53 million people will die from suicide - Gvion and Apter (2012). There is increasing evidence that this behaviour of using social media affects and changes people's lives, especially in teenagers. Suicide has been identified not only as an individual phenomenon, but it is influenced by social and environmental factors - Gvion and Apter (2012). As the internet becomes more ingrained in people's everyday life, they are desensitized to the mental and emotional issues it can cause to an individual Tingle (2015).

According to an article from the Journal of Neuroscience Research - Mining social networks to improve suicide preventions: A Scoping Review by Jorge Lopez – Castoman, Bilele Moulahi, Jerome Aza, Sandra Bringay, Julie Deninotti, Sebatian Guilame, Enrique Baca-Garcia, "Attention about the risks of online social networks has been called upon reports describing their use to express emotional distress and suicidal ideation or plans. On the Internet, cyberbullying, suicide pacts, Internet addiction, and "extreme" communities seem to increase suicidal behaviour".

According to the article "The role of online social networking on deliberate self-harm and suicidality in adolescents: A systematized review of the literature" Aksha M. Memon, Shiva G. Sharma, Satyajit S. Mohite, and Shailesh Jain in the Journal of psychiatry, social media is responsible for the following:

- "Cyberbullying: "Is an aggressive, intentional act, or behaviour that is carried out by an individual or group using electronic forms of contact, repeatedly and overtime against a victim who cannot easily defend himself/herself."
- "Social media advertisements expose adolescents to the substances of abuse including alcohol, tobacco, and marijuana which could lead to potential self-harm and suicide."
- "Adolescents on social media are at risk of being victims of sex crimes as sex offenders can use social media to lure adolescents for sexual exploitation, and these sexual experiences are associated with enhanced risk of adverse social, academic, and behavioural consequence".

"Another concern is the role of social media in the internalization of the "thin ideal" body image by adolescent females and according to the findings of a study conducted on high school girls using Facebook, users scored higher on all body image concerns than nonusers thus concluding a strong influence of this social media platform on body image."

The list is growing every day, and all the above may end up by triggering feelings and emotions that children and adolescents find it hard to understand, causing them to fall into depression, causing anxiety, etc.

Aja Romano author of the article "The frustrating, enduring debate over video games, violence, and guns" of the 26th of August 2019 states that "We cannot forget as well of the video games, such as Xbox and Power Stations, these games, most of the time, are violent games that can instigate violence in young people and adults. As was the case of the EL Passo – Texas where The El Paso shooter briefly referenced *Call of Duty*, a wildly popular game in which players assume the roles of soldiers during historical and fictional wartime, in his "manifesto."

It has been scientifically proven that gaming can change a person's brain. According to the article in Interesting Engineering by Christopher Mcfadden on the 22nd of April 2019 with the title "Playing Video Games Can Actually Change the Brain" - "It is official, gaming can, and does, change the brain of games, but it's not all for good". According to the article, gaming can have positives as children can interact with one and other, socialise. Christopher Mcfadden also mentions that "gaming does affect the brain in gamers. They have improved visuospatial skills, memory, attention and, it turns out, show signs of other brain change associated with some addictive disorders".

Finally, Digital Transformation has not only empowered consumers: it has empowered society, and now it is up to the exposed companies to manage their crises in an ethical way, gaming companies by thinking twice what games to launch, if it is continually focusing on violent games, social media platforms to see how they can restrict bullying, self-harming pages or forums, suicide pages, etc.

9   Ideological Segregation in the Digital Environment

A phenomenon already very present in the digital environment is what we call ideological segregation; this basically occurs because of our tendency to approach people with visions similar to ours. At the same time that networks give voice to everyone and that each ideological group can manifest itself freely, people prefer to interact within their own universe.

After all, isn't that what companies do when they determine their audience and develop actions focused on it? Don't they seek to customize the shopping experience and use to increase customer satisfaction and loyalty?

The most basic way to achieve this is by observing the contents that are being viewed the most. Based on them, it is possible to determine standard details to distribute similar messages. This type of tooling works well.

At the same time that this personalization pleases, society is bothered with the result: the low diversity of contents - which is what we call ideological segregation. As it becomes more evident, more people tend to bother with it; this is natural. To some extent, every trend generates some countertendency, that is, a defensive and contrary response. As this reaction grows, it is expected that there will be pressure on companies to reduce the level of customization.

Consequently, diversity within companies will be increasingly required, allowing employees of different races, ideologies and behaviours to understand an equally diverse audience better.

In fact, consumer pressure on company decisions is a determining aspect of the new society. The challenge for companies is to be able to incorporate this interference in the decision-making process - a definitive trend to respond to the enormous power of the customer.

A positive example is Smart Cities that with the use of technology, they allow involving the citizen in city planning. Thus, systems are developed that ensure the free flow of information seeking to find problems and develop solutions to promote economic development and quality of life.

10   The Positives of Technology

Of course, every negative has a positive, and technology has helped society in many ways, such as medical advancements, how technology can predict the climate crisis, easier communication, decreased emissions and greener environment keeping the earth, saving trees due to the use of less papers, safety, such as better police response, GPS, surveillance, digital security, 3D teaching in classrooms, etc. Nonetheless, if we stop to analyse the pros and cons of technology, we can see that the negative list is bigger.

11   Conclusion

It is still common for digital transformation to be considered exclusively as a technological issue, disregarding the significant impact that changes have on society.

The tremendous social change that has occurred is that people have already gotten involved and engaged with the transformation. That is why it is viable, possible and irreversible. Society is voluntarily willing to promote innovation - even if there are more resilient groups.

Moreover, to the context, we describe the influences of the government environment on the process.

It is foreseeable that interventions will take place. For better or worse, the concern with the social impact of digital transformation must guide regulations and incentive policies.

The economic and social impact of such a representative value is equally significant. Therefore, personal and business decisions will need to consider the impact of digital transformation on society increasingly. Our ability to manage life and business depends directly on our understanding of how we are moving towards interacting with each other.

The way society has been developing since the first computer, mobile phone, application, social media platform, online shopping, Artificial intelligence and so on, is quite worrying as people are becoming more and more dependent on them. Before when we would leave home without our watch, we would feel lost, now if we have forgotten our telephones, we go insane.

Decades ago, many predicted that technology would now be in charge of all the heavy work. We would have more free time and engage only in intellectual activities.

However, what we saw happen was a great change in the dynamics of our daily lives. At the same time that it creates facilities, technology accelerates the interactions and expands the channels. All the time, from anywhere and by various means, we are "connected".

Some have difficulty in adapting and others assume a compulsive behaviour, generating a psychological load that can create stress. However, the problem is not limited to these people. This affects everyone, and another great challenge is to think about the experience of use considering this effect on people.

This concern is justified by its social aspect and by the effects of anxiety. We already need to worry about writing short, objective messages, but there is a whole design experience that needs to be designed to lessen this stress.

It is necessary for those investing in technology to have a $360°$ vision rather than tunnel vision. Tunnel vision does not allow people to see the whole story, do the creators, innovators, scientists, companies, etc., stop to think of the pros and cons of technology and how their invention, innovation will impact on society. It is time to stop and think as the future belongs to the young ones, the question here is how we can do so? From an ethical point of view, when thinking of the utilitarianism approach, Stephen Nathanson, from the Northeastern University – USA - Act and Rule Utilitarianism, defines this approach as "best known and most influential moral theories. Like other forms of consequentialism, its core idea is that whether actions are morally right or wrong depends on their effects. More specifically, the only effects of actions that are relevant are the good and bad results that they produce", companies, creators, scientists, etc., should think not just about what is beneficial for their pockets, but as well how to deal with the bigger picture, on how this impacts on people on a day to day basis. Liz Soltan, from http://www.digitalresponsibility.org/technology-and-psychological-issues - states that "Whether or not changes in our behaviour due to technology use classify as a disorder, there is no denying that technology is affecting the way our minds operate. It remains to be seen exactly how technology will affect our psyches, but some changes are already starting to become apparent. Nowadays, Dr Larry Rosen argues that "this constant flow of information is more than the human mind was meant to handle." He shows, for example, that there is little difference between BlackBerry addicts and those suffering from obsessive-compulsive disorder. "Our technology use has sprouted a whole new array of symptoms of common disorders, from teenagers uploading their every move to Facebook to the 40-year-old who scours the Internet for information on the differences between freckles and melanoma, despite reassurances from his dermatologist." More importantly, Dr Rosen shows that there is a way to achieve harmony with technology without being controlled by the constant influx of information. IDisorder is the new mental health disease changes to your brain´s ability to process information and your ability to relate to the world due to your daily use of media and technology resulting in signs and **symptoms** of psychological disorders – such as stress, sleeplessness, and a compulsive need to check in with all of your technology. Nomophobia - the phobia of being out of cellular phone contact. It has been considered as a symptom or syndrome of problematic digital media use in mental health.

The question here is where do we go from here, how can we create awareness and help people healthily deal with Technology? Will mental health departments be able to cope with the influx of new patients?

Perhaps we need to relearn the teachings from the past. "Everything in moderation" as the saying goes.

References

Los Angeles Times, David Lazarus, a Business columnist on the 25th of September 2019 - Column: You may not be as attractive as that dating site would have you believe

The Daily mail - Mail Online on the 4th of August 2017 by "The mathematical chances of finding love will surprise you" Shivali Best

The Effects of Technology on Mental Health - September 18, 2018 | Fisher-Titus Healthy Living Team

More technology use linked to mental health issues in at-risk adolescents

George, M.J., Russell, M.A., Piontak, J.R., Odgers, C.L.: Technology use tied to increased attention and behaviour problems – but also to some positive behaviours. Global, Academics, 3 May 2017

Gvion, Y., Apter, A.: Suicide and suicidal behavior. Public Health Rev. (2012)

Tingle, J.: Preventing suicides: developing a strategy. Br. J. Nurs. (2015)

Lopez-Castroman, J., Moulahi, B., Azé, J., Bringay, S., Deninotti, J., Guillaume, S., Baca-Garcia, E.: Mining social networks to improve suicide prevention: a scoping review. J. Neurosci. Res. (2019)

McFadden, C.: Playing Video Games Can Actually Change the Brain-It's official, gaming can, and does, change the brain of gamers. But it's not all for the good, 22 April 2019

Aja Romano author of the article "The frustrating, enduring debate over video games, violence, and guns" of the 26th of August 2019 – VOX

Independent newspaper by Lizzie Dearden - Home Affairs Correspondent - Friday 27 April 2018- Why is knife crime increasing in England and Wales?

Regoli, N.: 16 Artificial Intelligence Pros and Cons. Vittana.org

Online dating lowers self-esteem and increases depression, studies say By Juliet Marateck, CNN, 29 May 2018

Combi, M.: The construction of flexible identities and negotiation of meanings on the Internet. In: Negrotti, M. (ed.) Yearbook of the Artificial. Kyosei, Culture and Sustainable Technology, pp. 10–16. Peter Lang, New York (2006)

Independent - Knife crime: Children as young as four among hundreds caught with blades at school, by Henry Vaughn

Stephen Nathanson, from the Northeastern University in the USA in Act and Rule Utilitarianism. https://www.iep.utm.edu/util-a-r/

Liz Soltan. http://www.digitalresponsibility.org/technology-and-psychological-issues

Rosen, L.D.: iDisorder: Understanding Our Obsession with Technology and Overcoming Its Hold on Us. Palgrave Macmillan, New York (2012)

Efficient Microcontroller Implementation of BIKE

Mario Bischof[1], Tobias Oder[2(✉)], and Tim Güneysu[2,3]

[1] Swiss Distance University of Applied Sciences (FFHS) Brig, Brig, Switzerland
mario.bischof@ffhs.ch
[2] Horst Görtz Institute for IT Security, Ruhr-Universität Bochum,
Bochum, Germany
{tobias.oder,tim.gueneysu}@rub.de
[3] DFKI, Bremen, Germany

Abstract. In the digital world, public-key cryptography is ubiquitous. Current public-key crypto schemes like RSA or Diffie-Hellmann are in widespread use and they represent an indispensable asset of our technological toolbox. However, the discovery of Shor's algorithm and the rapid progression in the field of quantum computers became a painful reminder of our alerting dependency on such technologies. At the same time, this realization started a demand for new cryptographic algorithms withstanding the power of quantum computers. The National Institute of Standards and Technology (NIST) aimed to satisfy this urge by initiating a standardization process in 2017 with a call for proposals of post-quantum key exchange mechanisms and signature algorithms. One of the submissions that made it to the second round is the key encapsulation mechanism BIKE.

This work investigates various techniques to achieve an efficient and secure implementation of BIKE on embedded devices. We show that it is possible for BIKE to run on a Cortex-M4 microcontroller using reduced data representation and adequate decoding algorithms. Our implementation achieves a performance of 6 million cycles for key generation, 7 million cycles for encapsulation, and 89 million cycles for decapsulation for BIKE-1.

Keywords: Post-quantum cryptography · Code-based cryptography · BIKE · KEM · Microcontroller · Timing attacks · Cortex-M4

1 Introduction

The advancements in the development of quantum computers impose an increasing threat [14,16] to most of the currently existing public-key crypto schemes. Already decades ago, Peter Shor [23] developed a quantum algorithm that is able to break them. Since current public-key cryptosystems like RSA are in such widespread use, it is crucial that extensive research for new cryptographic schemes is done before the arrival of large enough quantum computers. For

E. Simion and R. Géraud-Stewart (Eds.): SecITC 2019, LNCS 12001, pp. 34–49, 2020.
https://doi.org/10.1007/978-3-030-41025-4_3

this reason, the United States National Institute of Standards and Technology (NIST) announced a call for proposals in 2017 [12,17] to submit new cryptographic schemes able to withstand such attacks. One of these proposals is the **BI**t Flipping **K**ey **E**ncapsulation- or **BIKE**-suite [2]. The NIST standardization is a multi-round process aiming to select new algorithms and publish first drafted standards by the years 2022/2024 [18]. NIST announced a list of candidates that have been selected for the second round in early 2019 [19], with BIKE being among the selected schemes. The main NIST selection-criteria are security, cost and performance, as well as algorithm and implementation characteristics on a large variety of platforms [20]. We contribute to the NIST standardization process by presenting the first microcontroller implementation of BIKE.

1.1 Related Work

Most code-based cryptographic schemes nowadays are improved and/or optimized adaptations of the initial works of Robert McEliece [8] and Hermann Niederreiter [15], who published cryptographic schemes of the same names in the late seventies and eighties. Both of them are widely considered to be very well studied and remained essentially unbroken up until this day and provide sufficient security properties for the upcoming quantum computing age. To eliminate the major downside of these older schemes, being its very large key sizes, newer proposals often use codes that have some cyclic structure like quasi-cyclic (QC) low-density-parity-check (LDPC) or modest-density-parity-check (MDPC) codes [6,21]. This becomes especially essential when targeting embedded devices like we do in this work, due to their limited memory. The list of NIST submissions [19] shows that the majority of standardization candidates are either code- or lattice-based schemes. Examples of other code-based candidates closely related to BIKE are classic McEliece [3] or Hamming Quasi-Cyclic (HQC) [1].

The pqm4 post-quantum crypto library for the ARM Cortex-M4 [9] consolidates most microcontroller implementation efforts of post-quantum key exchange mechanisms and signature schemes. Great efforts towards efficient and side-channel attack resistant implementations of the McEliece crypto scheme using quasi-cyclic MDPC codes for embedded platforms has been made by von Maurich, Oder, Güneysu and Heyse [25,27–29] and is also a central topic of von Maurich's dissertation [26].

1.2 Contribution

In this work, we present the first microcontroller implementation of the NIST round 2 candidate BIKE. We replace any external dependencies that have been a major issue preventing microcontroller adoption of BIKE [9] with stand-alone components. Furthermore, we replace the decoding algorithm of the reference implementation with a more memory-efficient one to make the implementation fit the memory of our target device. Finally, we apply countermeasures to protect the implementation against timing side-channels. We implemented all three variants of BIKE, each at three different security levels, leading to a total number of 9 implementations. Up to our knowledge, no microcontroller implementations of code-based NIST round 2 candidates have been published so far. This work is therefore an important contribution to the evaluation of the practicability of code-based cryptography in the ongoing NIST standardization process. To allow independent verification of our results, we will make our source code publicly available with the publication of this work[1].

2   Preliminaries

In this section, we discuss the mathematical background that is necessary for the understanding of this paper. We use the following notation. n describes the size of the whole parity check matrix and r of one circulant block. w is the parity check matrix' row weight and t the weight of error, the code is able to correct. By H we denote the parity check matrix of a linear code and H^T denotes the transpose of the parity check matrix. The syndrome of an input vector e is defined as $s = eH^T$.

2.1   BIKE - Bit Flipping Key Encapsulation

BIKE is a key encapsulation mechanism (KEM) based on QC-MDPC codes. It is composed out of three different variants: BIKE-1, BIKE-2 and BIKE-3 that can be instantiated at three different security levels: Level 1, 3, and 5. These correspond to the security recommendations given by NIST. The suggested BIKE parameters are shown in Table 1. The three variants of BIKE are described in Figs. 1, 2 and 3. For a more detailed description of the scheme, we refer to the specification of the NIST submission [2].

Table 1. Parameters for every BIKE variant

Variant	Security	r	n	w	t
BIKE 1/2	Level 1	10,163	20,326	142	134
BIKE 1/2	Level 3	19,853	39,706	206	199
BIKE 1/2	Level 5	32,749	65,498	274	264
BIKE 3	Level 1	11,027	22,054	134	154
BIKE 3	Level 3	21,683	43,366	198	226
BIKE 3	Level 5	36,131	72,262	266	300

2.2   Decoding Using Bit Flipping Algorithms

To decode QC-MDPC codes we can use bit flipping algorithms. Many different bit flipping decoders do exist. Algorithm 1.1 [2] shows a classical variant. After

---

[1] https://www.seceng.ruhr-uni-bochum.de/research/publications/efficient-microcont roller-implementation-bike/.

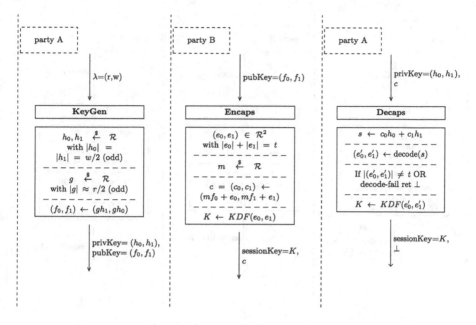

Fig. 1. BIKE-1 specification

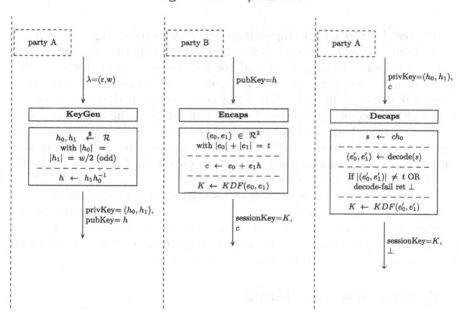

Fig. 2. BIKE-2 specification

termination, the algorithm should output an error pattern e which corresponds to the inputted syndrome s, e.g. $s = eH^T$.

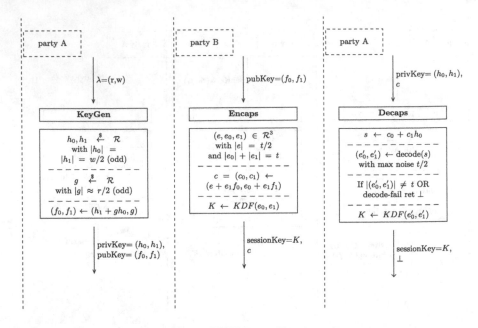

Fig. 3. BIKE-3 specification

Unsatisfied Parity Check Equations and Threshold. Algorithm 1.1 calculates the number of unsatisfied parity check equations per parity check matrix column h_j for all n columns of H and compares it to a given threshold $\tau|h_j|$ depending on the currently processed column h_j. h_j is the j-th column of the parity check matrix H interpreted as a row vector. $h_j \star s'$ is the component-wise product of two vectors and $|h_j \star s'|$ is the number of unchecked parity equations involving h_j. If the number of unsatisfied equations is higher than $\tau|h_j|$, the corresponding bit in the resulting error e_j is flipped. After all columns have been processed, the temporary syndrome s' gets updated $s' = s - eH^T$ with the current error pattern and the next round starts.

The stopping condition $|s'| > u$ specifies whether the correct error has been found. If $u = 0$ is used then $s' = s - eH^T = s - s = 0$. This also means that s is the exact syndrome of e. This is called *noiseless* syndrome decoding. If $u > 0$, the decoding is called *noisy*. In this case, the syndrome includes an additional error e' (or noise) and is not the exact syndrome of e.

3 Portable Implementation

The BIKE reference implementation relies on the NTL library [24] to perform arithmetic operations in finite fields, as well as OpenSSL for the AES-based pseudorandom number generators and the key derivation hash function SHA384. These external dependencies are the main reason, why there has not been a microcontroller implementation of BIKE yet [9]. The first step towards a microcontroller implementation is therefore to make the code portable. The source

Algorithm 1.1. BIT FLIPPING ALGORITHM

Input: $H \in \mathbb{F}_2^{(n-k) \times n}, s \in \mathbb{F}_2^{(n-k)}, u \geq 0$
Output: e.

```
1  begin
2  |    e ← 0;
3  |    s' ← s;
4  |    while |s'| > u do
5  |    |    τ ← Threshold ∈ [1, 0];
6  |    |    for j ← 0 to n − 1 do
7  |    |    |    if |h_j ⋆ s'| ≥ τ|h_j| then e_j ← e_j + 1 mod 2;
8  |    |    end
9  |    |    s' ← s − eH^T;
10 |    end
11 |    return e
12 end
```

code of our portable implementation will also be made available online with the publication of this work.

3.1 Replacing NTL Modules

Multiplication in GF2 has the most crucial impact on the performance of BIKE and is done with the help of the NTL library in the reference implementation of BIKE. The gf2x-library [5] is the result of extensive research [4] for efficient multiplication in finite fields. The gf2x-library has been integrated into NTL, after NTL was significantly outperformed by gf2x in the area of finite field operations. Another big advantage of gf2x is that almost everything is written in plain C (except very few C++ parts) and does not rely on any external dependencies, therefore we integrated the relevant software modules from the gf2x-library into our portable code.

3.2 Replacing OpenSSL Modules

To remove the platform dependent OpenSSL AES and SHA384 modules, we chose to adapt two alternatives [7,10] that are publicly available. According to the authors, both of these replacements for AES and SHA2 are validated against NIST test vectors and were designed in respect to portability, compactness and efficiency. This offered ideal conditions to be used for our portable BIKE implementation.

4   Cortex-M4 Implementation

After the development of a portable BIKE implementation, the next step is to develop an efficient Cortex-M4 implementation. Our evaluation platform is the

STM32F4-DISCOVERY board. It runs with a clock frequency of up to 168 MHz. The board offers 192 kB of RAM as well as 1 MB of flash memory. Furthermore, it features a true random number generator (TRNG) based on analog circuitry and a floating-point unit (FPU). NIST recommends to use the Cortex-M4F as target platform for microcontroller evaluations of post-quantum standardization candidates [13].

4.1   Bit Flipping in the BIKE Reference Implementation

BIKE-1 and BIKE-2 use *noiseless* syndrome decoding and BIKE-3 uses *noisy* syndrome decoding. BIKE operates with (2,1)-quasi-cyclic MDPC codes. Its decode-function, has the signature decode(e, s, h0, h1, u). The inputs are the syndrome s and the first two rows h_0 and h_1 of the two quasi-cyclic code blocks of the parity check matrix H. The integer u distinguishes between noiseless ($u = 0$) and noisy ($u > 0$) decoding. Decode outputs $e = e_0|e_1$ for which holds $|e_0 h_0 + e_1 h_1 + s| \leq u$, i.e. the *noise* of the syndrome must not be larger than u for decode to work. The secret key is of the form $sk = (h_0, h_1)$ for all BIKE variants, so the same decode function can be applied. The authors of BIKE suggest a one-round bit flipping algorithm [2] similar to the one illustrated in Algorithm 1.1.

4.2   Memory Requirements for Decoding

When the one round bit flipping algorithm is applied, the decoding becomes a major memory bottleneck. Table 2 shows the memory consumption of the largest data structures in the reference implementation of the decode operation for all BIKE variants. Clearly, this simple decoding mechanism can not be used on the microcontroller, since it requires way more memory than the 192 kB that are available, and needs to be substituted with a more adequate solution.

Table 2. Dynamic memory requirements of arrays in decode call for all BIKE variants in number of kB using the reference implementation.

Data structure	BIKE-1/2			BIKE-3		
	Level 1	Level 3	Level 5	Level 1	Level 3	Level 5
unsat_counter2[]	41	79	131	44	87	145
errorPos[]	41	79	131	44	87	145
unsat_counter[]	20	40	65	22	43	72
J[][]	813	1,271	2,620	882	1,735	2,890
e[]	20	40	65	22	43	72
syndrome	10	20	33	11	22	36
Overall	**945**	**1,529**	**3,046**	**1,026**	**2,017**	**3,360**

4.3   Decoding on Embedded Platforms

Extensive research on how to efficiently implement QC-MDPC McEliece on embedded devices has been done by von Maurich [26, Ch. 4]. Von Maurich evaluated and compared various different bit flipping decoders targeting constrained devices. In the following, we will shortly review the decoders that we adapted for our microcontroller implementation.

The primary idea [26, Ch. 4.4.1] is based on a decoding mechanism for LDPC codes first introduced by Gallager [6]. Similar to Algorithm 1.1, this strategy calculates the number of unsatisfied parity check equations for each bit of the received message and flips the corresponding bit, if a specific threshold b is reached. Thresholds of a given parameter set are pre-calculated for each iteration b_i of decoding, by calculating the probability P_i for a bit to be in error after iteration i. Decoding approaches using such types of thresholds are also called *hard decision bit flipping based* and mainly operate following these basic steps [26, p. 40]:

1. Calculate the syndrome of the inputted message and pass it to the decoder
2. Calculate the number of unsatisfied parity check equations for each bit of the input message
3. Flip those bits that violate at least b_i equations in iteration i
4. Recalculate the syndrome based on the updated message (since the message changed, the syndrome also changes)

A corresponding decoder $\mathcal{D}_1$ working the mentioned way is shown in Algorithm 1.2 in Appendix A. For BIKE-3, Line 2 in Algorithm 1.2 needs to check for the syndrome's hamming weight to be larger than some noise u, rather than 0. In case of BIKE-1/2, u will just be 0. Decoder $\mathcal{D}_1$ implements the following optimizations:

1. As proposed by Gallger [6], $\mathcal{D}_1$ uses precomputed thresholds b_i (Algorithm 1.2, Line 14), eliminating the need to calculate the maximum number of unsatisfied parity check equations for every invocation (like other decoders do).
2. The syndrome changes as follows if the threshold is reached: $s_{new} = s_{old} \oplus h_j$ [26, p. 41]. This crucial observation shows that it is not necessary to completely recalculate the syndrome every time it is updated. It can rather be computed by just adding the current h_j (Algorithm 1.2, Line 16), significantly speeding up syndrome recomputation.
3. Von Maurich points out [26, p. 46] that if about 4–6 iterations of the decoding algorithm have passed, it is extremely rare for it to still succeed without any adjustments to the threshold. So he suggests an ITERATIONS_MAX of 5 iterations for his QC-MDPC McEliece instance.

The decoding failure rate can be further reduced [26, p. 42–43] if in case of failure the thresholds b_i are increased by one, until a *threshold_delta_max* of 5 is reached. This concept is called decoder $\mathcal{D}_2$ shown in Algorithm 1.3 in Appendix A. $\mathcal{D}_2$ essentially just acts as a wrapper around $\mathcal{D}_1$, which upon failure increases the *threshold_delta* and starts decoding over again.

4.4   Microcontroller Optimizations

Instead of the simple decoding algorithm from the reference implementation, we use the proposed decoders $\mathcal{D}_1/\mathcal{D}_2$ [26, p. 62] for the microcontroller implementation which perform most of its computations in-place, omitting the necessity to store a lot of data at the cost of losing performance. This combination of decoders provides further failure rate reduction.

We can apply a time-memory tradeoff strategy [26, p. 61] to the sequential algorithm, turning it into a somewhat parallel method. *Parallel* in this sense means processing h_0 and h_1 in the same turn, using separate variables and counters. The parallel decoding method for decoder $\mathcal{D}_1$ is shown in Algorithm 1.4 in Appendix A. The same adjustments for the noise u as explained for the sequential algorithm are required for this method to work with BIKE. Using two variables current0 and current1, the parallel way counts the unsatisfied parity check equations for both h_0 and h_1 in violated0 and violated1 in the same loop iteration (Algorithm 1.4, Lines 10–15). Since this processes two vectors in the same turn, it has to finish the whole loop before doing the syndrome update outside the inner loop. If not stated otherwise, we will always refer to the parallel decoder for the remainder of this paper as it provides a superior performance.

The gf2x library proposes optimization-suggestions for ARMv7 (and other) platforms to speed up its implementation. Besides suggesting slightly different Karatsuba/Toom thresholds, the changes basically consist of a few optimized multiplication base cases gf2x_mul3, gf2x_mul5 and gf2x_mul6. In gf2x_mul3, we get an optimized version with 6 multiplications instead of 7. gf2x_mul5 now uses the formula of Peter Montgomery [11] allowing to multiply two 5-term polynomials with only 13 multiplications instead of 17. gf2x_mul6 implements the K_3 formula by Weimerskirch and Paar [30] which needs only 6 calls to gf2x_mul2, resulting in a total of 18 multiplications instead of 21. We furthermore replaced the AES implementation from [10] that we use as PRNG with the Cortex-M-optimized constant-time implementation from [22]. To seed the PRNG, we generate a random sample from the on-board TRNG.

The private key can be compressed by only storing the indices of the $\frac{w}{2}$ ones per vector, ending up with a $w * \lceil log_2(r) \rceil$-bit long representation [2]. We can then rotate the vector by just increasing all positions by one instead of shifting the whole vector by one bit. We take care of overflows by just setting a corresponding position to zero, if it was equal to r. The positions are reordered in case of an overflow, to keep them in an ordered fashion. This way, only the last position needs to be checked for overflow. We adapted the sparse representation [26, p. 108] to our code.

4.5   Hardening the Implementation Against Timing Attacks

We also investigated measures to secure the bit flipping decoding algorithm against timing attacks. Thorough research on how to secure QC-MDPC decoding has been done by von Maurich, Güneysu and Oder [26,29]. We adapted and extended the techniques from [26] for constant-time implementation of several components, like private key rotation, threshold comparison, syndrome and error update, and counting of unsatisfied parity check equations. Our tests showed that the overwhelming majority of decodings succeed after 2–4 iterations independent from the chosen BIKE variant. We hence fixed the number of iterations of the decoder to be always 5. That means that the decoder will always run 5 times, even if the decoding was successful in earlier runs already. However, the multiplication routine of the gf2x library is *not* constant-time. Our implementation therefore provides some resistance against timing-attacks but is not fully protected.

5   Results and Comparison

As environment, we used the Eclipse IDE for C/C++ developers, Version Photon Release 4.8.0 and Build id 20180619-1200 combined with the OpenSTM32 System Workbench for STM32 - C/C++ Embedded Development Tools for MCU 2.5.0.201807130628. For debugging purposes, we configured the internal eclipse debugger to use gdb via OpenOCD connecting to the STLink embedded debugger of the board. We counted clock cycles using the data watchpoint and trace unit (DWT) of the Cortex-M4 for performance measurements at 168 MHz.

5.1   Performance and Memory Evaluation

In Table 3, we show the cycle counts for all 9 implementations of BIKE. We also include the cycle counts for the case that the countermeasures against timing side-channels as described in Sect. 4.5 are applied to the decoding. The unusual high cost of the key generation in BIKE-2 is due to the expensive finite field inversion required in BIKE-2 only. Except for BIKE-2, the Decaps operation is the clear bottleneck regarding performance. In Table 4, we also show the dynamic memory consumption (heap and stack) of our implementations. The memory requirements range from 21 to 74 kB and therefore comfortably fit the memory of our evaluation platform. Encaps and Decaps have similar memory requirements and the increase in memory consumption is linear in the security level.

We compare our implementation with the evaluation results of several other NIST post-quantum candidates from the pqm4 library [9] in Table 5. In direct comparison with lattice-based schemes, the performance of BIKE is inferior. The only lattice-based scheme that performs worse is the Frodo KEM. Frodo is however a very conservative scheme. For a comparison with schemes with similar trust in the underlying security assumption, QC-MDPC-based schemes (like BIKE) should rather be compared to ideal lattice-based schemes (like NewHope). However, compared to isogeny-based cryptography, BIKE clearly has the superior performance and can therefore be seen as a backup alternative to lattice-based schemes.

Table 3. Final performance of KEM phases for all BIKE variants using parallel decoding, including timing attack countermeasures [TP]. Cycle counts are given in million cycles.

		KeyGen	Encaps	Decaps
BIKE-1	Level 1	6	7	89
	[TP]			305
	Level 3	15	17	228
	[TP]			773
	Level 5	28	30	569
	[TP]			1,685
BIKE-2	Level 1	918	4	87
	[TP]			303
	Level 3	3,345	9	222
	[TP]			766
	Level 5	8,763	15	557
	[TP]			1,673
BIKE-3	Level 1	4	7	86
	[TP]			309
	Level 3	10	18	234
	[TP]			795
	Level 5	20	37	774
	[TP]			1,819

Table 4. Final dynamic memory requirements of KEM phases for all BIKE variants in kB consisting of stack and heap memory. The maximum memory consumption of an implementation is highlighted in bold font.

		KeyGen	Encaps	Decaps
BIKE-1	Level 1	13.95	**21.59**	20.84
	Level 3	26.17	**41.07**	39.37
	Level 5	42.24	**66.83**	63.79
BIKE-2	Level 1	15.62	19.05	**20.84**
	Level 3	30.18	36.10	**39.37**
	Level 5	49.51	58.63	**63.79**
BIKE-3	Level 1	15.01	**23.30**	22.41
	Level 3	28.42	**44.71**	42.74
	Level 5	46.61	**73.75**	70.24

Table 5. Comparison of cycle counts of our implementations with results from pqm4 [9].

Scheme	Security	PQ family	KeyGen/10^3	Encaps/10^3	Decaps/10^3
BIKE-1 (our)	Level 1	Codes	6,437	6,867	89,131
NewHope-512	Level 1	Lattices	628	915	163
Kyber-512	Level 1	Lattices	514	653	621
Frodo-640	Level 1	Lattices	47,051	45,883	45,366
SIKEp434	Level 1	Isogenies	650,735	1,065,631	1,136,703
BIKE-1 (our)	Level 3	Codes	15,309	16,641	228,244
Kyber-768	Level 3	Lattices	977	1,147	1,095
SIKEp610	Level 3	Isogenies	1,819,652	3,348,669	3,368,114
BIKE-1 (our)	Level 5	Codes	27,605	29,797	568,517
NewHope-1024	Level 5	Lattices	1,035	1,495	206
Kyber-1024	Level 5	Lattices	1,575	1,779	1,709
SIKEp751	Level 5	Isogenies	3,296,225	5,347,056	5,742,522

6   Conclusion

In this work, we developed an efficient and secure implementation of the post-quantum standardization candidate BIKE. Our baseline was the reference implementation that depended on platform-specific third-party software libraries. A portable implementation was achieved by incorporating substitutions for the OpenSSL and NTL dependencies. Our analysis further revealed that the BIKE bit flipping decoding, as done in the reference implementation, is not feasible on the microcontroller and we provided adaptations of more adequate decoders that were able to satisfy the limiting memory constraints of the development board. We furthermore added countermeasures against timing attacks to our implementation. Our final implementation offers reasonable results in comparison with other Cortex-M4 post-quantum cryptography KEMs in terms of efficiency, security and memory requirements. Our work has successfully demonstrated that the BIKE standardization candidate can be implemented and run on an embedded microcontroller like the Cortex-M4. This result lives up to the expectation of NIST that the proposed algorithms are required to be implementable in a wide range of hardware and software platforms.

The finite field inversion resembles a heavy bottleneck for BIKE-2 key generation performance. As documented in the BIKE specification [2], batch key generation can reduce some performance loss generated by the inversion, in exchange for occupying more memory. We expect the benefit from batch key generation will be limited on embedded platforms due to memory restrictions but nonetheless, the exact limitations of these assumptions remained unknown and should still be verified in future work.

Acknowledgement. This work was supported in part through DFG Excellence Strategy grant 39078197 (EXC 2092, CASA), and by the Federal Ministry of Education and Research of Germany through the QuantumRISC project (16KIS1038).

A   Decoding Algorithms

Algorithm 1.2. DECODER $\mathcal{D}_1$ (SEQUENTIAL)

Input: syndrome s, private key h_0, h_1 and noise u
Output: error e

```
1  begin
2  |   while (|s| > u) & (iterations++ < ITERATIONS_MAX) do
3  |   |   for i ← 0 to 1 do
4  |   |   |   if !i then
5  |   |   |   |   current ← h0;
6  |   |   |   else
7  |   |   |   |   current ← h1;
8  |   |   |   end
9  |   |   |   for j ← 0 to R_BITS-1 do
10 |   |   |   |   violated ← 0;
11 |   |   |   |   for k ← 0 to R_BITS-1 do
12 |   |   |   |   |   if getBit(current,k) & getBit(syndrome,k) then
13 |   |   |   |   |   |   violated ← violated + 1;
14 |   |   |   |   |   |   if violated ≥ bi then
15 |   |   |   |   |   |   |   setBit(e,(i*R_BITS+j));
16 |   |   |   |   |   |   |   syndrome ← syndrome ⊕ current;
17 |   |   |   |   |   |   |   break;
18 |   |   |   |   |   |   end
19 |   |   |   |   |   end
20 |   |   |   |   end
21 |   |   |   |   rotate(current);
22 |   |   |   end
23 |   |   end
24 |   end
25 end
```

Algorithm 1.3. DECODER $\mathcal{D}_2$

Input: syndrome s, private key h_0,h_1 and noise u
Output: error e
1 **begin**
2   **for** *threshold_delta* $\leftarrow$ *0 to threshold_delta_max* **do**
3   // from here starts $\mathcal{D}_1$
4   ...;
5   // threshold needs to be considered in following line
6   **if** *violated* $\geq b_i$ + *threshold_delta* **then**
7   ...;
8   // check if decoding is successful and if so, leave function
9   **end**
10 **end**

Algorithm 1.4. DECODER $\mathcal{D}_1$ (PARALLEL)

Input: syndrome s, private key h_0,h_1 and noise u
Output: error e
1 **begin**
2   **while** $(|s| >u)$ & $(iterations + + < ITERATIONS\_MAX)$ **do**
3   **for** $i \leftarrow$ *0 to 1* **do**
4   current0 $\leftarrow h_0$;
5   current1 $\leftarrow h_1$;
6   **for** $j \leftarrow$ *0 to R_BITS-1* **do**
7   violated0 $\leftarrow 0$;
8   violated1 $\leftarrow 0$;
9   **for** $k \leftarrow$ *0 to R_BITS-1* **do**
10   **if** *getBit(current0,k)* & *getBit(syndrome,k)* **then**
11   violated0 $\leftarrow$ violated0 + 1;
12   **end**
13   **if** *getBit(current1,k)* & *getBit(syndrome,k)* **then**
14   violated1 $\leftarrow$ violated1 + 1;
15   **end**
16   **end**
17   **if** *violated0* $\geq b_i$ **then**
18   setBit(e,(i*R_BITS+j));
19   syndrome $\leftarrow$ syndrome $\oplus$ current0;
20   **end**
21   **if** *violated1* $\geq b_i$ **then**
22   setBit(e,(i*R_BITS+j));
23   syndrome $\leftarrow$ syndrome $\oplus$ current1;
24   **end**
25   **end**
26   rotate(current0);
27   rotate(current1);
28   **end**
29   **end**
30 **end**

References

1. Aguilar-Melchor, C., et al.: Hamming Quasi-Cyclic (HQC), November 2017. Submission to the NIST post quantum standardization process (2017)
2. Aragon, N., et al.: Bike: Bit Flipping Key Encapsulation (2018). http://bikesuite.org/files/BIKE.pdf. Accessed 18 Nov 2019
3. Bernstein, D.J., et al.: Classic McEliece: conservative code-based cryptography (2017). Submission to the NIST post quantum standardization process (2017)
4. Brent, R.P., Gaudry, P., Thomé, E., Zimmermann, P.: Faster multiplication in GF(2)[x]. In: van der Poorten, A.J., Stein, A. (eds.) ANTS 2008. LNCS, vol. 5011, pp. 153–166. Springer, Heidelberg (2008). https://doi.org/10.1007/978-3-540-79456-1_10
5. Brent, R.P., Gaudry, P., Thomé, E., Zimmermann, P.: InriaForge: gf2x: Project home (2018). https://gforge.inria.fr/projects/gf2x/. Accessed 18 Nov 2019
6. Gallager, R.G.: Low-density parity-check codes. IRE Trans. Inf. Theory **8**(1), 21–28 (1962)
7. Gay, O.: Fast software implementation in C of the FIPS 180–2 hash algorithms SHA-224, SHA-256, SHA-384 and SHA-512 (2018). https://github.com/ogay/sha2. Accessed 18 Nov 2019
8. McEliece, R.J.: A public-key cryptosystem based on algebraic coding theory. JPL DSN Progress Report 44 (1978)
9. Kannwischer, M.J., Rijneveld, J., Schwabe, P., Stoffelen, K.: pqm4: testing and benchmarking NIST PQC on ARM Cortex-M4. Cryptology ePrint Archive, Report 2019/844 (2019). https://eprint.iacr.org/2019/844
10. kokke. Small portable AES128/192/256 in C (2018). https://github.com/kokke/tiny-AES-c. Accessed 18 Nov 2019
11. Montgomery, P.L.: Five, six, and seven-term Karatsuba-like formulae. IEEE Trans. Comput. **54**(3), 362–369 (2005)
12. Moody, D.: The ship has sailed: the NIST post-quantum cryptography "competition". In: Invited talk at ASIACRYPT 2017, Hongkong (2017)
13. Moody, D.: Round 2 of NIST PQC competition. Invited talk at PQCrypto 2019, Chongqing, China (2019)
14. Moses, T.: Quantum Computing and Cryptography - Their impact on cryptographic practice. Technical report, Entrust, Inc. (2009). https://www.entrust.com/wp-content/uploads/2013/05/WP_QuantumCrypto_Jan09.pdf
15. Niederreiter, H.: Knapsack type cryptosystems and algebraic coding theory. Prob. Control Inf. Theory **15**(2), 159–166 (1986)
16. NIST. Post-Quantum Cryptography: NIST's Plan for the Future. Technical report, NIST (2016). https://csrc.nist.gov/csrc/media/projects/post-quantum-cryptography/documents/pqcrypto-2016-presentation.pdf
17. NIST. Call for Proposals - Post-Quantum Cryptography—CSRC. Technical report, NIST (2017). https://csrc.nist.gov/Projects/Post-Quantum-Cryptography/Post-Quantum-Cryptography-Standardization/Call-for-Proposals
18. NIST. Post-Quantum Cryptography - Workshops and Timeline. Technical report, NIST (2017). https://csrc.nist.gov/Projects/Post-Quantum-Cryptography/Workshops-and-Timeline
19. NIST. PQC Standardization Process: Second Round Candidate Announcement. Technical report, NIST (2019). https://csrc.nist.gov/News/2019/pqc-standardization-process-2nd-round-candidates

20. NIST. Status Report on the First Round of the NIST Post-Quantum Cryptography Standardization Process. Technical report, NIST (2019). https://csrc.nist.gov/publications/detail/nistir/8240/final
21. Ouzan, S., Be'ery, Y.: Moderate-density parity-check codes. CoRR, abs/0911.3262 (2009)
22. Schwabe, P., Stoffelen, K.: All the AES you need on Cortex-M3 and M4. In: Avanzi, R., Heys, H. (eds.) SAC 2016. LNCS, vol. 10532, pp. 180–194. Springer, Cham (2017). https://doi.org/10.1007/978-3-319-69453-5_10
23. Shor, P.: Polynomial-Time Algorithms for Prime Factorization and Discrete Logarithms on a Quantum Computer. Technical report, AT&T Research (1996). https://arxiv.org/abs/quant-ph/9508027
24. Shoup, V.: NTL: A library for doing number theory (2018). https://www.shoup.net/ntl/. Accessed 18 Nov 2019
25. Stehlé, D., Zimmermann, P.: A binary recursive Gcd algorithm. In: Buell, D. (ed.) ANTS 2004. LNCS, vol. 3076, pp. 411–425. Springer, Heidelberg (2004). https://doi.org/10.1007/978-3-540-24847-7_31
26. von Maurich, I.: Efficient implementation of code- and hash-based cryptography. Ph.D. thesis, Ruhr University Bochum, Germany (2017)
27. von Maurich, I., Güneysu, T.: Lightweight code-based cryptography: QC-MDPC McEliece encryption on reconfigurable devices. In: Design, Automation & Test in Europe Conference & Exhibition, DATE 2014, Dresden, Germany, 24–28 March 2014, pp. 1–6 (2014)
28. von Maurich, I., Güneysu, T.: Towards side-channel resistant implementations of QC-MDPC McEliece encryption on constrained devices. In: Mosca, M. (ed.) PQCrypto 2014. LNCS, vol. 8772, pp. 266–282. Springer, Cham (2014). https://doi.org/10.1007/978-3-319-11659-4_16
29. von Maurich, I., Oder, T., Güneysu, T.: Implementing QC-MDPC McEliece encryption. ACM Trans. Embedded Comput. Syst. 14(3), 44:1–44:27 (2015)
30. Weimerskirch, A., Paar, C.: Generalizations of the Karatsuba algorithm for efficient implementations. IACR Cryptology ePrint Archive, 2006:224 (2006)

Secure Deterministic Automata Evaluation: Completeness and Efficient 2-party Protocols

Giovanni Di Crescenzo[✉], Brian Coan, and Jonathan Kirsch

Perspecta Labs, Basking Ridge, NJ, USA
{gdicrescenzo,bcoan,jkirsch}@perspectalabs.com

Abstract. Secure computation (i.e., performing computation while keeping privacy of the inputs) is a fundamental research area in cryptography and a fundamental capability in the theory of computing. Deterministic automata evaluation is a fundamental computation problem, with numerous application areas, including regular expressions, string matching, constant-space computations.

In this paper, we investigate the complexity of achieving secure 2-party deterministic automata evaluation protocols. We show black-box reductions between this problem and the problem of constructing secure 2-party information retrieval protocols, and viceversa. Using previous results, this implies various interesting consequences: completeness of secure deterministic automata evaluation in the class of problems having 2-party and multi-party secure function evaluation protocols (previously, only 2 less natural problems were showed to be complete, or non-constructive characterizations of complete problems were given), and, under standard cryptographic assumptions, a communication-efficient secure protocol for automata evaluation (no such problem was given in the literature) and a time-efficient secure protocol faster than applying Yao's benchmark general solution.

1 Introduction

Deterministic automata evaluation is a fundamental computation problem, with numerous application areas, including regular expressions, string matching, constant-space computations. In the classical problem formulation, the automata is evaluated by a sequence of transactions, each going through a next state, chosen depending on the current state and the next symbol on its input string. At

This work was supported by the Defense Advanced Research Projects Agency (DARPA) via Air Force Research Laboratory (AFRL), contract number FA8750-14-C-0057. The U.S. Government is authorized to reproduce and distribute reprints for Governmental purposes notwithstanding any copyright annotation hereon. Disclaimer: The views and conclusions contained herein are those of the authors and should not be interpreted as necessarily representing the official policies or endorsements, either expressed or implied, of DARPA, AFRL or the U.S. Government.

© Springer Nature Switzerland AG 2020
E. Simion and R. Géraud-Stewart (Eds.): SecITC 2019, LNCS 12001, pp. 50–64, 2020.
https://doi.org/10.1007/978-3-030-41025-4_4

the end of the input string, the automata may be in a final state (thus, accepting the input string) or non-final state (thus, rejecting it). In one formulation of interest in this paper, the automata is called a *Moore automata*, and is also allowed to return an output symbol at each transaction, depending on the current state. In another formulation of interest for this paper, the computation is distributed between two parties, one holding the automata and one holding the input string.

Secure computation (i.e., performing computation while keeping privacy of the inputs) is a fundamental research area in cryptography and a fundamental capability in the theory of computing. In the formulation of interest for this paper, there are two parties, Alice and Bob, who would like to interactively compute a function f, expressible as a polynomial-size circuit, on their inputs x and y, such that at the end of the protocol: Bob obtains $f(x, y)$, an adversary corrupting Alice learns nothing new about Bob's input y, and an adversary corrupting Bob learns nothing new about Alice's input x, in addition to what is efficiently computable from $f(x, y)$. The first general solution to this problem for any function f having a polynomial-size circuit, was presented by Yao [21], assuming that the adversary is semi-honest (i.e., he follows the protocol as the corrupted party but may at the end try any polynomial-time algorithm to learn about the other party's input). Another important general solution for any function f having a polynomial-size circuit was given in [7], who studied the important multi-party scenario (i.e., where more than 2 parties run the protocol), and presented a compiler from any solution in the semi-honest adversary model to a solution where the adversary can be malicious (i.e., he may run an arbitrary polynomial-time strategy while deviating from the protocol). As of today, the area is still very active, and can be partitioned into two main sub-areas.

A first sub-area is concerned about *general-purpose* protocols, applicable to any function f expressible as a polynomial-size circuit. Questions studied for this type of protocols include, among others: (1) improving their time, communication, and round complexity; and (2) studying reduction and completeness questions for the class of functions having these protocols. With respect to (1), recent advances (see, e.g., [11,18] and follow-up papers) have moved these protocols significantly towards being usable in practice, at least in some specific scenarios (i.e., with the help of additional servers [2]). With respect to (2), [14] originally showed that Rabin's Oblivious Transfer protocol [20] is complete, meaning that it is possible to securely compute any efficient function if given a protocol securely computing oblivious transfer as a black box. Later, Private Information Retrieval was proved to be complete as well [4] and non-constructive characterizations have been given, some indicating that in some settings all problems are either complete or trivial [10,13,16].

A second sub-area is concerned about *special-purpose* protocols, applicable to specific functions f whose description is used by protocol designers to achieve improved results that are otherwise not achievable via general-purpose solutions. Even for this type of protocols improving their time, communication, and round complexity are among the most studied questions.

In this paper, we study secure 2 party computation protocols for the specific function of Deterministic Automata Evaluation, and show black-box reductions with (a stronger version of) the problem of Private Information Retrieval. This provides new insights on all above mentioned questions, including showing that this problem is complete for secure 2-party and multi-party protocols, and that has secure protocols with improved time-efficiency and communication-efficiency.

Our Contribution. In this paper, we investigate the complexity of achieving secure 2-party deterministic automata evaluation, and obtain the following results:

1. we show how to construct a secure 2-party deterministic automata evaluation protocol from any secure 2-party protocol for information retrieval and viceversa, and note 3 interesting consequences, as follows; no such reductions were presented in the literature;
2. combined with previous results, these results imply black-box constructions of any 2-party or multi-party problem solvable by a polynomial-size circuit from secure 2-party deterministic automata evaluation; previously, only 2 important but less natural problems (i.e., Oblivious Transfer and Information Retrieval from a database modeled as a string) were showed to be complete, or non-constructive characterizations of complete problems were given;
3. using secure information retrieval protocols from the literature with communication complexity sublinear in the number of data items, we obtain a secure deterministic automata evaluation protocol with communication complexity sublinear in the automata transition matrix; this is of special interest for problems with large automata matrices; we are not aware of any such result from the literature;
4. using secure information retrieval protocols from the literature with efficient time complexity, we obtain a secure deterministic automata evaluation protocol with time complexity faster than using Yao's protocol; this is of special interest even for problems with small automata matrices; previous efficient protocols with similar but somewhat different efficient properties were already given in [12,19].

Our main underlying techniques consist of expressing the secure deterministic automata evaluation problem as a problem of securely retrieving information from the automata transition matrix, and solving the latter problem using solutions that are either efficient in communication complexity (directly from the private information retrieval literature) or in time complexity, in the latter case using a circuit that is smaller than what would be generated by a conventional application of Yao's protocol.

Organization of the Paper. In Sect. 2 we detail definitions and models of interest. First, we give formal definitions for the automata evaluation problem and background cryptographic primitives like pseudo-random functions and symmetric encryption schemes. Then, we formally define secure computation protocols for arbitrary functions as well as specific functions like automata evaluation and functions related to background cryptographic primitives like information retrieval.

In Sect. 3 we present our first result: a reduction of secure 2-party information retrieval to secure 2-party deterministic Moore automata evaluation.

In Sect. 4 we present our second result: a reduction of secure 2-party deterministic automata evaluation protocol to secure 2-party information retrieval.

In Sect. 5 we present consequences of our results in the previous two sections: completeness of secure automata evaluation among 2-party and multi-party secure protocols, a communication-efficient secure protocol for 2-party automata evaluation, and a time-efficient secure protocol for 2-party automata evaluation.

2   Definitions and Background

In this section we recall definitions for automata evaluation, information retrieval problems, and secure 2-party protocols for arbitrary (and specific) functions.

2.1   Automata Evaluation and Information Retrieval

Automata Evaluation. A *deterministic automata* is formally defined as a tuple $DA = (S, s_0, F, A, \tau)$, where S is the set of automata *states*, $s_0 \in S$ is the *initial state*, F is a subset of S representing the set of *final states*, A is an *alphabet*, and $\tau : S \times A \to S$ is a *transition function* that maps any state and any alphabet element to the next state (when defined). We also denote as $|S| = s$ the number of states, as $|F| = f$ the number of final states, and as $|A| = a$ the number of alphabet symbols. An *input string* $x = (x_1, \ldots, x_n)$ is a sequence of alphabet symbols $x_i \in A$, for $i = 1, \ldots, n$, and n denotes the input length. The *automata evaluation* (briefly, AE) problem consists of computing $s_i = \tau(s_{i-1}, x_i)$, for $i = 1, \ldots, n$, and then returning as output $out_{ae} = 1$ if $s_{n+1} \in F$ (denoting that a final state is reached) or $out_{ae} = 0$ otherwise.

A *deterministic Moore automata* is defined as $mDA = (S, s_0, F, A_{in}, \tau, A_{out}, \lambda)$, where the tuple $(S, s_0, F, A_{in}, \tau)$ is a deterministic automata, A_{in} is the input alphabet, A_{out} is the output alphabet and $\lambda : S \to A_{out}$ is an *output function* that maps any state to an element of the output alphabet. The *Moore automata evaluation* (briefly, mAE) problem consists of computing $s_1, \ldots, s_n$ as in AE, and additionally returning as output $out_{mae} = (\lambda(s_0), \lambda(s_1), \ldots, \lambda(s_n))$, where $\lambda(s_i) \in A_{out}$, for $i = 0, \ldots, n$.

In a 2-party formulation of the mAE problem, the two parties, called Alice and Bob, are given as input the automata objects S, s_0, A_{in}, A_{out} and the parameters s, a, n; Alice is given as input F, τ, λ; Bob holds the input string x; and at the end of the 2-party protocol, Bob obtains the output of the mAE problem. A 2-party formulation of the AE problem is similarly derived.

Information Retrieval. A *database* is formally defined as a list of data blocks $x = (x[1], \ldots, x[m])$, where $|x[i]| = \ell$, for $i = 1, \ldots, m$. A *query index* is formally defined as a value $i \in \{1, \ldots, m\}$. The *Information Retrieval* (briefly, IR) problem is defined by returning as output, on input an m-block database x and a query index i, the data block $x[i]$. In a 2-party formulation of the problem, the two parties, called Alice and Bob, are given as input the parameters ℓ, m; Alice is given as input x; Bob is given as input index i; and at the end of the 2-party protocol, Bob obtains the output of the IR problem.

2.2 Secure Computation of Arbitrary and Specific Functions

Basic Definitions. Let σ denote a security parameter. A function over the set of natural numbers is *negligible* if for all sufficiently large natural numbers $\sigma \in \mathcal{N}$, it is smaller than $1/p(\sigma)$, for all polynomials p. Two distribution ensembles $\{D_\sigma^0 : \sigma \in \mathcal{N}\}$ and $\{D_\sigma^1 : \sigma \in \mathcal{N}\}$ are *computationally indistinguishable* if for any efficient algorithm A, the quantity $|\mathrm{Prob}[\,x \leftarrow D_\sigma^0 : A(x) = 1\,] - \mathrm{Prob}[\,x \leftarrow D_\sigma^1 : A(x) = 1\,]|$ is negligible in σ (i.e., no efficient algorithm can distinguish if a random sample came from one distribution or the other).

Secure 2-party Function Evaluation Protocols. Let f be a deterministic, 2-input, 1-output, function; that is, for any input pair (x, y), function f always returns one output z. In the 2-party formulation that we consider in the rest of the paper, string x is input to Alice, string y is input to Bob, and output z is returned to Bob. We use the simulation-based definition from [8] for security of 2-party function evaluation protocols in the presence of semi-honest adversaries (i.e., adversaries that corrupt one party, follow the protocol as that party and then attempt to obtain some information about the other party's input). In a 2-party protocol execution, a party's *view* is the sequence containing the party's input, the party's random string, and all messages received by or sent to the other party during the execution. According to this definition, a protocol π to evaluate a deterministic function f satisfies *simulation-based security* in the presence of a semi-honest adversary, if there exists two efficient algorithms Sim_A, Sim_B (called *simulators*), such that: (1) Sim_A's output on input Alice's input is computationally indistinguishable from Alice's view; and (2) Sim_B's output on input Bob's input and Bob's output is computationally indistinguishable from Bob's view. Here, the first (resp., second) condition says that a semi-honest adversary's view when corrupting Alice (resp., Bob), can be generated by an efficient algorithm not knowing Bob's (resp., Alice's) input, and thus the adversary does not learn anything about the uncorrupted party's input, other than the computation's output (when corrupting Bob).

Efficiency Requirements. We will target the following efficiency metrics (for a given secure 2-party protocol), expressed as a function of the security parameter σ: *time complexity* (briefly, *tc*), the time elapsed between the beginning and the end of a single protocol execution; *communication complexity* (briefly, *cc*), the length of all messages exchanged during a single protocol execution; and *round complexity* (briefly, *rc*), the number of messages exchanged during a single protocol execution.

Secure Evaluation Protocols for Specific Functions. In our solutions, we use or build constructions of 2-party secure evaluation protocols for the following functions: AE and IR.

A *secure automata evaluation protocol* (briefly, sAeval protocol) is a protocol between two parties: Alice, having as input a deterministic automata DA, and Bob, having as input a string x. The protocol is defined as a secure function evaluation of the output of the AE problem, returned to Bob (thus, without revealing any information about x to Alice, or any information about DA to Bob in addition to the DA evaluation on input x). Similarly, a *secure Moore automata evaluation protocol* (briefly, sMAeval protocol) is a protocol between two parties: Alice, having as input a Moore deterministic automata mDA, and Bob, having as input a string x. The protocol is defined as a secure function evaluation of the output of the AE problem, returned to Bob (thus, without revealing any information about x to Alice, or any information about mDA to Bob in addition to the mDA evaluation on input x).

A *secure information retrieval protocol* (briefly, sIReval protocol) is a protocol between two parties: Alice, having as input a database bl, and Bob, having as input a query index ind. The protocol is defined as a secure function evaluation of the output of the IR problem, returned to Bob (thus, without revealing any information about ind to Alice, or any information about bl to Bob in addition to the desired output $bl[ind]$).

3   From AE to IR

In this section we present our results on IR starting from analogue results on AE. Specifically, we first describe, in Sect. 3.1, a simple many-to-one reduction of the 2-party IR problem to the 2-party mAE problem, and then, in Sect. 3.2, describe a secure 2-party computation protocol by distributing the steps in this reduction.

3.1   A Privacy-Preserving Reduction

The basic steps underlying our reduction are as follows. Given a database bl and a query index ind, the reduction constructs a set of states S containing an initial state and one final state for each data block in bl. Then, a transition function τ and an output function λ are defined so that on input character i, the Moore automata moves from the initial state to the i-th final state and the latter outputs data block $bl[i]$, for $i = 1, \ldots, m$.

Since the computation of this reduction can be distributed between the two parties without any privacy violation, the reduction between problems can be extended to a reduction between protocols, where any protocol solving the 2-party mAE problem can be used to solve the 2-party IR problem.

We now proceed more formally. Given database $bl = (bl[1], \ldots, bl[m])$, and query index ind, we define a deterministic Moore automata

$$mDA = (S, s_0, F, A_{in}, \tau, A_{out}, \lambda),$$

as follows:

1. $s = m + 1$, $a = m$, $n = 1$ and $s_0 = 0$
2. $S = \{s_0, s_1, \ldots, s_m\}$
3. $A_{in} = \{1, \ldots, m\}$
4. $A_{out} = \{0, 1\}^\ell$
5. $F = \{1, \ldots, m\}$
6. $\tau(i, s_0) = s_i$, for $i = 1, \ldots, m$
7. $\lambda(0) = \emptyset$ and $\lambda(i) = bl[i]$, for $i = 1, \ldots, m$
8. $x_1 = ind$ and $x = (x_1)$.

3.2   A Secure 2-party Protocol

We show a communication-efficient secure information retrieval protocol based on any communication-efficient secure Moore automata evaluation protocol. Formally, we obtain the following

Theorem 1. Assume the existence of a 2-party sAeval protocol π_{ae}. There exists a (black-box) construction of a 2-party sIReval protocol π_{ir}, where $cc(\pi_{ir}) = cc(\pi_{ae})$, $rc(\pi_{ir}) = rc(\pi_{ae})$, and $tc(\pi_{ir}) = tc(\pi_{ae})$.

We prove Theorem 1 by showing protocol π_{ir} and its security and efficiency properties.

Formal Description. We observe that since the computation of the reduction presented in Sect. 3.1 can be distributed between the two parties without any privacy violation, the reduction between problems can be extended to a reduction between protocols, where any protocol solving the 2-party mAE problem can be used to solve the 2-party IR problem.

Based on the reduction steps defined in Sect. 3.1, given 2-party protocol π_{mae}, we define the following 2-party protocol π_{ir}:

Input to Alice: database $bl = (bl[1], \ldots, bl[m])$
Input to Bob: query index $ind \in \{1, \ldots, m\}$
Instructions for Alice and Bob in π_{ir}:

1. Alice and Bob generate $s, a, n, s_0, S, A_{in}, A_{out}$ as in above reduction steps 1–4
2. Alice generates F, τ, λ as in above reduction steps 5–7
3. Bob generates x as in the above reduction step 8
4. Alice and Bob run protocol π_{ae}, using the inputs generated in the previous 3 steps
   let $(\lambda(0), \lambda(ind))$ be the values obtained by Bob at the end of this protocol
5. Bob sets $bl[ind] = \lambda(ind)$ and outputs: $bl[ind]$.

Properties of π_{ir}. The showed reduction preserves both efficiency and security properties. Most notably: (1) if π_{ae} is a secure protocol then so is π_{ir}; and (2) the communication complexity of π_{ae} is the same as the communication complexity in π_{ir}. To prove (1), we show a simulator against any efficient semi-honest adversary Adv corrupting Alice and one against any efficient semi-honest adversary Adv corrupting Bob.

Adv Corrupts Alice. If π_{ae} is a secure protocol, there is an efficient simulator Sim_A^{ae} that, given Alice's input mDA in an execution of protocol π_{ae}, generates an output out_S^{ae} computationally indistinguishable from Alice's view during the protocol (note that Alice has no output in this protocol). Thus, in protocol π_{ir} we define Sim_A^{ir} as follows. Given Alice's input bl in an execution of protocol π_{ir}, Sim_A^{ir} does the following:

- generate mDA as in above reduction steps 1–7
- obtain out_S^{ae} by running Sim_A^{ae} on input mDA
- set $out_S^{ir} = out_S^{ae}$
- output: out_S^{ir}

By the analogue property of Sim_A^{ae}, we obtain that Sim_A^{ir} generates an output out_S^{ir} computationally indistinguishable from Alice's view during protocol π_{ir} (note that Alice has no output in this protocol).

Adv Corrupts Bob. If π_{ae} is a secure protocol, there is an efficient simulator Sim_B^{ae} that, given Bob's input x and Bob's output out_{Bob}^{ae} in a protocol for mAE, generates an output out_S^{ae} computationally indistinguishable from Bob's view during the protocol. Thus, in protocol π_{ir} we define Sim_B^{ir} as follows. Given Bob's input ind and Bob's output out_{Bob}^{ir} in an execution of protocol π_{ir}, runs the following steps:

- generate x as in above reduction step 8
- set $out_{Bob}^{ae} = 1$
- obtain out_S^{ae} by running Sim_B^{ae} on input x and out_{Bob}^{ae}
- set $out_S^{ir} = out_S^{ae}$
- output: out_S^{ir}

By the analogue property of Sim_B^{ae}, we obtain that Sim_B^{ir} generates an output out_S^{ir} computationally indistinguishable from Bob's view during protocol π_{ir}.

Efficiency Properties. By protocol inspection, we observe that protocol π_{ir}, when run on input length parameters m, ℓ, consists of running π_{ae} on input length parameters s, a, n, ℓ, where $s = m + 1$, $a = m$, and $n = 1$. These parameter relationships allow to directly compute the time complexity, round complexity and communication complexity of π_{ir} from those of π_{ae}. One interesting consequence is that if $cc(\pi_{ae}) = o(\max\{s, a\})$ then $cc(\pi_{ir}) = o(m)$; that is, sAeval protocols with communication sublinear in the number of automata states result in sIReval protocols with communication sublinear in the number of database blocks.

4   From Secure IR to Secure AE

In this section we present our second result: based on any secure information retrieval protocol, we construct a secure Moore automata evaluation protocol. Formally, we obtain the following

Theorem 2. Assume the existence of a 2-party sIReval protocol π_{ir} for IR. There exists a (black-box) construction of a 2-party sAeval protocol π_{ae} for AE, where

- $cc(\pi_{ae}) = O(n \cdot cc(\pi_{ir,s \cdot a}) + cc(\pi_{ir,n}) + san \log s)$
- $rc(\pi_{ae}) = n \cdot rc(\pi_{ir,s \cdot a}) + rc(\pi_{ir,n})$
- $tc(\pi_{ae}) = O(n \cdot tc(\pi_{ir,s \cdot a}) + tc(\pi_{ir,n}) + san \log s)$,

and where $\pi_{ir,q}$ denotes the protocol π_{ir} when run on a database with q data blocks.

We prove Theorem 2 by showing protocol π_{ae} and its security and efficiency properties.

Informal Description. We assume the existence of a 2-party sIReval protocol π_{ir} for IR. Although π_{ir} is defined to be usable by Alice to retrieve a value at index ind from an m-location array bl held by Bob, we will use for Alice to retrieve a value at row index ind_r and column index ind_c from an s-row, a-column matrix M held by Bob. This is simply done by representing M as a suitable vector bl and indices ind_r, ind_c as a suitable index ind. Specifically, define protocol π_{mir} as the protocol where Alice sets $ind = ind_r(m-1) + ind_c$, Bob sets $bl[i] = M[1 + \text{quotient}(i/m), 1 + i \bmod m]$, for $i = 1, \ldots, s \cdot a$, and finally the 2 parties run π_{ir}, with the computed inputs bl, for Bob, and ind, for Alice.

By directly applying the definition of finite automata, Alice and Bob can evaluate Alice's automata on input Bob's string x by a sequence of n retrievals from the automata's transition matrix, followed by one retrieval from the array denoting which state is final or not. Note that this defines a Turing reduction of the 2-party AE problem to the 2-party IR problem, and it is also possible to distribute this reduction between the two parties, similarly as done in the proof of Theorem 2 to create a candidate sAeval protocol.

However, this resulting protocol is not secure since at the end of a retrieval from the transition matrix, Bob obtains the next state, which leaks significant information about Alice's automata input. We avoid this problem by masking the state values in all entries of the transition matrix using a random permutation over the set of states. Since only one value output by this random permutation is ever shown to Bob, he only receives a random state.

This modification introduces a potential inconsistency on the automata computation, in that the permuted state received by Bob at the end of the retrieval protocol is not useful to retrieve the next state on the transition matrix. We avoid this inconsistency by using a copy of the transition matrix for each symbol of Bob's input string, by using a random and independent permutation over the set of states on each of these copies, and by permuting the rows of the next copy of the transition matrix by the same permutation used to mask the entries in the previous copy of the transition matrix.

We note that since an independent random permutation is used at each automata transition, Bob only receives a sequence of random and independent states as all outputs of the retrieval sub-protocols, and therefore these latter modifications maintain the protocol's privacy properties.

Formal Description. Let π_{ir} be a 2-party sIReval protocol and let π_{mir} be the corresponding 2-party secure protocol for information retrieval from a matrix, constructed as defined in the above informal description. We now proceed with a formal description of protocol π_{ae}.

Input to Alice: deterministic Moore automata $mDA = (S, s_0, F, A_{in}, \tau, A_{out}, \lambda)$
Input to Bob: string $x \in A_{in}^n$
Instructions for Alice and Bob in protocol π_{ae}:

1. For $h = 1, \ldots, n + 1$,
    Alice generates a random and independent permutation p_h of set $S = \{1, \ldots, s\}$
    Alice computes its inverse permutation p_h^{-1}
2. For $h = 1, \ldots, n$,
    Alice generates a permuted transition matrix ptM_h, as follows:
        for $i = 1, \ldots, s$
            for $j = 1, \ldots, a$
                set next state $ns_{i,j} = \tau(p_h^{-1}(i), j)$
                set matrix entry $ptM_h[i, j] = p_{h+1}(ns_{i,j})$
3. Alice generates a final state array fa, as follows:
        for $i = 1, \ldots, s$
        set $fa[i] = 1$ if $p_{n+1}^{-1}(i) \in F$
        set $fa[i] = 0$ if $p_{n+1}^{-1}(i) \notin F$
4. Bob sets the current permuted state cps_1 as the permuted initial state $p_1(s_0)$
5. For $h = 1, \ldots, n$
    Alice and Bob run protocol π_{mir}, where
        Alice uses as input matrix ptM_h
        Bob uses as input current permuted state cps_h
        Bob obtains a matrix entry as output
        Bob relabels the obtained output as cps_{h+1}
6. Alice and Bob run protocol π_{ir}, where
    Alice uses as input array fa
    Bob uses as input cps_{n+1}
    Bob obtains an array entry b as output
7. Bob returns: b

Properties of π_{ir}. The described protocol satisfies desirable efficiency and security properties. Most notably: (1) if π_{ir} is a secure protocol then so is π_{ae}; and (2) the communication complexity of π_{ae} is the same as the communication complexity in π_{ir}. To prove (1), we show a simulator for any efficient semi-honest adversary Adv corrupting Alice and one for any efficient semi-honest adversary Adv corrupting Bob.

Adv Corrupts Alice. If π_{ir} is a secure protocol, there is an efficient simulator Sim_A^{ir} that, given database array bl as Alice's input in an execution of protocol π_{ir}, generates an output out_S^{ir} which is computationally indistinguishable from Alice's view during the protocol (note that Alice has no output in this protocol). Under the same assumption, π_{mir} is a secure protocol, and thus there is an efficient simulator Sim_A^{mir} that, given matrix M as Alice's input in an execution of protocol π_{ir}, generates an output out_S^{ir} which is computationally indistinguishable from Alice's view during the protocol. Then, for protocol π_{ae} we define simulator Sim_A^{ae} as follows. Given Alice's input mDA in an execution of protocol π_{ae}, Sim_A^{ae} runs the following instructions:

– generate permutation p_h, p_h^{-1} as in step 1 of protocol π_{ae}, for $h = 1, \ldots, n$
– generate permuted transition matrix ptM_h as in step 2 of protocol π_{ae}, for $h = 1, \ldots, n$
– generate final state array fa as in step 3 of protocol π_{ae}, for $h = 1, \ldots, n$
– for $h = 1, \ldots, n$,
        obtain $out_{S,h}^{mir}$ by running Sim_A^{mir} on input ptM_h
– obtain out_S^{ir} by running Sim_A^{ir} on input fa
– output: $(out_{S,1}^{mir}, \ldots, out_{S,n}^{mir}, out_S^{ir})$

First of all we observe that values p_h, p_h^{-1}, ptM_h, and fa are generated by Sim_A^{ae} exactly as generated by Alice during protocol π_{ae}. Then, by the analogue property of Sim_A^{mir}, we obtain that Sim_A^{mir} generates an output $out_{S,h}^{mir}$ computationally indistinguishable from Alice's view during the h-th execution of protocol π_{mir} within protocol π_{ae}, for $h = 1, \ldots, m$. Similarly, we obtain that Sim_A^{ir} generates an output out_S^{ir} computationally indistinguishable from Alice's view during the execution of protocol π_{ir} within protocol π_{ae}. The claim that the entire output of Sim_A^{ae} is computationally indistinguishable from Alice's view during an execution of π_{ae} follows by a standard hybrid argument [9].

Adv Corrupts Bob. If π_{ir} is a secure protocol, there is an efficient simulator Sim_B^{ir} that, given index ind as Bob's input in an execution of protocol π_{ir} and Bob's output out_{Bob}^{ir}, generates an output out_S^{ir} which is computationally indistinguishable from Bob's view during the protocol. Under the same assumption, π_{mir} is a secure protocol, and thus there is an efficient simulator Sim_B^{mir} that, given indices ind_r, ind_c as Bob's input in an execution of protocol π_{mir} and Bob's output out_{Bob}^{mir}, generates an output out_S^{mir} which is computationally indistinguishable from Bob's view during the protocol. Then, for protocol π_{ae} we define simulator Sim_B^{ae} as follows. Given Bob's input x in an execution of protocol π_{ae}, and Bob's output $b \in \{0,1\}$, Sim_B^{ae} runs the following instructions:

– generate permutation p_1 as in step 1 of protocol π_{ae}
– generate current permuted state cps_1 as in step 4 of protocol π_{ae}
– for $h = 1, \ldots, n$,

randomly and independently choose $cps_{h+1} \in \{1, \ldots, s\}$
set $out_{Bob,h}^{mir} = cps_{h+1}$
obtain $out_{S,h}^{mir}$ by running Sim_B^{mir} on input cps_h and $out_{Bob,h}^{mir}$
- set $out_{Bob}^{ir} = b$
- obtain out_S^{ir} by running Sim_B^{ir} on input cps_{n+1} and out_{Bob}^{ir}
- output: $(out_{S,1}^{mir}, \ldots, out_{S,n}^{mir}, out_S^{ir})$

First of all we observe that values p_1 and cps_1 are generated by Sim_B^{ae} exactly as generated by Bob during protocol π_{ae}.

Then, by induction over h, we can prove that the values cps_h generated by Sim_B^{ae} are computationally indistinguishable from the values cps_h computed by Bob during π_{ae}. The base case, when $h = 1$, follows by the fact that cps_1 is generated by Sim_B^{ae} exactly as done by Bob during protocol π_{ae}. For the inductive case, first assume the claim is true for cps_h; and then observe that cps_{h+1} is randomly chosen from $\{1, \ldots, s\}$ in Sim_B^{mir} and computed as the output of protocol π_{mir} on input cps_h from Bob during an execution of π_{ae}. Note that by the induction hypothesis and the security property of π_{mir}, the value cps_{h+1} computed by Bob is computationally indistinguishable from the output of a random permutation on input cps_h, which is uniformly distributed in $\{1, \ldots, s\}$.

Then, by the analogue property of Sim_B^{mir}, we obtain that Sim_B^{mir} generates an output $out_{S,h}^{mir}$ computationally indistinguishable from Bob's view during the h-th execution of protocol π_{mir} within protocol π_{ae}, for $h = 1, \ldots, m$. Similarly, we obtain that Sim_B^{ir} generates an output out_S^{ir} computationally indistinguishable from Bob's view during the execution of protocol π_{ir} within protocol π_{ae}. Finally, the claim that the entire output of Sim_B^{ae} is computationally indistinguishable from Bob's view during an execution of π_{ae} follows by a standard hybrid argument [9].

Efficiency Properties. By protocol inspection, we observe that protocol π_{ae}, when run on input length parameters s, a, n, ℓ, consists of running n times π_{mir} on input length parameters m, ℓ, where $m = s \cdot a$, and of running once π_{ir} on input length parameters $m = n$. These parameter relationships allow to easily compute the time complexity, round complexity and communication complexity of π_{ae} from those of π_{ir}. One interesting consequence is that if $cc(\pi_{ir}) = o(m)$ then $cc(\pi_{ae})/n = o(s \cdot a)$; that is, sIReval protocols with communication complexity sublinear in the number of database blocks result in sAeval protocols with communication complexity (per Bob's input symbol) sublinear in the transition matrix.

5   Extensions and Applications

We discuss some extensions and/or applications of our results in Sects. 3 and 4.

5.1   Completeness of sMAeval Protocols

We show that any sMAeval protocol can be used to construct a secure (against semi-honest adversaries) 2-party or multi-party protocol for any polynomial-size boolean circuit.

The 2-Party Case. The notion of 1-out-of-2 oblivious transfer protocols was introduced in the seminal paper [20] and has been since then used in a very large number of cryptographic protocols. Notably, the foundational result from [21] shows that 1-out-of-2 oblivious transfer protocols and symmetric encryption schemes can be used to construct a 2-party secure protocol for any polynomial-size circuit. We note that sIReval protocols are, by definition, secure 1-out-of-n oblivious transfer protocols, for any desired $n \geq 2$. By implementing a 1-out-of-2 oblivious transfer protocol with the sIReval protocol which we presented in the proof of Theorem 1, we obtain the following result.

Corollary 1. Assuming the existence of an sMAeval protocol and of symmetric encryption schemes, there exists, constructively, a secure (against efficient and semi-honest adversaries) 2-party protocol for any polynomial-size circuit.

The Multi-party Case. Oblivious transfer has been used to construct secure multi-party computation protocols for any polynomial-size circuit [7]. In fact, it has been shown to be complete for secure multi-party computation, in the sense that any polynomial-size circuit can be securely computed given a black-box securely computing oblivious transfer [15]. By implementing a 1-out-of-2 oblivious transfer protocol with the sIReval protocol which we presented in the proof of Theorem 1, we obtain the following result.

Corollary 2. Assuming the existence of an sMAeval protocol, there exists, constructively, a secure (against efficient and semi-honest adversaries) multi-party protocol for any polynomial-size circuit.

5.2   Communication-Efficient sAeval Protocols for Large Automata

There is a large literature on 2-party private information retrieval protocols, focusing on designing protocols that achieve communication complexity sublinear in the number of database blocks. We remark that information retrieval protocols satisfying security when only one of the 2 parties are corrupted (often going under the acronym PIR protocols) or only satisfying a privacy requirement, even for both parties (often called symmetrically private PIR protocols), may not satisfy the simulation-based security against any adversary that can corrupt any one of the two parties, which we consider here. Protocols satisfying simulation-based security are, by definition, 1-out-of-n OT protocols with simulation-based security, and have been proposed, in the semi-honest adversary model, under standard cryptographic assumptions, in [5] and in [1,17]. By implementing the sIReval protocol used in the proof of Theorem 2 using any one of these results, we obtain the following result, which is of special interest in instances of the AE problem having large transaction matrices.

Corollary 3. Under standard cryptographic assumptions, there exists, constructively, an sAeval protocol with communication complexity (per symbol in Bob's input string) sublinear in the size of the transaction matrix in Alice's input automata.

5.3   Time-Efficient sAeval Protocols for Small Automata

There is a large literature on 2-party keyword search protocols, focusing on designing protocols that achieve time efficient protocols (and communication complexity linear in the number of database blocks). We remark that such keyword search protocols can be used to obtain time-efficient linear-communication information retrieval protocols. For instances, protocols in [3,6] achieve this goal by only assuming the existence of oblivious pseudo-random functions protocols and of symmetric encryption schemes. By implementing the sIReval protocol used in the proof of Theorem 2 using this result, we obtain the following result, which is of special interest in instances of the AE problem having small transaction matrices.

Corollary 4. Under the existence of oblivious pseudo-random functions protocols and of symmetric encryption schemes, there exists, constructively, an sAeval protocol with time complexity equal to $O(n \log a)$ modular exponentiations and $O(nas)$ block cipher evaluations.

We remark that the time complexity of the obtained sAeval protocol compares favorably with that obtained by a direct application of Yao's general-purpose protocol [21], which would require $O(n \log a)$ modular exponentiation and $O(nas \log s)$ block cipher evaluations. On the other hand, previous efficient protocols with similar but somewhat different efficiency properties were already given in [12,19].

References

1. Aiello, B., Ishai, Y., Reingold, O.: Priced oblivious transfer: how to sell digital goods. In: Pfitzmann, B. (ed.) EUROCRYPT 2001. LNCS, vol. 2045, pp. 119–135. Springer, Heidelberg (2001). https://doi.org/10.1007/3-540-44987-6_8
2. Bogetoft, P., et al.: Secure multiparty computation goes live. In: Dingledine, R., Golle, P. (eds.) FC 2009. LNCS, vol. 5628, pp. 325–343. Springer, Heidelberg (2009). https://doi.org/10.1007/978-3-642-03549-4_20
3. Di Crescenzo, G., Cook, D.L., McIntosh, A., Panagos, E.: Practical and privacy-preserving information retrieval from a database table. J. Comput. Secur. **24**(4), 479–506 (2016)
4. Di Crescenzo, G., Malkin, T., Ostrovsky, R.: Single database private information retrieval implies oblivious transfer. In: Preneel, B. (ed.) EUROCRYPT 2000. LNCS, vol. 1807, pp. 122–138. Springer, Heidelberg (2000). https://doi.org/10.1007/3-540-45539-6_10
5. Even, S., Goldreich, O., Lempel, A.: A randomized protocol for signing contracts. Commun. ACM **28**(6), 637–647 (1985)

6. Freedman, M.J., Ishai, Y., Pinkas, B., Reingold, O.: Keyword search and oblivious pseudorandom functions. In: Kilian, J. (ed.) TCC 2005. LNCS, vol. 3378, pp. 303–324. Springer, Heidelberg (2005). https://doi.org/10.1007/978-3-540-30576-7_17
7. Goldreich, O., Micali, S., Wigderson, A.: Proofs that yield nothing but their validity or all languages in NP have zero-knowledge proof systems. J. ACM **38**(1), 691–729 (1991)
8. Goldreich, O.: The Foundations of Cryptography: Volume 2, Basic Applications. Cambridge University Press, Cambridge (2004)
9. Goldwasser, S., Micali, S.: Probabilistic encryption. J. Comput. Syst. Sci. **28**(2), 270–299 (1984)
10. Harnik, D., Naor, M., Reingold, O., Rosen, A.: Completeness in two-party secure computation: a computational view. J. Cryptol. **19**(4), 521–552 (2006)
11. Huang, Y., Evans, D., Katz, J., Malka, L.: Faster secure two-party computation using garbled circuits. In: Proceedings of the 20th USENIX Security Symposium, San Francisco, CA, USA, 8–12 August 2011 (2011)
12. Ishai, Y., Paskin, A.: Evaluating branching programs on encrypted data. In: Vadhan, S.P. (ed.) TCC 2007. LNCS, vol. 4392, pp. 575–594. Springer, Heidelberg (2007). https://doi.org/10.1007/978-3-540-70936-7_31
13. Ishai, Y., Prabhakaran, M., Sahai, A.: Founding cryptography on oblivious transfer – efficiently. In: Wagner, D. (ed.) CRYPTO 2008. LNCS, vol. 5157, pp. 572–591. Springer, Heidelberg (2008). https://doi.org/10.1007/978-3-540-85174-5_32
14. Kilian, J.: A note on efficient proofs and arguments. In: Proceedings of ACM STOC 1992 (1992)
15. Kilian, J.: Founding cryptography on oblivious transfer. In: Proceedings of the 20th Annual ACM Symposium on Theory of Computing, Chicago, Illinois, USA, 2–4 May 1988, pp. 20–31 (1988)
16. Kilian, J., Kushilevitz, E., Micali, S., Ostrovsky, R.: Reducibility and completeness in private computations. SIAM J. Comput. **29**(4), 1189–1208 (2000)
17. Kushilevitz, E., Ostrovsky, R.: Replication is NOT needed: SINGLE database, computationally-private information retrieval. In: 38th Annual Symposium on Foundations of Computer Science, FOCS 1997, Miami Beach, Florida, USA, 19–22 October 1997, pp. 364–373 (1997)
18. Malkhi, D., Nisan, N., Pinkas, B., Sella, Y.: Fairplay - secure two-party computation system. In: Proceedings of the 13th USENIX Security Symposium, San Diego, CA, USA, 9–13 August 2004, pp. 287–302 (2004)
19. Mohassel, P., Niksefat, S., Sadeghian, S., Sadeghiyan, B.: An efficient protocol for oblivious DFA evaluation and applications. In: Dunkelman, O. (ed.) CT-RSA 2012. LNCS, vol. 7178, pp. 398–415. Springer, Heidelberg (2012). https://doi.org/10.1007/978-3-642-27954-6_25
20. Rabin, M.O.: How to exchange secrets with oblivious transfer. IACR Cryptology ePrint Archive 2005:187 (2005)
21. Yao, A.C.-C.: How to generate and exchange secrets (extended abstract). In: FOCS, pp. 162–167 (1986)

Detecting Malicious Websites by Query Templates

Satomi Kaneko[1]([✉]), Akira Yamada[2], Yukiko Sawaya[2], Tran Phuong Thao[3], Ayumu Kubota[2], and Kazumasa Omote[1]

[1] University of Tsukuba, 1-1-1 Tennoudai, Tsukuba, Ibaraki 305-8573, Japan
`s1820578@s.tsukuba.ac.jp, omote@risk.tsukuba.ac.jp`
[2] KDDI Research, Inc., 2-1-15 Ohara, Fujimino, Saitama 356-8502, Japan
`{ai-yamada,yu-sawaya,kubota}@kddi-research.jp`
[3] The University of Tokyo, 7-3-1 Hongo, Bunkyo, Tokyo 113-8656, Japan
`tpthao@yamagula.ic.i.u-tokyo.ac.jp`

Abstract. With the development of the Internet, web content is exponentially increasing. Along with this, web-based attacks such as drive-by download attacks and phishing have grown year on year. To prevent such attacks, URL blacklists are widely used. However, URL blacklists are not enough because they lack the ability to detect newly generated malicious URLs. In this paper, we propose an automatic query template generation method to detect malicious websites. Our method focus on URL query strings that contained similarities on malicious website groups. Additionally, we evaluate our proposed method with large-scale dataset and verify effectiveness. Consequently, our proposed method can grasp the characteristics of malicious campaigns; it can detect 11,292 malicious unique domains not detected by Google Safe Browsing. Moreover, our method achieved high precision in the seven months of experiments.

Keywords: Web security · Web-based attacks · Phishing · Malicious websites detection

1 Introduction

Currently, web contents become increasingly important in daily life. According to a research by VeriSign, Inc. [14], the fourth quarter of 2018 closed with approximately 348.7 million domain name registrations across all top-level domains, an increase of approximately 6.3 million domain name registrations compared to the third quarter of 2018. This also gives rise to a considerable number of malicious domains. Web-based attacks such as drive-by download attacks and phishing also increase along with the number of malicious domains [12]. Therefore, web security has become a hot topic both in research and in the industry. Currently, URL blacklists are widely used as a means to prevent web-based attacks. URL blacklists collect already-known malicious URLs and manage the reputation of various URLs. When a client accesses the domain in URL blacklists, the request

© Springer Nature Switzerland AG 2020
E. Simion and R. Géraud-Stewart (Eds.): SecITC 2019, LNCS 12001, pp. 65–77, 2020.
https://doi.org/10.1007/978-3-030-41025-4_5

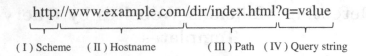

Fig. 1. Components of a URL

is blocked. One of the most famous URL blacklists is Google Safe Browsing [5] provided by Google. Google Safe Browsing examines billions of URLs and contents on web pages and discovers thousands of new malicious software sites and phishing sites daily. However, malicious websites are known to be very short-lived in order to avoid detection by URL blacklists. Therefore, simple URL blacklist methods using URLs and IP addresses cannot efficiently discover malicious websites. On the other hand, a case has been reported that a URL query string parameter containing a specific string appears on a compromised website used in drive-by download attacks [7]. This report indicates that the possibility of detecting a group of malicious URLs by focusing on query string parameters of short-lived domains.

In this paper, we propose a new method to generate query templates that generalize query string parameters, focusing on query string parameters of malicious websites. Our method detects short-lived malicious URLs by using specific strings included in the query template. We evaluate our proposed detection method using a real-world dataset, which is a large-scale web access log dataset. Query templates generated by our proposed method detect malicious URLs that are not detected by Google Safe Browsing. Furthermore, our proposed method can grasp the characteristics of malicious campaigns; it can detect 11,292 malicious unique domains not detected by Google Safe Browsing with only four query templates. Therefore, we consider that our proposed method is more efficient than a URL blacklist method.

2   Background

2.1   URL Components

Figure 1 shows an example of URL components. URL, which stands for Uniform Resource Locator, is a global address for documents and other resources on the World Wide Web. A URL has four main components: (I) A scheme: it identifies the protocol to be used to access the resource on the Internet, (II) A hostname: it identifies the host that holds the resource, (III) A path: it identifies the specific resource in the host that the web client wants to access, (IV) A query string: it follows the path component and provides a string of information that the resource can use for some purpose (e.g., parameters for a search, data to be processed). In this paper, we focus on a query string. A query string comprises two elements: parameter name and parameter value. In the case of Fig. 1, the parameter names and parameter values are "q" and "value", respectively.

2.2   Google Safe Browsing

Google Safe Browsing is a blacklist service provided by Google that was launched in 2007 to protect users across the web from web-based attacks. Currently, Google Chrome, Safari, and Firefox use the blacklists from the Google Safe Browsing service for page checking against potential threats. In addition, a client application can check URLs against Google's constantly updated lists of unsafe web resources by using the API.

Thao et al. [13] analyzed 14 popular blacklists such as malwaredomains, phishtank, urlblacklist and Google Safe Browsing (version 3/version 4). They found that Google is developing GSBv3 and GSBv4 independently and GSBv4 can detect younger domains compared to the other blacklists. Owing to this research result, we used GSBv4 in this study to collect malicious websites.

3   Related Work

The research approach on malicious URL detection can be divided into three categories [2]: detection method based on blacklists, heuristic rules, and machine learning. The detection method based on blacklist is a common and classical technique [10]. When a user visits a website, blacklists refer to confirmed malicious website domain names and IP addresses. If the domain name or IP address is present in the blacklist, it is considered to be malicious and access is blocked. However, attackers have registered domain names using low-cost methods such as Domain Generation Algorithm (DGA) [11]. Consequently, it is difficult for blacklists to detect new threats. The detection method based on heuristic rules is an extension type of blacklist-based method. Such a method uses data mining and machine learning algorithms to build a heuristic rule base to detect malicious attempts [1]. Heuristic rules have the ability to detect threats in new URLs. However, this method would fail to detect novel attack when the signature detection is often evaded by attackers by changing patterns and obfuscation techniques. The detection method based on machine learning is currently the most popular one. This method is used to classify malicious websites through the features from URLs, host, web contents, and network activity. However, the detection of malicious URLs using machine learning requires computational resources for feature extraction and model training. Therefore, it is unsuitable for real-time detection of large-scale data. To perform real-time detection on large-scale data, generating a URL signature without host information or web contents is effective. However, detection through URL signatures tends to have high false positive rates as well as heuristic rule-based detection. Therefore, our approach aims to extract only features effective for detection from URLs. The closest research to the direction of our approach is *ARROW* developed by Zhang et al. [15]. *ARROW* found the central server of malware distribution network by inputting the HTTP trace log and generated a set of regular expression-based signatures based on the URLs of each central server of malware distribution network. However, this method has the disadvantage that it needs to input HTTP trace log and can only generate signatures of the URL of the central server.

Table 1. Sample of the dataset

Element	Attribute	Content
(i)	Timestamp	2019-07-10 08:24:06
(ii)	USER ID	e9fb7ffa-12b7-1e4b-8224-3f2075002e67
(iii)	URL	http://www.example.com/dir/index.html?q=value

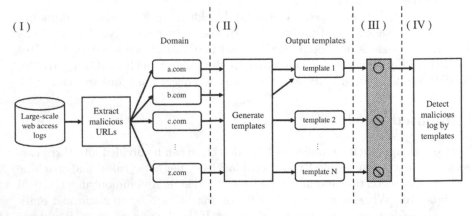

(I) Malicious URLs extraction phase (II) Template generation phase   (III) Template filtering phase   (IV) Detection phase

Fig. 2. Process of the proposed method

Mizuno et al. [8] generated signatures automatically, an approach different than that of Zhang et al. [15] Mizuno et al. proposed a system called *BotDetector* for detecting malicious traffic, which searches for malware-infected devices. The method automatically generates a template by generalizing the information in each HTTP header field. In addition, the method not only reduces the amount of information to be kept but also extracts useful features. Therefore, we generate URL signatures based on the Mziuno et al.'s generalization method.

4   Dataset

The dataset is provided by security software installed in several client PCs. A security vendor that provided the software collected large-scale web access logs on each client PC. The security software is a browser extension that can be downloaded and used by users. As the browser extension is used by hundreds of thousands of people, collecting large-scale web access logs is possible. The log is created when a user accesses a website and comprises the following elements: (i) A timestamp, (ii) a anonymized unique user ID, and (iii) an access destination URL. Table 1 shows a sample of the dataset.

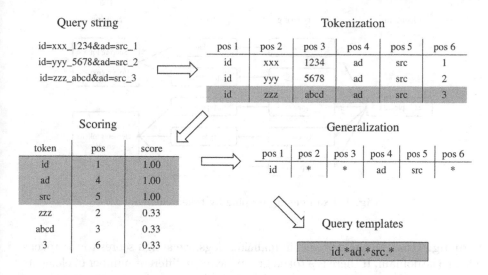

Fig. 3. Process of query template generation ($\delta = 0.1$, $\beta = 0.6$)

5 Proposed Method

Figure 2 shows the outline process of our proposed method. Our technique, named query template, provides efficient detection of short-lived malicious websites, which is difficult to detect with a blacklist method. Our method is divided into four phases: (I) Malicious log extraction phase, (II) template generation phase, (III) filtering phase, and (IV) detection phase.

5.1 Malicious URL Extraction Phase

In our proposed method, a query template is generated based on a known malicious URL. The Google Safe Browsing API is used to extract malicious URLs from dataset access logs in this phase.

5.2 Template Generation Phase

In this phase, a generalization is performed on the query string of the URL extracted in the previous phase to generate a query template. Figure 3 shows the outline process of the query template generation.

Tokenization of Query String. Query strings collected in the malicious log extraction phase are divided into tokens for each domain using delimiters. We defined delimiters such as "+", ".", ",", ":", ";", "=", "?", "#", "&", "/", "_", "-", "|". When the URL is percent-encoded, it is converted from an encoded string to a decoded string. Specifically, the tokenization is performed as follows. When "?q=value &a=type_x&b=type_y" is given as a query string, "q, value, a, type, x, b, type, y" is generated via tokenization.

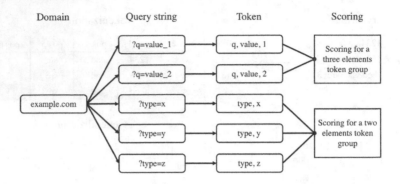

Fig. 4. Example of grouping by token elements

Scoring. Using all the domains in malicious logs, we assign scores to the tokens within the domain. If there is a token group having a different number of elements in the same domain, the score is calculated after grouping by the number of elements of the token group. This is done as shown in Fig. 4. We calculate the conditional probability of the tokens for each domain. For a token t in a given domain D, the score of the token $S(t; D)$ is given by the following conditional probability:

$$S(t; D) = P(t \mid \text{pos}(t, \ D), \ \text{len}(D)) = \frac{n(t, \ \text{pos}(t, \ D), \ \text{len}(D))}{n(\text{pos}(t, \ D), \ \text{len}(D))}, \qquad (1)$$

where $\text{pos}(t, \ D)$ is the position of the token in a given domain, D, and $\text{len}(D)$ is the number of tokens in the domain, D, respectively. If $D = \{$"q", "value", "a", "type", "x", "b", "type", "y"$\}$ and $t = $"value", $\text{pos}(t, D) = 2$ and $\text{len}(D) = 8$. $n(X)$ denotes the number of occurrences of the variate X over the entire domains.

DBSCAN. DBSCAN [3] is one of the clustering algorithms that does not require a predefined number of clusters and its algorithm extracts clusters with any shape. The threshold for the maximum distance and the minimum number of elements in a cluster are denoted by ϵ and m, respectively. Given the two elements p and q, the set $N_\epsilon(p)$ is defined as

$$N_\epsilon(p) = \{q \in D \mid d(p, q) \le \epsilon\}, \qquad (2)$$

where $d(x, y)$ denotes the Euclidean distance between x and y. If p and q satisfy the following condition, they are grouped into the same cluster.

$$p \in N_\epsilon(q) \qquad (3)$$

$$|N_\epsilon(q)| \ge m \qquad (4)$$

In our proposed method, $d(x, y)$ is defined as the absolute value of the difference of the score of the token group.

Table 2. Aggregate by regular expression

Generated template	Output template
q value * * *	q.*value.*
q value * *	q.*value.*

Output Query Templates. We introduce two thresholds δ ($\delta \geq 0$) and β ($0 < \beta < 1$). The thresholds are empirically determined. δ is the maximum distance between clusters and it affects the number of template outputs, and β is a threshold for determining the degree of template generalization when the template provides an output. The query template output process comprises the following steps.

Step 1: Sort tokens
Each token is sorted in descending order of its score.

Step 2: Cluster generation
Using DBSCAN based algorithm, the tokens are clustered. More precisely, when the score of the token differs from the mean score of a cluster by less than δ, the token is clustered into the current cluster. Otherwise, the token is assigned to a new cluster. This clustering process is repeated until all tokens are included in either cluster.

Step 3: Output templates
We generate a template using tokens whose score rank is higher than $\beta \times$ len(D) in a cluster. The remaining tokens whose score rank is lower than the threshold, are replaced with the wild character "*".

Step 4: Aggregate by regular expression
We aggregate the tokens that were replaced with "*" in Step 3 using a regular expression. Table 2 shows an example of aggregates using a regular expression.

5.3   Template Filtering Phase

In our proposed method, two-step filtering is performed on query templates in order to perform efficient extraction of short-lived malicious websites.

Step 1: Query template string length
Malicious URLs tend to be longer than benign URLs [6]. Filtering by the string length of the query template is performed to reduce the false-positives of filtering in the Step 2. Note that the string length does not include "*".

Step 2: Correspondence of domain and query template
We presume the group of short-lived malicious websites has the same characteristics in query parameters even if the domains are different. Thus, the same query template is generated from multiple domains. Therefore, we match the malicious URLs with the query template and filter by the correspondence between the domain and the query template. If the domain and query template correspond one to one, the filtering process is performed because a query

template can be replaced by the domain. Therefore, only the query template in which the domain and query template correspond to many-to-one is used in the next phase.

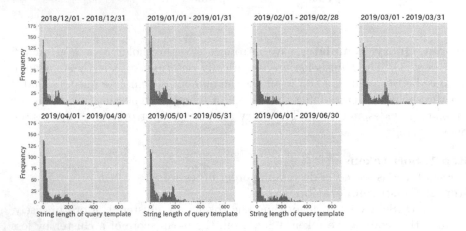

Fig. 5. Distribution of string length of query templates

5.4 Detection Phase

The detection phase only detects URLs that match the query template that has passed the filtering phase from the dataset. Specifically, the detection as follows. When "id.*ad.*src.*" is given as a query template, for example URLs such as "a.com/?id=xxx_1234&ad=src_1", "z.com/ index.html?id=yyy&ad=src", among others, can be detected from the access log.

6   Experimental Evaluation

We conduct experiments to evaluate the effectiveness of our proposed method. Concretely, we evaluate the total number of malicious URLs detected by the query template. We also use the number of malicious URLs detected by Google Safe Browsing as a baseline for comparison.

6.1 Experimental Procedure

We describe the experimental procedure for evaluating our proposed method.

Collection of Malicious URLs. We extracted malicious URLs from the dataset using the Google Safe Browsing API. The period for extracting malicious URLs is seven months from 2018/12/01 to 2019/06/30.

Table 3. List of query template samples

Pattern	Query template	String length
1	visitid.*11e9.*type.*js.*browserWidth.*browserHeight.*iframeDetected.*false.*	61
2	sourceid.*match.*ron.*carrier.*wifi.*mob.*pf.*windows.*	39
3	type.*sc.*ts.*1434261996.*z.*c65586175e50fb9495c3b87g9zfc5zdo1q7g4tft8g.*	61
4	x.*context.*pxl.*MSM3550.*MSM3478.*RUNT.*utm.*pubid.*RSTRST.*x.*at.*	46
5	utm.*medium.*oxxGrJ1EO8rl.*lkgHhDHtdaJe.*6y3ml38Z.*	41
6	*true.*ad.*673873.*f.*a.*cri.*s.*u.*si.*di.*ci.*16.*h.*cc.*JP.*https.*1.*useAf.*loaded.*string.*ar.*	58
7	hfghf.*vLMG24eIARq.*EzBlGmfzGd.*QJXocHt8RZwDsgaUYGDY.*cid.*	49
8	version.*1.*t.*imp.*trs.*filter.*1.*nf.*14.*nf2.*16.*fwidth.*fheight.*fiframe.*fiframesandbox.*ftype.*js.*end.*	75
9	hash.*type.*iframe.*cookie.*true.*sandblaster.*true.*html5.*sreenWidth.*	54
10	initialCallTimestamp.*adRefreshCount.*refreshTimeStamp.*	50
11	partnersCode.*701ac9ce.*bu.*http.*donstick.*com.*	37
12	ip.*device.*brand.*Desktop.*device.*model.*Desktop.*browser.*name.*Internet.*Explorer.*	65
13	shu.*pst.*rmtc.*t.*uuid.*1.*pii.*in.*false.*key.*9ca601a9f47c735df76d5ca46fa26a66.*psid.*	65

Table 4. List of query templates used in the detection phase

Pattern	Period	Query template
I	2018/12 - 2019/06	ip.*device.*brand.*Desktop.*device.*model.*Desktop.*browser.*name.*Internet.*Explorer.*
II	2018/12	utm.*medium.*oxxGrJ1EO8rl.*lkgHhDHtdaJe.*6y3ml38Z.*
III	2019/01 - 2019/02	utm.*campaign.*oxxGrJ1EO8rl.*lkgHhDHtdaJe.*6y3ml38Z.*
IV	2019/02 - 2019/06	utm.*campaign.*bKMuT7EMVXU5Z6UvvSHONGlfu.*yV43iC8T8uYixAFxs1.*

Query Template Generation. We generate query templates for each month's malicious URLs. We empirically set query template generation parameters δ and β to 0.1 and 0.6, respectively. In addition, the threshold value of the character string length in the filtering phase is the median character string length of the query template generated each month. Figure 5 shows the distribution of string lengths of the query templates for each month.

Detection. We detect URLs that match our query template from the dataset for the month following the period in which the malicious URLs were extracted to generate the query template. For example, when a query template is generated using the malicious log extracted from 2018/12/01 to 2018/12/31, we detect URLs matching our query template from the dataset from 2019/01/01 to 2019/01/31.

Evaluation. First, we manually label URLs that match query templates as benign or malicious based on website availability and domain name composition. If the website is available, we additionally obtain website content and take screenshots using Selenium [9]. This information is also used for labeling. Second, we use Google Safe Browsing to detect malicious URLs from URLs that match query templates and set a baseline for evaluation. Finally, we compare and evaluate the number of malicious URLs detected by our query templates and the number of malicious URLs detected by Google Safe Browsing.

6.2 Experimental Results

We describe the experimental results of our proposed method.

Table 5. Detection results

Period	Our method detection (unique)	Malicious URLs		Our method precision (unique)
		GSB (unique)	Our method (unique)	
2019/01	48452 (2169)	3977 (867)	25485 (1924)	0.5260 (0.8870)
2019/02	21594 (2049)	2383 (597)	18522 (1972)	0.8577 (0.9624)
2019/03	22561 (2469)	3766 (487)	22166 (2458)	0.9825 (0.9955)
2019/04	8154 (1950)	1613 (441)	7823 (1939)	0.9594 (0.9943)
2019/05	15972 (2279)	2059 (368)	15631 (2232)	0.9787 (0.9794)
2019/06	16082 (2072)	1476 (142)	15516 (2005)	0.9648 (0.9677)
2019/07	12872 (1945)	405 (98)	12483 (1894)	0.9698 (0.9738)
All Period	145687 (14657)	15679 (2988)	117626 (14280)	0.8074 (0.9743)

Table 6. Sample of detected domains

Detected by Pattern I	Detected by Pattern II, III, IV
dm16i8sauoo45[.]cloudfront[.]	game5419[.]cccgates41[.]
esugolb8[.]sightcomputer[.]	best4948[.]tthsrv53[.]
3zyssao0[.]craftedcomputerservice[.]	app9266[.]mmcgateway89[.]
7kpafrpz[.]productionpcservice[.]	prize0106[.]wtflife74[.]
6v1bwjc8[.]nutritioncomputer[.]	reward8277[.]hardway21[.]
x01fcj93[.]intactcomputer[.]	competition1343[.]easysearch16[.]

Query Template Generation. Table 3 shows the query templates samples generated based on the malicious URLs extracted from 2018/12/01 to 2018/12/31 and filtered it with the rule in Step 1 of the template filtering phase. We filter the query template in Table 3 with the rule in Step 2 of the template filtering phase. As a result, only the patterns 5 and pattern 12 have a many-to-one correspondence between the domain and the query template. Therefore, the detection phase uses the query template of pattern 5 and pattern 12. Similarly, query templates are generated for all periods and filtered. Table 4 shows query templates used in the detection phase.

Detection. Table 5 shows the detection results of the detection phase. Table 6 shows the domain information detected by our query templates. Moreover, Fig. 6 shows an actual sample of a phishing website detected using the pattern IV query template. This particular webpage tries to steal client credit card information.

Evaluation. Our method detected 14,280 unique malicious domains, and Google Safe Browsing detected 2,988 unique malicious domains. Therefore, our method has detected 11,292 unique malicious domains that are not detected by Google Safe Browsing. Moreover, we confirmed that our proposed method has reached high detection results in periods other than 2019/01 from the Table 5.

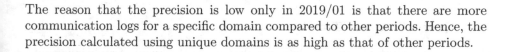

Fig. 6. Example of phishing website (play5191[.]checkingyourbrowser51[.]█████)

The reason that the precision is low only in 2019/01 is that there are more communication logs for a specific domain compared to other periods. Hence, the precision calculated using unique domains is as high as that of other periods.

7 Discussion

In this section, we discuss the validity of query templates, causes of errors, query template efficiency, query template trends and limitation on query template generation.

7.1 Validity of Query Templates

Many websites detected by the pattern I query template are warned by fake antivirus software. Therefore, we consider that the client information contains the query string for a realistic warning. The "utm.*medium" and "utm.*campaign" in the query templates of the pattern II, III and IV are the "utm_medium" and the "utm_campaign" parameter of Google Analytics [4]. The "utm_medium" parameter is used to identify the marketing media, and the parameter values such as "cpc", "banner", "social" and "email" are usually set. However, an unusual parameter value is used in the pattern II query template. The "utm.*campaign" parameter is also used to identify the campaign, and parameter values such as individual campaign name, slogan and promo code are used. The query templates for patterns III and IV contained the parameter value considering the campaign name. As a result, even if the parameter name is common, we consider that it is possible to use it for detecting malicious websites by focusing on the parameter value.

7.2 Causes of Errors

Errors in this experiment are divided into two categories: (I) The query template happens to match the query string of a benign URL; (II) A benign URL query string contains a malicious URL to be detected. The error of (I) is confirmed with the query template of pattern I, and the error of (II) is confirmed with the query template of all patterns. The error of (II) included many communication logs to the localhost through security software and communications from a security vendor's security diagnostic service. Therefore, reducing the error of (I) is difficult, but we consider that the error of (II) can be reduced by registering a specific domain as a white list and ignoring that domain.

7.3   Query Template Efficiency

In our proposed method, we detected 14,280 unique domains by four query templates. From these result, we consider that detection using query templates is superior in efficiency when compared with the URL blacklist method that requires registration of 14,280 rules for similar detection.

7.4   Query Template Trends

Our proposed method can flexibly grasp changes in the trend of malicious campaign, so we confirmed the change in a query string trend from the query templates II, III and IV in Table 4.

7.5   Limitation on Query Template Generation

During query template generation in our proposed method, the query parameters are divided using delimiters to generate tokens. Therefore, if the token itself is a feature, we can generate a valid query template. However, if part of the token contains the feature, namely, if the delimiter cannot successfully tokenize the feature, the token itself is generalized. Consequently, we consider that generating a valid query template is difficult.

8   Conclusion

In this paper, we proposed a method of generating query templates to detect short-lived URLs that are generally difficult to detect with a blacklist. We evaluated our approach with an experiment using large-scale web access logs. As a result, our proposed method detected 11,292 malicious unique domains not detected by Google Safe Browsing. In addition, our method achieved high precision in the seven months of experiments. However, we could evaluate true positives and false positives, but not false negatives and true negatives. The following points can be given as the reasons: (I) We need to know all malicious URLs in the dataset to evaluate false negatives. (II) The malicious URLs detected using our proposed method in this experiment are only a part of all malicious URLs in the dataset. Therefore, the evaluation of the false positive rate and false negative rate of our proposed method is left for future work.

Acknowledgments. The research results have been achieved by WarpDrive: Web-based Attack Response with Practical and Deployable Research InitiatiVE, the Commissioned Research of National Institute of Information and Communications Technology (NICT), JAPAN.

References

1. Abdelhamid, N., Ayesh, A., Thabtah, F.: Phishing detection based associative classification data mining. Expert Syst. Appl. **41**(13), 5948–5959 (2014). https://doi.org/10.1016/j.eswa.2014.03.019. http://www.sciencedirect.com/science/article/pii/S0957417414001481
2. Ding, Y., Luktarhan, N., Li, K., Slamu, W.: A keyword-based combination approach for detecting phishing webpages. Comput. Secur. **84**, 256–275 (2019). https://doi.org/10.1016/j.cose.2019.03.018. http://www.sciencedirect.com/science/article/pii/S0167404819300707
3. Ester, M., Kriegel, H.P., Sander, J., Xu, X.: A density-based algorithm for discovering clusters a density-based algorithm for discovering clusters in large spatial databases with noise. In: Proceedings of the Second International Conference on Knowledge Discovery and Data Mining, KDD 1996, pp. 226–231. AAAI Press (1996). http://dl.acm.org/citation.cfm?id=3001460.3001507
4. Google: Collect campaign data with custom URLs. https://support.google.com/analytics/answer/1033863
5. Google: Google safe browsing. https://safebrowsing.google.com
6. Kim, S., Kim, J., Kang, B.: Malicious URL protection based on attackers' habitual behavioral analysis. Comput. Secur. (2018). https://doi.org/10.1016/j.cose.2018.01.013
7. Malwarebytes: Cybercrime tactics and techniques Q1 2017. https://www.malwarebytes.com/pdf/labs/Cybercrime-Tactics-and-Techniques-Q1-2017.pdf
8. Mizuno, S., Hatada, M., Mori, T., Goto, S.: Detecting malware-infected devices using the http header patterns. IEICE Trans. Inf. Syst. **E101D**(5), 1370–1379 (2018). https://doi.org/10.1587/transinf.2017EDP7294
9. SeleniumHQ: Selenium WebDriver. https://docs.seleniumhq.org/projects/webdriver
10. Sheng, S., Wardman, B., Warner, G., Cranor, L.F., Hong, J.I., Zhang, C.: An empirical analysis of phishing blacklists. In: Conference on Email and Anti-Spam (2009)
11. Sood, A.K., Zeadally, S.: A taxonomy of domain-generation algorithms. IEEE Secur. Privacy **14**(4), 46–53 (2016). https://doi.org/10.1109/MSP.2016.76
12. Symantec: Internet security threat report volume 24. https://www.symantec.com/content/dam/symantec/docs/reports/istr-24-2019-en.pdf
13. Thao, T.P., Makanju, T., Urakawa, J., Yamada, A., Murakami, K., Kubota, A.: Large-scale analysis of domain blacklists. In: Proceedings of the 11th International Conference on Emerging Security Information, Systems and Technologies (2017)
14. Verisign: Internet grows to 348.7 million domain name registrations in the fourth quarter of 2018. https://investor.verisign.com/news-releases/news-release-details/internet-grows-3487-million-domain-name-registrations-fourth
15. Zhang, J., Seifert, C., Stokes, J., Lee, W.: Arrow: generating signatures to detect drive-by downloads. In: Proceedings of the International Conference on World Wide Web (2011). https://www.microsoft.com/en-us/research/publication/arrow-generating-signatures-to-detect-drive-by-downloads/

A Deep Learning Attack Countermeasure with Intentional Noise for a PUF-Based Authentication Scheme

Risa Yashiro[1,2]([⊠]), Yohei Hori[1], Toshihiro Katashita[1], and Kazuo Sakiyama[2]

[1] National Institute of Advanced Industrial Science and Technology (AIST),
Tsukuba, Ibaraki 305-8568, Japan
[2] The University of Electro-Communications, Chofu, Tokyo 182-8585, Japan
`yashiro@uec.ac.jp`

Abstract. We propose a scheme to prevent the machine learning (ML) attacks against physically unclonable functions (PUFs). A silicon PUF is a security primitive in a semiconductor chip that generates a unique identifier by exploiting device variations. However, some PUF implementations are vulnerable to ML attacks, in which an attacker tries to obtain the mathematical clone of the target PUF to predict its responses. Our scheme adds intentional noise to the responses to disturb ML by an attacker so that the clone fails to be authenticated, while the original PUF can still be correctly authenticated using an error correction code (ECC). The effectiveness of this scheme is not very obvious because the attacker can also use the ECC. We apply the countermeasure to n-XOR arbiter PUFs to investigate the feasibility of the proposed scheme. We explain the relationship between the prediction accuracy of the clone and the number of intentional noise bits. Our scheme can successfully distinguish a clone from the legitimate PUF in the case of 5-XOR PUF.

Keywords: Physical unclonable function · Machine learning attack · Authentication · Noise · Fuzzy extractor

1 Introduction

1.1 Background

Nowadays, a vast number of electronic devices including sensors, consumer electronics, and automobiles are connected to the network to form the so-called the Internet of Things (IoT). In the IoT, the pervasively deployed devices collect, transfer, and share various data, some of which are confidential or private. Therefore, the security of the devices and data is very important in the IoT. Furthermore, a large number of counterfeit integrated circuit (IC) chips are circulated in the market [3]. Since IC chips are widely used in critical infrastructure and in daily life, counterfeit IC chips can cause serious damage to the society.

A silicon physically unclonable function (PUF) [16,17] is one of the promising approaches for IoT security to protect the devices and the data. A silicon PUF

© Springer Nature Switzerland AG 2020
E. Simion and R. Géraud-Stewart (Eds.): SecITC 2019, LNCS 12001, pp. 78–94, 2020.
https://doi.org/10.1007/978-3-030-41025-4_6

(hereinafter, PUF) is a circuit or a memory element that exploits the device variations to generate a chip-specific random output. Usually, a PUF receives an input (*challenge*) and generates a unique output (*response*) under the influence of device variations. Since a PUF is unclonable and its responses are unique and unpredictable, it can be used for entity authentication [21] and cryptographic key generation [14,15]. As the PUF responses are noise-prone, usually an error correction scheme called the *fuzzy extractor* [5] is used for key generation in which even a single-bit error is not allowed.

However, unclonability of some PUF implementations can be compromised by machine learning (ML) attacks [12,18]. By learning the model of a PUF from a large number of challenge-response pairs (CRPs), an attacker can obtain the mathematical clone of the PUF. Recently, deep learning (DL) attacks that use deep neural network (DNN) models have been also proposed to attack arbiter PUFs (APUFs) and its derivations [1,10,20,23].

1.2 Contribution

The purpose of this study is to develop a countermeasure to DL attacks against a PUF. We propose a PUF-based authentication scheme that prevents DL attacks by adding intentional noise to the responses.

Our contributions can be summarized as follows:

- Develop the PUF-based authentication scheme with a countermeasure to DL attacks against arbiter-type PUFs by adding intentional noise.
- Evaluate the effectiveness of the proposed authentication scheme for n-XOR arbiter PUFs using the open-source dataset [19].
- Explain the relationship between the prediction accuracy of the clone and the number of intentional noise bits.

2 Related Work

There have been several studies on modeling attacks against APUFs [6] and their variants, e.g., the n-XOR PUF [21], FF-PUF [11], and DAPUF [13]. For details of these PUFs, see Appendix A.1.

Lim [12] showed that the internal delay of an APUF can be estimated with a linear delay model and successfully attacked the APUF for the first time. Rühmair and Sehnke [18] successfully attacked the APUFs, n-XOR PUFs, and FF-PUFs. For details of the modeling attack [18], see Appendix A.2.

Delvaux and Verbauwhede [4] suggest that reliability of a response is more useful in some cases than the response itself. An unstable response of an APUF indicates that the delay difference of the two selector lines is quite small; in other words, the reliability leaks some amount of information about the internal delay. They reported that the *reliability-based attack* against an APUF was successful. In the reliability-based attack, the key technique used is the linear equation; thus, it is not an ML attack.

Becker [2] extended the reliability-based attack and applied an evolutional algorithm called the covariance matrix adaption evolution strategy (CMAES). The CMAES decreases the complexity of the attack against n-XOR PUFs from exponential to linear in n. The noise in [2] is the environmental noise, unlike our random noise. Thus, we do not focus on reliability-based attacks in this study.

Yashiro and Machida [23] pioneered the deep learning (DL) attack against a PUF in 2016. They attacked APUFs and their variants with the DL attack and reported that all except the DAPUFs were broken. However, Khalafalla and Gebotys successfully attacked DAPUFs using the DL attack with a larger neural network [10]. In the same year, Awano and Iizuka [1] also succeeded in attacking DAPUFs with DL using only raw CRPs for DL without transforming the challenge based on the knowledge of the internal structure of the DAPUF. Santikellur and Bhattacharyay [20] mounted a DL attack against n-XOR PUF using a neural network as small as possible.

The learning parity with noise (LPN)-based PUF authentication has also been previously proposed [7,9]. The responses in this scheme are generated by adding intentional noise to the ordinal PUFs. Previous studies adopted the fuzzy extractor; thus, the systems are relatively large. In this study, we adopt the reverse fuzzy extractor [22] to realize a lightweight PUF token. Yuejiang [24] has also reported that adding noise can be a countermeasure to the attacks.

3   Proposed PUF-Based Authentication Scheme

3.1   Supposed PUF-Based Authentication System

The purpose of our scheme is to prevent ML attacks in PUF-based authentication systems. In ML attacks against a PUF, an attacker is supposed to be able to collect a large number of CRPs during the authentication procedure. The key idea of the countermeasure is that, during the verification phase, we intentionally add noise to the PUF responses to disturb the machine learning by an attacker. The goal is to sufficiently decrease the prediction accuracy of the clone, while the tempered responses are still authentic for legitimate players. Note that the attacker can also use the fuzzy extractor and thus the guessed responses by the attacker should be erroneous beyond the error correction capability of the applied error correcting code (ECC).

In our countermeasure, an ECC decoder with a high error correcting capability is essential. Therefore, we adopt a *reverse* fuzzy extractor [22] for error correction in which the resource-consuming ECC decoder is implemented in the verifier side; the encoder for generating helper data is implemented in the PUF token. For details of the fuzzy extractor and the reverse fuzzy extractor, see Appendix A.3.

3.2   Details of the Authentication Procedure with Intentional Noise

In this section, we introduce the PUF-based cryptographic authentication with the countermeasure against ML attacks. The block diagram of the PUF-based

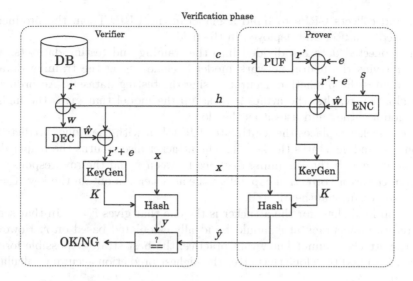

Fig. 1. Verification phase of the supposed PUF-based authentication scheme.

authentication scheme is illustrated in Fig. 1. Here, the *raw response* from a PUF and the *intentional noise* are represented by r and e, respectively. *KeyGen* is the key generation module which can be a universal hash function. *Hash* is a keyed-hashing function. The enrollment phase is omitted in Fig. 1.

In the enrollment phase, the verifier gives x-bit challenge (c) to the prover (e.g., a PUF token) and collects the corresponding response r from the PUF. The verifier registers c and r to the database.

In the verification phase, the verifier pulls the set of the c and r from the database and sends c to the prover. The prover gives c to the PUF and obtains the new raw response (r'), and then intentionally adds the noise bit e to r' at random. The prover generates the helper data h from the noisy response $r' + e$, and sends h to the verifier. Then, the verifier tries to generate $r' + e$ from r with the help of h. Note that, when the Hamming distance between r and $r' + e$ is less than or equal to the error correction capability, the verifier can reproduce $r' + e$. In this case, the prover and verifier can generate the same key K from the shared secret $r' + e$. After the key K is shared, the verifier sends a random number x to the prover. The prover generates the hash tag $\hat{y}$ from x with the key K, and returns $\hat{y}$ to the verifier. The verifier generates hash tag y from x with his/her own K to generate y, and check if $y == \hat{y}$.

3.3 Attack Scenario

In this study, we assume that an attacker is able to collect as many CRPs (c and $r' + e$) as possible. For example, an attacker can collect CRPs from a PUF product in the supply chain. The attacker picks up a PUF product in the supply chain, and collects CRPs to build a model of the PUF. Then, the product is distributed to a user and deployed in the field.

The collected data are divided into the training and testing datasets. The attacker trains the neural network model (=clone) using the training dataset and evaluates the prediction accuracy using the testing datasets. According to the evaluation results, the attacker picks up the model that gives the highest prediction accuracy and uses it as the clone.

The attacker replaces the legitimate PUF token with the clone, predicts the response $\tilde{r}$, and generates the key $\tilde{K}$. The attacker also returns the helper data $\tilde{h}$ to the verifier. If the Hamming distance between $\tilde{r}$ and the raw response r is less than the error correction capability, the attacker can obtain the key $\tilde{K} = K$ and be successfully authenticated.

The optimal clone for the attacker is the one that gives $\tilde{r} = r$. In that sense, the prediction accuracy of $\tilde{r}$ should be ideally calculated based on r. However, since the attacker cannot know r in practice, the best strategy possible for the attacker is to find the clone that gives the highest prediction accuracy calculated based on $r' + e$.

4   Evaluation and Results

4.1   Evaluation Setup

We evaluate the feasibility of the proposed authentication scheme with the countermeasure using the open-source dataset [19]. To make a fair comparison, the sizes of training data in our experiments are the same as ones in [20], namely, 32,000, 37,600, 255,000, and 655,000 for 2-XOR, 3-XOR, 4-XOR, and 5-XOR PUFs, respectively. The training data are tampered with intentional noise e and then used to train PUF clones.

The ECC used in the reverse fuzzy extractor is the 255-bit Bose-Chaudhuri-Hocquenghem (BCH) code, which can correct up to 63 bits error. As a consequence, the added intentional noise e ranges from 0 through 63 bits per codeword. The positions of the inserted noise e are randomly chosen.

While the training data contain intentional noise, the testing data are raw responses newly collected from the dataset because the prediction accuracy should be evaluated based on r, as mentioned above. For this purpose, another 10,000 CRPs are collected from the original dataset for each evaluation.

The DL engine is built using the Keras library. The DL attack is run on the Intel Core-i9 9900K with 32 GB memory and Nvidia GeForce RTX 2080.

4.2   Evaluation of the Effectiveness of the Intentional Noise

First, we examine the effectiveness of intentional noise in disturbing a DL attack. The hyperparameters are taken from the previous work [20]; the activation function used for the hidden layer is the *Rectified Linear Unit (ReLU)*; for the last layer, the *sigmoid* function; the optimizer is *Adam*. The number of hidden layers and nodes per layer are provided in Table 1.

Table 1. Hyperparameters of the deep learning in Santikellur et al. [20] and our work.

		$h1$	$h2$	$h3$	$h4$	Dropout
2-XOR	[20]	5	5	–	–	–
(32,000 CRP)	Our work	500	200	100	–	0.1
3-XOR	[20]	10	10	–	–	–
(37,600 CRP)	Our work	1000	500	200	100	0.1
4-XOR	[20]	53	53	53	–	–
(255,000 CRP)	Our work	1000	500	200	100	0.1
5-XOR	[20]	100	100	100	100	–
(655,000 CRP)	Our work	5000	500	200	100	0.1

Note that the PUF responses r and r' usually include environmental noise in practice. However, as the environmental noise is not considered in the datasets [19], all error bits in the training data here are caused by intentional noise. The influence of environmental noise is discussed later in Sect. 4.4.

Figure 2 shows the prediction accuracy in training and testing of the clone of the 3-XOR PUF, with the hyperparameters defined in [20]. As space is limited, only the results of one clone out of five are displayed in the figure, but the other clones also show similar results. The blue lines represent the accuracy in training (hereinafter, *training accuracy*); the orange lines represent the prediction accuracy. The number of noise bits inserted to the 255-bit codeword is 15, 31, 47, and 63 bits, respectively. The horizontal and vertical axes are the number of epochs and the training/prediction accuracies of the clone, respectively.

The best strategy for an attacker is to use the clone that gives the highest prediction accuracy in a testing phase (orange line). As Fig. 2 depicts, the prediction accuracy reduces as the number of noise bits increases. Therefore, adding intentional noise is quite effective in preventing a DL attack with the hyperparameters given in [20].

Figure 3 illustrates the relationship between the number of intentional noise bits (horizontal axis) and the mean prediction accuracy of clones (the line graphs that refer to the right axis). The bar graphs are the number of error bits in the predicted responses by the clone and refer to the left axis. The shaded area shows the number of correctable error bits of 255-bit BCH code with error correction capability $t = 7, 15, 31, 42, 47, 55$, and 63, respectively. The case of 0-bit noise is also provided for reference. If the bar is in the shaded area, the response of the clone cannot be distinguished from one of a legitimate PUF, resulting in a successful attack by the clone. Conversely, if the bar exceeds the shaded area, the clone's responses cannot pass authentication, while ones from a legitimate PUF are correctly authenticated.

As Fig. 3 shows, the prediction accuracies of the 2-XOR PUF clone are more than 95%, and consequently the numbers of error bits in the predicted responses are quite small, irrespective of intentional noise bits. This means that, even

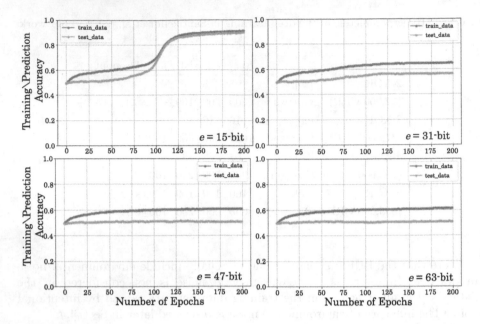

Fig. 2. Prediction accuracy of the cloned 3-XOR PUF with the hyperparameters in [20]. The intentional noise added is 15, 31, 47, and 63 bits, respectively. (Color figure online)

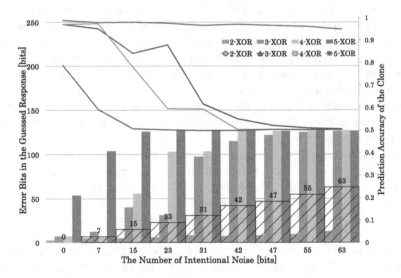

Fig. 3. Relationship between the prediction accuracy, the prediction error bits, and the intentional noise bits, with the hyperparameters in [20].

trained with 63-bit (=25% of a codeword) intentional noise, the 2-XOR PUF clone can predict a 255-bit codeword with an error rate of less than 5%. The total error bits in this case is 13 on average, which is within the error correction capability. Therefore, a 2-XOR PUF cannot be protected with intentional noise against a DL attack.

In the cases of 3-XOR and 4-XOR PUF clones, the prediction accuracies are more than 95% for 7-bit intentional noise, indicating a successful attack by the clones. However, the prediction accuracies significantly reduce with intentional noise of 15 bits and more.

For example, the prediction accuracy of the 3-XOR PUF clone for 15-bit intentional noise is 84.3%, resulting in 40 bits error in a predicted codeword on average. Let p_e be the bit error rate (BER) of a PUF response and X_e be the number of error bits in a predicted codeword. Here, $p_e = 1 - 0.843 = 0.157$. The probability that the number of error bits in a predicted codeword is less than 15 is

$$\Pr[X_e \leq 15; p_e = 0.157] = \sum_{i=0}^{15} \binom{255}{i} \cdot p_e^i \cdot (1 - p_e)^{255-i} = 1.28\mathrm{e}{-6}. \quad (1)$$

Therefore, the probability that an attacker obtains a codeword with less than a 15-bit error is negligible. Consequently, adding 15-bit intentional noise and using $(255, 139, t = 15)$ BCH code, a 3-XOR PUF can be protected against a DL attack. Likewise, a 4-XOR PUF can be protected by adding 15-bit noise and using $(255, 139)$ BCH code, though a detailed explanation is omitted.

In the case of 5-XOR PUF clone, the prediction accuracies are approximately 80 and 60% for 0-bit and 7-bit intentional noise, respectively. Examined in detail, for 0-bit intentional noise, the prediction accuracies of three 5-XOR PUFs out of five are 97%, and the remaining two are around 50%. For 7-bit intentional noise, the prediction accuracy of one 5-XOR PUF out of five is 97%, and the remaining four are around 50%. When the intentional noise is 15 bits and more, all five 5-XOR-PUF clones show prediction accuracies around 50%. These results indicate that adding a 15-bit or more intentional noise is effective in protecting a 5-XOR-PUF against a DL attack.

4.3   Evaluation with the Improved Hyperparameters

In the previous subsection, it is found from the results that adding intentional noise is quite effective in preventing a DL attack against 3-XOR, 4-XOR, and 5-XOR PUFs. The hyperparameters of the DL are taken from [20]; however, the prediction accuracy of the clone can be possibly improved by adjusting the hyperparameters. In this section, we evaluate the prediction accuracies of XOR-PUF clones with optimized hyperparameters. Here, the activation function used for the first hidden layers is *Hyperbolic Tangent (tanh)* and for the other hidden layers, the *sigmoid* function. The optimizer used is *Adam*. The dropout rate is set to 0.1. The hyperparameters in our DL attack are also provided in Table 1.

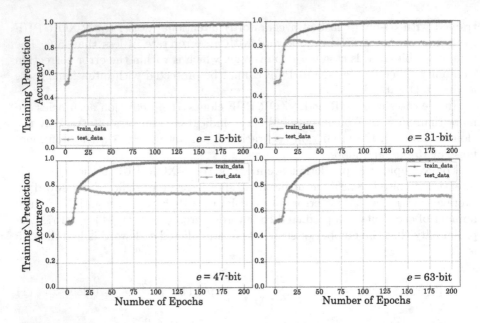

Fig. 4. Prediction accuracy of the cloned 3-XOR PUF with our improved hyperparameters. (Color figure online)

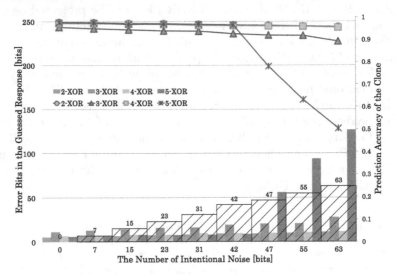

Fig. 5. Relationship between the prediction accuracy and the number of intentional noise bits with our improved hyperparameters.

Figure 4 shows the prediction accuracy in training and testing of the clone of the 3-XOR PUF, with our improved hyperparameters. Similarly to Fig. 2, the best strategy for an attacker is to use the clone that gives the highest prediction accuracy in a testing phase (orange line). As Fig. 4 depicts, the prediction accuracy reduces as the number of noise bit increases. Therefore, adding intentional noise is quite effective in preventing a DL attack with our improved hyperparameters.

As the blue lines in Figs. 2 and 4 show, the training accuracies are significantly different between [20] and our work. Since the dataset is the same, the difference is caused by the hyperparameters. The number of hidden layers in [20] is only 2 and the number of the nodes per layer is only 10, while our model has 3 hidden layers and more than 100 nodes per layer. This result indicates that the small neural network model is insufficient to learn the features of XOR PUFs, especially under noisy inputs.

As the orange lines in Figs. 2 and 4 illustrate, the prediction accuracies are also considerably different between [20] and our work. Looking at the peak of the orange lines, the prediction accuracy in our work is almost the same as [20] for the intentional noise of 15 bits. In contrast, the prediction accuracies in our work with 31-, 47- and 63-bits noise achieve higher prediction accuracy than [20]. These results indicate that a neural network model should be large enough to build an accurate clone from noisy inputs.

Figure 5 illustrates the relationship between the number of intentional noise bits and the mean prediction accuracy of clones with the optimized hyperparameters. The bar graphs are the number of error bits in the predicted responses by the clone. The shaded area shows the number of correctable error bits.

In Fig. 5, the prediction accuracies of 2-XOR, 3-XOR, and 4-XOR PUF clones are maintained quite high for error bits 0 through 63, indicating a successful attack. Since the dataset used in [20] and our work are the same, the difference is caused by the hyperparameters. These results show that, by using a sufficiently large neural network, a DL can model 2-, 3-, and 4-XOR PUFs quite effectively even with noisy training data.

Note that the prediction accuracy of the 3-XOR PUF clone is lower than other PUFs, which would be because the size of the training data (37,600) is insufficient. In the experiment, the data size is set to the same one as [20] to make a fair comparison. When the training is performed with 100,000 data, the prediction accuracy of the 3-XOR PUF clone is improved (*cf.* Appendix B).

In the case of 5-XOR PUF clone, the prediction accuracies are maintained high for error bits 0 through 42. However, the prediction accuracies significantly decrease to 78.0%, 63.1%, and 50.4% for the error bits 47, 55, and 63, respectively. When the intentional noise is 47 bits, the BER of the clone's response is $p_e = 1 - 0.780 = 0.220$, and the probability $\Pr[X_e \leq 47]$ is

$$\Pr[X_e \leq 47;\, p_e = 0.220] = \sum_{i=0}^{47} \binom{255}{i} \cdot p_e^i \cdot (1 - p_e)^{255-i} = 0.0949. \qquad (2)$$

The result shows that the 5-XOR PUF clone trained with 47-bit noise can be authenticated with a 9.49% probability. In this case, by using multi-query verification, the probability of the clone being authenticated can be drastically reduced.

When the 5-XOR PUF clone is trained with 55- and 63-bit noise, BERs are 0.369 and 0.496, respectively, and

$$\Pr[X_e \le 55; p_e = 0.396] = 9.63\mathrm{e}{-8}, \tag{3}$$
$$\Pr[X_e \le 63; p_e = 0.496] = 3.41\mathrm{e}{-16}. \tag{4}$$

Consequently, the probabilities that an attacker obtains a codeword with less than 55- and 63-bit error are negligible.

From the above consideration, adding intentional noise is highly effective in preventing a DL attack against 5-XOR PUF even if an attacker optimizes the hyperparameters of the neural network.

4.4   Discussion

In Sects. 4.2 and 4.3, it is demonstrated that the countermeasure with intentional noise is effective in preventing a DL attack against some kinds of XOR PUFs. However, the environmental noise is not considered in the previous subsections. Here, we discuss the effectiveness of the countermeasure under environmental noise.

We consider the 5-XOR PUF clone trained with the optimized hyperparameters (Fig. 5). Let p_{env} be the BER of a response caused by environmental noise. Considering the performance of the APUF in [8] (intra-Hamming distance 0.832 bit for 128-bit APUF, etc.), the environmental noise-derived BER is set to 1%. In this case, the number of error bits in a predicted codeword is 2.55 bits on average and less than 8 bits in most cases, which is explained as follows:

$$\Pr[X_e \le 8; p_{env} = 0.01] = \sum_{i=0}^{8} \binom{255}{i} \cdot p_{env}^i \cdot (1 - p_{env})^{255-i} = 0.999. \tag{5}$$

Suppose we use $(255, 21, t = 55)$ BCH code. For a legitimate PUF to be authenticated with a 99.9% probability, the added intentional noise should not exceed $47\ (= 55 - 8)$ bits. Because the mean environmental noise is 2.55 bits, the total error bits in a codeword is around 49 bits on average. In this case, the countermeasure could be used for multi-query verification, similarly to the case of 47-bit noise discussed in Sect. 4.3.

When we use $(255, 9, t = 63)$ BCH code, we can add up to $55\ (= 63 - 8)$ bits intentional noise. As already discussed in Sect. 4.3, 55-bit noise is sufficient for disturbing a DL attack against 5-XOR PUF. Therefore, using $(255, 9)$ BCH code, the countermeasure with 55-bit intentional noise is quite effective even under environmental noise.

5   Conclusion and Future Work

We developed a PUF-based authentication scheme with the countermeasure for a DL attack. The countermeasure intentionally adds noise to the PUF responses to disturb a DL attack. The feasibility of the authentication scheme was evaluated in the practical attack scenario. The countermeasure was applied to the n-XOR PUFs ($1 \leq n \leq 5$) from the open-source dataset to investigate its effectiveness in the developed scheme. The experimental results show that the authentication scheme with the countermeasure is quite feasible. The scheme prevents the PUFs from being cloned by DL attacks while enabling the verifier to authenticate the legitimate PUF.

Although the graphs for all n-XOR PUFs could not be provided in this paper, the results that show the effectiveness of the noise insertion varies from PUF to PUF. In our experiments, the noise is randomly added to the responses. However, the effectiveness of the countermeasure may be improved by adding noise to specific bits based on some rationale. Investigating the rationale is the focus of the future work. In this study, several XOR PUFs were also investigated as a case study. Evaluating a larger number of XOR PUFs and other types of PUFs, to find optimal hyperparameter for each PUFs are also future work topics.

Acknowledgment. This paper is based on the results obtained from the project commissioned by the New Energy and Industrial Technology Development Organization (NEDO).

Appendix A: Preliminaries

A.1 Arbiter PUF and Its Derivations

An arbiter PUF (APUF) is a typical PUF that exploits the delay variation of the signal paths. Figure 6 shows the structure of the APUF and its derivation, a 4-XOR arbiter PUF.

An APUF consists of a pair of selector lines, and each line has x selectors and an arbiter. The arbiter determines the response according to which the signal reaches the arbiter first; e.g., the response is 1 if the upper signal is faster and 0 otherwise. An APUF receives x-bit challenge that determines the path of the selector lines. In Fig. 6, the signals in the i-th selectors go straight if the i-th challenge bit is 0 and go across if the challenge bit is 1. The delay of the two selectors is greatly affected by device variations and thus the CRPs of APUFs are different from each other.

An n-XOR arbiter PUF [21] (hereinafter, n-XOR PUF) consists of n APUFs, and the outputs from each APUF are XORed to obtain a 1-bit response. The resistance of n-XOR PUFs against ML attacks is improved exponentially in n.

A feed-forward arbiter PUF [11] (FF-PUF) has an APUF circuit and several feed-forward arbiters. The feed-forward arbiter is inserted to certain positions in the selector lines of the APUF circuit and generates the intermediate response that becomes the challenge to the selector at a later stage. The challenge generated by the feed-forward arbiter cannot be obtained by an attacker, which makes it difficult to attack the FF-PUF with ML.

A double arbiter PUF (DAPUF) is composed of several APUF circuits and XOR gates. In 2-XOR PUF, the responses of the two APUFs, say APUF1 and APUF2, are XORed to generate a 1-bit response. In DAPUF, the upper and lower selector lines in APUF1 and APUF2 are XORed. This structure is useful for improving the uniqueness of the DAPUF implemented on an FPGA [13].

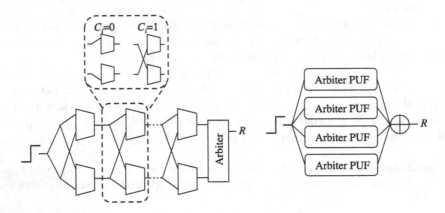

Fig. 6. Structure of arbiter PUF and 4-XOR arbiter PUF.

A.2 Machine Learning Attack Against Arbiter PUF

The response of an APUF is determined by the delay difference of the two selector chains, which is mathematically modeled by the cumulative delay differences of each stage. An ML attack aims to reveal the delay parameters of each stage from CRPs.

The model of an APUF is explained as follows [18]. Let c_l be the l-th bit of the x-bit challenge. The delay difference of the l-th stage is represented by δ_l^0 for $c_l = 0$ and δ_l^1 for $c_l = 1$.

The challenge vector is transformed into the *parity vector* $\overrightarrow{\Phi}$, which is expressed as

$$\overrightarrow{\Phi}(\overrightarrow{C}) = (\Phi^1(C), \dots, \Phi^x(\overrightarrow{C}), 1)^T, \tag{6}$$

where $\Phi^l(\overrightarrow{C}) = \prod_{i=l}^{x}(1 - 2c_i)$ for $l = 1, \dots, x$.

The delay difference of each stage, $\overrightarrow{w}$, is defined as

$$\overrightarrow{w} = (w^1, w^2, \dots, w^x, w^{x+1})^T, \tag{7}$$

where $w^1 = (\delta_1^0 - \delta_1^1)/2$ and $w^i = (\delta_{i-1}^0 + \delta_{i-1}^1 + \delta_i^0 - \delta_i^1)/2$ for $i = 2, \dots, x$, and $w^{x+1} = (\delta_x^0 - \delta_x^1)/2$. The total delay difference Δ between the two selector chains is expressed as

$$\Delta = \overrightarrow{w}^T \overrightarrow{\Phi}. \tag{8}$$

Consequently, response r of an APUF is given by

$$r = \text{sgn}(\Delta) = \text{sgn}(\overrightarrow{w}^T \overrightarrow{\Phi}), \tag{9}$$

where sgn is the sign function.

To summarize, an ML attack aims to reproduce the delay parameter $\overrightarrow{w}$ from the collected challenges $\overrightarrow{\Phi}$ and responses. Once the delay parameter is obtained, an attacker can easily predict the response to a new challenge by calculating $\text{sgn}(\Delta)$. In that sense, the obtained $\overrightarrow{w}$ is the very mathematical clone of the PUF.

A.3 Fuzzy Extractor and Reverse Fuzzy Extractor

Since a PUF exploits subtle variation of devices, the responses are error-prone due to the environmental noise. Therefore, in a PUF-based authentication with key sharing, an error correction scheme called the fuzzy extractor is often implemented.

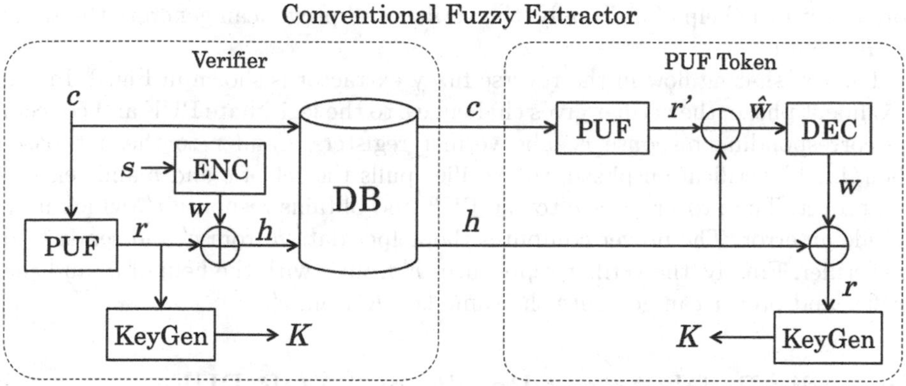

Fig. 7. Key generation flow of a conventional fuzzy extractor.

A PUF-based key sharing flow is usually separated into two phases: enrollment and verification phase. The enrollment phase is supposed to be performed in a trusted area by a verifier, e.g., a PUF manufacturer, vendor, and a service provider. The verifier collects CRPs of the PUF and register the CRPs to a database. The verification phase is performed after the shipment of the PUF product. The verifier checks if the target PUF is authentic by collating the returned PUF response with the database.

The key sharing flow in the conventional fuzzy extractor is shown in Fig. 7. In the enrollment phase, the verifier gives challenge c to a legitimate PUF and collects the corresponding response r. The verifier calculates the helper data h for error correction. The verifier registers the c and h to the database. Then, in

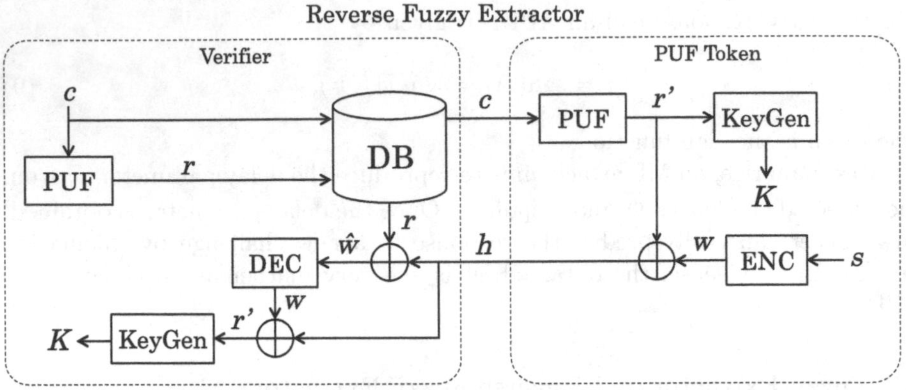

Reverse Fuzzy Extractor

Fig. 8. Key generation flow of a reverse fuzzy extractor.

the verification phase, the verifier pulls the set of c, r, and h from the database, and sends c and h to a prover (e.g., a PUF token). The prover gives c to the PUF and obtains response r', which may include an error. The prover reproduces r from r' with the help of h. Finally, the verifier and prover can generate the same key K from r.

The key sharing flow in the reverse fuzzy extractor is shown in Fig. 8. In the enrollment phase, the verifier gives challenge c to the legitimate PUF and collects the corresponding response r. The verifier registers c and r to the database. Then, in the verification phase, the verifier pulls the set of c and r and sends c to a prover. The prover gives c to the PUF and obtains response r', which may include an error. The prover computes the helper data h from r' and sends h to the verifier. Finally, the verifier reproduces r' from r with the help of h, and the verifier and prover can generate the same key K from r'.

Appendix B: DL Attack Results of 3-XOR PUFs

In Fig. 5, the prediction accuracies of the 3-XOR PUF clone are lower than those of other PUF clones. This is not intuitive because 4-XOR PUF has more complicated structure than 3-XOR PUF does. This could be because the size of the training data for the 3-XOR PUF (37,600) was too small. Therefore, we train the 3-XOR PUF clone with 100,000 CRPs and evaluate its prediction accuracy.

Figure 9 shows the results of DL of the 3-XOR PUF using 100,000 training data. The prediction accuracies are increased to 97%, which is almost the same as the 2-XOR and 4-XOR PUF clones. The results indicate that the size of training data was not sufficient in Fig. 5, while the hyperparameters were suitable.

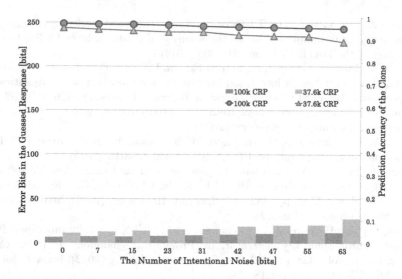

Fig. 9. DL attack results of 3-XOR PUFs with different size of training dataset.

References

1. Awano, H., Iizuka, T., Ikeda, M.: PUFNet: a deep neural network based modeling attack for physically unclonable function. In: Proceedings of the ISCAS 2019, pp. 1–4 (2019)
2. Becker, G.T.: The gap between promise and reality: on the insecurity of XOR arbiter PUFs. In: Güneysu, T., Handschuh, H. (eds.) CHES 2015. LNCS, vol. 9293, pp. 535–555. Springer, Heidelberg (2015). https://doi.org/10.1007/978-3-662-48324-4_27
3. Chaudhry, P.E., Zimmerman, A.: Protecting Your Intellectual Property Rights: Understanding the Role of Management, Governments, Consumers and Pirates. Springer, New York (2012). https://doi.org/10.1007/978-1-4614-5568-4
4. Delvaux, J., Verbauwhede, I.: Side channel modeling attacks on 65nm arbiter PUFs exploiting CMOS device noise. In: Proceedings of the HOST 2013, pp. 137–142 (2013)
5. Dodis, Y., Reyzin, L., Smith, A.: Fuzzy extractors: how to generate strong keys from biometrics and other noisy data. In: Cachin, C., Camenisch, J.L. (eds.) EUROCRYPT 2004. LNCS, vol. 3027, pp. 523–540. Springer, Heidelberg (2004). https://doi.org/10.1007/978-3-540-24676-3_31
6. Gassend, B., Clarke, D., Van Dijk, M., Devadas, S.: Silicon physical random functions. In: Proceedings of the CCS 2002, pp. 148–160 (2002)
7. Herder, C., Ren, L., Van Dijk, M., Yu, M., Devadas, S.: Trapdoor computational fuzzy extractors and stateless cryptographically-secure physical unclonable functions. IEEE Trans. Dependable Secure Comput. **14**, 65–82 (2016)
8. Hori, Y., Katashita, T., Kang, H., Satoh, A., Kawamura, S., Kobara, K.: Evaluation of physical unclonable functions for 28-nm process field-programmable gate arrays. J. Inf. Process. **22**(2), 344–356 (2014)
9. Jin, C., et al.: FPGA implementation of a cryptographically-secure PUF based on learning parity with noise. Cryptography **1**(3), 23 (2017)

10. Khalafalla, M., Gebotys, C.: PUFs deep attacks: enhanced modeling attacks using deep learning techniques to break the security of double arbiter PUFs. In: Proceedings of the DATE 2019, pp. 204–209 (2019)
11. Lee, J.W., Lim, D., Gassend, B., Suh, G.E., Van Dijk, M., Devadas, S.: A technique to build a secret key in integrated circuits for identification and authentication applications. In: VLSI Circuits. Digest of Technical Papers, pp. 176–179 (2004)
12. Lim, D.: Extracting secret keys from integrated circuits. Master's thesis, Massachusetts Institute of Technology (2004)
13. Machida, T., Yamamoto, D., Iwamoto, M., Sakiyama, K.: A new arbiter PUF for enhancing unpredictability on FPGA. Sci. World J. **2015** (2015)
14. Maes, R., Tuyls, P., Verbauwhede, I.: Low-overhead implementation of a soft decision helper data algorithm for SRAM PUFs. In: Clavier, C., Gaj, K. (eds.) CHES 2009. LNCS, vol. 5747, pp. 332–347. Springer, Heidelberg (2009). https://doi.org/10.1007/978-3-642-04138-9_24
15. Maes, R., Van Herrewege, A., Verbauwhede, I.: PUFKY: a fully functional PUF-based cryptographic key generator. In: Prouff, E., Schaumont, P. (eds.) CHES 2012. LNCS, vol. 7428, pp. 302–319. Springer, Heidelberg (2012). https://doi.org/10.1007/978-3-642-33027-8_18
16. Pappu, R.: Physical one-way functions. Ph.D. thesis, Massachusetts Institute of Technology (2001)
17. Pappu, R., Recht, B., Taylor, J., Gershenfeld, N.: Physical one-way functions. Science **297**(5589), 2026–2030 (2002)
18. Rührmair, U., Sehnke, F., Sölter, J., Dror, G., Devadas, S., Schmidhuber, J.: Modeling attacks on physical unclonable functions. In: Proceedings of the CCS 2010, pp. 237–249 (2010)
19. Santikellur, P., Bhattacharyay, A., Chakraborty, R.S.: Modeling_of_APUF_compositions. https://github.com/Praneshss/Modeling_of_APUF_Compositions
20. Santikellur, P., Bhattacharyay, A., Chakraborty, R.S.: Deep learning based model building attacks on arbiter PUF compositions. Cryptology ePrint Archive, Report 2019/566 (2019). https://eprint.iacr.org/2019/566
21. Suh, G.E., Devadas, S.: Physical unclonable functions for device authentication and secret key generation. In: Proceedings of the DAC 2007, pp. 9–14 (2007)
22. Van Herrewege, A., et al.: Reverse fuzzy extractors: enabling lightweight mutual authentication for PUF-enabled RFIDs. In: Keromytis, A.D. (ed.) FC 2012. LNCS, vol. 7397, pp. 374–389. Springer, Heidelberg (2012). https://doi.org/10.1007/978-3-642-32946-3_27
23. Yashiro, R., Machida, T., Iwamoto, M., Sakiyama, K.: Deep-learning-based security evaluation on authentication systems using arbiter PUF and its variants. In: Ogawa, K., Yoshioka, K. (eds.) IWSEC 2016. LNCS, vol. 9836, pp. 267–285. Springer, Cham (2016). https://doi.org/10.1007/978-3-319-44524-3_16
24. Yuejiang, W.: Improving security and reliability of physical unclonable functions using machine learning. Master's thesis, Clemson University (2018)

Implementing Cryptography Pairings over Ordinary Pairing-Friendly Curves of Type $y^2 = x^5 + a\,x$

Mohammed Zitouni$^{(\boxtimes)}$ and Farid Mokrane

Laboratory Analysis, Geometry and Applications CNRS (UMR 7539),
Galilee Institute, Paris 13 University, Villetaneuse, France
zitounimohammmed@gmail.com, mokrane@math.univ-paris13.fr

Abstract. In this paper, we describe an efficient implementation in Sage of the Tate pairing over ordinary hyperelliptic curves of type $y^2 = x^5 + a\,x$. First, we describe a method of construction of these curves according to Kawazoe and Takahashi [8]. Then, we describe an efficient formula for computing pairings on such curves over prime fields, and develop algorithms to compute Tate pairing. We provide a faster optimisation of the final exponentiation in particular for the embedding degree $k = 28$.

Keywords: Hyperelliptic curve · Tate pairing · Finite field · Embedding degree · Final exponentiation

1 Introduction

In 1989, three years after the introduction of elliptic curves cryptography, Koblitz suggest to use hyper-elliptic curves as a generalization to higher genus curves [8]. He extended the idea of abelian points group on elliptic curves over finite field to the Jacobian of a hyperelliptic curves, since the Jacobian is a finite abelian group on which the arithmetic operations are applied.

The algebraic curves-based cryptography has divided the cryptographers community [11] into two teams. The first one which argues that the problems of factorization and discrete logarithm problem (DLP) over finite field have already been intensively studied; and that it would require more time before the community can really apprehend the nature of elliptic curves. The other team was ambitious, started working in it and proposed their first protocols.

The first protocols proposed are based on a mathematical tool called pairing, the oldest of them being the Weil pairing. This mathematical protocol has received a great attention by the researchers and is now among the majors topics in cryptography. In order to realize protocols based on pairings, it is essential to have Pairing-friendly-curves which have parameters such as p the large prime fields $\mathbb{F}_p$ and the embedding degree k. The embedding degree plays an important role in ensuring a certain desired level security. In this context, the security of the pairing-based cryptosystems depends on finding curves whose Jacobian order

© Springer Nature Switzerland AG 2020
E. Simion and R. Géraud-Stewart (Eds.): SecITC 2019, LNCS 12001, pp. 95–108, 2020.
https://doi.org/10.1007/978-3-030-41025-4_7

over the finite fields $\mathbb{F}_{p^k}$, is divisible by a larger prime number ℓ (a condition necessary for resisting attacks such as Pohling-Hellman attacks).

In this paper, we consider Kawazoe-Takahashi [8] genus two ordinary pairing-friendly curves of type $y^2 = x^5 + a\,x$ which are generated over a finite field $\mathbb{F}_{p^k}$ using a method introduced by Kachisa [7]. These curves are characterized by simple and fast complex multiplications. It is also possible to have curves with a known odd prime factor ℓ of the Jacobian order with different embedding degrees and offer a small $\rho_{-value} = 2\,log(p)/log(\ell)$ between 2 and 3.

The paper is organized as follows. First, we recall some backgrounds on pairings over hyperelliptic curves, Jacobian group structure, and representation of divisors classes. We describe a method to construct ordinary pairing-friendly of Kawazoe and Takahashi curves with simple method proposed by Kachisa [7] to obtain curves with small ρ_{-value}. Then, we recall the Tate-Lichtenbaum pairing definition and present implementation techniques for pairings on hyperelliptic curves. We provide a new approach to the final exponentiation when the embedding degree is $k = 28$. The critical computational task of evaluating a function at a divisor is also provided.

Finally, we give some implementation results in Sage using Intel Core i5-7300HQ CPU @ 2.50 GHz processor on several security levels. We conclude that for most applications there exits an efficient algorithm for computing pairings on hyperelliptic curves that is better that on ordinary elliptic curves from the point of view of efficiency and security.

2   Preliminaries

In this section, we briefly recall the definition of the hyperelliptic curves, pairings and the definition of the Tate-Lichtenbaum pairing.

2.1   Hyperelliptic Curves

A genus g hyperelliptic curves over a prime finite field $\mathbb{F}_p$ are non-singular curves of a general form:

$$\mathcal{H}: \qquad y^2 + h(x)\,y = f(x) \qquad\qquad (1)$$

with h, $f \in \mathbb{F}_p[x]$, $deg(f) = 2\,g + 1$, $deg(h) \leq g$ and $f(x)$ is monic. For any algebraic extension $\mathbb{K}$ of $\mathbb{F}_p$, there is a special point at infinity, which is denoted by P_∞, and we can consider the set of K-rational points on $\mathcal{H}$:

$$\mathcal{H}(K) := \{(x,y) \in K \times K \mid y^2 + h(x)\,y - f(x) = 0\} \cup \{\infty\}. \qquad (2)$$

2.2   Pairings

The concept of a pairing was introduced in cryptography for the fitst time by Menezes et al. [11] to attack instances of the Discrete Logarithm Problem on elliptic curves and hyperelliptic curves. In 2000, pairing was used as bilinear application by Joux [6] to build cryptographic protocols.

Let $\mathbb{G}_1$ and $\mathbb{G}_2$ two additive abelian groups of prime order ℓ, $\mathbb{G}_3$ a multiplicative abelian group of order also ℓ. A bilinear pairing on $(\mathbb{G}_1, \mathbb{G}_2, \mathbb{G}_3)$ is a map:

$$e : (\mathbb{G}_1, +) \times (\mathbb{G}_2, +) \longrightarrow (\mathbb{G}_3, \times)$$

that satisfies the following requirements:

1. Bilinearity : $\forall D_1, D_1' \in \mathbb{G}_1, \forall D_2, D_2' \in \mathbb{G}_2$,
    i. $e(D_1 + D_1', D_2) = e(D_1, D_2)\, e(D_1', D_2)$,
    ii. $e(D_1, D_2 + D_2') = e(D_1, D_2)\, e(D_1, D_2')$,
    iii. $e(a\, D_1, D_2) = e(D_1, a\, D_2) = e(D_1, D_2)^a, a \in \mathbb{N}^*$.
2. Non-degeneracy:
    i. $\forall D_1 \in \mathbb{G}_1 - \{0\}, \exists D_2 \in \mathbb{G}_2 : e(D_1, D_2) \neq 1$,
    ii. $\forall D_2 \in \mathbb{G}_2 - \{0\}, \exists D_1 \in \mathbb{G}_1 : e(D_1, D_2) \neq 1$.
3. Easily and efficiently calculable.

We recall here the definition of the Tate-Lichtenbaum pairing as it is stated in the literature, which is an explicit version described by Lichtenbaum.

Let $Jac_{\mathcal{H}}(\mathbb{F}_{p^k})$ be the Jacobian group of the hyperelliptic curve $\mathcal{H}$ over $\mathbb{F}_{p^k}$, ℓ be a prime with $\ell \mid \sharp Jac_{\mathcal{H}}(\mathbb{F}_{p^k})$ and let k be the smallest integer such that $\ell \mid (p^k - 1)$, then k is called the embedding degree (dependent on ℓ).

Definition 1. *The Tate-Lichtenbaum pairing is a bilinear and non-degeneracy map defined by:*

$$T_\ell : \quad Jac_{\mathcal{H}}(\mathbb{F}_{p^k})[\ell] \times Jac_{\mathcal{H}}(\mathbb{F}_{p^k})/\ell\, Jac_{\mathcal{H}}(\mathbb{F}_{p^k}) \longrightarrow \mathbb{F}_{p^k}^\times / (\mathbb{F}_{p^k}^\times)^\ell$$

$$(D_1, D_2) \longmapsto T_\ell(D_1, D_2) = f_{\ell, D_1}(D_2)^{(p^k - 1)/\ell}.$$

f_{ℓ, D_1}: *the function given by the divisor* $\ell\, D_1 - \ell\,(\infty) = div(f)$.

3 Pairing-Friendly Curves of Type $y^2 = x^5 + a\,x$

3.1 Curve Choice

We can give here explicit constructions of pairing-friendly hyperelliptic curves with ordinary Jacobian proposed by Kawazoe and Takahishi [8], we show also such that curves are suitable to construct genus 2 pairing at the high security levels.

We consider p an odd prime number, $\mathbb{F}_p$ is a finite field of characteristic $p \neq 2$, so we can define equation of the curve $\mathcal{H}$ as $y^2 = f(x)$ where $f(x)$ is a polynomial $\in \mathbb{F}_p[x]$ of degree 5. Let Jac_H be the Jacobian variety of a hyperelliptic curve $\mathcal{H}$. We denote the group of rational points on Jac_H over $\mathbb{F}_p$ by $Jac_{\mathcal{H}}(\mathbb{F}_p)$.

To compute the Jacobian order, we need the characteristic polynomial of p−th power Frobenius endomorphism of $\mathcal{H}$. Then the order is given by

$$\sharp\, Jac_{\mathcal{H}}(\mathbb{F}_p) = \chi_p(1)$$

It is very difficult to evaluate the characteristic polynomial of p−th power Frobenius endomorphism of $\mathcal{H}$ in 1 for hyperelliptic curves over height level bits fields, there are very few results on it, Gaudry and Harley [3] compute the group order over 80-bits fields but their algorithm needs very long running time. To solve this problem, there are a very special curves with complex multiplication, they are known by the existence of efficient algorithms called CM-methods to construct such curves. The best example of such ordinary pairing-friendly curves is curves of type $y^2 = x^5 + a\,x$ given by Kawazoe and Takahashi [8]. They proposed also a fast algorithm to compute the Jacobian group order over a prime finite field.

3.2   Counting Points

In [3] Gaudry presented a method to compute the Jacobian order modulo the characteristic p of the base field by using the Hasse-Witt matrix. Two main theorems in [10] and [16] quoted below:

Theorem 1. *Let* $y^2 = f(x)$ *with* $deg(f) = 2g + 1$ *be the equation of a genus g hyperelliptic curve. Denote by c_i the coefficient of x^i in the polynomial $f(x)^{(p-1)/2}$. Then the Hasse-Witt matrix is given by*

$$A = (c_{ip-j})_{1 \leq i,j \leq g}.$$

The following theorem give the link between the characteristic polynomial of the Frobenius endomorphism and the Hasse-Witt matrix.

Theorem 2. *Let $\mathcal{H}$ be a curve of genus g defined over a finite field $\mathbb{F}_{p^k}$. Let A be the Hasse-Witt matrix of $\mathcal{H}$, and let $A_\phi = AA^{(p)}...A^{(p^{k-1})}$. Let $\kappa(t)$ be the characteristic polynomial of the matrix A_ϕ and $\chi(t)$ the characteristic polynomial of the Frobenius endomorphism. Then*

$$\chi(t) \equiv (-1)^g\, t^g\, \kappa(t)(mod\, p).$$

This method is difficult in general when p is very large, but if we consider a special form of $f(x) = x^5 + a\,x \in \mathbb{F}_p[x]$ of degree 5 we can easily compute the Hasse-Witt matrix, $A = \begin{bmatrix} c_{p-1} & c_{p-2} \\ c_{2p-1} & c_{2p-2} \end{bmatrix}$, the element (c_i) is coefficient of x^i in polynomial $f(x)^{(p-1)/2}$. The characteristic polynomial of the Frobenius endomorphism of the genus 2 curve $y^2 = f(x)$ over $\mathbb{F}_p$ is

$$\chi(t) = t^4 - s_1 t^3 + s_2 t^2 - s_1 pt + p^2, \qquad |s_1| \leq 4\sqrt{p}, \quad |s_2| \leq 6p$$

The s_1 and s_2 are two integers (for more details see Theorem 3, [3]), they are given by

$$s_1 \equiv c_{p-1} + c_{2p-2}(mod\, p) \quad and \quad s_2 \equiv c_{p-1}\, c_{2p-2} + c_{p-2}\, c_{2p-1}(mod\, p)$$

3.3   Pairing-Friendly Curves of the Cocks-Pinch Method

By using results in [Theorem 3, [3]] and Cocks-Pinch method for hyperelliptic curve $\mathcal{H} : y^2 = x^5 + a\,x$. We can construct pairing-friendly curves of this type over a prime field $\mathbb{F}_p$, with parameters c and d integers such that: $p = c^2 + 2\,d^2$, ℓ large prime factor of the Jacobian order over $\mathbb{F}_p$ and k embedding degree, satisfying the following conditions:

1. $p \equiv 1,\ 3\ (mod\ 8)$,
2. $\chi \equiv 0\ (mod\ \ell)$,
3. $\phi_k(p) \equiv 0\ (mod\ \ell)$,
4. $p = c^2 + 2\,d^2$,   with $c \equiv 1\ (mod\ 4)$.

We did the implementation in Sage of the algorithm presented by Kawazoe and Takahashi which is the analog of Cocks-Pinch method to obtain genus 2 ordinary hyperelliptic curves of the form $y^2 = x^5 + a\,x$. By using generalization of Kachisa [7] which he parametrized the parameters c, d, r and p as polynomials $c(z)$, $d(z)$, $\ell(z)$ and $p(z)$ in a variable z. By using this approach, we can obtain curves with small $\rho - value = 2\,log(p)/log(\ell)$.

Algorithm 1. Kawazoe Takahashi pairing-friendly hyperelliptic curves with Cocks-Pinch method construction.

1: **Require:** $k \in \mathbb{Z}$
2: **Ensure:** A genus 2 hyperelliptic curve defined by $y^2 = x^5 + a\,x$ with Jacobian subgroup order ℓ.
3: Choose a prime number ℓ such that: $lcm(k, 8)$ divides $(\ell - 1)$
4: Choose α, β and γ such that: α is a primitive k^{th} root of unity in $(\mathbb{Z}/l\ \mathbb{Z})^{\times}$, $\beta^2 \equiv -1\ (mod\ \ell)$ and $\gamma^2 \equiv 2\ (mod\ \ell)$.
5: Compute c and d integers such that:
6: $c \equiv (\alpha + \beta)(\gamma(\beta + 1))^{-1}\ (mod\ \ell)$ and $c \equiv 1\ (mod\ 4)$,
7: $d \equiv (\alpha\,\beta + 1)(2\,(\beta + 1))^{-1}\ (mod\ \ell)$
8: Compute $p = c^2 + 2\,d^2$
9: **if** (p is a prime satisfying $p \equiv 1\ (mod\ 8)$) **then**
10:    Compute a such that:
11:    $a^{(p-1)/2} \equiv -1\ (mod\ p)$,
12:    $2\,(-1)^{(p-1)/8}\,d \equiv (a^{(p-1)/8} + a^{3(p-1)/8})\,c\ \ (mod\ p)$.
13: **else**
14:    Go to step **3:**
15: **end if**
16: **return** k, p, ℓ, a, d, c.

---

4   Group Structure of Hyperelliptic Curve

4.1   General Group Element

The group structure of a hyperelliptic curve $\mathcal{H}$ over a finite field $\mathbb{F}_q$, $(q = p^k)$, p : prime odd number $(p \geq 5)$ and k integer $(k \geq 1)$, recapitulates on the representation of his Jacobian. The following theorem show the unique representation of the Jacobian element.

Definition 2. *A divisor D is a finite formal sum of points on the curve $\mathcal{H}$ such that:*

$$D := \sum_{i=1}^{m}(P_i) \tag{3}$$

We can also define the **reduced divisor** D_r associated with D as follows:

Theorem 1. *Let D an element on the Jacobian of the curve $\mathcal{H}$, the element D has a **unique** representation D_r of the form:*

$$D_r := \sum_{i=1}^{m}(P_i) - m(\infty), \tag{4}$$

such that:

1. *$m \neq g$,*
2. *P_i are affine points,*
3. *The involution $\imath$, satisfy: $\imath(P_i) \neq \imath(P_j)$, for all i, j such that $i \neq j$.*

All elements on Jacobian form an abelian variety, Mumford [13] introduced a way of representing such that elements, it's extremely useful for implementation.

Theorem 2 *(Mumford representation). Let $\mathcal{H}$: $y^2 + h(x)\, y = f(x)$ a hyperelliptic curve of genus g define over a finite field $\mathbb{F}_q$, $q = p^k$ p: primer $(p \geq 5)$ and k integer $(k \geq 1)$. Let K an algebraic extension of $\mathbb{F}_q$, then any element D of the Jacobian of the curve $\mathcal{H}$, can be represented in a **unique** way by two polynomials $(u(x), v(x)) \in K[x]^2$ such that:*

1. *u is monic, with $\deg(u(x)) \leq g$,*
2. *$\deg(v(x)) \leq \deg(u(x))$, and*
3. *$u(x)$ divides $\{v(x)^2 + v(x)\, h(x) - f(x)\}$.*

As we saw before, we have two representations for a divisor D on the Jacobian, a natural representation $D = \sum_{i=1}^{m}(P_i) - m(\infty)$ and a Mumford representation $D = (u(x), v(x))$. To do implementation, we must understand how to manipulate the two representations. For example to pass from the Mumford representation to the natural one, we compute the coordinates of the points $P_i = (x_i, v(x_i))$ with x_i the roots of the polynomial $u(x)$. In the case of genus 2 hyperelliptic curve $\mathcal{H}$, the Mumford representation of divisor of degree 0 whose effective part E is the sum of the points $P1 = (x_1, y_1)$ and $P2 = (x_2, y_2)$, $(E = P_1 \pm P_2)$ is obtained by multiplying and dividing by:

$$u(x) = x^2 - (x_1 + x_2)x + x_1 x_2 \quad and \quad v(x) = \frac{y_1 - y_2}{x_1 - x_2}(x - x_1) + y_1. \tag{5}$$

The set of torsion points are the points whose order is finite, which is the case for all element on the Jacobian $Jac_{\mathcal{H}}$ over $\mathbb{F}_q$. The set of ℓ-torsion points is defined as follows:

1. $[\ell]D = \underbrace{D + D + ... + D}_{\ell \text{ terms}} \qquad if \quad \ell > 0,$

2. $[\ell]D = -([-\ell]D) \quad if \quad \ell < 0,$
3. $[0]D = (\infty).$

By definition, we say that D is an ℓ-torsion divisor if $[\ell]D = (\infty)$. The subgroup of ℓ-torsion divisors on the Jacobian of hyperelliptic curve $\mathcal{H}$ over a finite field $\mathbb{F}_q$ is denoted by $Jac_{\mathcal{H}}(\mathbb{F}_q)[\ell]$, with $q = p^k$, p: prime number ($p \geq 5$) and k integer ($k \geq 1$).

4.2   Jacobian Subgroup Operations

To do pairing implementation, we need to perform operations on the Jacobian group $Jac_{\mathcal{H}}(\mathbb{F}_{p^k})[\ell]$, Cantor [1] developed and showed efficient algorithms to manipulate elements of the Jacobian $Jac_{\mathcal{H}}[\ell](\mathbb{F}_{p^k})$, by using the Mumford representation, assuming that $h(x) = 0$ and $p \neq 2$. These algorithms was later generalised by Koblitz [9] to remove these conditions.

We will show here the two algorithms implemented in Sage, the first one is to give a semi-reduced divisor D equivalent to $D_s \simeq D_1 + D_2$ from two semi-reduced divisors D_1 and D_2 (represented by Algorithm 2), and the other algorithm is to reduce the divisor semi-reduced D_s (given by Algorithm 2) to obtain a reduced divisor D_r equivalent (represented by Algorithm 3).

Algorithm 2. Divisor Composition.

1: **Require:** $D_1 = [u_1(x), v_1(x)]$ and $D_2 = [u_2(x), v_2(x)]$
2: **Ensure:** $D_s \simeq D_1 + D_2$, $D_s = [u_s(x), v_s(x)]$.
3: Compute: $d_1 = gcd(u_1(x), u_2(x)) = a_1 \, u_1(x) + a_2 \, u_2(x)$
4: Compute: $d = gcd(d_1, v_1(x) + v_2(x) + h(x)) = b_1 \, d_1 + b_2 \, (v_1(x) + v_2(x) + h(x))$
5: $c_1 \leftarrow b_1 \, a_1, \, c_2 \leftarrow b_1 \, a_2, \, c_3 \leftarrow b_2$
6: $u_s(x) \leftarrow (u_1(x) \, u_2(x)) \, / \, (d^2)$
7: $v_s(x) \leftarrow (c_1 \, u_1(x) \, v_2(x) + c_2 \, u_2(x) \, v_1(x) + c_3 \, (v_1(x) \, v_2(x) + f(x))) \, / \, d \, mod \, (u_s(x))$
8: **return** $[u_s(x), v_s(x)]$.

Algorithm 3. Divisor Reduction.

1: **Require:** $D = [u(x), v(x)]$, semi-reduced divisor.
2: **Ensure:** $D_r = [u_r(x), v_r(x)]$ reduced with $D_r \simeq D$.
3: Compute: $u_r(x) \leftarrow (f(x) - v(x) \, h(x) - v(x)^2) \, / \, u(x)$
4: Compute: $v_r(x) \leftarrow (-h(x) - v(x)) \, mod \, u_r(x)$
5: **if** $(deg(u_r(x)) > g)$ **then**
6:     $u(x) \leftarrow u_r(x),$
7:     $v(x) \leftarrow v_r(x)$
8:     Go to step **3:**
9: **end if**
10: Make $u_r(x)$ monic.
11: **return** $[u_r(x), v_r(x)]$.

5   Our Work

To compute pairing we need Miller algorithm [12] which makes it possible to calculate the function $f_{\ell,D_1}(D_2)$, this algorithm was applied for the elliptic case and quickly it has been generalised on hyperelliptic curves. We define the group law $\oplus$ on the Jacobian $Jac_{\mathcal{H}}(\mathbb{F}_{p^k})$, let D_1 and $D_2 \in Jac_{\mathcal{H}}(\mathbb{F}_{p^k})$, there is a function $h \in \mathbb{F}_p(\mathcal{H})$ with its divisor:

$$div(h_{D_1,D_2}) = D_1 + D_2 - (D_1 \oplus D_2),$$

The main task involved in computing the evaluation $f_{\ell,D_1}(D)$ in D_1, Miller has shown how to efficiently compute it, this function appearing in

$$Div(f_{\ell,D}) = \ell\, D - D_\ell.$$

For $\ell = n + m$, n and m integers, we find:

$$Div(f_{\ell,D}) = Div(f_{n+m,D}) = f_{n,D} \cdot f_{m,D} \cdot h_{D_n,D_m},$$

With h a function such that:

$$div(h_{D_n,D_m}) = D_n + D_m - \rho(D_n + D_m),$$

$\rho(D_n + D_m)$: the reduced divisor of $(D_n + D_m)$.

This immediately leads to the following algorithm:

Algorithm 4. Miller's Algorithm for hyperelliptic curves

1: **Require:** $\ell \in \mathbb{N}$ *and* $D_1, D_2 \in Jac_{\mathcal{H}}(\mathbb{F}_{p^k})$, reduced-divisors with disjoint support.
2: **Ensure:** $f_{\ell,D_1}(D_2)$
3: Write ℓ in binary form: $\ell = \Sigma_{j=0}^{s}\, \ell_j 2^j$, with $\ell_j \in \{0,1\}$ and $\ell_s = 1$
4: $D \leftarrow D_1$
5: $f \leftarrow 1$
6: **for** (j from $s-1$ to 0) **do**
7:     Compute $D \leftarrow [2]\, D$ and extract $h_{(D,D)}$
8:     $f \leftarrow f^2 \cdot h_{(D,D)}(D_2)$
9:     **if** ($\ell_j == 1$) **then**
10:         Compute $D \leftarrow D \oplus D_1$ and extract $h_{(D,D_1)}$
11:         $f \leftarrow f \cdot h_{(D,D_1)}(D_2)$
12:     **end if**
13: **end for**
14: **return** f

We can clearly see that the execution of the Miller algorithm requires the existence of an algorithm that allows the evaluation of the function $h \in \mathbb{F}_q(\mathcal{H})$, $q = p^k$ p: primer ($p \geq 5$) and k integer ($k \geq 1$). We called this algorithm "evaluatefunction()", it's the crucial step of Miller's algorithm, it allows to calculate the value of the function in a point $D \in Jac_{\mathcal{H}}(\mathbb{F}_q)$, such that D is a reduced divisor represented in Mumford representation. For this work, we will focus only on the evaluation of the function h in an effective divisor that we note $E = [u_E(x), v_E(x)]$. There are two different methods to compute $h(E)$ (we use in general a norm computation and resultants).

The first method requires a polynomial factorisation of $u_E(x)$, it can be summarized by the following algorithm:

Algorithm 5. Method 1, function evaluation of h in E.

1: $E \leftarrow \Sigma_{i=1}^{i=d}(P_i)$, $P_i = (x_i, y_i) \in \mathcal{H}$, $D = E - d(\infty)$.
2: Compute the support of E.
3: Factoring $u_E(x)$, as $u_E(x) = \prod_{i=1}^{i=d}(x - x_i)$
4: Setting $y_i = v_E(x_i)$.
5: Note that $(x_i, y_i) \in \mathbb{F}_{q^{g_i}}$, $with$ $g_i \leq g$.
6: Compute $h(E) = \prod_{i=1}^{i=d} h(x_i, y_i) = h(x_1, y_1) \times h(x_2, y_2) \times ... \times h(x_d, y_d)$.

The above method is not the best because it didn't take in consideration the fact that the result of the evaluation has to be in $\mathbb{F}_q$ Instead, one could partition the support into distinct Galois orbits as follows:

$$\{(x_i, y_i), (x_i^q, y_i^q), ..., (x_i^{q^{g_i-1}}, y_i^{q^{g_i-1}})\}$$

And the last step **(6.)** of the algorithm is simply reduced by calculating the norm $N_{\mathbb{F}_{q^{g_i}}/\mathbb{F}_q}(h(x_i, y_i))$.

The second method is faster than the first one, since it does not require any polynomial factorisation. It is based on the observation of $\tilde{h}(x) = h(x, v_E(x))$ which verified for all x_i root of $u_E(x)$, $\tilde{h}(x_i) = h(x_i, v_E(x_i))$ so instead of calculating the product $h(E) = \prod_{i=1}^{i=d} h(x_i, y_i)$, the problem is reduced to the computation of $h(E) = \prod_{i=1}^{i=d} \tilde{h}(x_i)$, with x_i the zeros of $u_E(x)$, but this corresponds exactly to the definition of the resultant of the two polynomials $u_E(x)$ and $\tilde{h}(x)$, and we can write:

$$h(E) = Resultant(u_E(x), h(x, v_E(x)))$$

As we work on hyperelliptic curves of genus g, the polynomials degree $deg(u_E(x))$ of the Mumford representation of $E = [u_E(x), v_E(x)]$ is smaller than g, so we can write:

$$h(E) = Resultant(u_E(x), \tilde{h}(x) \bmod u_E(x))$$

We consider $\mathcal{H}$ a hyperelliptic curve of genus 2, defined over a finite field $\mathbb{F}_q$ by $y^2 + h_x y = f_x$, $(q = p^k)$, p : prime odd number $(p \geq 5)$ and k integer $(k \geq 1)$, let D, D_1 and $D_2 \in Jac_{\mathcal{H}}(\mathbb{F}_q)$, $D = E - d(\infty)$, E effective divisor.

As $h_{D_1,D_2} = h(x,y)$ is a rational function $h(x,y) \in \mathbb{F}(\mathcal{H})$, we can write:

$$h(x,y) = \frac{h_1(x,y)}{h_2(x,y)}$$

So,

$$\tilde{h}(x) = h(x,v_E(x)) = \frac{h_1(x,v_E(x))}{h_2(x,v_E(x))} = \frac{\tilde{h}_1(x)}{\tilde{h}_2(x)}$$

Algorithm evaluation of the rational function $h = h_{D_1,D_2}(D)$ in E is given by:

Algorithm 6. Method **2**, evaluation of the function h_{D_1,D_2} in E

1: **Require:** $E = [u_E(x), v_E(x)], D_1 = [u_1(x), v_1(x)]$ and $D_2 = [u_2(x), v_2(x)],$
2: $f_x, h_x, d = deg(u_E(x)).$
3: **Ensure:** $h_{D_1,D_2}(E).$
4: $\tilde{h}_1 \leftarrow u_2(x) \bmod u_E(x), \tilde{h}_2 \leftarrow 1, \tilde{h}_3 \leftarrow 1$
5: $D = [u,v] = D_1 + D_2,$ divisors composition D_1 and D_2
6: **while** degree of $u > g$ **do**
7:    $u \leftarrow (f_x - v\,h_x - v^2)/u$
8:    $v \leftarrow (-h_x - v) \bmod u$
9:    Make u monic.
10:    $\tilde{h}_1 \leftarrow (\tilde{h}_1(v_E - v)) \bmod u_E$
11:    $\tilde{h}_2 \leftarrow (\tilde{h}_2.u) \bmod u_E$
12:    **if** degree of $v > g$ **then**
13:       $\tilde{h}_3 \leftarrow -\tilde{h}_3 \times coef,$ $coef$: the leading coefficient of the polynomial $v(x).$
14:    **end if**
15: **end while**
16: Compute R_1 : resultant of the two polynomials $u_2(x)$ and $\tilde{h}_1$
17: Compute R_2 : resultant of the two polynomials $u_2(x)$ and $\tilde{h}_2$
18: $\tilde{h}_3 = \tilde{h}_3^{\,d}$
19: **return** $\frac{R_1}{\tilde{h}_3.R_2}.$

---

6 Final Exponentiation

Tate pairing algorithm requires computation of final exponentiation after the Miller loop. The optimisation of this computation is to factor the term $(p^k - 1)/\ell$ combined with the p-th power Frobenius operations. So the final exponentiation can be written as

$$\frac{p^k - 1}{\ell} := \frac{\phi_k(p)}{\ell} \cdot \prod_{s|k,\ s<k} \phi_s(p) \tag{6}$$

We note that this exponent is determined by fixed system parameters. This final exponent can be broken down into three components. Let $e = \frac{k}{2}$ then

$$\frac{p^k - 1}{\ell} := (p^e - 1) \cdot [\frac{(p^e + 1)}{\phi_k(p)}] \cdot [\frac{\phi_k(p)}{\ell}] \tag{7}$$

For example for $k = 28$ the final exponent becomes

$$\frac{p^{28} - 1}{\ell} = (p^{14} - 1) \cdot [\frac{(p^{14} + 1)}{\phi_{28}(p)}] \cdot [\frac{\phi_{28}(p)}{\ell}]$$

With $\phi_{28}(p) = p^{12} - p^{10} + p^8 - p^6 + p^4 - p^2 + 1$, so

$$\frac{p^{28} - 1}{\ell} = (p^{14} - 1) \cdot (p^2 + 1) \cdot [\frac{(p^{12} - p^{10} + p^8 - p^6 + p^4 - p^2 + 1)}{\ell}]$$

There are two parts of the exponentiation, the first one is an easy exponentiation to the power of $exp_1 = (p^{14} - 1) \cdot (p^2 + 1)$ (because of the Frobenius), it also simplifies the rest of the final exponentiation because after raising to the power $(p^{14} - 1)$ the field element becomes "unitary". The other part $exp_2 = (p^{12} - p^{10} + p^8 - p^6 + p^4 - p^2 + 1)/\ell$ is the very hard part of the final exponentiation can be calculated using a fast multi-exponentiation algorithm [5]. However, we can use the polynomial description of $p(z)$ and $\ell(z)$ given by Kachisa in [7]. In this case the hard part of the final exponentiation is to the power of $(p^{12} - p^{10} + p^8 - p^6 + p^4 - p^2 + 1)/\ell$. After substituting the polynomials for $p(z)$ and $\ell(z)$, after it can be expressed to the base p.

7   Implementation Results

We have implemented the Tate pairing for the different level security on ordinary genus two curves in SageMath version 8.1. Our aim was not to provide an optimal ad-hoc implementation for any one of the curves or pairings, but rather to keep a sufficient level of security appropriate for a general purpose system, while still implementing algorithmic optimisations that apply in a broader context. All were performed on Intel Core i5-7300HQ CPU @ 2.50 GHz processor.

In the following, we will compute the execution time needed to calculate Tate's pairing for different embedding degree and several levels of security. The following Table 1 shows the calculation time in milliseconds of all Tate's large pairing computation steps on ordinary Kawazoe curves of type $y^2 = x^5 + a\ x$. So we compute the times: t_g, t_J, t_p, t_r, t_m and t_e such that: t_g: time generation of the curve equation, t_J: time computation of the Jacobian on $\mathbb{F}_q$, t_p: Construction time of Jacobian two points, t_r: reducing time of the two divisors, t_m: execution time of the Miller loop, t_e: time required for the final exponentiation.

For t_g, t_J and t_p, we will directly give the time needed by predefined algorithms in Sage to generate the desirable curves, compute Jacobian and to construct two points on the Jacobian $Jac_\mathcal{H}(\mathbb{F}_p)$ over prime finite field. On the other hand, the times t_r and t_m are the conclusion of the implementation of the different executable algorithms proposed by Galbraith [2], Granger et al. [4] and others.

To vary the embedding degree, we will always work on genus two Kawazoe and Takahashi curves of type $y^2 = x^5 + a\ x$ generated by Kachisa [7], these parameters are chosen in order to have the desirable ordinary pairing-friendly curves.

Table 1. Execution times in milliseconds (ms) to compute Tate's pairing.

	$k=7$	$k=8$	$k=10$	$k=28$
p (bits)	336	387	378	379
ℓ (bits)	254	257	249	255
t_g	1.163	1.228	1.187	1.779
t_J	0.084	0.076	0.033	0.083
t_p	18112,942	14364,803	44049.245	221412.49
t_r (1 D)	0.294	0.337	0.381	1.042
t_m	808.031	10555.84	1221.53	5163.32
t_e	32.1519	57.774	97.863	1561.75

For cryptography applications, the discrete logarithm problems in $Jac_{\mathcal{H}}(\mathbb{F}_{p^k})$ and in the multiplicative group $\mathbb{F}_{p^k}$ must both be computationally infeasible. For Jacobian varieties of hyperelliptic curves of genus 2 the best known discrete logarithm problem (DLP) algorithm is the parallelized rho-Pollard algorithm in [14] and [15], which has running time $O(\sqrt{\ell})$ where ℓ is the size of the largest prime-order subgroup of $Jac_{\mathcal{H}}(\mathbb{F}_{p^k})$. In the following Table 2, we will give the security level for genus two curves according to the size of the curve parameters (k, p, ℓ) and the $\rho - value = \dfrac{g \, log(p)}{log(\ell)}$.

Table 2. Embedding degrees for hyperelliptic curves of genus $g = 2$ required to obtain commonly desired levels of security.

Security level (bits)	Subgroup size (ℓ)	Extension field size (p^k)	Embedding degree(k)			
			$\rho \simeq 1$	$\rho \simeq 2$	$\rho \simeq 3$	$\rho \simeq 4$
80	160	1024	12	6	4	3
128	256	3072	24	12	8	6
192	384	7680	40	20	13	10
256	512	15360	60	30	20	14

Now, we calculate the execution time in Sage needed to compute Tate pairing for different security levels (128, 192 and 256 bits), the following Table 3 lists the execution time of Miller loop and final exponentiation required to compute pairing in milliseconds (ms).

Table 3. Execution times in milliseconds (ms) required to compute Tate's pairing for different security levels.

Security level (bits)	128	192	256
Miller loop	1055.840	1221.53	5163.32
Final exponentiation	57.774	97.863	1561.75
Total	1113.614	1319.393	6725.07

8   Conclusions

In this work, we discuss an implementation of pairings over pairing-friendly hyperelliptic curves. In particular, we focus on Kawazoe-Takahashi genus 2 curves of the form $y^2 = x^5 + a\,x$. We provide the necessary background to have sufficient understanding of pairings on hyperelliptic curves, discuss the algorithm to sample curves of the desired type, and describe the group structure of these curves. We then continue and present details of the Miller algorithm that are involved in the efficient evaluation of the pairing.

First, we present the analogue of the Cocks-Pinch method to obtain ordinary Kawazoe-Takahashi pairing-friendly curves using approach of Kachisa to have curves with a small $\rho - value$, we have implemented this method in Sage, the ordinary Jacobian order over $\mathbb{F}_p$, $\mathbb{F}_{p^k}$ and the various curve parameters are calculated.

Second, we gave several techniques for pairing computation more precisely for Tate pairing case, operations on Jacobian subgroup, Miller loop and we have provided explicit formulae for the evaluation of the function $f_{D_1,D_2}(E)$ in effective divisor required by the Miller algorithm. We then continue and give a performance method for final exponentiation in order to speed up the pairing, generally applicable and which is calculated in two parts, an easy part given a unitary field element and a hard part using polynomial description of curve parameters.

Finally, we gave the implementation results in Sage for different levels of security according to the embedding degree of the curve. Our studies indicates that pairing on hyperelliptic curves is computable and we can have pairing applications efficient and competitive to the pairing on elliptic curves in performance and security level.

As the main contribution here is the evaluation of the rational function h in the point on the Jacobian of the curve over prime field, that appears in the evaluation of $f_{\ell,D_1}(D)$ in algorithm of Miller. We present one method, that is based on the factorization of polynomials, and a faster one, that instead of factorization of polynomials is based on the resultant of polynomials The includes some interesting ideas to improve the evaluation of pairings on hyperelliptic curves. We also gave a fast method to calculate the final exponentiation by using the parametrization of the curve parameters p and l.

108   M. Zitouni and F. Mokrane

References

1. Cantor, D.G.: Computing in the Jacobian of a hyperelliptic curve. Math. Comput. **48**(177), 95–101 (1987)
2. Galbraith, S.D., Hess, F., Vercauteren, F.: Hyperelliptic pairings. In: Takagi, T., Okamoto, T., Okamoto, E., Okamoto, T. (eds.) Pairing 2007. LNCS, vol. 4575, pp. 108–131. Springer, Heidelberg (2007). https://doi.org/10.1007/978-3-540-73489-5_7
3. Gaudry, P., Harley, R.: Counting points on hyperelliptic curves over finite fields. In: Bosma, W. (ed.) ANTS 2000. LNCS, vol. 1838, pp. 313–332. Springer, Heidelberg (2000). https://doi.org/10.1007/10722028_18
4. Granger, R., Hess, F., Oyono, R., Thériault, N., Vercauteren, F.: Ate pairing on hyperelliptic curves. In: Naor, M. (ed.) EUROCRYPT 2007. LNCS, vol. 4515, pp. 430–447. Springer, Heidelberg (2007). https://doi.org/10.1007/978-3-540-72540-4_25
5. Granger, R., Page, D., Smart, N.P.: High security pairing-based cryptography revisited. In: Hess, F., Pauli, S., Pohst, M. (eds.) ANTS 2006. LNCS, vol. 4076, pp. 480–494. Springer, Heidelberg (2006). https://doi.org/10.1007/11792086_34
6. Joux, A.: A one round protocol for Tripartite Diffie–Hellman. In: Bosma, W. (ed.) ANTS 2000. LNCS, vol. 1838, pp. 385–393. Springer, Heidelberg (2000). https://doi.org/10.1007/10722028_23
7. Kachisa, E.J.: Generating more kawazoe-takahashi genus 2 pairing-friendly hyperelliptic curves. In: Joye, M., Miyaji, A., Otsuka, A. (eds.) Pairing 2010. LNCS, vol. 6487, pp. 312–326. Springer, Heidelberg (2010). https://doi.org/10.1007/978-3-642-17455-1_20
8. Kawazoe, M., Takahashi, T.: Pairing-friendly hyperelliptic curves with ordinary Jacobians of Type $y^2 = x^5 + ax$. In: Galbraith, S.D., Paterson, K.G. (eds.) Pairing 2008. LNCS, vol. 5209, pp. 164–177. Springer, Heidelberg (2008). https://doi.org/10.1007/978-3-540-85538-5_12
9. Koblitz, N.: Hyperelliptic cryptosystems. J. Cryptol. **1**(3), 139–150 (1989)
10. Manin, J.I.: The Hasse-Witt matrix of an algebraic curve. In: Selected Papers of Yu I Manin, pp. 3–22. World Scientific (1996)
11. Menezes, A.J., Okamoto, T., Vanstone, S.A.: Reducing elliptic curve logarithms to logarithms in a finite field. IEEE Trans. Inf. Theory **39**(5), 1639–1646 (1993)
12. Miller, V., et al.: Short programs for functions on curves. **97**(101–102), 44 (1986, Unpublished manuscript)
13. Mumford, D.: Tata Lectures on Theta i, ii. Birkhäuser, Boston (1984)
14. Pollard, J.M.: Monte carlo methods for index computation. Math. Comput. **32**(143), 918–924 (1978)
15. Van Oorschot, P.C., Wiener, M.J.: Parallel collision search with cryptanalytic applications. J. Cryptol. **12**(1), 1–28 (1999)
16. Yui, N.: On the Jacobian varieties of hyperelliptic curves over fields of characteristic $p > 2$. J. Algebra **52**(2), 378–410 (1978)

Towards Practical Deployment of Post-quantum Cryptography on Constrained Platforms and Hardware-Accelerated Platforms

Lukas Malina[✉][iD], Sara Ricci[iD], Petr Dzurenda[iD], David Smekal[iD], Jan Hajny[iD], and Tomas Gerlich[iD]

Brno University of Technology, Technicka 12, Brno, Czech Republic
{malina,ricci,dzurenda,smekald,hajny,gerlich}@feec.vutbr.cz

Abstract. Most of the cryptographic constructions deployed in practical systems today, in particular digital signatures and key-establishment schemes, are vulnerable to attacks using quantum computers. Post-quantum cryptography (PQC) deals with the design and implementation of cryptographic algorithms that are resistant to these attacks. In this paper, we evaluate the NIST's PQC competition candidates with respect to their suitability for the implementation on special hardware platforms. In particular, we focus on the implementability on constrained platforms (e.g., smart cards, small single-board computers) on one side and on the performance on very fast hardware-accelerated platforms (i.e., field-programmable gate arrays - FPGAs) on the other side. Besides the analysis of the candidates' design features affecting the performance on these devices and security aspects, we present also the practical results from the existing implementation on contemporary hardware.

Keywords: Applied cryptography · Constrained device · FPGA · Performance · Post-Quantum Cryptography · Smartcard · Security

1 Introduction

Post-Quantum Cryptography (PQC) brings together cryptographic primitives, schemes, and systems that are designed to withstand potential attacks using quantum computers. On one hand, the Shor's algorithm running on a quantum computer with a sufficient number of qubits could allow attackers to solve the current security assumptions of asymmetric cryptosystems that are based on discrete logarithm and factorization problems. On the other hand, the Shor's algorithm requires 4000 logical qubits to break 2048-bit RSA keys [28], and current quantum computers (QCs) capable to run Shor's algorithm only have about 20 logical qubits [25] (current QCs have 72 physical qubits). It is important

This work is supported by the National Sustainability Program under grant LO1401 and Ministry of Interior under grant VI20192022126.

© Springer Nature Switzerland AG 2020
E. Simion and R. Géraud-Stewart (Eds.): SECITC 2019, LNCS 12001, pp. 109–124, 2020.
https://doi.org/10.1007/978-3-030-41025-4_8

also to mention that the biggest QC is D-WAVE2000Q with 2048 qubits that are based on a different technology, i.e. quantum annealing. The Shor's algorithm cannot be executed on the D-WAVE2000Q. In addition to the Shor's algorithm which could compromise conventional asymmetric cryptosystems, there is the Grover algorithm that streamlines the collision or symmetric key brute force search on $O(\sqrt{N})$, where N is the domain size of the function. Many security experts and practitioners are addressing these potential threats by proposing schemes based on different assumptions (quantum resistant). Their focus and activities are united under a knowledge area called Post-Quantum Cryptography.

This paper aims to help security experts with the practical deployment of PQC into heterogeneous networks that can contain many computational and memory constrained end nodes (e.g. sensors with SAM modules - smart cards, embedded devices etc.) and powerful central back-end servers or application servers. These servers usually terminate hundreds to thousands connections from end nodes by using many-to-one communication model. Therefore, these central servers can be supported by FPGA platforms that are used for a hardware acceleration of expensive operations in order to increase the computational capacities and the number of user connections.

This paper is organized as follows: the rest of this section contains related work and our contribution. Section 2 introduces PQC and discusses the implementation aspects of PQC. Section 3 presents recent implementations of PQC schemes on smart cards and presents our performance assessment of NIST PQC candidates on a small single-board computer. Section 4 deals with the deployment of PQC schemes on FPGA and presents our assessment on the updated hardware platform. In the last section, we conclude this work.

1.1 Related Work

There are several research and survey papers dealing with the implementation of PQC schemes on smart cards and FPGA platforms. Due to the memory and computational limits of smart cards, there are only few papers that study and present the implementation of PQC schemes on the cards. For instance, the paper [38] deals with the implementation of the McEliece cryptosystem on a chip card (Infineon SLE76) where the encryption operation takes 0.97 s. Section 3 presents more papers dealing with the implementations of PQC on smart cards. The hardware implementation of post-quantum cryptography schemes on FPGA platforms have been studied in several papers, e.g., [22,23,30,34]. A recent survey paper [30] studies lattice-based cryptographic schemes (LBC schemes) and their software and hardware implementations. The paper describes several works dealing with hardware implementations on a FPGA platform. Nevertheless, the paper does not compare practical results (e.g. occupied HW resources, etc.). The authors of the paper [4] employ the High-Level Synthesis method to make the hardware implementation of the 11 PQC schemes of the second round of the NIST PQC on Xilinx Virtex-7 FPGA. The article compares 7 key exchange schemes: Newhope, Frodokem, Crystals-KYBER, NTRU-HRSS,

Classic McEliece, Saber, LEDACrypt, and 4 signature schemes: CRYSTALS-Dilithium, qTESLA, SPHINCS+, MQDSS. Benchmark results include data on captured HW resources, e.g., Look-up Tables (LUT), Flip-flop registers (FF), latency, and Latency-Area Product (LAP) values on side A (encapsulation) and side B (decapsulation) with and without optimization methods (Loop unrolling, Loop pipelining). More papers dealing with the hardware implementations of PQC on FPGA are presented in Sect. 4. In our work we explore recent state of the art and we add our experimental results of PQC schemes on the contemporary Xilinx UltraScale+ FPGA platform and on ARM platform.

1.2   Contribution

The contribution of this paper is twofold:

- We present the overview of existing PQC implementations on constrained devices and smart cards. We also present our experimental results of NIST PQC semifinals on a constrained device (i.e. ARM device).
- We present the overview of existing hardware implementations PQC on FPGA platforms and we present our experiment results of 6 chosen PQC schemes on the current FPGA platform UltraScale+. We do not use a HLS method as some related works but we directly run the existing scheme implementations in VHDL (VHSIC-HDL) (Very High Speed Integrated Circuit Hardware Description Language).

2   Application Pros and Cons of Post Quantum Cryptography Schemes

This section discusses the maturity, advantages, disadvantages and basic parameters of PQC, such as key sizes, signature/ciphertext sizes, memory requirements, and expensive operations that can cause obstacles in hardware implementations or within implementations on constrained platforms such as smart cards.

PQC schemes can be divided into 6 areas:

- **Lattice**-based cryptography (LBC) is based on lattice-based computational problems, e.g., the Shortest Vector Problem (SVP) and the Ring Learning With Errors (RLWE) problem. A lattice $L \subset R^n$ is defined as the set of all integer linear combinations of basis vectors. LBC schemes are usually used for public key encryption, key exchange and digital signatures. Well known LBC cryptosystems are the Frodo scheme [9], and Ring-Learning with Errors (Ring-LWE) schemes such as NTRU [18], New Hope [3], Kyber [10].
- **Multivariate** cryptography (MVC) is based on systems of multivariate polynomial equations over a finite field $\mathbb{F}$. There are several variants of MVC schemes based on Hidden Field Equations (HFE) trapdoor functions [33] such as the Unbalanced Oil and Vinegar Cryptosystems (UOV) [21]. UOV schemes are used for signatures. Other examples of multivariate public-key cryptosystems (MPKC) are the Rainbow scheme [13] and Tame Transformation Signatures [11].

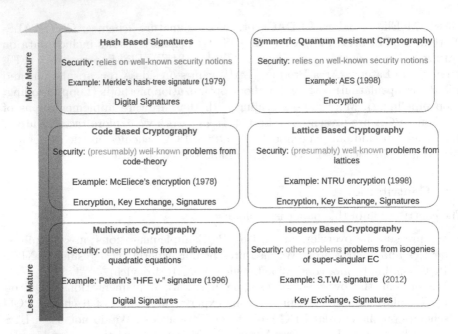

Fig. 1. Post-quantum cryptography family.

- **Hash**-based cryptography (HBC) is based on the security of hash functions (as a one-way function). Ralph Merkle introduced the Merkle Signature Scheme (MSS) [27] based on a one-time signatures (e.g., the Lamport signature scheme [24]) and a binary hash tree (a Merkle tree) in 1979. MSS is resistant against quantum computer algorithms.
- **Code**-based cryptography (CBC) is based on using error correcting codes to construct a one-way function. The security is based on the hardness of decoding a message which contains random errors and recovering the code structure. The McEliece public key encryption scheme [26] is based on binary Goppa codes with high error correction capability and works with matrices. A receiver secretly chooses a private key that is a binary Goppa code. The public key is generator matrix **G** that describes a scrambled and randomly permuted variant of the Goppa code. A sender first encodes the plain text using **G** and adds t random errors during the encryption. Then, the receiver who knows the private key (the hidden algebraic structure of the Goppa code) is able to correct the errors and recover the message. The McEliece scheme [26] is considered as secure for 40 years. The Niederreiter cryptosystem [31] as a McEliece variant provides both encryption and signature schemes. Many McEliece variants require large public keys.
- **Supersingular** elliptic curves - **Isogeny**-based cryptography (IBC) is based on supersingular elliptic curve isogenies which are secure against quantum adversaries. These schemes are secured under the problem of constructing an isogeny between two supersingular curves with the same number of points.

Isogeny-based schemes may serve as digital signatures or key exchange such as Supersingular Isogeny Diffie-Hellman (SIDH) scheme [20].
– **Symmetric** quantum resistant cryptography (SQRC) is based on the principles of diffusion and confusion. The leading example is the Advanced Encryption Standard (AES) which applies several rounds of substitutions and permutations on the key and plaintext to produce the ciphertext [12]. Doubling the key size provides an adequate security level against QC attacks. Remarkable is that this family offers the smallest key sizes for PQC.

PQC offers a secure alternative to traditional cryptography by relying on hard problems which cannot be speed up by a quantum computer. Moreover, PQC can be implemented in current infrastructure unlike the quantum cryptography which requires QCs. In fact, only quantum-key distribution based on photons are nowadays possible. However, some PQC schemes are not ready and time is required to improve their efficiency (e.g., long key size and slow algorithms), improve their usability (e.g., software and hardware implementations), and build confidence in it (standards are under development). The maturity of these 6 PQC areas with basic information is depicted in Fig. 1. As shown in the figure, HBC and SQRC are the families with higher maturity. These families come from well study and currently used cryptographic schemes, and therefore standards are already developed and their efficiency is known. The only sort of disadvantage of these families is that their security is not based on hard problems which means that they are not provably secure. In case of CBC and LBC families, even if they are mostly based on hard problems which bring confidence on their security, they are a bit below in the ranking. The main reason is that their efficiency is still under development, in particular their keysizes need to be reduced as well as their computational cost in order to be competitive with the current schemes and can be applied on constrained devices. MVC family presents the same issues of CBC and LBC and, moreover, in terms of provable security, there exist hardly any rigorous proofs which reduce their security to hard mathematical problems. At last, IBC is the newest one among PQC families and is very computationally expensive even compared to LBC.

Table 1. NIST PQC competition.

NIST 2019			
	Signature	KEM/encryption	Overall
Lattice-based	5(3)	21(9)	26(12)
Code-based	2(0)	17(7)	19(7)
Multi-variate	7(4)	2(0)	9(4)
Symmetric/hash-based	3(2)	None	3(2)
Other	2(0)	5(1)	7(1)
Total	19(9)	45(17)	64(26)

There are many proposals of PQC schemes and PQC studies, e.g. [5]. In 2016, NIST initiated a process to solicit, evaluate, and standardize one or more PQC schemes [1]. In 2019, NIST announced 17 second-round candidates (semifinals) for key establishment and 9 schemes for quantum resistant digital signatures. Table 1 summarizes the NIST PQC competition. Each column shows how many proposals received NIST in 2016 and how many survived until now (between parenthesis). In order to compare the strength of the different NIST competitors, their efficiency in term of key sizes and computational costs has to be considered. In Appendix A, Table 6 shows key pair, signature and ciphertext sizes of 2nd round NIST schemes. The performance assessment on various platforms could be found in the next sections.

3   Post Quantum Cryptography on Constrained Devices

This section discusses the current state of PQC deployment on smart cards and similar constrained devices, and presents some recommendations for the future deployment. The section also contains our experiments on constrained devices.

Different issues arise when PQC meets constrained devices such as smart cards (SCs). In fact, PQC schemes are generally memory and power consuming, and therefore pose a challenge for devices with bounded resources. Moreover, these schemes require the implementation of primitives which are not supported by the current SCs. Therefore, off-the-shelf smart card platforms (Java Card, Basic Card, MultOS) with constrained memory and API limits are not very appropriate for the implementation of PQC schemes. For instance, Strenzke [38] could not fully implement McEliece scheme (the key generation algorithm is missing) on a microprocessor due to the involvement of operations on matrices that by far exceed the RAM size. Also the realization of LBC schemes on contemporary computing platforms requires careful design choices and trade-offs. The majority of the LBC schemes require the implementation of at least one of the following algorithms: discrete Gaussian sampling, matrix multiplication, polynomial multiplication and number theoretic transform. For standard LWE schemes, matrix multiplication algorithms are adopted, whereas number theoretic transform is a better choice for polynomial multiplication in RLWE [29].

3.1   Current Implementations of PQC on Constrained Platforms

The current software and hardware implementations on SCs (or microprocessors) are summarized in Table 2. More specifications are given below.

Lattice-Based PQC on Smartcards: In 2014, Boorghany *et al.* [7] adapted 3 identification schemes based on LP-LWE scheme to work on SCs. Their implementation provides 128-bit security on three environment settings: Java Card (contact), Java Card (contactless) and AVR ATxmega64A3 microcontroller. The main encountered issues are fast Fourier transformation and discrete Gaussian sampling implementations which are high time consuming. In 2015, Boorghany

Table 2. Recent PQC implementations on constrained devices (microcontroller, smart cards), the sizes of EEPROM and RAM are given in kilobytes.

Scheme	Type	Device	Chip	EEPROM	RAM
McEliece [38]	Code	SC chip	16-bit Infineon SLE76CF5120P	310	4.4
LPR [40]	Lattice	Java Card	JCOP v2.4.1 NXP	≪80	≪10
			J3A081 Dual Interface Card		
GLP12 [7]	Lattice	Java Card	Feitian FT-Java/H10CR Java Card	11.4	4.2
		Micro	AVR ATxmega64A3 microcontroller	13.8	
DDLL13 [7]	Lattice	Java Card	Feitian FT-Java/H10CR Java Card	55.5	5.2
		Micro	AVR ATxmega64A3 microcontroller	13.8	
DJ13 [7]	Lattice	Java Card	Feitian FT-Java/H10CR Java Card	12.1	1.9
		Micro	AVR ATxmega64A3 microcontroller	13.9	
NTRU [8]	Lattice	Property Card	32-bit ARM7TDMI processor	55.8	3.5
		Micro	AVR ATxmega64A3 microcontroller	13.4	
LP-LWE [35]	Lattice	Micro	AVR ATmega328P microcontroller	0.3	1.1
Kyber [2]	Lattice	SC chip	16-bit Infineon SLE78CLUFX5000	<500	<16

et al. [8] published the SC implementation of three authentication schemes on LBC. These schemes are based on the same primitives, e.g. GLP and BLISS signature schemes, considered in the identification schemes in [7]. Furthermore, the authors also executed the NTRU encryption scheme on SCs. Their implementation provides 128-bit security. In a more recent work, Yuan *et al.* [40] present a RLWE based encryption scheme on Java Card providing 128 bit security. Polynomial multiplication is solved by applying Montgomery modular multiplication and number theoretic transform instead of fast Fourier transform. To be noted that long integers are not supported on SCs. Saarinen [35] shows how a compression technique of Ring-LWE ciphertexts can help with PQC implementations on constrained devices. They reduce ciphertext size by more than 40% at equivalent security level (128-bit security). Furthermore, they avoid NTT in the decryption operation. Albrecht *et al.* [2] present how to use RSA co-processors on standard smart cards to speed-up lattice-based cryptography. In particular, they convert polynomials to big integers which are processed on a RSA co-processor and then the results are converted back to the polynomials.

Code-Based PQC on Smartcards: Strenzke and Falko [38] present the implementation of the McEliece scheme for the 100 bit security level using a microcontroller. They could not reach higher security due to memory problems. Moreover, the key generation algorithm could not be implemented on the microprocessor for exceeding card's RAM size.

3.2 Experimental Results on Constrained Platforms

In order to get a complete overview of PQC schemes complexity on constrained devices, we evaluate PQC schemes efficiency on ARM Cortex-A53 processor which is utilized in some versions of single-board computers. In particular, we employ a Raspberry Pi 3 Model B (1.2 GHz CPU, 1 GB RAM) with Raspbian

9 operating system (32-bit version) to execute PQC NIST competitors [1]. Each competing scheme includes a zip file with C/C++ implementations, a mandatory *"reference implementation"* and optional optimized versions. In our comparison, we consider only *"reference implementation"* of each scheme with 128-bit security level. Therefore, each scheme was downloaded, built, and executed on our Raspberry Pi device. We compute executing time as an arithmetic mean from ten measurements. Our experimental results are shown in Table 3. In order to run the PQC algorithms, the following libraries need to be pre-installed: OpenSSL [16] (used mostly for calling AES algorithm functions), NTL [36] (computations with vectors, matrices and polynomials), GMP (big number operations) [17] and XKCP [6] (Keccak sponge function family). Moreover, Linux packages `make`, `gcc` and `g++` are used to make and build C/C++ applications.

Table 3. Performance of selected signature and KEM/Encryption schemes from 2nd NIST round [1]. The elapsed time is given in ms and is computed from an average of 100 measurements of algorithm run on ARM Cortex-A53 processor.

NIST KEM/encryption					
Scheme	Type	Sec	Key pair generation	Encryption	Decryption
BIKE	Code	128	2.1	2.2	10.8
Kyber	Lattice	128	2.2	3.1	8.7
FrodoKEM	Lattice	128	40.4	78.3	78.8
HQC	Code	128	4.1	8.2	12.7
NewHope	Lattice	128	2.0	2.9	0.5
NTRU	Lattice	128	11.7	2.3	3.5
ROLLO-I	Code	128	19.4	2.6	10.1
FrodoKEM	Lattice	128	40.4	78.2	78.8
NIST signatures					
Scheme	Type	Sec	Key pair generation	Signing	Verification
Dilithium	Lattice	125	0.1	0.5	0.1
Falcon	Lattice	$\gg$128	34.8	3.2	0.3
MQDSS	Multivariate	128	1.2	98.4	72.9
Picnic	Symmetric /hash	128	0.1	61.7	41.9
qTESLA	Lattice	$\gg$128	1.1	0.8	0.2
SPHINCS+	Hash	128	3.5	110.0	4.7

The results indicate that lattice-based KEM schemes (e.g., NewHope, NTRU) and lattice-based digital signatures (e.g., Dilithium, qTESLA,) are more efficient than PQC schemes based on other types (e.g., code-based, multivariate-based).

4 Post Quantum Cryptography on Hardware-Accelerated Platforms

The hardware implementation on FPGA can overcome the computational expensiveness of some PQC schemes. In this section, we present the overview of recent PQC implementations on FPGA and add our results from updated FPGA platform, Xilinx UltraScale+. We use the following notation: LUT indicates the number of Look-Up Tables and FF denotes the number of Flip-Flop registers on chip. I/O presents the number of input and output ports. DSP is module Digital Signal Processor and BRAM (Block Random Access Memory) is used for storing the large amounts of data inside of FPGA. Frequency denotes the maximum frequency at which the unit is able to run.

4.1 Current Implementations of PQC on FPGA

The following text overviews recent PQC hardware implementations on FPGA cards. The performance results and hardware requirements of chosen PQC implementations are summarized in Table 4.

Lattice-Based PQC on FPGA: Kuo *et al.* [23] present the first hardware implementation of the NewHope scheme for key establishment. The paper describes implemented blocks and operations of NewHope including the discrete version of fast fourier transformation (NTT operation) and pseudo-random PRNG generator using SHA-3 hash function. Their NewHope implementation (128-bit security) utilizes 6098 FFs, 12340 LUTs, 29 DSPs (Digital Signal Processors), 14 BRAMs (block memories) at 114 MHz on the Xilinx 7 FPGA platform (dual core ARM Cortex A9 with 667 MHz and 28 nm Artix-7 Z-7020 FPGA providing 46,000 LUTs). The key establishment scheme runs within three phases (2 on side A and 1 on side B). The total time is given by the sum of all phases, i.e., $75.4 + 99.1 + 24.6$ µs. Subsequently, Oder and Guneysu [32] design the HW implementation of the NewHope scheme that emphasize the efficiency of the size of used FPGA HW resources. Their implementation utilizes 5142 LUTs, 4452 FFs, 4 18Kb-BRAMs and 2 server-side DSPs at 125 MHz on the Xilinx 7 platform. Overall, their NewHope implementation takes 1.4 ms on the server side and 1.5 ms on the client side. In 2017, Howe *et al.* [19] published the first HW implementation of the Ring-TESLA signature scheme on the FPGA Xilinx Spartan-6 platform. The authors designed 4 versions occupying different HW resources. Their implementation oriented on a small number of HW resources (4447 LUTs, 3345 FFs, 1257 slice registers, BRAM 3x, DSP 6x at 190 MHz) performs 104 signing operations/s. Their speed-oriented implementation performs 785 signing operations/s (1.273 ms) and takes 6848 LUTs, 5457 FFs, 2254 register slices, BRAM 4x, DSP 16x at 180 MHz. To be noted, that a signing process has similar performance and takes similar HW resources as a verification process. Ebrahimi *et al.* [14] introduce a hardware-optimized implementation of the Ring-BinLWE variant based on lattice problems. Their implementation on the

FPGA platform is compared with other HW implementations (McBits scheme, NTRU scheme, Isogeny SIKE scheme, and the classic ECC implementation). Their implementation of InvRBLWE in 140-bits post-quantum security occupies 5k LUT, 5K FF, 1292 slice registers and 0 DSP/BRAM on Virtex-7. At 524 MHz, the encryption time is only 1.97 µs. The survey [37] deals with a comparison of HW implementations of post-quantum digital signature schemes, namely, qTESLA and CRYSTALS-Dilithium schemes. Authors use Xilinx Vivado High-Level Synthesis (HLS) method and present the results of both schemes on FPGA (Xilinx Artix-7). They show that CRYSTALS-Dilithium at lower security levels has slightly lower hardware requirements than qTESLA.

Code-Based PQC on FPGA: In 2018 Wang *et al.* [39] published the FPGA implementation of a code-based scheme, namely, the Niederreiter cryptosystem using binary Goppa codes. Their implemented scheme provides 128-bit post-quantum security on the Stratix V (5SGXEA7N). Their implementation takes up 52% of the available logic, i.e., 121806 ALMs and 961 RAM blocks (38% of resources) at a clock rate of 250 MHz. The number of cycles for key generation is 966400, and 14291 cycles are required for decryption. Their implementation is synthesized on the Virtex-6 XC6VLX240T where the implementation needs 6571 slice registers at 267 MHz. The decryption takes 0.04 ms.

Multivariate PQC on FPGA: In 2018 Ferozpuri and Gaj [15] introduced the design and hardware implementation of the Rainbow signature scheme on the FPGA Xilinx Virtex 7 (XC7VX1140) and Kintex-7 (XC7K480) platforms. The Rainbow scheme is based on multivariant equations and the Unbalanced Oil and Vinegar (UOV) problem and is a candidate in the NIST PQC competition (the second round). Their version of the Rainbow-80 implementation on Virtex-7 occupies 17048 LUTs, 5878 register slices, 9033 FFs, 0 DSPs, 18 BRAMs. At 200 MHz, the signing operation takes 0.61 µs (148 clock cycles per operation).

Other PQC Schemes on FPGA: The first hardware implementation of SIDH (Supersingular Isogeny Diffie-Hellman) based on supersingular eliptic curves is introduced in the article [22]. The paper describes a design and implementation of fast and scalable architecture. The paper further describes the concrete algorithms for operations and the options of parallel computation processing. The implementation of the scheme (85 bit post-quantum security) on FPGA Xilinx Virtex-7 at 177.1 MHz utilizes 3 dual multipliers, 30031 FFs, 24499 LUTs, and 10298 slices. The total time of the scheme is 33.7 ms (i.e., 30 SIDH operations/s).

Table 4 shows that recent Ebrahimi *et al.*'s [14] implementation of the InvR-BLWE scheme is the most efficient (1.97 µs) in compare with other observed schemes.

Table 4. Current hardware FPGA implementations of 2nd round NIST PQC schemes.

PQC scheme	FPGA	HW resources						Perform on A side	Perform on B side
		LUTs	FFs	Slices	DSPs	BRAMs	Freq.[MHz]		
KEM/encryption PQC schemes on FPGA									
New Hope Kuo et al. [23]	Xilinx 7	12340	6098	-	29	14	114	100 µs	99.1 µs
New Hope Oder et al. [32]	Xilinx 7	5142	4452	-	2	4 × 18 Kb	2 × 125	1.5 ms	1.4 ms
InvRBLWE-n-512 Ebrahimi et al. [14]	Xilinx 7	5k	5K	1292	0	0	524	1.97 µs for enc	0.95 µs for enc.
SIDH Koziel [22]	Xilinx Virtex 7	24499	30031	10298	192	27	3 × 177.1	17.88 ms	15.82 ms
PQC digital signatures schemes on FPGA									
Ring-TESLA Signing reduced HW Howe et al. [19]	Xilinx Spartan-6	4447	3345	1257	6	3	190	104 signing ops/s	-
Ring-TESLA Verify reduced HW Howe et al. [19]	Xilinx Spartan-6	3714	3023	1172	6	3	188	-	102 verify ops/s
Ring-TESLA signing Signing speed Oriented Howe et al. [19]	Xilinx Spartan-6	6848	5457	2254	16	4	180	785 signing ops/s	-
Ring-TESLA Verify speed Oriented Howe et al. [19]	Xilinx Spartan-6	6473	5582	2103	16	3	178	-	776 verify ops/s
qTESLA-2SL Soni et al. [37]	Xilinx Artix-7	137559	39086	-	-	-	-	3696400 clock cycles	-
CRYSTALS-Dilithium-2SecLev Soni et al. [37]	Xilinx Artix-7	89933	21023	-	-	-	-	1259801 clock cycles	-
Rainbow-80 signature Ferozpuri and Gaj [15]	Xilinx Virtex-7	17048	9033	5878	0	18	200	0.61 µs	-

4.2 Deployment Issues and Setup of PQC Implementations on FPGA UltraScale+

Many related works employ HLS (High Level Synthesis) which is using a high level abstraction for a general algorithm description. Because the C/C++ programming languages are widely used, it is easier to specify desired functions in these languages, less errors are made, and the circuit verification is more effective. Moreover, the simulation of HLS is faster than a conventional VHDL simulation. Nonetheless, there are few constructions which are not compatible with HLS synthesis: system calling, dynamic allocation of resources, few operations with pointers (reallocation, array of pointers), and standard template library. The C implementations of NIST PQC semifinalists often depend on external libraries that are not a part of the code and they could not be converted directly by HLS. Furthermore, a simple conversion of C codes of PQC schemes by HLS produces non-optimized hardware implementations. To be noted that many implementations of PCQ digital signature schemes (their C sources are also available at their websites) also contain non-compatible parts and constructions for VHDL. For instance, most of these digital schemes employ the OpenSSL library which could not be easily converted and synthesized on FPGA platforms. We test PQC schemes directly in VHDL. The direct hardware implementations in VHDL could produce more efficient implementations. We use Vivado 2019.1.3 to synthesize the implementations of 6 chosen schemes. The HDL implementations are mostly taken from the author's websites or from the official website of the NIST's PQC competition. We implement algorithms on the Xilinx UltraScale+ chip and test the correct functionality of the output. Further, we optimize each algorithm separately to get it working properly.

4.3 Experimental Results on Virtex FPGA Platform

We present the comparison of 6 NIST semifinalists: SIKE, BIKE, NewHope, SABER, classic McEliece and FrodoKEM schemes. We compare hardware resources and maximum working frequency. The results of the synthesis utilized on the Virtex UltraScale+ are summarized in Table 5. The classic McEliece scheme with 76k LUTs and 129 FFs requires the most HW resources from implemented schemes. KEM schemes, BIKE and NewHope, require less than 10k LUTs and FF registers. Nevertheless, both schemes require units of BRAM modules. In our experiment, the BIKE scheme requires the lowest numbers of HW resources on the FPGA UltraScale+ platform.

Table 5. Our experimental synthesis results of PQC schemes on FPGA.

PQC schemes on FPGA UltraScale+						
PQC Scheme	LUT	FF	I/O	DSP	BRAM	Frequency [MHz]
SIKE[a]	36481	51092	175	-	-	421
BIKE[b]	5195	3259	145		6	368
NewHope[c]	9069	9369	53	4	4	258
SABER[d]	20218	36123	160	-	-	66
Classic McEliece[e]	76382	129000	-	-	530	128
FrodoKEM[f]	21360	10606	-	-	40	160

[a] The VHDL implementation from https://sike.org/#implementation.
[b] The HDL files for the designs taken from https://bikesuite.org/#implementation.
[c] Implementations for the FPGAs taken from https://github.com/mupq/pqhw.
[d] Source code are available on the website https://csrc.nist.gov/CSRC/media/Projects/Post-Quantum-Cryptography/documents/round-2/submissions/SABER-Round2.zip.
[e] HW implementation in VHDL from https://classic.mceliece.org/hardware.html.
[f] HLS and VHDL core taken from https://github.com/Microsoft/PQCrypto-LWEKE.

5   Conclusion

This work maps the current state of PQC implementations on constrained plat-forms and on FPGA platforms. FPGA, which enables communication nodes to accelerate some computationally expensive operations, can be very useful tech-nology for the dissemination of PQC schemes in heterogeneous networks. Our analysis shows that several works have successfully implemented and tested PQC schemes on FPGA platforms. This work presents our synthesis results of 6 PQC schemes on the updated FPGA UltraScale+ platform. We do not employ the HLS procedure and we use directly the VHDL synthesis. Our results indicate that New Hope and BIKE schemes require less HW resources than the code based Classic McEliece scheme and other schemes such as SIKE, SABER and FrodoKEM. Further, this paper focuses on PQC on smart cards and constrained devices. Our analysis shows that there are only few works dealing with the PQC implementation on smart cards that are specifically customized. Neverthe-less, there are no known implementations that could be run on current off-the-shelf programmable smart cards. The limited memory resources of smart cards and non-trivial functions such as polynomial multiplication prevent the imple-mentation of PQC schemes on smart card platforms. Our experimental results measured on the ARM platform indicate that lattice-based schemes such as NewHope, NTRU, Dilithium and qTesla are more efficient than other compared PQC schemes. In our future work, we plan to implement and optimize suitable PQC schemes, e.g. NewHope, Dilithium, on an off-the-shelf smart cards.

A   Post Quantum Cryptography Size Requirements

This section discusses the current size requirements of the 2nd round NIST competitors. Our overview on current PQC schemes deals with implementations on devises which have limited memory capacity. Therefore, the suitability of a PQC scheme depends at first on its memory requirements. If the scheme is too demanding, it can not be directly implemented. Table 6 shows key pair, signature and ciphertext sizes of 2nd round NIST schemes. Regarding signature schemes, Dilithium and Falcon are the proposals which require less storage. Note that both the schemes belong to LBC group.

In case of KEM schemes, ROLLO-I and Round5 are the most promising ones. Therefore, the less demanding schemes between LBC and CBC groups have comparable memory requirements for KEM. Observe that NewHope also demands small memory capacity.

It is important to notice that memory capacity is only one of the component which have to be taken in consideration when schemes are compared.

Table 6. Size requirements of 2nd round NIST signature schemes and KEM/Encryption schemes.

Scheme	Type	Sec. Level [b]	Secret key [B]	Public key [B]	Signature [B]
NIST signatures					
Dilithium	Lattice	125	-	1 472	2 701
Falcon	Lattice	≫128	-	1 441	993.91
GeMSS	Multivariate	128	14 208	417 408	48
LUOV	Multivariate	128	32	7 300	1 700
MQDSS	Multivariate	128	32	62	32 882
Picnic	Symmetric/hash	128	32	64	195 458
qTESLA	Lattice	≫128	12 320	39 712	6 176
Rainbow	Multivariate	≫128	511 400	206 700	156
SPHINCS+	Hash	128	64	32	16 976
NIST KEM/encryption					
BIKE	Code	128	249	2 541	2 541
McEliece	Code	128	6 452	261 120	128
Kyber	Lattice	128	1 632 (or 32)	800	736
FrodoKEM	Lattice	128	19 888	9 616	9 720
HQC	Code	128	252	6 170	6 234
LAC	Lattice	128	512	544	712
LEDAcrypt	Code	128	452	1 872	1 872
NewHope	Lattice	128	869	928	1 088
NTRU	Lattice	128	1 452	1 138	1 138
NTRU Prime	Lattice	128	1 125	897	1 025
NTS-KEM	Code	128	9 248	319 488	1 024
ROLLO-I	Code	128	40	465	465
Round5	Lattice	128	16	634	682
RQC	Code	128	40	853	1690
SABER	Lattice	≫128	1 568	672	736
SIKE	Isogeny	128	374	330	346
Three Bears	Lattice	128	40	804	917
FrodoKEM	Lattice	128	19872	9616	9736

References

1. NIST - Computer Security Resource Center (CSRC). https://csrc.nist.gov/Projects/Post-Quantum-Cryptography/round-2-submissions
2. Albrecht, M.R., Hanser, C., Hoeller, A., Pöppelmann, T., Virdia, F., Wallner, A.: Implementing RLWE-based schemes using an RSA co-processor. IACR Trans. Cryptograph. Hardware Embedded Syst. **2019**(1), 169–208 (2019)
3. Alkim, E., Ducas, L., Pöppelmann, T., Schwabe, P.: Post-quantum key exchange-a new hope. In: USENIX Security Symposium, vol. 2016 (2016)
4. Basu, K., Soni, D., Nabeel, M., Karri, R.: NIST post-quantum cryptography-a hardware evaluation study. IACR Cryptol. ePrint Archive **2019**, 47 (2019)
5. Bernstein, D.J.: Post-quantum cryptography. In: van Tilborg, H.C.A., Jajodia, S. (eds.) Encyclopedia of Cryptography and Security, pp. 949–950. Springer, Heidelberg (2011). https://doi.org/10.1007/978-1-4419-5906-5
6. Bertoni, G., Daemen, J., Hoffert, S., Peeters, M., Van Assche, G., Van Keer, R.: Extended keccak code package. https://github.com/XKCP/XKCP

7. Boorghany, A., Jalili, R.: Implementation and comparison of lattice-based identification protocols on smart cards and microcontrollers. IACR Cryptol. ePrint Archive **2014**, 78 (2014)
8. Boorghany, A., Sarmadi, S.B., Jalili, R.: On constrained implementation of lattice-based cryptographic primitives and schemes on smart cards. ACM Trans. Embedded Comput. Syst. (TECS) **14**(3), 42 (2015)
9. Bos, J., et al.: Frodo: take off the ring! practical, quantum-secure key exchange from LWE. In: Proceedings of the 2016 ACM SIGSAC Conference on Computer and Communications Security, pp. 1006–1018. ACM (2016)
10. Bos, J., et al.: CRYSTALS-kyber: a CCA-secure module-lattice-based KEM. In: 2018 IEEE European Symposium on Security and Privacy (EuroS&P). IEEE (2018)
11. Chen, J.-M., Yang, B.-Y.: A more secure and efficacious TTS signature scheme. In: Lim, J.-I., Lee, D.-H. (eds.) ICISC 2003. LNCS, vol. 2971, pp. 320–338. Springer, Heidelberg (2004). https://doi.org/10.1007/978-3-540-24691-6_24
12. Daemen, J., Rijmen, V.: The Design of Rijndael: AES-the Advanced Encryption Standard. Springer, Berlin (2013)
13. Ding, J., Schmidt, D.: Rainbow, a new multivariable polynomial signature scheme. In: Ioannidis, J., Keromytis, A., Yung, M. (eds.) ACNS 2005. LNCS, vol. 3531, pp. 164–175. Springer, Heidelberg (2005). https://doi.org/10.1007/11496137_12
14. Ebrahimi, S., Bayat-Sarmadi, S., Mosanaci-Boorani, H.: Post-quantum cryptoprocessors optimized for edge and resource-constrained devices in IoT. IEEE IoT J. **6**, 5500–5507 (2019)
15. Ferozpuri, A., Gaj, K.: High-speed FPGA implementation of the NIST round 1 rainbow signature scheme. In: 2018 International Conference on ReConFigurable Computing and FPGAs (ReConFig), pp. 1–8. IEEE (2018)
16. OpenSSL Foundation: OpenSSL cryptography and SSL/TLS toolkit. https://www.openssl.org/
17. Granlund, T.: The GNU multiple precision arithmetic library. https://gmplib.org/
18. Hoffstein, J., Pipher, J., Silverman, J.H.: NTRU: a ring-based public key cryptosystem. In: Buhler, J.P. (ed.) ANTS 1998. LNCS, vol. 1423, pp. 267–288. Springer, Heidelberg (1998). https://doi.org/10.1007/BFb0054868
19. Howe, J., Rafferty, C., Khalid, A., O'Neill, M.: Compact and provably secure lattice-based signatures in hardware. In: 2017 IEEE International Symposium on Circuits and Systems (ISCAS), pp. 1–4. IEEE (2017)
20. Jao, D., De Feo, L.: Towards quantum-resistant cryptosystems from supersingular elliptic curve isogenies. In: Yang, B.-Y. (ed.) PQCrypto 2011. LNCS, vol. 7071, pp. 19–34. Springer, Heidelberg (2011). https://doi.org/10.1007/978-3-642-25405-5_2
21. Kipnis, A., Patarin, J., Goubin, L.: Unbalanced oil and vinegar signature schemes. In: Stern, J. (ed.) EUROCRYPT 1999. LNCS, vol. 1592, pp. 206–222. Springer, Heidelberg (1999). https://doi.org/10.1007/3-540-48910-X_15
22. Koziel, B., Azarderakhsh, R., Kermani, M.M., Jao, D.: Post-quantum cryptography on FPGA based on isogenies on elliptic curves. IEEE Trans. Circuits Syst. I Regul. Pap. **64**(1), 86–99 (2016)
23. Kuo, P.C., et al.: Post-quantum key exchange on FPGAs. IACR Cryptol. ePrint Archive **2017**, 690 (2017)
24. Lamport, L.: Constructing digital signatures from a one-way function. Technical report, Technical Report CSL-98, SRI International Palo Alto (1979)
25. Martín-López, E., Laing, A., Lawson, T., Alvarez, R., Zhou, X.Q., O'brien, J.L.: Experimental realization of Shor's quantum factoring algorithm using qubit recycling. Nat. Photonics **6**(11), 773 (2012)

26. Mceliece, R.J.: A public-key cryptosystem based on algebraic. Coding Thv **4244**, 114–116 (1978)
27. Merkle, R.C.: A certified digital signature. In: Brassard, G. (ed.) CRYPTO 1989. LNCS, vol. 435, pp. 218–238. Springer, New York (1990). https://doi.org/10.1007/0-387-34805-0_21
28. Moses, T.: Quantum computing and cryptography. Entrust Inc., January 2009
29. Nejatollahi, H., Dutt, N., Ray, S., Regazzoni, F., Banerjee, I., Cammarota, R.: Software and hardware implementation of lattice-cased cryptography schemes (2017)
30. Nejatollahi, H., Dutt, N., Ray, S., Regazzoni, F., Banerjee, I., Cammarota, R.: Post-quantum lattice-based cryptography implementations: a survey. ACM Comput. Surv. **51**(6), 129:1–129:41 (2019). https://doi.org/10.1145/3292548. http://doi.acm.org.ezproxy.lib.vutbr.cz/10.1145/3292548
31. Niederreiter, H.: Knapsack-type cryptosystems and algebraic coding theory. Prob. Control Inf. Theory **15**(2), 159–166 (1986)
32. Oder, T., Güneysu, T.: Implementing the newhope-simple key exchange on low-cost FPGAs. In: Lange, T., Dunkelman, O. (eds.) LATINCRYPT 2017. LNCS, vol. 11368, pp. 128–142. Springer, Cham (2019). https://doi.org/10.1007/978-3-030-25283-0_7
33. Patarin, J.: Hidden Fields Equations (HFE) and Isomorphisms of Polynomials (IP): two new families of asymmetric algorithms. In: Maurer, U. (ed.) EUROCRYPT 1996. LNCS, vol. 1070, pp. 33–48. Springer, Heidelberg (1996). https://doi.org/10.1007/3-540-68339-9_4
34. Pöppelmann, T.: Efficient implementation of ideal lattice-based cryptography. IT-Inf. Technol. **59**(6), 305–309 (2017)
35. Saarinen, M.J.O.: Ring-LWE ciphertext compression and error correction: tools for lightweight post-quantum cryptography. In: Proceedings of the 3rd ACM International Workshop on IoT Privacy, Trust, and Security, pp. 15–22. ACM (2017)
36. Shoup, V.: NTL: a library for doing number theory. https://shoup.net/ntl/
37. Soni, D., Basu, K., Nabeel, M., Karri, R.: A hardware evaluation study of NIST post-quantum cryptographic signature schemes (2020)
38. Strenzke, F.: A smart card implementation of the McEliece PKC. In: Samarati, P., Tunstall, M., Posegga, J., Markantonakis, K., Sauveron, D. (eds.) WISTP 2010. LNCS, vol. 6033, pp. 47–59. Springer, Heidelberg (2010). https://doi.org/10.1007/978-3-642-12368-9_4
39. Wang, W., Szefer, J., Niederhagen, R.: FPGA-based niederreiter cryptosystem using binary goppa codes. In: Lange, T., Steinwandt, R. (eds.) PQCrypto 2018. LNCS, vol. 10786, pp. 77–98. Springer, Cham (2018). https://doi.org/10.1007/978-3-319-79063-3_4
40. Yuan, Y., Fukushima, K., Kiyomoto, S., Takagi, T.: Memory-constrained implementation of lattice-based encryption scheme on standard Java card. In: 2017 IEEE International Symposium on Hardware Oriented Security and Trust (HOST), pp. 47–50. IEEE (2017)

White-Box Traitor-Tracing from Tardos Probabilistic Codes

Sandra Rasoamiaramanana[1,2]($\boxtimes$), Gilles Macario-Rat[1], and Marine Minier[2]

[1] Orange Labs, Applied Crypto Group, Châtillon, France
{sandra.rasoa,gilles.macariorat}@orange.com
[2] Université de Lorraine, CNRS, Inria, LORIA, 54000 Nancy, France
marine.minier@loria.fr

Abstract. In this paper, we address the problem of tracing traitors in the white-box model. A traitor tracing system generally comes with a broadcast encryption scheme where each user is equipped with a secret that allows him to decrypt broadcast data. When a broadcast encryption scheme is provided with a tracing procedure, the user's key is used to uniquely identify him. A white-box model refers to a context where an attacker shares the host with a software implementation of a cryptographic algorithm and controls the execution environment. Thus, a traditional broadcast encryption scheme will fail in this context since an adversary may steal the user's decryption key and illegally decrypts broadcast contents. In this work, we describe a traitor tracing system where each user is provided with a distinct key generation function instead of a secret key. The key generator is made user-specific and enables to generate a content key which is used to decrypt the encrypted content. We use techniques of White-Box Cryptography to build the key generation function and use a collusion-secure code to derive the user-specific key generators. Finally, we prove that the system is collusion-resilient.

Keywords: Traitor tracing · White-Box Cryptography · Tardos code

1 Introduction

A broadcast encryption scheme is a cryptographic method used to distribute encrypted data over an insecure channel[1]. Such a scheme is used, e.g., for digital content distribution and users of the system generally own a decryption box to decrypt the data. To allow the users to decrypt the data, a broadcast information is sent and each user is provided with a secret key that enables him to decrypt the encrypted data. The decryption box can be a tamper-resistant device such as a smart-card or a software on a personal computer or a smart-phone. Because tamper-resistant devices are hard and expensive to produce, software decryption boxes are more and more spread. For both cases, the main issue encountered is

---

[1] In particular used by the Advanced Access Content System (AACS) standard.

© Springer Nature Switzerland AG 2020
E. Simion and R. Géraud-Stewart (Eds.): SecITC 2019, LNCS 12001, pp. 125–141, 2020.
https://doi.org/10.1007/978-3-030-41025-4_9

the illegal redistribution of the decryption key. In the case of a software decryption box, key extraction is within the reach of a white-box attacker. Illegal redistribution of decryption keys may then lead to a substantial financial loss and one solution to this threat is traitor tracing. A traitor tracing scheme is a broadcast encryption provided with a tracing procedure. In a traitor tracing system, each user's decryption box is provided with a distinct secret key which uniquely identifies him. Sometimes, some misbehaved users called the traitors collude to forge and redistribute a decryption key. The system is collusion-resilient if the tracing procedure retrieves at least one those traitors.

The problem of traitor tracing was first introduced in [5] by Chor, Fiat and Naor who proposed a combinatorial scheme. Since the problem statement numerous works proposed collusion-resilient schemes which can be classified into three classes: combinatorial scheme, public key scheme (first introduced in [13]) and, collusion-secure code-based scheme. Kiayias and Yung [12] first introduced collusion-secure code-based scheme to solve the problem of traitor tracing and many papers followed the trend [3,10]. One advantage of such schemes is that the ratio of the ciphertexts and the plaintexts is constant. In particular, Billet and Phan introduced in 2008 a collusion-resilient traitor tracing scheme based on a Tardos code [2]. A Tardos code is a binary code that was introduced by Tardos in 2008 for watermarking digital documents [15]. Each document is identified with a mark which is a codeword embedded within the document and if some malicious users collude to produce a pirate version of the document, an accusation algorithm retrieves at least one of the misbehaved users. Billet and Phan harnessed the fact that traitor tracing and collusion-secure codes may share some properties. Actually, both have a collusion strategy that is constrained by an assumption called a "marking assumption". In brief the marking assumption states that a coalition of users are only able to identify the positions where their codewords differ. Our traitor tracing scheme belongs to the class of collusion-secure code-based scheme and uses a Tardos code. The main difference with Billet and Phan's work is that the bits of the codeword are hidden. Consequently the collusion strategy that we describe is completely different and is not constrained by the standard marking assumption. In particular, the proof of the collusion resistance does not directly depend on the collusion resistance of the code. Besides, the code length is shorter than the "optimal" length suggested by G. Tardos.

Solving the problem of traitor tracing in the white-box model was suggested by Delerablée et al. in [8]. They presented the desired "white-box security notions", i.e. the security notions that should be proved to state the security of an encryption scheme in the white-box model. Specifically, the problem of traitor tracing is rephrased by the traceability property of a white-box program. Authors stated that "a program can be made traceable by unnoticeably modifying its functionality", i.e. if the set of inputs for which the modified program unusually behaves is negligible compared to the whole set of inputs then the program can be traced using these inputs. In the same paper, Delerablée et al. defined an encryption scheme that is collusion-resilient using a primitive first introduced in [4] called a Private Linear Broadcast Encryption (PLBE) scheme. Yet they did not instantiate the encryption scheme in the white-box model and we are not aware if it can be practically instantiated with known white-box implementations. The work of Delerablée et al. aimed to bring a theoretical foundation of White-Box Cryptography. WBC refers to a research area that focuses on proving the security of a cryptographic implementation in the white-box model. It was first introduced in 2002 by Chow et al. [6,7] to enable a secure distribution of a digital content in a broadcasting system or through an application with Digital Rights Management enforcement. In their seminal paper, Chow et al. proposed a "white-box" implementation of two standard algorithms: the Advanced Encryption Standard and the Data Encryption Standard. A white-box implementation is an implementation of a cryptographic algorithm that hides a key, i.e. the secret key is obfuscated in the source code such that it cannot be extracted. The technique described by Chow et al. is to represent the algorithm with a network of randomized lookup tables which each embeds a part of the secret key.

Related Work. Billet and Gilbert proposed in [1] a "traceable block cipher" that can be used in a broadcasting system. Their scheme is non combinatorial and relies on the hardness of the Isomorphism of Polynomials (IP) problem. Actually, each user of the broadcasting system receives a distinct description of the block cipher as systems of multivariate polynomials. Even if the description of the block cipher differs from a user to another, the evaluation of the block cipher gives the same result for all users which ensures correctness. Unfortunately, the scheme is unlikely a weak instance of the IP problem and can be solved efficiently [9].

Our Contribution. In this work we describe a traitor tracing system with a key generation function, i.e. instead of using a decryption algorithm to decrypt a content key, we use the key generator. We use a probabilistic Tardos code to encode the identity of each user of the system. The codewords are then used to compute a user-specific key generator. In order to derive distinct user-specific key generators that correctly "hide" the codewords, we use techniques of WBC to construct the key generator. We describe a collusion strategy that is completely different from the strategy associated to a Tardos code. Indeed we show that either the collusion retrieves the (untraceable) broadcaster key generator or it exposes the identity of one traitor.

Organization of the Paper. Our paper starts with some preliminaries about the Tardos code. Then, in Sect. 3, we describe our construction of a key generator that will be used in the system. Finally, we prove the collusion resistance of the construction in Sect. 4.

2   Tardos Code

A Tardos code [15] is a binary code used for watermarking digital document. The code is composed of l codewords, where l is the number of users who receive a copy of the document with a unique embedded codeword. If some dishonest users collude to create a pirate version of the document then the distributing entity executes an accusation algorithm which outputs a non-empty set of users or $\emptyset$. The code is collusion-resilient if the accusation algorithm outputs a subset of the set of colluding users. Tardos proved that for at most c colluding users a code of length $L = 100c^2\lceil\log(1/\epsilon)\rceil$ provides c-collusion resilience with a probability of failure strictly lower than ϵ. Besides, Tardos proved that the length is optimal regardless of the collusion strategy. The code is probabilistic i.e. each codeword is constructed from a sequence of probabilities. A c-collusion ϵ-resilient binary code $\mathcal{C}[L, c, \epsilon]$ of length L is defined as follows:

- For $\tau = 1/(300c)$, let $0 < \tau' < \pi/4$ s.t. $\sin^2\tau' = \tau$. Let $r_i \in [\tau', \pi/2 - \tau']$ some random values. Define the probability p_i as $p_i = \sin^2 r_i$. The p_i are independent, identically distributed (i.i.d.) random variables from $[\tau, 1 - \tau]$.
- A codeword $\omega = \omega_0 \ldots \omega_{L-1}$ is constructed s.t. $Pr[\omega_i = 1] = p_i$.

This way l codewords $\omega_1, \ldots, \omega_l$ are constructed and represented as a $l \times L$ matrix M where for $u \in [1, l]$, each entry $\omega_{u,i}$ is independent:

$$M = \begin{bmatrix} \omega_{1,0} & \cdots & \omega_{1,L-1} \\ \omega_{2,0} & \cdots & \omega_{2,L-1} \\ \vdots & \ddots & \vdots \\ \omega_{l,0} & \cdots & \omega_{l,L-1} \end{bmatrix}$$

Each of these codewords is embedded in the user's document and allows to identify the owner of the document. The collusion-resistance of the code depends on an accusation algorithm and a "marking condition". In a nutshell, the marking condition ensures that a collusion of users T which compare their codewords are only able to modify the bits where their codewords differ, i.e. if $y \in \{0,1\}^L$ is the binary word forged by the collusion then y is such that $\omega_{u,i} = b$ implies $y_i = b$ for $u \in T$ and $i \in [0, L-1]$. The accusation algorithm relies on a $l \times l$ matrix U defined as follows: $\forall u \in [1, l], i \in [0, L-1]$, $U_{u,i} = \begin{cases} \sqrt{\frac{1-p_i}{p_i}} & \text{if } \omega_{u,i} = 1 \\ -\sqrt{\frac{p_i}{1-p_i}} & \text{if } \omega_{u,i} = 0 \end{cases}$

Given a forged codeword y, the distributing entity is able to retrieve a subset of the set of colluding users T by computing an accusation sum $\sum_{i=0}^{L-1} y_i U_{u,i}$ for each user u. For any bit number i, if $y_i U_{u,i}$ is positive then $y_i = \omega_{u,i}$ and the accusation algorithm tends to accuse the user u. Otherwise, if $y_i U_{u,i}$ is negative that means that $y_i \neq \omega_{u,i}$ and the user u is considered as an innocent. This way, the accusation algorithm determines how much a user can be considered guilty. If $\sum_{i=0}^{L-1} y_i U_{u,i} > Z$ where $Z = 20c\lceil\log(1/\epsilon)\rceil$ is a fixed threshold then u is accused. Thus, the accusation algorithm does not need to compute the accusation sums for all users of the system but outputs the index of a user as soon as the corresponding sum is sufficiently high.

The work of Tardos aimed to provide the optimal code length that enables collusion resistance regardless of the collusion strategy. Besides, the code length does not depend on the number of users of the system but only on the number of colluding users tolerated which makes it practical for a large system. In his work, Tardos proved that:

(i) For an arbitrary user $u \in [1, l]$ and a coalition $\mathcal{T} \subseteq [1, l] \setminus \{u\}$ the probability that u is wrongly accused is lower than ϵ.
(ii) For a coalition $\mathcal{T} \subseteq [1, l]$ of size c, the probability that no users of the coalition is accused is lower than $\epsilon^{c/4}$.

In other words, the probability of false-positive when all other users collude is at most ϵ and the probability of non-detection for a coalition of size at most c is at most $\epsilon^{c/4}$.

We give some details about the Tardos code to understand the intuition behind the construction of the code. Actually, we do not use the same accusation algorithm since the marking condition does not hold in our case. We only take advantage of the probabilistic generation of the code.

3 Broadcast Encryption Scheme with a Tracing Procedure

3.1 Broadcasting Encrypted Information

One method to secure digital content distribution is broadcast encryption. Such a method is used, e.g., for pay TV systems or distribution of encrypted musics, videos and documents over the Internet. Each user owns a decryption box (smart-card or software) and needs a decryption key to enjoy digital contents. Generally, the system is subject to subscription or digital management licenses before the key is delivered or updated. To avoid key distribution (a legitimate user shares his key to allow someone to decrypt content without subscribing), a unique personal decryption key is given to each user and unambiguously identifies him. Given any user key or a key forged by a subset of users, a tracing procedure retrieves the identity of the user (or at least one traitor when the key has been forged by a collusion). This way, the broadcast encryption scheme becomes a traitor tracing scheme. We first introduce our definition of a broadcast encryption scheme.

Definition 1 (Broadcast encryption (BE)). *A BE scheme is composed of three algorithms:*

- *Setup(l, K) takes as input the number of users l and a randomly drawn secret key K and outputs a key generator KG and l derived key generators $KG_1, \ldots, KG_l$: $(KG, KG_1, \ldots KG_l) \leftarrow$ Setup(l, K).*
- *Encrypt(EB, C) takes as input an enabling block EB and a content C and outputs a pair (EB, CB) s.t. CB is the result of the encryption of a content C under a secret CW called a control word and generated by KG from the input EB. CB is called the cipher block: $(EB, CB) \leftarrow$ Encrypt(EB,C).*
- *Decrypt(u, EB, CB) takes as input an index u and the broadcast information (EB, CB) and outputs C_u which is the result of the decryption of CB under a control word $CW_u = KG_u(EB)$: $C_u \leftarrow$ Decrypt(u,EB,CB).*

The broadcast encryption scheme should be correct, i.e. for any user $u \in [1, l]$:
   if $(KG, KG_1, \ldots, KG_l) \leftarrow Setup(l,K)$ and $(EB, CB) \leftarrow Encrypt(EB,C)$ then,
$C_u = C$ *for $C_u \leftarrow Decrypt(u,EB,CB)$.*

The correctness property guarantees that all users of the system can recover the content C even if the key generators are all distinct. Here, the correctness of the BE is tied to the specificity of the key generators and the way the enabling block EB is chosen. Actually, EB is randomly drawn from a subset of the input domain. We will give the details of the constructions of the key generator and of the enabling block respectively in Sects. 3.2 and 3.3. For now, we describe our system as follows. Let l be the number of users. The setup algorithm outputs a key generator KG and l user-specific key generators $KG_1, \ldots, KG_l$. The broadcaster chooses an enabling block EB computes CW using KG and computes CB using a block cipher E instantiated with the key CW. Any user u is given a decryption box provided with a key generator KG_u and the decryption algorithm E^{-1}. Given an enabling block EB, u computes the control word CW and then decrypts the cipher block CB into C. Thus, the broadcaster and the users of the system each generate the control word separately but agree on the same control word. Figure 1 illustrates the difference between the decryption boxes of two users.

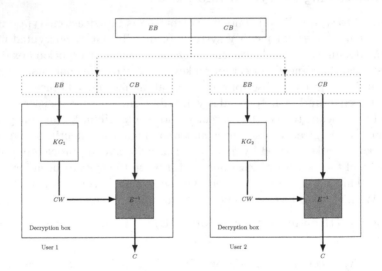

Fig. 1. The system with user-specific key generators.

3.2   Description of the Key Generator

As we said before, the correctness of the scheme depends on the key generator. Thus, we introduce in this section our construction which is at the heart of the system. Before going into details, let us give the ideas behind the construction. We construct a function which outputs a N-bit key[2]. As the key should be random i.e. indistinguishable from a N-bit random sequence, the function should output any key with probability $\frac{1}{2^N}$. Let m, t be such that $N = mt$ and $f_1, \ldots, f_t$ be t permutation functions over $\mathbb{F}_{2^m}$. Then, each output of the function $f = (f_1, \ldots, f_t)$ given an input $(x_1, \ldots, x_t) \in \mathbb{F}_{2^m}^t$ appears with probability $(\frac{1}{2^m})^t = \frac{1}{2^N}$. Thus, the key generator makes call to t permutation functions. Besides, we want to derive user-specific description of the key generator. We chose to implement the permutation functions with m-bit lookup tables and so used white-box techniques[3]. This way, the key generator makes use of t m-bit lookup tables which describe t distinct permutations over $\mathbb{F}_{2^m}$. As we will see in Sect. 3.3, the lookup tables will "embed" a Tardos codeword and become user-specific. For each lookup table, we use the AES-128 in counter mode to generate $2^m \cdot m$ pseudo-random bits and then use the Fisher-Yates shuffle algorithm [11] to generate a m-to-m bits pseudo-random permutation[4].

Let $f \colon \mathbb{F}_2^{128} \times (\mathbb{F}_2^m)^t \rightarrow (\mathbb{F}_2^m)^t$ be a function defined for any input (K, X) with $X = (x_1, \ldots, x_t)$ as: $f(K, X) = (T_{K \oplus 1}(x_1), \ldots, T_{K \oplus t}(x_t))$, where $T_{K \oplus 1}, \ldots, T_{K \oplus t}$ are lookup tables that each describes a random permutation. Each lookup table $T_{K \oplus i}$ for $1 \leqslant i \leqslant t$ maps m bits to m bits and can be seen as a random permutation over the range $\{0, 1, \ldots, 2^m - 1\}$. The tables are computed using the AES-128 in counter mode with the key $K \oplus i$ and with some plaintexts $P_i = i$. The generated pseudo-random sequence of $2^m \cdot m$ bits is used to compute an array of 2^m m-bit values using the Fisher-Yates shuffle algorithm. We illustrate the tables generation in Fig. 2.

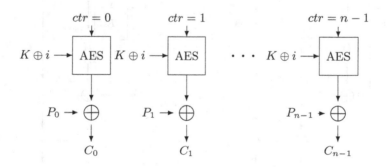

Fig. 2. Generation of $n = \frac{2^m \cdot m}{128}$ ciphertexts before the Fisher-Yates shuffle algorithm.

---

[2] "Key" here refers to the control word CW.

[3] A popular technique used in White-Box Cryptography to hide a part of a secret key is to compute some lookup tables that are key-dependent and then make table calls to execute the algorithm. Actually, our construction is a white-box implementation of a key generation algorithm.

[4] We chose this method as it is an elegant way to generate a permutation from a random binary sequence. Other methods exists and can be used for this construction.

Since the key K is fixed and the tables are precomputed, we write $T_1, \ldots, T_t$ for $T_{K\oplus 1}, \ldots, T_{K\oplus t}$ and f_K in place of $f(K, \cdot)$. For $d \geqslant 2$, the key generator (Fig. 3) $KG: (\mathbb{F}_2^{mt})^{2^d} \to \mathbb{F}_2^{mt}$ is defined for any $(X_1, \ldots, X_{2^d})$ s.t $X_k = (x_{k,1}, \ldots, x_{k,t})$ as

$$KG(X_1, \ldots, X_{2^d}) = \left(\sum_{k=1}^{2^d} T_1(x_{k,1}), \ldots, \sum_{k=1}^{2^d} T_t(x_{k,t}) \right) = \sum_{k=1}^{2^d} f_K(X_k) \quad (1)$$

Remark 1. As we see in (1), the output of the key generator is a vector of t "sums". Each "sum" is the result of the XOR of 2^d permutations. Thus, the value of the sum can be distinguished from random with $O(2^m)$ input/output values. As concluded in [14] the XOR of some permutations allows to generate a random function from random permutations. Hence, the output of the key generator is random.

Remark 2. The key generator is a white-box dedicated algorithm and provides the unbreakability security [8], i.e. the master key K cannot be recovered by an adversary having access to the lookup tables. Indeed, the key extraction security reduces to the security of AES-128 in counter mode (Fig. 2).

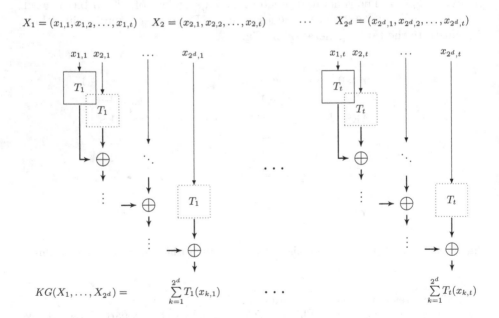

Fig. 3. The key generator.

3.3   User-Specific Key Generator

The key generator KG described in Sect. 3.2 is the broadcaster's generator. We describe in this section how the users' key generators are derived from KG. This is where the Tardos code comes in. We "encode" the identity of each user using the Tardos code of Sect. 2. The user-specific key generator is then computed according to the codeword associated to the user. For a user u, the key generator KG_u makes use of lookup tables $T_1^{(u)}, \ldots, T_t^{(u)}$ derived from the original lookup tables $T_1, \ldots, T_t$ by modifying all the tables values. However, this modification is done such that the user's key generator outputs the same output as the broadcaster's one on a specified set of inputs.

User's Identification. Let a system with l users. Each user u is represented as a binary codeword of a c-collusion ϵ-resilient Tardos code $\mathscr{C}[L, c, \epsilon]$, i.e. $u = (u_0, \ldots, u_{L-1})$ s.t $Pr[u_i = 1] = p_i$ for a sequence of probabilities p_i outputted by a distribution $\mathcal{P}$. The users of the system are represented by a matrix with l rows and L columns. The main idea of the personalization is to use all bits of each user codeword to compute all the tables values. First, the codeword is divided into t sub-words of length L/t and each sub-word is used for each table. The parameters (L, d, m, t) of the scheme verify $L = td2^{\lceil m/d \rceil}$ where d is called the "dimension" of the system. d is a parameter chosen to ensure the collusion resistance of the system. We will see in Sect. 4 how it should be chosen.

User's Perturbation Function. Now that each user of the system is identified with a codeword, we define a user's perturbation function that depends on that codeword and allows to compute the user's tables accordingly.

Definition 2 (User's perturbation function). *Let L, t, d, m be defined as above. Let $e_0, \ldots, e_{L-1}$ be L distinct non-zero m-bit values randomly drawn from $\mathbb{F}_2^m \setminus \{0\}$. For $d \geqslant 2$, let A be a d-dimensional array with $v = \frac{L}{td}$ cells which randomly contains the elements of $\mathbb{F}_2^m$. Let index be a function that takes $x \in \mathbb{F}_2^m$ as input and returns a d-uple $(i_1^{(x)}, \ldots, i_d^{(x)})$ of indices. index gives the coordinates of x in the d-dimensional array A, i.e. $0 \leqslant i_j^{(x)} \leqslant v - 1$ for any $1 \leqslant j \leqslant d$.*

For any user u associated to a codeword $(u_0, \ldots, u_{L-1})$ and any $1 \leqslant i \leqslant t$, a perturbation function is defined as

$$\forall x \in \mathbb{F}_2^m \; m_u(i, x) = \sum_{j=1}^{d} \left(u_{i_j^{(x)} + jv + \frac{(i-1)L}{t}} \right) \left(e_{i_j^{(x)} + jv + \frac{(i-1)L}{t}} \right).$$

The values $e_0, \ldots, e_{L-1}$ are random secret values that will be used to transform the permutation implemented by T_i into a pseudo-random function. For any $x \in \mathbb{F}_2^m$, a mask value $m_u(i, x)$ is computed as a sum of at most d secret values among $e_0, \ldots, e_{L-1}$, i.e. if the bit u_* is equal to 1 then e_* contributes to the mask value, otherwise e_* does not contribute.

User's Lookup Table. For $1 \leqslant i \leqslant t$, the i-th table $T_i^{(u)}$ is computed from the original table T_i as follows: $\forall x \in \mathbb{F}_2^m \; T_i^{(u)}(x) = T_i(x) + m_u(i, x)$. m_u is a "perturbation function" used to mask the value of $T_i(x)$ for any x. Since $m_u(i, x)$ is random then $T_i^{(u)}$ implements a pseudo-random function.

The user-specific key generator is then defined for any $(X_1, \ldots, X_{2^d})$ as

$$KG_u(X_1, \ldots, X_{2^d}) = \left(\sum_{k=1}^{2^d} T_1^{(u)}(x_{k,1}), \ldots, \sum_{k=1}^{2^d} T_t^{(u)}(x_{k,t}) \right).$$

The idea behind the construction can be summarized as follows. For any user, each table value is a masked (perturbed) version of the broadcaster table value. The perturbation added to each table value is random and depends on the user codeword. However, the perturbation function is defined such that the sum $\sum_{k=1}^{2^d} m_u(i, x_k)$ is equal to 0 for some inputs $(x_1, \ldots, x_{2^d})$ and this way guarantees the correctness of the user's key generator. This is stated by the following lemma.

Lemma 1. *For any user u, KG_u is correct iff for any $(X_1, \ldots, X_{2^d}) \in (\mathbb{F}_2^{mt})^{2^d}$, $\sum_{k=1}^{2^d} m_u(i, x_{k,i}) = 0$ for all $1 \leqslant i \leqslant t$.*

Definition 3 (Partial correctness). *For any u, KG_u is partially correct if there exists a set $I \subset (\mathbb{F}_2^{mt})^{2^d}$ such that for any $(X_1, \ldots, X_{2^d}) \in I$, $KG_u(X_1, \ldots, X_{2^d}) = KG(X_1, \ldots, X_{2^d})$. We say that KG_u is I-correct and that I is a perturbation canceler.*

The following proposition gives a sufficient condition on the set I to allow the partial correctness.

Proposition 1. *Let $d \geqslant 2$. For any $1 \leqslant i \leqslant t$, let a set $I_i \subset (\mathbb{F}_2^{mt})^{2^d}$ such that for any $(x_{1,i}, \ldots, x_{2^d,i}) \in I_i$, for any $1 \leqslant j \leqslant d$ there exists a partition $\mathcal{P}_{1,i}^j, \ldots, \mathcal{P}_{2^{d-1},i}^j$ of the set $\{x_{1,i}, \ldots, x_{2^d,i}\}$ defined as follows*

$$\begin{cases} \left| \mathcal{P}_{k,i}^j \right| = 2 \\ i_j^{(x)} = i_j^{(x')} \text{ for } x, x' \in \mathcal{P}_{k,i}^j \end{cases} \quad \text{and if } x \in \mathcal{P}_{k,i}^j \text{ and } y \in \mathcal{P}_{k,i'}^j \text{ then } i_j^{(x)} \neq i_j^{(y)}.$$

Then, for any u, P_u is I-correct for $I = I_1 \times \ldots \times I_t$.

Example 1. Let $d = 2$ and $m = 4$. Then A is a 4×4 matrix containing all the elements of $\mathbb{F}_2^4$ (which we represent with $*$). Without loss of generality, let $i = 1$. For simplicity, we write (x_1, x_2, x_3, x_4) instead of $(x_{1,1}, x_{2,1}, x_{3,1}, x_{4,1})$. Assume that the matrix A is defined as follows

$$A = \begin{bmatrix} * & * & * & * \\ * & x_1 & * & x_2 \\ * & * & * & * \\ * & x_3 & * & x_4 \end{bmatrix}$$

Since $\begin{cases} i_1^{(x_1)} = i_1^{(x_2)} = 1 \\ i_1^{(x_3)} = i_1^{(x_4)} = 3 \end{cases}$ and $\begin{cases} i_2^{(x_1)} = i_2^{(x_3)} = 3 \\ i_2^{(x_2)} = i_2^{(x_4)} = 1 \end{cases}$, we get the following

partitions of $\{x_1, x_2, x_3, x_4\}$: $\mathcal{P}_1^1 = \{x_1, x_2\}$, $\mathcal{P}_2^1 = \{x_3, x_4\}$ and $\mathcal{P}_1^2 = \{x_1, x_3\}$, $\mathcal{P}_2^2 = \{x_2, x_4\}$. Then, (x_1, x_2, x_3, x_4) belongs to the set I_1.

Proposition 2. *Let $d \geqslant 2$. Let I be the set as defined in Proposition 1. Then for any $1 \leqslant i \leqslant t$, $|I_i| \geqslant \prod_{k=1}^{2^{d-1}} (2^m - (k-1)d2^{(d-1)m/d})$.*

The proofs of Lemma 1, Propositions 1 and 2 can be found in Appendix.

3.4 Broadcast Information Generation and Decryption Procedure

The broadcaster needs to generate a broadcast information (EB, CB) that allows all users of the system to recover a content B. Since each user has a distinct description of the key generator, we define the enabling block EB with a special structure. Actually, we take EB in the perturbation-canceler set I, thus the key generator removes all perturbations added to the user-specific description and enables each user to recover CW and the content C.

Let $E \colon \mathbb{F}_2^n \times \mathbb{F}_2^n \to \mathbb{F}_2^n$ be a block cipher, i.e. E is the encryption function and E^{-1} is the decryption function. The system consists of the following steps:

1. The broadcaster randomly picks an enabling block EB in the perturbation-canceler set I, then generate a control word CW using KG: $CW = KG(EB)$.
2. The broadcaster encrypts a content block C using a block cipher E instantiated with the secret key CW. He computes the cipher block $CB = E_{CW}(C)$.
3. The broadcaster sends (EB, CB) to all users of the system.
4. Any user u generates the control word CW using his key generator KG_u: $CW = KG_u(EB)$ and decrypts the cipher block to obtain the content C: $C = E_{CW}^{-1}(CB)$.

3.5 The Tracing Procedure

A tracing procedure is executed by the tracing entity to identify the owner of a decryption box. We assume that the tracing procedure is executed in a white-box way, i.e. the tracing entity has access to the pirate decryption box and executes the tracing procedure on the key generator, namely on the set of lookup tables. The pirate decryption box embeds a key generator with forged tables $T_i^{\hat{u}}$ so the tracing procedure takes as input a set of pirate tables $T_i^{\hat{u}}$ and outputs a user index $\hat{u}$. For all $1 \leqslant i \leqslant t$, the tracing entity executes the following steps:

1. For any $x \in \mathbb{F}_2^m$ look at the value $T_i^{\hat{u}}(x)$ and compare with the 2^d possible values $T_i(x) + \sum_{j=1}^{d} (\hat{u}_{\mathbf{i}_j^{(\mathbf{x})} + jv + \frac{(i-1)L}{t}})(e_{\mathbf{i}_j^{(\mathbf{x})} + jv + \frac{(i-1)L}{t}})$.
2. Deduce the values of the bits $\hat{u}_{\mathbf{i}_j^{(\mathbf{x})} + jv + \frac{(i-1)L}{t}}$ for all $1 \leqslant j \leqslant d$.
3. When $(\hat{u}_0, \ldots, \hat{u}_{L-1})$ is fully determined, search the user in the matrix M.

The key generator is traceable in the sense that the identity of its owner can be retrieved by the tracing entity. We assume that even if some traitors collude either they expose the identity of one of them or they cannot create a functional pirate decryption box. Thus, the tracing procedure only needs to reconstitute the codeword associated to a key generator and then search in the matrix of all codewords. The details of the collusion strategy are described in Appendix A.4.

4   Collusion Resistance

The advantage of the broadcast encryption scheme described is Sect. 3.4 is the traceability of the key generators. This property enables to find the owner of an illegally redistributed decryption box. Besides, we prove that even if several dishonest users collude, they cannot produce an untraceable and functional key generator. We first define the notion of traceability against an arbitrary collusion.

Definition 4 (Traceability game against an arbitrary collusion). *Let an adversary A and a challenger B playing the following game:*

1. *B randomly picks a key $K \in \mathcal{K}$ and a set of secret parameters param^5.*
2. *B computes the key generator KG as in Sect. 3.2.*
3. *A chooses a set $T = \{u_1, \ldots, u_c\} \subseteq \{1, \ldots, l\}$ of traitors and queries the corresponding key generators with q chosen inputs $(X_1, \ldots, X_{2^d})$.*
4. *If $(X_1, \ldots, X_{2^d})$ is valid, i.e. $(X_1, \ldots, X_{2^d}) \in I$, then B outputs the corresponding tables outputs. Otherwise, B outputs $\perp$.*
5. *A outputs a key generator $\widehat{KG}$.*
6. *If $\widehat{KG}$ is I-correct, B runs the tracing procedure Trace on $\widehat{KG}$ and outputs a set $S \subseteq \{1, \ldots, l\}$.*
7. *A wins if $\widehat{KG}$ is I-correct and $S = \emptyset$ or $S \nsubseteq T$.*

We say that a (L, d, m, t)-key generator satisfies (q, ϵ)-traceability against a c-collusion if the probability that A wins is lower than ϵ.

Theorem 1. *Consider our construction of a (L, m, d, t)-key generator where L is the length of a Tardos code, m is the table input length, d is the dimension and t is the number of tables. We claim that if the adversary makes at most $q \leqslant |I_i|$ queries with q_v valid queries then no coalition of users less than $\frac{d}{2} + 1$ can produce a functional pirate key generator with probability higher than $\left(\frac{1}{2^m}\right)^{t(|I_i| - q_v)}$.*

The proof of Theorem 1 where the collusion strategy is described is sketched in Appendix A.4.

Table 1. Examples of parameters: m is the table input length, t is the number of tables, d is the dimension, L is the code length and is defined as $L = td2^{\lceil m/d \rceil}$ and c is the collusion size. WB size is the total size of the key generator.

t	d	m	L	c	WB size	Upper bound on q	Size of EB (bits)
8	2	16	2^{12}	1	2 MB	2^{63}	512
8	3	16	2^{10}	2	2 MB	2^{63}	1024
4	2	32	2^{19}	1	64 GB	2^{127}	512
4	3	32	2^{15}	2	64 GB	2^{127}	1024
4	4	32	2^{12}	2	64 GB	2^{127}	2048

---

[5] param are the parameters of the Tardos code and the random m-bit values $e_1, \ldots, e_{L-1}$.

Examples of Parameters. Some parameters for implementation are given in Table 1. The block cipher E is the AES-128 and the control word length is 128 bits.

Conclusion

In this work, we proposed a traitor tracing system that resists a collusion of c traitors for small values of c. We described a broadcast encryption scheme that uses a key generator to generate the control words. Even if each user receives a personalized key generator, the special structure of the enabling information allows all users to generate the correct control word as the broadcaster. One advantage of our construction is that the code length is lower than the optimal length computed by G. Tardos and so storing system's users is less costly. The main drawback of our construction is that it does not allow the revocation of traitors and we let this as a future work.

Proofs

A.1   Lemma 1

Proof. Let $(X_1, \ldots, X_{2^d}) \in (\mathbb{F}_2^{mt})^{2^d}$.

$$\left(\sum_{k=1}^{2^d} T_1^{(u)}(x_{k,1}), \ldots, \sum_{k=1}^{2^d} T_t^{(u)}(x_{k,t}) \right) = \left(\sum_{k=1}^{2^d} T_1(x_{k,1}), \ldots, \sum_{k=1}^{2^d} T_t(x_{k,t}) \right)$$

$$\Leftrightarrow \forall i \sum_{k=1}^{2^d} T_i^{(u)}(x_{k,i}) = \sum_{k=1}^{2^d} T_i(x_{k,i}) \Leftrightarrow$$

$$\forall i \sum_{k=1}^{2^d} (T_i(x_{k,i}) + m_u(i, x_{k,i})) = \sum_{k=1}^{2^d} T_i(x_{k,i}) \Leftrightarrow$$

$$\forall i \sum_{k=1}^{2^d} (T_i(x_{k,i}) + m_u(i, x_{k,i})) - \sum_{k=1}^{2^d} T_i(x_{k,i}) = 0 \Leftrightarrow \forall i \sum_{k=1}^{2^d} m_u(i, x_{k,i}) = 0$$

A.2   Proposition 1

Proof. We prove that for any $(x_{1,i}, \ldots, x_{2^d,i}) \in I_i$, $\sum_{k=1}^{2^d} m_u(i, x_{k,i}) = 0$.
For any i, let $(x_{1,i}, \ldots, x_{2^d,i}) \in I_i$. Then,

$$\sum_{k=1}^{2^d} m_u(i, x_{k,i}) = \sum_{k=1}^{2^d} \left(\sum_{j=1}^{d} (u_{i_j}^{(x_{k,i})} {}_{+jv+ \frac{(i-1)L}{t}})(e_{i_j}^{(x_{k,i})} {}_{+jv+ \frac{(i-1)L}{t}}) \right)$$

$$= \sum_{j=1}^{d} \left(\sum_{k=1}^{2^{d-1}} \sum_{x \in \mathcal{P}_{k,i}^j} (u_{i_j}^{(x)} {}_{+jv+ \frac{(i-1)L}{t}})(e_{i_j}^{(x)} {}_{+jv+ \frac{(i-1)L}{t}}) \right)$$

Since for any $x, x' \in \mathcal{P}_{k,i}^j$, $\mathbf{i}_j^{(\mathbf{x})} = \mathbf{i}_j^{(\mathbf{x}')}$ then $u_{\mathbf{i}_j^{(\mathbf{x})} + jv + \frac{(i-1)L}{t}} = u_{\mathbf{i}_j^{(\mathbf{x}')} + jv + \frac{(i-1)L}{t}}$
and $e_{\mathbf{i}_j^{(\mathbf{x})} + jv + \frac{(i-1)L}{t}} = e_{\mathbf{i}_j^{(\mathbf{x}')} + jv + \frac{(i-1)L}{t}}$.

Thus, for any i, j, k, $\sum\limits_{x \in \mathcal{P}_{k,i}^j} (u_{\mathbf{i}_j^{(\mathbf{x})} + jv + \frac{(i-1)L}{t}})(e_{\mathbf{i}_j^{(\mathbf{x})} + jv + \frac{(i-1)L}{t}}) = 0$.

Hence, $\sum_{k=1}^{2^d} m_u(i, x_{k,i}) = 0$ for all i.

A.3   Proposition 2

Proof. – $d = 2$. Let us count all 4-uple $(x_{1,i}, x_{2,i}, x_{3,i}, x_{4,i}) \in (\mathbb{F}_2^m)^4$ s.t. there exits two partitions as defined in Proposition 1: $x_{1,i}$ can be any element of $\mathbb{F}_2^m$ so we have 2^m possible choices; $x_{2,i}$ can be chosen s.t. $\mathbf{i}_1^{(\mathbf{x}_{2,i})} \neq \mathbf{i}_1^{(\mathbf{x}_{1,i})}$ and $\mathbf{i}_2^{(\mathbf{x}_{2,i})} \neq \mathbf{i}_2^{(\mathbf{x}_{1,i})}$, thus we have $2^m - 2 \cdot 2^{m/2}$ possible choices. Since we get $x_{1,i}$ and $x_{2,i}$, without loss of generality we can set $x_{1,i} \in \mathcal{P}_1^1, \mathcal{P}_1^2$ and $x_{2,i} \in \mathcal{P}_2^1, \mathcal{P}_2^2$ then $x_{3,i}$ and $x_{4,i}$ are fixed as the second elements of each set.

– $d = 3$. We count all 8-uple $(x_{1,i}, \ldots, x_{8,i}) \in (\mathbb{F}_2^m)^8$. Following the same reasoning as above: there are 2^m possible choices for $x_{1,i}$, $2^m - 3 \cdot (2^{m/3})^2$ possible choices for $x_{2,i}$, at most $2^m - 6 \cdot (2^{m/3})^2$ possible choices for $x_{3,i}$ and at most $2^m - 9 \cdot (2^{m/3})^2$ possible choices for $x_{4,i}$. Each of these elements is set as the first element of each set $\mathcal{P}_k^j$, for $1 \leqslant j \leqslant 3$ and $1 \leqslant k \leqslant 4$, then $x_{5,i}, x_{6,i}, x_{7,i}, x_{8,i}$ are fixed as the second elements.

The same reasoning is used for any value of d, i.e. choose one element for each set $\mathcal{P}_k^j$, for $1 \leqslant j \leqslant d$ and $1 \leqslant k \leqslant 2^{d-1}$, then the 2^{d-1} remaining coordinates are fixed to be the second elements of each set.

A.4   Theorem 1

Proof. We consider two cases: $c = 1$ and $c > 1$ and for both cases we describe two possible strategies that make the pirate key generator untraceable. First, the adversary records the outputs $(\sum\limits_{i=1}^{2^d} T_1(x_{k,1}), \ldots, \sum\limits_{i=1}^{2^d} T_t(x_{k,t}))$ for all valid inputs for later use and, second, the adversary recovers the original table values $T_i(x)$.

– $c = 1$. We assume that the adversary is a single user. He adopts the first strategy, i.e. records the outputs $(\sum\limits_{i=1}^{2^d} T_1(x_{k,1}), \ldots, \sum\limits_{i=1}^{2^d} T_t(x_{k,t}))$ for all valid inputs.

Let q, q_v be respectively the number of input queries made by the adversary such that $q \leqslant |I_i|$ and the number of valid queries. One query can be seen as t simultaneous queries to the tables. For a query $\mathbf{q}$, we write $\mathbf{q_1}, \ldots, \mathbf{q_t}$ for the corresponding table queries. We say that a query $\mathbf{q}$ is valid iff all of the queries $\mathbf{q_1}, \ldots, \mathbf{q_t}$ are valid. If the query is valid, then the adversary gets the output $(\sum\limits_{i=1}^{2^d} T_1(x_{k,1}), \ldots, \sum\limits_{i=1}^{2^d} T_t(x_{k,t}))$ corresponding to an input $(\mathbf{q_1}, \ldots, \mathbf{q_t})$. Otherwise, he does not gain any information. Thus, if the adversary makes

q_v valid queries then he gets q_v values $\sum_{i=1}^{2^d} T_i(x_{k,i})$ for each table. If $q_v < |I_i|$ then the adversary needs to guess the sum values for the $|I_i| - q_v$ remaining table inputs for each table. Since for any i, $(x_{1,i}, \ldots, x_{2^d,i}) \mapsto \sum_{i=1}^{2^d} T_i(x_{k,i})$ is a pseudo-random function, the probability that the adversary produces a functional pirate key generator, i.e. that the adversary guesses the unknown sum values is equal to $\left(\frac{1}{2^m}\right)^{t(|I_i|-q_v)}$. To ensure that the probability is negligible, it is sufficient to show that $|I_i| - q_v \geqslant 1$.

Let X be the random variable that gives the number of valid queries among q. X follow the hypergeometric distribution with parameter $(q, p = \frac{|I_i|}{2^{m2^d}}, 2^{m2^d})$. Indeed, we calculate the probability of successes in q draws (q queries) without replacement from a population of size 2^{m2^d}. $p2^{m2^d}$ corresponds to the number of valid inputs (for one table), i.e. $|I_i|$. Thus, the probability of the event $\{X = q_v\}$ is given by: $\mathbb{P}(q_v) = \frac{\binom{|I_i|}{q_v}\binom{2^{m2^d}-|I_i|}{q-q_v}}{\binom{2^{m2^d}}{q}}$. If $q = |I_i|$ then $\mathbb{P}(|I_i|) = \frac{1}{\binom{2^{m2^d}}{q}}$.

Hence, $q_v < |I_i|$ and $|I_i| - q_v \geqslant 1$.

Now assume that the adversary adopts the second strategy, i.e. recovers all the table values $T_i(x)$. For simplicity, let us consider one table $T(x)$ (i.e. we omit the index i since the same technique can be applied independently to all tables).

For a valid tuple $(x_1, \ldots, x_{2^d})$, the adversary knows the table outputs. Let s be the index of the adversary, for $1 \leqslant k \leqslant 2^d$, $1 \leqslant j \leqslant d$, we denote by $\alpha_{s,k,j}$ the unknown $u_{s,i_j^{(x_k)}+jv+\frac{(i-1)L}{t}}$ and by $\beta_{k,j}$ the unknown $e_{s,i_j^{(x_k)}+jv+\frac{(i-1)L}{t}}$ for a fixed i. The adversary constructs the following system of equations:

$$\begin{cases} T^{(u_s)}(x_1) = T(x_1) + \sum_{j=1}^{d} \alpha_{s,1,j} \cdot \beta_{1,j} \\ T^{(u_s)}(x_2) = T(x_2) + \sum_{j=1}^{d} \alpha_{s,2,j} \cdot \beta_{2,j} \\ \vdots \\ T^{(u_s)}(x_{2^d}) = T(x_{2^d}) + \sum_{j=1}^{d} \alpha_{s,2^d,j} \cdot \beta_{2^d,j} \end{cases}$$

Since $\alpha_{s,k,j} \in \{0,1\}$, the adversary can construct 2^{d2^d} systems of 2^d equations where there are at most $2^m + d2^m$ unknowns in the case where all the $\alpha_{s,k,j}$ are equal to 1. With $q_v < |I_i|$ valid inputs, each system is composed of at most 2^m equations with $2^m(\frac{d}{2}+1)$ unknowns[6].

The adversary can solve the correct system iff $2^m \geqslant 2^m(\frac{d}{2}+1) \Leftrightarrow \frac{d}{2}+1 \leqslant 1$ which is impossible for $d \geqslant 2$.

- $c > 1$. We assume that the adversary is a collusion of c users. Let $q_v < |I_i|$ be the number of valid queries. As above the adversary can store the sum

---

[6] Only one of these systems is correct and since there are approximatively as many as "1" values as "0" values in a codeword, the correct system has in average $2^m + \frac{d}{2}2^m$ unknowns.

values and guesses the other sum values. Hence, the probability to produce a functional pirate key generator is equal to $\left(\frac{1}{2^m}\right)^{t(|I_i|-q_v)}$.

Besides, the adversary may leverage the coalition to retrieve the original values $T_i(x)$ for all i, x and thus reduce the storage size, this is the second strategy.

For a tuple $(x_1, \ldots, x_{2^d})$, the adversary knows the table outputs of all members of $\mathcal{T}$. For $1 \leqslant s \leqslant c$, $1 \leqslant k \leqslant 2^d$, $1 \leqslant j \leqslant d$, we denote by $\alpha_{s,k,j}$ the unknown $u_{s,i_j^{(x_k)}+jv+\frac{(i-1)L}{t}}$ and by $\beta_{k,j}$ the unknown $e_{s,i_j^{(x_k)}+jv+\frac{(i-1)L}{t}}$ for a fixed i. The adversary constructs the following system of equations:

$$
\begin{cases}
T^{(u_1)}(x_1) = T(x_1) + \sum_{j=1}^{d} \alpha_{1,1,j} \cdot \beta_{1,j} \\
T^{(u_1)}(x_2) = T(x_2) + \sum_{j=1}^{d} \alpha_{1,2,j} \cdot \beta_{2,j} \\
\vdots \\
T^{(u_1)}(x_{2^d}) = T(x_{2^d}) + \sum_{j=1}^{d} \alpha_{1,2^d,j} \cdot \beta_{2^d,j} \\
\vdots \\
T^{(u_c)}(x_1) = T(x_1) + \sum_{j=0}^{d} \alpha_{c,1,j} \cdot \beta_{1,j} \\
\vdots \\
T^{(u_c)}(x_{2^d}) = T(x_{2^d}) + \sum_{j=0}^{d} \alpha_{c,2^d,j} \cdot \beta_{2^d,j}
\end{cases}
$$

As above, the adversary can construct 2^{cd2^d} systems of $2^d c$ equations where there are at most $2^m + d2^m$ unknowns and in average $2^m + \frac{d}{2}2^m$ unknowns. With $q_v < |I_i|$ valid inputs, each system is composed of at most $2^m c$ equations with $2^m(\frac{d}{2}+1)$ unknowns.

The adversary can solve the correct system iff $2^m c \geqslant 2^m(\frac{d}{2}+1) \Leftrightarrow c \geqslant \frac{d}{2}+1$.

References

1. Billet, O., Gilbert, H.: A traceable block cipher. In: Laih, C.-S. (ed.) ASIACRYPT 2003. LNCS, vol. 2894, pp. 331–346. Springer, Heidelberg (2003). https://doi.org/10.1007/978-3-540-40061-5_21
2. Billet, O., Phan, D.H.: Efficient traitor tracing from collusion secure codes. In: Safavi-Naini, R. (ed.) ICITS 2008. LNCS, vol. 5155, pp. 171–182. Springer, Heidelberg (2008). https://doi.org/10.1007/978-3-540-85093-9_17
3. Boneh, D., Naor, M.: Traitor tracing with constant size ciphertext. In: Proceedings of the 15th ACM Conference on Computer and Communications Security, pp. 501–510. ACM (2008)
4. Boneh, D., Sahai, A., Waters, B.: Fully collusion resistant traitor tracing with short ciphertexts and private keys. In: Vaudenay, S. (ed.) EUROCRYPT 2006. LNCS, vol. 4004, pp. 573–592. Springer, Heidelberg (2006). https://doi.org/10.1007/11761679_34
5. Chor, B., Fiat, A., Naor, M.: Tracing traitors. In: Desmedt, Y.G. (ed.) CRYPTO 1994. LNCS, vol. 839, pp. 257–270. Springer, Heidelberg (1994). https://doi.org/10.1007/3-540-48658-5_25

6. Chow, S., Eisen, P., Johnson, H., Van Oorschot, P.C.: White-box cryptography and an AES implementation. In: Nyberg, K., Heys, H. (eds.) SAC 2002. LNCS, vol. 2595, pp. 250–270. Springer, Heidelberg (2003). https://doi.org/10.1007/3-540-36492-7_17

7. Chow, S., Eisen, P., Johnson, H., van Oorschot, P.C.: A white-box DES implementation for DRM applications. In: Feigenbaum, J. (ed.) DRM 2002. LNCS, vol. 2696, pp. 1–15. Springer, Heidelberg (2003). https://doi.org/10.1007/978-3-540-44993-5_1

8. Delerablée, C., Lepoint, T., Paillier, P., Rivain, M.: White-box security notions for symmetric encryption schemes. In: Lange, T., Lauter, K., Lisoněk, P. (eds.) SAC 2013. LNCS, vol. 8282, pp. 247–264. Springer, Heidelberg (2014). https://doi.org/10.1007/978-3-662-43414-7_13

9. Faugère, J.-C., Perret, L.: Polynomial equivalence problems: algorithmic and theoretical aspects. In: Vaudenay, S. (ed.) EUROCRYPT 2006. LNCS, vol. 4004, pp. 30–47. Springer, Heidelberg (2006). https://doi.org/10.1007/11761679_3

10. Fazio, N., Nicolosi, A., Phan, D.H.: Traitor tracing with optimal transmission rate. In: Garay, J.A., Lenstra, A.K., Mambo, M., Peralta, R. (eds.) ISC 2007. LNCS, vol. 4779, pp. 71–88. Springer, Heidelberg (2007). https://doi.org/10.1007/978-3-540-75496-1_5

11. Fisher, R.A., Yates, F.: Statistical Tables for Biological, Agricultural and Medical Research, 6th edn. Hafner Publishing Company, New York (1963)

12. Kiayias, A., Yung, M.: Traitor tracing with constant transmission rate. In: Knudsen, L.R. (ed.) EUROCRYPT 2002. LNCS, vol. 2332, pp. 450–465. Springer, Heidelberg (2002). https://doi.org/10.1007/3-540-46035-7_30

13. Kurosawa, K., Desmedt, Y.: Optimum traitor tracing and asymmetric schemes. In: Nyberg, K. (ed.) EUROCRYPT 1998. LNCS, vol. 1403, pp. 145–157. Springer, Heidelberg (1998). https://doi.org/10.1007/BFb0054123

14. Patarin, J.: Generic attacks for the Xor of k random permutations. In: Jacobson, M., Locasto, M., Mohassel, P., Safavi-Naini, R. (eds.) ACNS 2013. LNCS, vol. 7954, pp. 154–169. Springer, Heidelberg (2013). https://doi.org/10.1007/978-3-642-38980-1_10

15. Tardos, G.: Optimal probabilistic fingerprint codes. J. ACM **55**(2), 10 (2008)

Generic Construction of Anonymous Deniable Predicate Authentication Scheme with Revocability

Hiroaki Anada[1(✉)] and Yoshifumi Ueshige[2]

[1] Department of Information Security, University of Nagasaki,
1-1-1, Manabino, Nagayo-cho, Nagasaki 851-2195, Japan
anada@sun.ac.jp
[2] Center for Information and Communication Technology, Nagasaki University,
1-14, Bunkyo-cho, Nagasaki-city, Nagasaki 852-8521, Japan
yueshige@nagasaki-u.ac.jp

Abstract. We propose a syntax and security definitions of an anonymous deniable predicate authentication scheme with *revocability* (rADPA). This new cryptographic primitive is to attain revocation function as well as strong privacy guarantee concerning authentication. Anonymity is for privacy in the authentication protocol, while deniability is for anti-forensics after completion of the protocol. Then, we give a generic construction of our rADPA scheme. Our approach is to build-in the revocable attribute-based encryption scheme proposed by K. Yamada et al. (ESORICS2017) into the anonymous deniable predicate authentication scheme proposed by S. Yamada et al. (PKC2012). Finally, we discuss how our rADPA scheme can be instantiated by employing concrete building blocks in our generic construction.

Keywords: Anonymous authentication · Attribute · Deniability · Revocation

1 Introduction

Authentication is one of the three fundamental processes (i.e. identification, authentication and authorization) for security of both private devices and networks; we have already been receiving benefits of information devices and communication infrastructures such as smartphones and the internet in daily life, and those benefits are mostly after logging-in to the devices and networks. There the authentication mechanisms is running with hash functions, symmetric-key systems, public-key infrastructures and various protocols with them.

Recently, more need of privacy protection is arising among participants of networks. One big motivating trend is expansion of social networking services. The participants, using pseudonyms, are communicating with each other on the networks, but they are under the fear of being traced and punished due to some wrong behavior. This actually a serious problem because there was news of a

© Springer Nature Switzerland AG 2020
E. Simion and R. Géraud-Stewart (Eds.): SecITC 2019, LNCS 12001, pp. 142–155, 2020.
https://doi.org/10.1007/978-3-030-41025-4_10

famous SNS company giving participants' personal data including pseudonyms in response to the demand issued by a government.

In this paper, we propose a cryptographic tool for solving the above problem on privacy protection: Anonymous deniable predicate authentication scheme with revocability. An anonymous authentication is already well-known technique based on tokens issued by authorities. Especially, a cryptographic notion of attribute-based encryption (ABE) [17] can be used as the technique to execute a challenge-and-response authentication protocol. In key-policy ABE (KP-ABE) introduced by the subsequent work of Goyal, Pandey, Sahai and Waters [12,16], a secret key is associated with an access policy which is a boolean formula over attributes, while a ciphertext is associated with a set of attributes. In a dual manner, in ciphertext-policy ABE (CP-ABE) [12,18], a ciphertext is associated with access policy over attributes, while a secret key is associated with a set of attributes. In a KP-ABE or CP-ABE scheme, a secret key works to decrypt a ciphertext if and only if the associated set of attributes satisfies the associated access policy, and hence the challenge-and-response protocol works for a prover to be authenticated based on attributes and policies. This protocol resembles the traditional role-based access control (RBAC). However, the feature of the ABE-based protocol is that it attains *attribute privacy*; the verifier in the authentication cannot decide which satisfying assignment of attributes is used for the boolean formula (the access policy) in CP-ABE, and vice versa in KP-ABE. Attribute privacy is a strong privacy notion and anonymity is realized as a part of the property of it [12]. We note that currently the notion of an ABE scheme is sophisticated into a predicate encryption scheme (PE) [21], where a more general notions of key-attributes and ciphertext attributes are used.

Deniability is a different aspect of privacy protection. As is defined in Dodis et al. [8], a deniable authentication scheme guarantees a seemingly paradoxical property: upon completion of the protocol the verifier in an authentication server is convinced that the prover is certainly a one who has satisfying key-attributes in our scenario. However, neither party can convince anyone else (a third entity) that the other party took part in the protocol. Thus, deniability is a property of anti-forensics, and it is useful for participants who want to feel free of putting any message in SNS without any fear. We stress that deniability is not implied by anonymity and vice versa. This is because anonymity of a prover might be broken by the server log-data and timing analysis, but deniability guarantees that the log-data cannot be witness for the server to claim to a third entity that the prover actually logged in. Conversely, if the timing analysis is prevented by a network design like TOR, then anonymity actually blinds the server from identifying the prover, and this is beyond the deniability property.

Anonymous deniable predicate authentication schemes (ADPAs) with the above two properties were studied by S. Yamada et al. [21]. Actually they gave a generic construction of an ADPA scheme, and discussed instantiations. The idea in [21] is to enhancing the challenge-and-response authentication protocol which uses a predicate encryption scheme by adding another four rounds of message-transactions employing a perfectly binding commitment scheme.

1.1 Our Contribution

In this paper, following this previous work [21], we further pursue a must function in an authentication scheme; *revocation*. Needless to say, in an authentication scheme an authority has to activate a participant, and has to revoke a participant when it become to be needed. because of reasons such as expiration of attributes. To attain the revocability we look at another important previous work by K. Yamada et al. [19,20], in which they proposed a revocable attribute-based encryption scheme (rABE).

We propose an anonymous deniable predicate authentication scheme with revocability (rADPA) by employing (as the predicate encryption scheme) a revocable attribute-based encryption scheme rABE. That is, we substitute the pair of a ciphertext attribute and a revocation list $(Y, \mathcal{RL})$ of rABE with the original ciphertext attribute Y of the predicate encryption scheme.

We finally note that, in our rADPA scheme, a revocation list $\mathcal{RL}$ should be maintained as a certificate revocation list (CRL) by a certificate authority (CA). This is unavoidable for now, but the maintenance by, for example, a blockchain [13,15] would be our future work.

1.2 Organization of This Paper

In Sect. 2 we summarize the needed notions and notations. In Sect. 3 we define the syntax and security of our rADPA. In Sect. 4 we give a generic construction of our rADPA. In Sect. 5 we discuss how our rADPA can be instantiated. In Sect. 6 we conclude our work, and mention our future work.

2 Preliminaries

In this section, we prepare for the needed notions and notations to describe and discuss our scheme in the remaining sections.

The set of natural numbers is denoted by $\mathbb{N}$. The security parameter is denoted by λ, where $\lambda \in \mathbb{N}$. We put $\mathbb{N}_0 := \mathbb{N} \cup \{0\}$. The residue class ring of integers modulo a prime number p is denoted by $\mathbb{Z}_p$. The number of elements of a set S is denoted by $|S|$. The bit length of a string s is denoted by $|s|$. The inverted value of a bit b is denoted by $\bar{b}$ (i.e. $\bar{b} := 1 - b$). A uniform random sampling of an element a from a set S is denoted as $a \in_R S$. The expression $a =_? b$ returns a value 1 when $a = b$ and 0 otherwise. When an algorithm A on input a outputs z, we denote it as $z \leftarrow A(a)$, or, $A(a) \rightarrow z$. When a probabilistic algorithm A on input a and with randomness r returns z, we denote it as $z \leftarrow A(a; r)$ When two probabilistic interactive algorithms A and B, on common input x and private input a to A, interact with each other and B outputs z, we denote it as $z \leftarrow \langle A(a), B \rangle(x)$. When an algorithm A accesses an oracle $\mathcal{O}$, we denote it as $A^{\mathcal{O}}$. A probability P is said to be negligible in λ if for any given positive polynomial $\text{poly}(\lambda)$ $P < 1/\text{poly}(\lambda)$ for sufficiently large λ. Two probabilities P and Q are said to be computationally indistinguishable if $|P - Q|$ is negligible in λ, which is denoted as $P \approx_c Q$.

2.1   Terminologies

- $\mathcal{ID} = \{0,1\}^k$: The space of identity strings of bit-length k.
- $m := |\mathcal{ID}|$: The total number of possible identity strings; $m = 2^k$.
- $\mathcal{RL}$: The revocation list, which is a subset of $\mathcal{ID}$.
- B: The upper bound of the number of revoked identity strings. That is, $|\mathcal{RL}|$ should be less than B ($|\mathcal{RL}| < B$).
- κ: The index which describes an attribute set and also a predicate function. $\kappa \in \mathbb{N}^c$ for a constant c.
- $\mathbb{X}^\kappa$: The set of all key-attributes under the index κ.
- $\mathbb{Y}^\kappa$: The set of all ciphertext-attributes under the index κ.
- $\mathsf{R}^\kappa : \mathbb{X}^\kappa \times \mathbb{Y}^\kappa \to \{0,1\}$: A predicate function on $\mathbb{X}^\kappa \times \mathbb{Y}^\kappa$, which determines a relation under the index κ (i.e. a subset $R^\kappa := \{(X,Y) \in \mathbb{X}^\kappa \times \mathbb{Y}^\kappa \mid \mathsf{R}^\kappa(X,Y) = 1\}$).
- $\mathcal{R} := \{\mathsf{R}^\kappa\}^{\kappa \in \mathbb{N}^c}$: The family of predicate functions.

2.2   Revocable Attribute-Based Encryption Scheme [19, 20]

A revocable attribute-based encryption scheme rABE is defined with a given family of predicate functions $\mathcal{R}$. rABE consists of four probabilistic polynomial-time algorithms (PPTs for short): rABE = (Setup, KeyGen, Enc, Dec).

- Setup$(1^\lambda, \kappa) \to (\mathrm{PK}, \mathrm{MSK})$. This PPT algorithm takes as input the security parameter 1^λ and the index κ which describes a predicate function. It returns a public key PK and a master secret key MSK.
- KeyGen$((X, \mathrm{id}), \mathrm{PK}, \mathrm{MSK}) \to \mathrm{SK}_{\mathrm{id}}^X$. This PPT algorithm takes as input a key-attribute X, an identity string id, the public key PK and the master secret key MSK. It returns a private secret key $\mathrm{SK}_{\mathrm{id}}^X$.
- Enc$((Y, \mathcal{RL}), \mathrm{PK}, M) \to CT$. This PPT algorithm takes as input a ciphertext attribute Y, the revocation list $\mathcal{RL}$, the public key PK and a plaintext M. It returns a ciphertext CT.
- Dec$(\mathrm{SK}_{\mathrm{id}}^X, (Y, \mathcal{RL}), \mathrm{PK}, CT) \to \tilde{M}$. This deterministic polynomial-time algorithm takes as input a private secret key $\mathrm{SK}_{\mathrm{id}}^X$, the public key PK and a ciphertext CT. It returns a decryption result $\tilde{M}$.

Correctness of Revocable Attribute-Based Encryption Scheme. Correctness of rABE is defined as the correctness as an attribute-based encryption scheme in the following way. First we extend the predicate function R^κ on a key-attribute X and a ciphertext attribute Y into $\bar{\mathsf{R}}^\kappa$ by doing substitution $X \leftarrow (X, \mathrm{id})$ and $Y \leftarrow (Y, \mathcal{RL})$ so that $\bar{\mathsf{R}}^\kappa$ captures whether the $\mathrm{id} \in \mathcal{RL}$ holds or not:

$$\bar{\mathsf{R}}^\kappa((X, \mathrm{id}), (Y, \mathcal{RL})) \stackrel{\mathrm{def}}{=} \begin{cases} 1 \text{ if } \mathsf{R}^\kappa(X,Y) = 1 \wedge \mathrm{id} \notin \mathcal{RL}, \\ 0 \text{ otherwise.} \end{cases}$$

rABE is said to be correct when, for any $\lambda \in \mathbb{N}$, any $\kappa \in \mathbb{N}^c$, any $(X, \mathrm{id}) \in \mathbb{X}^\kappa \times \mathcal{ID}$ and any $(Y, \mathcal{RL}) \in \mathbb{Y}^\kappa \times 2^{\mathcal{ID}}$, s.t. $\bar{\mathsf{R}}^\kappa((X, \mathrm{id}), (Y, \mathcal{RL})) = 1$, and any message M, it holds that $\Pr[M = \tilde{M} \mid \mathsf{Setup}(1^\lambda, \kappa) \to (\mathrm{PK}, \mathrm{MSK}), \mathsf{Enc}((Y, \mathcal{RL}), \mathrm{PK}, M) \to CT, \mathsf{KeyGen}((X, \mathrm{id}), \mathrm{PK}, \mathrm{MSK}) \to \mathrm{SK}_{\mathrm{id}}^X, \mathsf{Dec}(\mathrm{SK}_{\mathrm{id}}^X, (Y, \mathcal{RL}), \mathrm{PK}, CT) \to \tilde{M}] = 1$.

IND-CCA Security of Revocable Attribute-Based Encryption Scheme.
Security of indistinguishability against chosen-ciphertext attacks (IND-CCA security) of rABE is defined by the following experimental algorithm on rABE and a given algorithm **A**.

$$\mathsf{Expr}_{\mathsf{rABE},\mathbf{A}}^{\text{ind-cca}}(1^\lambda, \kappa)$$

$$(\mathrm{PK}, \mathrm{MSK}) \leftarrow \mathsf{Setup}(1^\lambda, \kappa)$$

$$((M_0, M_1), (Y^*, \mathcal{RL}^*), St) \leftarrow \mathbf{A}^{\mathcal{DEC}, \mathcal{KG}}(\mathrm{PK}, \kappa)$$

$$b \in_R \{0, 1\}, CT^* \leftarrow \mathsf{Enc}((Y^*, \mathcal{RL}^*), \mathrm{PK}, M_b)$$

$$b^* \leftarrow \mathbf{A}^{\mathcal{DEC}, \mathcal{KG}}(CT^*, St)$$

If $b = b^*$ then return WIN else return LOSE

The two chosen plaintexts should be equal length: $|M_0| = |M_1|$. **A** accesses two oracles. One is the decryption oracle $\mathcal{DEC}$. Sending $((X_i, \mathrm{id}_i), (Y_i, \mathcal{RL}_i, CT_i))$, **A** queries $\mathcal{DEC}$ for the decryption of CT_i. The other is the key-generation oracle $\mathcal{KG}$. Sending (X_j, id_j), **A** queries $\mathcal{KG}$ for a private secret key $\mathrm{SK}_{\mathrm{id}_j}^{X_j}$. The numbers q_{dec} and q_{key} of the both queries $(i = 1, \ldots, q_{\mathrm{dec}}, j = 1, \ldots, q_{\mathrm{key}})$ are bounded by a polynomial in λ. (M_0, M_1) is a pair of chosen-plaintexts, which is the target plaintexts. $(Y^*, \mathcal{RL}^*)$ are called the target ciphertext-attribute and the target revocation list, respectively. Two restrictions are imposed: First, **A** is not allowed to issue a decryption query $((X_i, \mathrm{id}_i), (Y_i, \mathcal{RL}_i, CT_i))$ s.t. $\bar{\mathsf{R}}^\kappa((X_i, \mathrm{id}_i), (Y_i, \mathcal{RL}_i)) = 1$ and $(Y_i, \mathcal{RL}_i, CT_i) = (Y^*, \mathcal{RL}^*, CT^*)$. Second, **A** is not allowed to issue a key-extraction query (X_j, id_j) s.t. $\bar{\mathsf{R}}^\kappa((X_j, \mathrm{id}_j), (Y^*, \mathcal{RL}^*)) = 1$. The advantage $\mathbf{Adv}_{\mathsf{rABE},\mathbf{A}}^{\text{ind-cca}}(\lambda, \kappa)$ of **A** over rABE is defined as the winning probability: $\mathbf{Adv}_{\mathsf{rABE},\mathbf{A}}^{\text{ind-cca}}(\lambda, \kappa) \stackrel{\text{def}}{=} \Pr[\mathsf{Expr}_{\mathsf{rABE},\mathbf{A}}^{\text{ind-cca}}(1^\lambda, \kappa) \text{ returns WIN}]$. rABE is said to be IND-CCA secure if, for any given PPT algorithm **A**, $\mathbf{Adv}_{\mathsf{rABE},\mathbf{A}}^{\text{ind-cca}}(\lambda, \kappa)$ is negligible in λ.

The notion of *semi-adaptive* IND-CCA security [7,11] is defined by imposing **A** to declare the target *after* seeing PK and public parameters but *before* issuing any queries.

$$\mathsf{Expr}_{\mathsf{rABE},\mathbf{A}}^{\text{ind-semiad-cca}}(1^\lambda, \kappa)$$

$$(\mathrm{PK}, \mathrm{MSK}) \leftarrow \mathsf{Setup}(1^\lambda, \kappa)$$

$$((M_0, M_1), (Y^*, \mathcal{RL}^*), St) \leftarrow \mathbf{A}(\mathrm{PK}, \kappa)$$

$$b \in_R \{0, 1\}, CT^* \leftarrow \mathsf{Enc}((Y^*, \mathcal{RL}^*), \mathrm{PK}, M_b)$$

$$b^* \leftarrow \mathbf{A}^{\mathcal{DEC}, \mathcal{KG}}(CT^*, St)$$

If $b = b^*$ then return WIN else return LOSE

The advantage $\mathbf{Adv}_{\mathsf{rABE},\mathbf{A}}^{\text{ind-semiad-cca}}(\lambda, \kappa)$ is defined in the same way.

Verifiability of Revocable Attribute-Based Encryption Scheme [21].
Verifiability of rABE is defined as the following property. For any $\lambda \in \mathbb{N}$, any
$\kappa \in \mathbb{N}^c$, any $(\text{PK}, \text{MSK}) \leftarrow \text{Setup}(1^\lambda, \kappa)$, any $(X, \text{id}), (X', \text{id}') \in \mathbb{X}^\kappa \times \mathcal{ID}$, any
$(Y, \mathcal{RL}) \in \mathbb{Y}^\kappa \times 2^{\mathcal{ID}}$, any $\text{SK}_{\text{id}}^X \leftarrow \text{KeyGen}((X, \text{id}), \text{PK}, \text{MSK})$ and any $\text{SK}_{\text{id}'}^{X'} \leftarrow$
$\text{KeyGen}((X', \text{id}'), \text{PK}, \text{MSK})$, if $\bar{R}^\kappa((X, \text{id}), (Y, \mathcal{RL})) = \bar{R}^\kappa((X', \text{id}'), (Y, \mathcal{RL}))$,
then for any $CT \in \{0, 1\}^*$ it holds that $\text{Dec}(\text{SK}_{\text{id}}^X, (Y, \mathcal{RL}), \text{PK}, CT) =$
$\text{Dec}(\text{SK}_{\text{id}'}^{X'}, (Y, \mathcal{RL}), \text{PK}, CT)$.

2.3 Commitment Scheme [6,10]

A commitment scheme CmtSch consists of three PPT algorithms: CmtSch =
(Cmt.Setup, Cmt.Com, Cmt.Open).

- Cmt.Setup$(1^\lambda) \rightarrow$ CK. This PPT algorithm takes as input the security parameter 1^λ. It returns a commitment key CK.
- Com$(\text{CK}, M; \gamma) \rightarrow C$. This PPT algorithm takes as input the commitment key CK and a message M. It returns a commitment C and an opening key γ which is the randomness used to generate C.
- Open$(C, \gamma) \rightarrow \hat{M}$. This deterministic polynomial-time algorithm takes as input a commitment C and the opening key γ It returns an opened message $\hat{M}$.

Definition 1 (Perfectly Binding [10]**).** *A commitment scheme CmtSch is
said to be perfectly binding if it satisfies the following condition for some
unbounded algorithm Cmt.Open: For any security parameter 1^λ, any commitment key $CK \leftarrow Cmt.Setup(1^\lambda)$ and any message M,*

$$\Pr[M = M' \mid (C, \gamma) \leftarrow Cmt.Com(M; \gamma), M' \leftarrow Cmt.Open(C)] = 1.$$

Definition 2 (Computationally Hiding [10]**).** *A commitment scheme
CmtSch is said to be computationally hiding if it satisfies the following condition:
For any security parameter 1^λ, any commitment key $CK \leftarrow Cmt.Setup(1^\lambda)$ and
any PPT algorithm $\mathbf{A}$,*

$$\Pr[\mathbf{A}(St, C) = 1 \mid (M, M', St) \leftarrow \mathbf{A}(CK), (C, \gamma) \leftarrow Cmt.Com(M)]$$
$$\approx_c \Pr[\mathbf{A}(St, C') = 1 \mid (M, M', St) \leftarrow \mathbf{A}(CK), (C', \gamma') \leftarrow Cmt.Com(M')]. \quad (1)$$

3 Syntax and Security Definitions of Anonymous Deniable Predicate Authentication Scheme with Revocability

In this section, we give a syntax of an anonymous deniable predicate authentication scheme that has the function of revocability. We denote the scheme by
rADPA. Then we define three security notions: concurrent soundness, anonymity
and deniability. The syntax and security definitions are in accordance with the
previous work [21].

3.1 Syntax

Our rADPA consists of four PPTs: rADPA = (Setup, KeyGen, P, V).

- Setup$(1^\lambda, \kappa) \to$ (PK, MSK). This PPT algorithm takes as input the security parameter 1^λ and the index κ which describes a predicate function. It returns a public key PK and a master secret key MSK.
- KeyGen$((X, \texttt{id}), \text{PK}, \text{MSK}) \to \text{SK}_{\texttt{id}}^X$. This PPT algorithm takes as input a key-attribute X, an identity string $\texttt{id}$, the public key PK and the master secret key MSK. It returns a private secret key $\text{SK}_{\texttt{id}}^X$.
- $\langle \text{P}(\text{SK}_{\texttt{id}}^X), \text{V}\rangle((Y, \mathcal{RL}), \text{PK}) \to 1/0$. These interactive PPT algorithms take as common input a ciphertext attribute and a revocation list $(Y, \mathcal{RL})$ and the public key PK, and as private input to P a private secret key $\text{SK}_{\texttt{id}}^X$. P and V interact with each other for at most a polynomial number of rounds in λ. Then V finally returns a decision 1 or 0.

3.2 Security Definitions

Concurrent Soundness. Intuitively, concurrent soundness means security against misauthentication caused by an adversary which does not have a satisfying private secret key. Formally a definition is given via the following experimental algorithm $\text{Expr}_{\text{rADPA}, \mathbf{A}}^{\text{c-sound}}$.

$$\text{Expr}_{\text{rADPA}, \mathbf{A}}^{\text{c-sound}}(1^\lambda, \kappa)$$
$$(\text{PK}, \text{MSK}) \leftarrow \text{Setup}(1^\lambda, \kappa)$$
$$((Y^*, \mathcal{RL}^*), St) \leftarrow \mathbf{A}^{\mathcal{P}_i(\text{SK}_{\texttt{id}_i}^{X_i})|_{i=1}^{q_{\text{P}}}, \mathcal{KG}}(\text{PK}, \kappa)$$
$$b \leftarrow \langle \mathbf{A}^{\mathcal{P}_i(\text{SK}_{\texttt{id}_i}^{X_i})|_{i=1}^{q_{\text{P}}}, \mathcal{KG}}(St), \text{V}\rangle((Y^*, \mathcal{RL}^*), \text{PK})$$
$$\text{If } b = 1 \text{ then return WIN else return LOSE}$$

Two restrictions are imposed: First, $\mathbf{A}$ is not allowed to relay the messages even in partial. Second, $\mathbf{A}$ is not allowed to issue a key-extraction query $(X_j, \texttt{id}_j)$ s.t. $\bar{\text{R}}^\kappa((X_j, \texttt{id}_j), (Y^*, \mathcal{RL}^*)) = 1$.

The advantage $\mathbf{Adv}_{\text{rADPA}, \mathbf{A}}^{\text{c-sound}}(\lambda, \kappa)$ of $\mathbf{A}$ over rADPA is defined as the winning probability: $\mathbf{Adv}_{\text{rADPA}, \mathbf{A}}^{\text{c-sound}}(\lambda, \kappa) \stackrel{\text{def}}{=} \Pr[\text{Expr}_{\text{rADPA}, \mathbf{A}}^{\text{c-sound}}(1^\lambda, \kappa) \text{ returns WIN}]$. rADPA is said to be (adaptively) concurrently sound if, for any given PPT algorithm $\mathbf{A}$, $\mathbf{Adv}_{\text{rADPA}, \mathbf{A}}^{\text{c-sound}}(\lambda, \kappa)$ is negligible in λ.

The notion of *semi-adaptive* concurrent soundness is defined by imposing $\mathbf{A}$ to declare the target *after* seeing PK and public parameters but *before* issuing any queries.

$$\mathsf{Expr}^{\text{semiad-c-sound}}_{\text{rADPA,A}}(1^\lambda, \kappa)$$

$$(\mathrm{PK}, \mathrm{MSK}) \leftarrow \mathsf{Setup}(1^\lambda, \kappa)$$

$$((Y^*, \mathcal{RL}^*), St) \leftarrow \mathbf{A}(\mathrm{PK}, \kappa)$$

$$b \leftarrow \langle \mathbf{A}^{\mathcal{P}_i(\mathrm{SK}^{X_i}_{\mathrm{id}_i})|^{q_p}_{i=1}, \mathcal{KG}}(St), \mathsf{V} \rangle ((Y^*, \mathcal{RL}^*), \mathrm{PK})$$

If $b = 1$ then return WIN else return LOSE

The advantage $\mathbf{Adv}^{\text{semiad-c-sound}}_{\text{rADPA,A}}(\lambda, \kappa)$ is defined in the same way.

$$\mathbf{Adv}^{\text{semiad-c-sound}}_{\text{rADPA,A}}(\lambda, \kappa) \stackrel{\text{def}}{=} \Pr[\mathsf{Expr}^{\text{semiad-c-sound}}_{\text{rADPA,A}}(1^\lambda, \kappa) \text{ returns WIN}].$$

Anonymity. Intuitively, anonymity means privacy which is indistinguishability between satisfying two patterns of key-attributes. Formally a definition is given via the following experimental algorithm $\mathsf{Expr}^{\text{anonym}}_{\text{rADPA,A}}$.

$$\mathsf{Expr}^{\text{anonym}}_{\text{rADPA,A}}(1^\lambda, \kappa)$$

$$(\mathrm{PK}, \mathrm{MSK}) \leftarrow \mathsf{Setup}(1^\lambda, \kappa)$$

$$((X_0^*, \mathrm{id}_0^*), (X_1^*, \mathrm{id}_1^*), St) \leftarrow \mathbf{A}(\mathrm{PK}, \mathrm{MSK})$$

$$\mathrm{SK}^{X_0^*}_{\mathrm{id}_0^*} \leftarrow \mathsf{KeyGen}((X_0^*, \mathrm{id}_0^*), \mathrm{PK}, \mathrm{MSK}), \mathrm{SK}^{X_1^*}_{\mathrm{id}_1^*} \leftarrow \mathsf{KeyGen}((X_1^*, \mathrm{id}_1^*), \mathrm{PK}, \mathrm{MSK})$$

$$((Y^*, \mathcal{RL}^*), St) \leftarrow \mathbf{A}(St, \mathrm{SK}^{X_0^*}_{\mathrm{id}_0^*}, \mathrm{SK}^{X_1^*}_{\mathrm{id}_1^*}) \text{ s.t.}$$

$$\bar{\mathsf{R}}^\kappa((X_0^*, \mathrm{id}_0^*), (Y^*, \mathcal{RL}^*)) = \bar{\mathsf{R}}^\kappa((X_1^*, \mathrm{id}_1^*), (Y^*, \mathcal{RL}^*))$$

$$b \in_R \{0,1\}, b^* \leftarrow \mathbf{A}^{\mathcal{P}(\mathrm{SK}^{X_b^*}_{\mathrm{id}_b^*})}(St)$$

If $b = b^*$ then return WIN else return LOSE

The advantage $\mathbf{Adv}^{\text{anonym}}_{\text{rADPA,A}}(\lambda, \kappa)$ of $\mathbf{A}$ over rADPA is defined as the winning probability: $\mathbf{Adv}^{\text{anonym}}_{\text{rADPA,A}}(\lambda, \kappa) \stackrel{\text{def}}{=} |\Pr[\mathsf{Expr}^{\text{anonym}}_{\text{rADPA,A}}(1^\lambda, \kappa) \text{ returns WIN}] - \frac{1}{2}|$. rADPA is said to have anonymity if, for any given PPT algorithm $\mathbf{A}$, $\mathbf{Adv}^{\text{anonym}}_{\text{rADPA,A}}(\lambda, \kappa)$ is negligible in λ.

Deniability. Intuitively, deniability means privacy which states anti-forensic property that a third party is not able to confirm whether a prover actually participate in the authentication protocol. Formally a definition is given via the indistinguishability of the following two probability distributions Real and Sim, where $\mathbf{A}$ is any given algorithm and S is an adaptively given algorithm to $\mathbf{A}$.

$$\mathrm{Real}(\lambda, \kappa, (X, \mathsf{id}), (Y, \mathcal{RL})) \overset{\text{def}}{=} \mathsf{View}(\langle \mathsf{P}(\mathrm{SK}_{\mathsf{id}}^X), \mathbf{A}\rangle((Y, \mathcal{RL}), \mathrm{PK})$$
$$| \; \mathsf{Setup}(1^\lambda, \kappa) \to (\mathrm{PK}, \mathrm{MSK}); \mathsf{KeyGen}((X, \mathsf{id}), \mathrm{MSK}) \to \mathrm{SK}_{\mathsf{id}}^X),$$

$$\mathrm{Sim}(\lambda, \kappa, (X, \mathsf{id}), (Y, \mathcal{RL})) \overset{\text{def}}{=} \mathsf{View}(\langle \mathsf{S}, \mathbf{A}\rangle((Y, \mathcal{RL}), \mathrm{PK})$$
$$| \; \mathsf{Setup}(1^\lambda, \kappa) \to (\mathrm{PK}, \mathrm{MSK}); \mathsf{KeyGen}((X, \mathsf{id}), \mathrm{MSK}) \to \mathrm{SK}_{\mathsf{id}}^X).$$

rADPA is said to have deniability if, for any given PPT algorithm $\mathbf{A}$, there exists a PPT algorithm S s.t. for any given PPT algorithm $\mathbf{D}$ it holds that

$$\Pr[\mathbf{D}(\mathrm{Real}(\lambda, \kappa, (X, \mathsf{id}), (Y, \mathcal{RL}))) = 1]$$
$$\approx_c \Pr[\mathbf{D}(\mathrm{Sim}(\lambda, \kappa, (X, \mathsf{id}), (Y, \mathcal{RL}))) = 1].$$

4   Generic Construction of Anonymous Deniable Predicate Authentication Scheme with Revocability

In this section, we give a generic construction of an rADPA scheme in Sect. 3 following the idea of previous work [21].

4.1   Construction

The idea in [21], which originates from the work of Naor [14], is to combine an IND-CCA secure verifiable predicate encryption scheme with a perfectly binding commitment scheme. In our case, we follow the above idea, but we employ a revocable attribute-based encryption scheme rABE as the predicate encryption scheme. That is, we substitute the original ciphertext attribute Y of the predicate encryption scheme with the pair of a ciphertext attribute and a revocation list $(Y, \mathcal{RL})$ of rABE.

Figure 1 shows our construction of rADPA. Intuitively, the prototype of rADPA is a challenge-and-response protocol in which rABE is employed. Next we modify it by, for each $i = 1$ to λ, dividing the "response" $\tilde{r}$ into two random strings r_{i0} and r_{i1} with a linear constraint $\tilde{r} = r_{i0} \oplus r_{i1}$. Then we execute "commit and open" protocol with randomly selected bits b_i for $i = 1$ to λ.

4.2   Security

Theorem 1 (Concurrent Soundness). *If rABE is IND-CCA secure and verifiable, and if Com is perfectly binding, then our rADPA is concurrently sound. More precisely, for any given PPT algorithm $\mathbf{A}$ which is in accordance with $\mathsf{Expr}_{rADPA,\mathbf{A}}^{c\text{-}sound}(\lambda, \kappa)$, there exists a PPT algorithm $\mathbf{B}$ such that*

$$\mathbf{Adv}_{rADPA,\mathbf{A}}^{c\text{-}sound}(\lambda, \kappa) < \mathbf{Adv}_{rABE,\mathbf{B}}^{ind\text{-}cca}(\lambda, \kappa). \tag{2}$$

Proof. See the full version of this extended abstract.   □

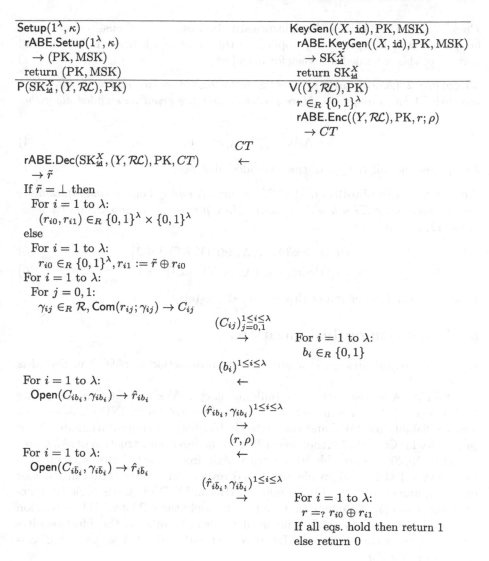

Fig. 1. Our generic construction of anonymous deniable predicate authentication scheme with revocability, rADPA.

Corollary 1 (Semi-adaptive Concurrent Soundness). *If rABE is semi-adaptively IND-CCA secure and verifiable, and if Com is perfectly binding, then our rADPA is semi-adaptively and concurrently sound. More precisely, for any given* PPT *algorithm* **A** *which is in accordance with* $\mathsf{Expr}_{rADPA,\mathbf{A}}^{semiad\text{-}c\text{-}sound}(\lambda,\kappa)$, *there exists a* PPT *algorithm* **B** *such that*

$$\mathbf{Adv}_{rADPA,\mathbf{A}}^{semiad\text{-}c\text{-}sound}(\lambda,\kappa) < \mathbf{Adv}_{rABE,\mathbf{B}}^{ind\text{-}semiad\text{-}cca}(\lambda,\kappa). \tag{3}$$

Proof (Sketch). This is straightforward because the discussion of semi-adaptiveness is independently applied to the proof of Theorem 1. See the full version of this extended abstract for detail.   ☐

Theorem 2 (Anonymity). *If rABE is IND-CCA secure and verifiable, then our rADPA has anonymity. More precisely, for any given unbounded algorithm* **A**,

$$\mathbf{Adv}_{rADPA,\mathbf{A}}^{anonym}(\lambda, \kappa) = 0. \tag{4}$$

Proof. See the full version of this extended abstract.   ☐

Theorem 3 (Deniability). *If rABE is correct, and if Com is computationally hiding, then our rADPA has deniability. More precisely, for any given* PPT *algorithm* **D**,

$$\Pr[\mathbf{D}(Real(\lambda, \kappa, (X, id), (Y, \mathcal{RL}))) = 1] \tag{5}$$
$$\approx_c \Pr[\mathbf{D}(Sim(\lambda, \kappa, (X, id), (Y, \mathcal{RL}))) = 1]. \tag{6}$$

Proof. See the full version of this extended abstract.   ☐

5   Discussion on Instantiations

In this section, we discuss how our generic construction of rADPA in Sect. 4 is instantiated.

Our rADPA consists of the two building blocks: rABE and CmtSch. According to Theorems 1, 2 and 3 in Sect. 4, we need the correctness, IND-CCA security and verifiability for rABE and the perfectly binding and computationally hiding properties for CmtSch. Further, according to the (first) construction of rABE proposed in [19,20], we are able to construct rABE from an attribute-based encryption scheme (ABE) and an identity-based revocation scheme (IBR) in the pair encoding framework [2], which combines ABE and IBR via the generic conjunctive conversion [5]. Note here that we have to apply the CPA-to-CCA conversion [21] to the component ABE scheme, if needed. Thanks to the functionality-preserving property [19,20], if ABE is correct and IND-CCA secure, then so is the converted rABE.

As for verifiability, most of selectively secure ABE schemes such as [16] (KP-ABE) and [18] (CP-ABE) are publicly verifiable, and hence verifiable [21]. Applying the generic transformation [11] to a selectively secure ABE scheme, we obtain a semi-adaptively IND-CCA secure rABE which is also verifiable. In contrast, the adaptively secure ABE schemes such as [2,3], which depend on the dual-system encryption technique, are not verifiable in their proposed forms, but they can be modified into verifiable ones [21]. Hence we obtain an adaptively IND-CCA secure rABE which is also verifiable.

Among the instantiations discussed in the previous work [19,20], we are interested in rABE with the selective security which yields the semi-adaptive security [11], or with constant size ciphertexts. The former is because, in the semi-adaptive security model, adversaries choose the target (in our case (M_0, M_1) and

Table 1. Instantiations

IND-CCA Secure rABE ABE (Flavor), IBR	CmtSch	Verifiability	Message Len.	Security	Assumptions
[11,16,21] (KP-ABE), [2]	EG [9]	Public	Non-const.	Semi-adap.	DBDH, EDHE
[11,16,21] (KP-ABE), [4]	EG [9]	Public	Non-const.	Semi-adap.	DBDH, EDHE
[11,18,21] (CP-ABE), [2]	EG [9]	Public	Non-const.	Semi-adap.	DPBDHE, EDHE
[11,18,21] (CP-ABE), [4]	EG [9]	Public	Non-const.	Semi-adap.	DPBDHE, EDHE
[2,21] (KP-ABE), [2]	EG [9]	via [21]	Const.	Adap.	EDHE
[2,21] (KP-ABE), [4]	EG [9]	via [21]	Const.	Adap.	EDHE
[3,21](CP-ABE), [2]	EG [9]	via [21]	Const.	Adap.	MDH, EDHE
[3,21](CP-ABE), [4]	EG [9]	via [21]	Const.	Adap.	MDH, EDHE

$(Y^*, \mathcal{RL}^*))$ after seeing PK and public parameters but before issuing any queries. This model is considered to be natural and often sufficient in the case of *authentication* (see Sect. 2.2), which makes a contrast to the case of encryption. The ABE schemes with the selective security are known; for example, KP-ABE [16] and CP-ABE [18]. The IND-CCA security of the ABE schemes (after applying the CPA-to-CCA conversion [21]) is under the decisional bilinear Diffie-Hellman assumption (DBDH) and the decisional parallel bilinear Diffie-Hellman Exponent assumption (DPBDHE), respectively.

The latter is because, when an authentication scheme is applied in a real network protocol, the message length should preferably be constant. It is notable that ABE schemes with constant size ciphertexts are known (KP-ABE [2] and CP-ABE [3]). The IND-CCA security of the ABE schemes (after applying [21]) is under the matrix Diffie-Hellman assumption (MDH) and the expanded Diffie-Hellman exponent assumption (EDHE), respectively. Also, there are IBR schemes with constant size ciphertexts [2,4]. The IND-CCA security of the IBR schemes (after applying [21]) is under the EDHE assumption. Hence we can actually instantiate our rADPA with constant message length.

As for a commitment scheme CmtSch with the perfectly binding and computationally hiding properties, we can employ the ElGamal encryption scheme (EG) [9]. The computationally hiding property is obtained from the indistinguishability against chosen-plaintext attacks, which is under the decisional Diffie-Hellman assumption (DDH).

Table 1 summarizes the above discussion.

6   Conclusion

We proposed an anonymous deniable predicate authentication scheme with revocability, rADPA, which has strong privacy protection properties. We gave the syntax and formal security definitions of rADPA; concurrent soundness, anonymity and deniability. Then we showed a generic construction of rADPA, whose building blocks are a revocable attribute-based encryption scheme, rABE, and a commitment scheme, CmtSch. We stated that, when rABE and CmtSch have suitable properties, then our rADPA attains the security properties. Finally, we discussed how our generic construction of rADPA is instantiated.

Our future work would be a feasibility study of our rADPA by implementation. Also, we have to examine how the six-round authentication protocol of our rADPA is feasible in real scenarios in the internet.

Acknowledgements. This work was supported by JSPS KAKENHI Grant Number JP18K11297. We would like to express our sincere thanks to Keita Emura for his suggestions on the semi-adaptive security. We would like to express our sincere thanks to Nuttapong Attrapadung for his comments on the instantiations.

References

1. Agrawal, S., Chase, M.: A study of pair encodings: predicate encryption in prime order groups. In: Kushilevitz, E., Malkin, T. (eds.) TCC 2016. LNCS, vol. 9563, pp. 259–288. Springer, Heidelberg (2016). https://doi.org/10.1007/978-3-662-49099-0_10
2. Attrapadung, N.: Dual system encryption via doubly selective security: framework, fully secure functional encryption for regular languages, and more. In: Nguyen, P.Q., Oswald, E. (eds.) EUROCRYPT 2014. LNCS, vol. 8441, pp. 557–577. Springer, Heidelberg (2014). https://doi.org/10.1007/978-3-642-55220-5_31
3. Attrapadung, N.: Dual system encryption framework in prime-order groups via computational pair encodings. In: Cheon, J.H., Takagi, T. (eds.) ASIACRYPT 2016. LNCS, vol. 10032, pp. 591–623. Springer, Heidelberg (2016). https://doi.org/10.1007/978-3-662-53890-6_20
4. Attrapadung, N., Libert, B., de Panafieu, E.: Expressive key-policy attribute-based encryption with constant-size ciphertexts. In: Catalano, D., Fazio, N., Gennaro, R., Nicolosi, A. (eds.) PKC 2011. LNCS, vol. 6571, pp. 90–108. Springer, Heidelberg (2011). https://doi.org/10.1007/978-3-642-19379-8_6
5. Attrapadung, N., Yamada, S.: Duality in ABE: converting attribute based encryption for dual predicate and dual policy via computational encodings. In: Nyberg, K. (ed.) CT-RSA 2015. LNCS, vol. 9048, pp. 87–105. Springer, Cham (2015). https://doi.org/10.1007/978-3-319-16715-2_5
6. Brassard, G., Chaum, D., Crépeau, C.: Minimum disclosure proofs of knowledge. J. Comput. Syst. Sci. **37**(2), 156–189 (1988). https://doi.org/10.1016/0022-0000(88)90005-0
7. Chen, J., Wee, H.: Semi-adaptive attribute-based encryption and improved delegation for Boolean formula. In: Abdalla, M., De Prisco, R. (eds.) SCN 2014. LNCS, vol. 8642, pp. 277–297. Springer, Cham (2014). https://doi.org/10.1007/978-3-319-10879-7_16
8. Dodis, Y., Katz, J., Smith, A., Walfish, S.: Composability and on-line deniability of authentication. In: Reingold, O. (ed.) TCC 2009. LNCS, vol. 5444, pp. 146–162. Springer, Heidelberg (2009). https://doi.org/10.1007/978-3-642-00457-5_10
9. ElGamal, T.: A public key cryptosystem and a signature scheme based on discrete logarithms. In: Blakley, G.R., Chaum, D. (eds.) CRYPTO 1984. LNCS, vol. 196, pp. 10–18. Springer, Heidelberg (1985). https://doi.org/10.1007/3-540-39568-7_2
10. Goldreich, O.: The Foundations of Cryptography - Volume 1, Basic Techniques. Cambridge University Press, Cambridge (2001)

11. Goyal, R., Koppula, V., Waters, B.: Semi-adaptive security and bundling functionalities made generic and easy. In: Hirt, M., Smith, A. (eds.) TCC 2016. LNCS, vol. 9986, pp. 361–388. Springer, Heidelberg (2016). https://doi.org/10.1007/978-3-662-53644-5_14
12. Goyal, V., Pandey, O., Sahai, A., Waters, B.: Attribute-based encryption for fine-grained access control of encrypted data. In: Proceedings of the 13th ACM Conference on Computer and Communications Security, CCS 2006, Alexandria, VA, USA, 30 October–3 November 2006, pp. 89–98 (2006). https://doi.org/10.1145/1180405.1180418
13. Nakamoto, S.: Bitcoin: a peer-to-peer electronic cash system (2008). http://bitcoin.org/bitcoin.pdf
14. Naor, M.: Deniable ring authentication. In: Yung, M. (ed.) CRYPTO 2002. LNCS, vol. 2442, pp. 481–498. Springer, Heidelberg (2002). https://doi.org/10.1007/3-540-45708-9_31
15. Narayanan, A., Bonneau, J., Felten, E., Miller, A., Goldfeder, S.: Bitcoin and Cryptocurrency Technologies: A Comprehensive Introduction. Princeton University Press, Princeton (2016)
16. Ostrovsky, R., Sahai, A., Waters, B.: Attribute-based encryption with non-monotonic access structures. In: Proceedings of the 2007 ACM Conference on Computer and Communications Security, CCS 2007, Alexandria, Virginia, USA, 28–31 October 2007, pp. 195–203 (2007). https://doi.org/10.1145/1315245.1315270
17. Sahai, A., Waters, B.: Fuzzy identity-based encryption. In: Cramer, R. (ed.) EUROCRYPT 2005. LNCS, vol. 3494, pp. 457–473. Springer, Heidelberg (2005). https://doi.org/10.1007/11426639_27
18. Waters, B.: Ciphertext-policy attribute-based encryption: an expressive, efficient, and provably secure realization. In: Catalano, D., Fazio, N., Gennaro, R., Nicolosi, A. (eds.) PKC 2011. LNCS, vol. 6571, pp. 53–70. Springer, Heidelberg (2011). https://doi.org/10.1007/978-3-642-19379-8_4
19. Yamada, K., Attrapadung, N., Emura, K., Hanaoka, G., Tanaka, K.: Generic constructions for fully secure revocable attribute-based encryption. In: Foley, S.N., Gollmann, D., Snekkenes, E. (eds.) ESORICS 2017. LNCS, vol. 10493, pp. 532–551. Springer, Cham (2017). https://doi.org/10.1007/978-3-319-66399-9_29
20. Yamada, K., Attrapadung, N., Emura, K., Hanaoka, G., Tanaka, K.: Generic constructions for fully secure revocable attribute-based encryption. IEICE Trans. 101–A(9), 1456–1472 (2018). https://doi.org/10.1587/transfun.E101.A.1456
21. Yamada, S., Attrapadung, N., Santoso, B., Schuldt, J.C.N., Hanaoka, G., Kunihiro, N.: Verifiable predicate encryption and applications to CCA security and anonymous predicate authentication. In: Fischlin, M., Buchmann, J., Manulis, M. (eds.) PKC 2012. LNCS, vol. 7293, pp. 243–261. Springer, Heidelberg (2012). https://doi.org/10.1007/978-3-642-30057-8_15

Physical Cryptography

Mariana Costiuc[1] , Diana Maimuţ[1]([✉]) , and George Teşeleanu[1,2]

[1] Advanced Technologies Institute, 10 Dinu Vintilă, Bucharest, Romania
{mariana.safta,diana.maimut,tgeorge}@dcti.ro
[2] Simion Stoilow Institute of Mathematics of the Romanian Academy,
21 Calea Grivitei, Bucharest, Romania

Abstract. We recall a series of physical cryptography solutions and provide the reader with relevant security analyses. We mostly turn our attention to describing attack scenarios against schemes solving Yao's millionaires' problem, protocols for comparing information without revealing it and public key cryptosystems based on physical properties of systems.

Keywords: Security education · Recreational cryptography · Physical cryptography · Decoy based cryptography · Yao's millionaires' problem · Public key cryptography

1 Introduction

In our paper we present a security analysis to a series of problems that can be seen as abstract games. Our main motivation for studying such protocols is their teaching utility. Note that we are not aware of any real-world application of any sort, as these problems fall in the category of "recreational cryptography". Although recreational, these protocols can provide interesting insight and techniques that can be useful for understanding the concepts on which the underlying problems are based.

Physical cryptography [4,11,17,20] makes use of physical properties of systems for encrypting and/or exchanging information (*i.e.* without using one-way functions). Although a very interesting teaching tool, it can be shown that some of the proposed methods are not safe in practice. Thus, our aim is to attack such physical protocols using methods similar to classical side channel techniques.

Besides the obvious cryptographic teaching utility of physical cryptography schemes, we believe that some of the schemes tackled in the current paper may be successfully used for introducing concepts corresponding to other domains. We provide the reader with such examples in the following sections.

Although some authors acknowledge that their proposed protocols are only useful for playing with children or introducing new concepts to non-technical audiences, the authors of [9–11,21] claim that their schemes can be securely implemented in real-life scenarios. In [6], Courtois attacks one of the protocols proposed in [10], but the authors contest his results in [11]. We independently conducted a simulation of the attack and our results acknowledge Courtois' claim.

E. Simion and R. Géraud-Stewart (Eds.): SecITC 2019, LNCS 12001, pp. 156–171, 2020.
https://doi.org/10.1007/978-3-030-41025-4_11

Structure of the Paper. In Sect. 2 we describe various schemes proposed in [9–11,21] which aim at solving Yao's millionaires' problem and provide the reader with their corresponding security analyses. In Sect. 3 we present a set of protocols which act as solutions for comparing information without revealing it and discuss their security. In Sect. 4 we describe a public key cryptosystem constructed by means of an electrical scheme and tackle its security. We conclude and discuss future work ideas in Sect. 5. Due to the page number restriction, we recall various physical cryptographic solutions which appeared in the literature in Appendix A. Also, in Appendix B we present a generic physical public key encryption scheme useful for introducing students to different properties of physical systems.

Notations. We denote by U and V the private spaces of Alice and, respectively, Bob. By "impenetrable" we further refer to an object that can not be broken or looked into no matter the means employed by an adversary. Note that, in practice, "impenetrable" objects do not exist, but we use this concept for presenting the philosophical aspects of different cryptographic problems.

2   Yao's Millionaires' Problem

In [24] Yao introduced "Two Millionaires' Problem". The problem can be defined as follows. Alice has a private number a and Bob has a private number b. The goal of the two parties is solving the inequality $a \leqslant b$ without revealing the actual values. We further assume that $a, b \in [0, n]$ are integers.

In [9–11,21] the authors present a number of solutions for the previously mentioned problem based on physical principles. In this section we focus on describing their proposed protocols together with our security analyses.

According to the original security model, during the following we consider Alice and Bob as being *honest but curious* users, *i.e.* they can observe, measure and compute whatever they like and try to get a hold on the other party's private numbers while following the protocol's steps.

2.1   "Elevator" Solution

Description. To recall the scheme we follow the descriptions given in [9,11]. We start by assuming that we have at our disposal a building with at least n floors. Moreover, we consider that the chosen building is equipped with an elevator. Alice positions herself on floor number a while Bob goes to floor number b. Then, Bob takes an elevator (from Bob's private space V) going down and stopping at every floor. Alice watches the elevator doors on her floor, making sure that Bob does not see her if the elevator doors open (here is Alice's private space U). If she sees the elevator doors open, she knows that Bob's number is larger. If not, then his number is smaller. Using such a protocol, Bob will not know the result of the comparison until Alice shares it with him.

Security Analysis. The only security considerations of [9, 11] are that Bob can lock the stairs and disable all elevators except one. This may prevent Alice from cheating by running between different floors to get a better estimate of Bob's number.

During our analysis we found other various attack scenarios. We consider the steps of the protocol as being sequential (*i.e.* first Alice gets to floor a and then Bob gets to floor b).

1. If Alice uses the same elevator as Bob she can simply conceal a small camera[1] while ascending to floor a. Thus, she can recover b as soon as Bob ascends to his designated floor. In order to mitigate such an attack, Bob must be ensured that Alice uses a different elevator or the stairs (*i.e.* making sure that Bob's elevator remains somewhat protected).
2. If the floor doors of Bob's elevator are not secured then Alice can open one of the doors and attach a motion sensor to the elevator. By analyzing the elevator's movement Alice can deduce b. Hence, Bob must be ensured that all the floor doors are secured against unauthorized access.
3. If Alice has access only to the stairs then she can install cameras on each of the n floors[2]. If Bob limits Alice's access to only one floor (a) for security reasons, then he can always check the access readers installed on each floor and find a. These attacks can also be mounted by Alice if Bob takes the stairs. As a result, the only viable solution would be for Alice and Bob to use separate elevators.
4. Once Alice reaches a then she can use a microphone to detect the sound made by the elevator's movement. By counting the number of times the elevator's engine starts or the doors open Alice can deduce b. Hence, to prevent such an attack, Bob can use a device for generating noise in order to mask the other relevant sounds. This attack can also be mounted by Bob for deducing a.

When Alice and Bob simultaneously ascend to their designated floors, the attack scenarios Items 3 and 4 are still feasible.

We do not claim that the protocol is feasible in practice (the doors must be "impenetrable" and the noise source must perfectly mask the sound of the elevator's movement). We only claim that the example can be practically used to introduce Yao's problem to non-specialized audiences and also to make people think of different methods of attacking the system.

2.2   "Race Track" Solution

Description. For recalling the scheme we follow the description from [11]. Let us consider that Alice and Bob have at their disposal a race track of length n. Then, the two parties run toward each other from the opposite ends of the race track,

---

[1] We can also consider all types of small devices which incorporate cameras.
[2] If the building already has security cameras, a simpler solution is bribing the security guard and watching the security footage to obtain b.

maintaining the speeds of a m/s (Alice), respectively b m/s (Bob). The party which reaches first the midpoint of the track leaves a mark there and runs back, knowing that he/she was faster[3]. When the other party gets to the midpoint, he/she will know that he/she was slower[4]. In order to create their private spaces in this scenario, Alice and Bob have to construct an "impenetrable" fence across the track at the midpoint.

The authors of [11] state that the "race track" idea can be implemented on a computer if two different programs are allowed to work with the same file at the same time. Thus, consider that the shared file is a bit string of length n, with all bits initially equal to 1. Alice provides a program that goes over this bit string left to right, replacing the current 1 symbol by 0 at the speed of one symbol per a time units. Bob provides a similar program going over the same bit string right to left, at the speed of one symbol per b time units. When either of the two programs replaces $n/2$ symbols, it replaces the current symbol by X and stops. In such a way, the two parties will know that whose program stops first has the bigger number. Both programs will have to use the computer's internal clock.

Security Analysis. In [11] the authors mention that the "race track" solution only works if both parties are honest and provide the reader with an attack scenario otherwise. More precisely, the party who reaches the fence first does not run back but just waits to see when the other party arrives, thus figuring out the other party's speed.

During our analysis we found that another restriction must hold. If Alice and Bob run on a circular track when they are "close enough"[5] to the midpoint they will be able to see each other. Thus, even if the parties are honest, the previous attack is still valid. To avoid such a scenario, a possible solution would be to put an "impenetrable"[6] fence such that both private spaces are isolated one from the other and also from the outside world[7].

The digital variant of the "race track" idea on a computer is, unfortunately, flawed. In order for the protocol to be valid both users need read/write access to the file. This implies that any of the parties can choose two positions of the other parties' half of the file, continuously read the symbols corresponding to these positions and record the time needed for the symbols to change. This can be easily extended to monitoring multiple positions. Thus, each user can compute the other party's value.

Teaching Utility. Although the digital variant is not secure, it can be used by teachers as an implementation task. Thus, students can implement two programs that race each other and also a third program that monitors the speed of either Alice and/or Bob.

---

[3] Without knowing the actual speed of the other party.

[4] Again, without knowing the actual speed of the other party.

[5] The precise difference between a and b depends on the race track's radius.

[6] From both a visual and acoustic point of view.

[7] If, for example, we isolate the two areas using only a wall, one of the parties can use a drone for spying the other.

2.3 "Communicating Vessels" Solution

Description. To recall the scheme we follow the description from [11]. We start by assuming that Alice has a communicating vessel C_A in her private space U, while Bob has a communicating vessel C_B in his private space V. C_A and C_B are connected by a horizontal pipe attached to their bottoms and, thus, a working system is constructed. The shapes of the vessels are part of the parties' private keys. In the beginning the system is "almost" filled with water. Then, Alice starts pumping the water out of her vessel at the speed of a gallons[8] per second, while Bob starts pumping the water in his vessel at the speed of b gallons per second. The parties are simply watching whether the level of water is decreasing or increasing. If it is decreasing, then $a > b$; if it is increasing, then $a < b$.

Security Analysis. According to the authors of [21] the final level of water in the system depends not only on a and b, but also on the shapes of both vessels. Also, the relation between a and quantities that can be measured outside of Alice's vessel depends on the shape of Alice's vessel, which is unknown to anybody except Alice herself.

During our analysis we observed two main issues of the proposed protocol. First of all, if the participants pump water in and out of the system the shapes of their communicating vessels become irrelevant. In such a case, the authors might have thought about *pouring* water instead of pumping it while constructing their scheme. Secondly, the shapes of the vessels must be considered in such a way that the two parties can precisely measure fluctuations in their corresponding vessels. To explain this type of phenomena we can consider the following exaggerated example: the shapes of Alice and Bob's vessels correspond to those of two small artificial lakes and they pump water in and out with negligible speeds (*e.g.* a milliliter per hour). Then, they can not accurately detect which speed is greater than the other.

The scheme enhanced with our previous comments becomes equivalent with: Alice and Bob have two cylinder shaped vessels such that they can accurately measure fluctuations of the system. To detect Alice's value, Bob can use a graduated cylinder and measure the volume's fluctuation. Then, using his own speed value b he can compute a. Hence, the scheme is insecure for solving Yao's problem but it can be used as a public key encryption scheme (see Appendix B).

Teaching Utility. Communicating vessels are a common example in physics teaching (see for example [12]). More precisely, the scheme provides a good opportunity for a teacher to introduce students to the dynamics of (ideal) fluids.

2.4 "Rope" Solution

Description. For recalling the scheme we follow the description given in [10]. Alice and Bob privately select $c < 0$ and, respectively, $d > 0$. We position Alice

---

[8] Or whatever units.

and Bob in a plane, Alice at point $A = (a, c)$ and Bob at point $B = (b, d)$. Also, we give them both long pieces of rope. We assume that the scaling is such that Alice and Bob cannot see each other's point.

First, Alice fixes one end of her rope at point A and selects as her private space U a neighborhood of point A that cannot be seen by Bob. Bob, too, selects V as a neighborhood of his point B. Then, Alice fixes the other end of her rope to a random point C in the plane, far enough so that her neighborhood U can not be seen from C. After fixing the rope, she positions the part of the rope inside U so that this part is not a straight line. She then communicates the coordinates of point C to Bob.

Bob walks to point C, ties one end of his rope to Alice's rope, then walks back to his point B, while unwinding (not pulling) his rope along the way. When Bob reaches his B, he starts pulling the rope until Alice tells him to stop, which is as soon as Alice sees that the part of the rope inside her neighborhood U is a straight line. To make sure that it is not by accident that the part of the rope inside her neighborhood U is a straight line, Alice asks Bob whether or not the part of the rope inside his neighborhood V is a straight line. If it is not, then Alice starts pulling her end of the rope toward her point A until Bob tells her to stop, which is as soon as Bob sees that the part of the rope inside his neighborhood V is a straight line.

When the parts of the rope inside both neighborhoods U and V are straight, Alice and Bob assume that their points A and B are connected by a straight rope, and they find the slope s of the corresponding straight line by selecting any two points on the parts of the line inside their private neighborhoods. Then, $a < b$ if and only if $s > 0$.

Security Analysis. Some parts of the scheme described in [10] may seem redundant according to the authors. As pointed out by them, if both parties are honest the protocol can be simplified. To mitigate dishonest parties attacks, *e.g.* Alice must tell Bob to stop as soon as she sees that the part of the rope inside her neighborhood U is a straight line. Otherwise, Bob could triangulate Alice's point A by straightening the rope between A and two different points of his choice.

Since we do not consider the honest but curious attack model for this precise protocol, another simple attack can be mounted. Bob can walk along Alice's rope until he is able to determine the coordinates of point A. To prevent Alice from seeing Bob while he tries to find A, he can use, for example, either a small drone or a powerful telescopic sight. To avoid such a vulnerability of the protocol, the neighborhood U must be covered by an "impenetrable" material and, also, to contain a large number of points such that it is impossible for Bob to determine the exact position of A. When selecting the number of points in U we also need to take into account the following scenario. After determining the precise position of U in the plane Bob gets back to point C and follows the initial protocol for determining s. Then, Bob can narrow down the number of possibilities for A.

Teaching Utility. A variation of this protocol for key exchange may be the following. Ted, a trusted third party, takes an infinite rope and fixes one end of it at Alice's point A. Similarly, Ted fixes another rope at Bob's point B. After fixing the ropes, Ted walks to a random point T such that the distance to A and B is equal and then cuts the ropes at point T. In the last step of the protocol Ted returns the ropes to Alice and, respectively, Bob. The common key is the length of the two ropes.

Besides a good reason for a discussion about analytic geometry, this variations of the protocol can be the starting point for describing the secure key exchange protocol for the Internet of Things networks introduced in [18].

2.5   "Laboratory Scale" Solution

Description. To recall the scheme we follow the description from [9]. We assume that Alice and Bob have access to a laboratory scale[9]. Each of the two parties manufacture a weight corresponding to their private number (*e.g.* in grams). We also assume that they have identical boxes[10] where each of them can put their corresponding weight. Alice enters the room where the scale is positioned and puts her box on one of the plates. Then, Bob enters and puts his box on the other plate. If his plate goes down, then his number is larger; otherwise, it is Alice's number that is larger.

Security Analysis. The authors argue in [9] that Alice and Bob do not have to be in the same place at the same time to perform the comparison, but they still have to be in the same place at some point, which may be inconvenient. In fact, if, say, Alice is worried about Bob cheating (by putting different weights on his plate to zoom in on Alice's weight), then she would have to stay in the room and watch what Bob is doing.

Note that when we analyzed the solution we assume that the box is "impenetrable". Compared to the "rope" solution where Bob needs to cheat in order to detect the dimensions of U, here Bob knows the precise size of the covering box. This gives him an upper limit of the weight's volume. If he knows the material of the weight, then he has an upper limit of the value a. This could be easily mitigated by keeping the weight's material secret.

3   Comparing Information Without Revealing It

The initial problem from which the study in [8] started is the following. Charlie complains to one of his managers, Alice, about a sensitive matter and asks her to keep it secret. A few months later, another manager, Bob, tells Alice that someone complained to him, also with a confidentiality request, about the same matter. Alice and Bob need a way to determine if the same person complained to them without revealing the identity of the complainer. The authors of [8] describe a series of complex protocols that try to accomplish this task. But, the simplest solution was actually provided by the 13 year old son of the first author:

---

[9] A simple mechanism with two plates that are in balance when no weight is placed on either of them.

[10] Which, in this case, are considered their private spaces.

"Why not just ask Charlie whether he complained to Bob?". This proves that sometimes experts try to find too complicated solutions for simple things.

We further present a few solutions that can still work when implemented using our current technology. A legacy example may be considered the "airline reservation" solution. While Bob is not in the same room Alice calls a specific airline and makes a particular reservation in the name of her complainer. Then, Bob tries to cancel the reservation in his complainer's name. Finally, Alice cancels or tries to cancel the reservation she made. It is obvious that nowadays such a version of the protocol can not be functional anymore, due to the fact that in order to cancel a reservation one needs to have extra pieces of information (*e.g.* the reservation code).

For uniformity, we consider, as in Sect. 2, that Alice and Bob are honest but curious.

3.1   Message for Bob

Description. We assume that Alice and Bob associate each candidate with a random telephone number. Alice dials the number[11] assigned to the person who complained to her (Charlie) and asks to leave a message for Bob. It is clear that the one answering the phone does not know who Bob is. A while after, Bob dials the number of the person who complained to him and asks if anyone has left him a message.

Security Analysis. The authors of [8] provide a short security analysis. More precisely: (1) if Alice does not supervise Bob, then Bob might try several candidates and (2) Dave might deny that a message was left for Bob.

The protocol was designed in a period of time in which telephones were only analog. But, nowadays, we also have digital and mobile phones. Thus, we further consider all the three cases when analyzing the security of the scheme. If Alice and Bob use the same phone to run the protocol, then, in the digital and mobile cases, Bob can check the call history of the phone to find out the identity of the complainer. Thus, to prevent such an attack, Alice must delete the call history. Even if she does this, there is a small probability that Dave will call back and, if Bob, is near the phone at that particular time, he can see the phone number and deduce the identity of the complainer. This problem can be easily rectified if Alice hides her number. Note that the previously mentioned problems do not happen in the analog case.

If Alice and Bob use different analog phones and Bob is nearby, he can redial the last number and ask Dave which is his phone number. Thus, in the analog case Alice needs to call another number afterwards[12]. In the digital case, Alice simply has to delete the call history to avoid the redialing attack. If the protocol is run using mobile phones, such an attack is even harder because Bob has to

---

[11] We denote the owner by Dave.
[12] To overwrite the call history.

physically take Alice's phone. Even if he manages to snatch Alice's phone, the device might be locked.

We conclude that in the analog case either version is secure (*i.e.* with one or two phones) as long as Alice overwrites the call logs, while in the digital case it is better to use two phones. We believe that the protocol is secure as long as the initial scenario is valid[13] and our proposed countermeasures are taken into account.

3.2   Password

Description. We assume that Alice chooses to change her password in accordance with Charlie's name. Next, Bob tries to log in as Alice. In order to do so, Bob uses the name of the person who complained to him as a password.

Security Analysis. As in Sect. 3.1, Bob might try several candidates [8]. Additional to the initial security analysis, there is always the possibility that Alice installs either a key logger on the computer or a video camera inside the room and directly finds out Bob's password. Thus, the protocol is insecure.

Teaching Utility. In one version of the protocol, the authors of [8] suggest using the "passwd" Linux command to run the scheme. This provides a good opportunity for a teacher to introduce students to the Linux terminal basics and also how passwords are stored in Linux.

3.3   Cups

Description. We start by assuming that we have a small number s of candidates. Alice and Bob get s identical containers (*e.g.* by acquiring disposable cups), line them up and label them[14]. Then, Alice puts a folded slip of paper saying "yes" in the cup of Charlie and a slip saying "no" in the other $s - 1$ cups. Bob does the same. Next, Alice and Bob remove the labels and shuffle the cups. To complete the protocol, both the parties look inside the cups to see whether one of them contains two slips saying "yes".

Security Analysis. If Alice and Bob use the suggested containers, Bob can always check which cup contains the slip saying "yes". Thus, it is better to use secure containers, for example ballot boxes which are tamper-evident. Hence, even if Bob manages to break into all the secure containers, Alice can detect that Bob cheated.

Teaching Utility. The secure version of the protocol may be seen as a toy version of the voting process. Thus, it can be used as an introduction to elections and electoral fraud.

---

[13] A powerful enough Bob can always eavesdrop the landline or ask the operator for Alice's call history.

[14] One for each candidate.

4 Public Key Encryption

Several public key cryptosystems based on different laws of physics[15] can be found in [11][16]. Although these solutions are hard to implement in the real world[17], they provide a very good teaching tool. More precisely, a teacher can interactively transition from these toy protocols to precise explanations of the underlying physical laws.

Given the attack possibilities we observed while analyzing the schemes in [11], we chose to only discuss the "capacitors" solution during the following.

4.1 "Capacitors" Solution

Description. Assume that Alice wishes to send a secret positive number q_a to Bob. Let us consider that Alice has a capacitor C_1 of the capacitance c_A (denoting her *public key*) and charge q_A (denoting her *secret message*) in U. Similarly, Bob has a capacitor C_2 of the capacitance c_B (denoting his *long-term private key*) and a randomly chosen charge q_B (denoting his *session private key*) in V. Note that the private key is selected by Bob randomly before each transmission from Alice. The capacitors are connected in such a way that the plates holding the positive charges are connected by one wire, and the plates holding the negative charges are connected by another wire (see Fig. 1). Alice has a switch that keeps the circuit disconnected until the actual transmission begins. Also, Alice has an ammeter to monitor the electric current in the circuit. Bob has a rheostat included in the circuit in V. This allows him to randomly change the resistance of the whole circuit, and therefore also to change parameters of the electric current during transmission.

According to the authors, Alice uses her switch to connect the circuit, starting the redistribution of the electric charges between the two capacitors. When this process is complete, she disconnects the circuit. After redistribution of charges, both Alice and Bob, have new charges: Q_A and Q_B. Now, all that Bob has to do in order to compute the secret of Alice is to apply the following mathematical expression: $q_A = Q_B \cdot (1 + \frac{c_A}{c_B}) - q_B$.

Security Analysis. To promote an idea which might be relevant in practice, some experimental results should be presented. In this case, the authors gave an example of a system used for information transmission based on physical properties of passive components. Although the authors are theoretically right, Courtois contested the strength of their model in [6]. In our analysis, we propose a complete, yet simple way to demonstrate both theories. The proposed scheme is represented in Fig. 2. In order to do so, we extended the electrical circuit proposed in [10] so that we could prove its functionality by simulating it. Based on the fact that the authors gave no technical specifications regarding the circuit,

---

[15] We refer the reader to Appendix B.
[16] A similar solution for Yao's problem is described in [9].
[17] The authors assume that only Alice and Bob interferes with the system.

we analyzed several scenarios. The first one concerns the type of capacitors used in the circuit. We tested the scheme using polarized and non-polarized capacitors with specific given input values and concluded that, in simulation, the differences are not significant. Nevertheless, in practice, the type of capacitor used is very important in order to avoid damaging the circuit.

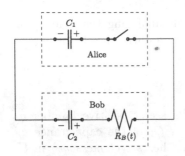

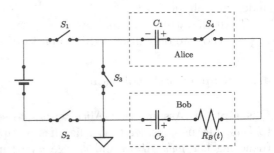

Fig. 1. "Capacitors" solution   **Fig. 2.** Proposed "capacitors" solution

To ease description, in order to validate the functionality of the "capacitors" solution we randomly choose a set of parameters for the scheme. Our example can directly be used in class to experimentally show that the solution is a viable one.

For obtaining a functional "capacitors" solution, we propose adding a power supply and 3 more switches (see Fig. 2). The voltage generated by the power supply is $1\,V$. We use a $10\,\mu F$ capacitance for Alice's capacitor and a $1\,\mu F$ capacitance for Bob's capacitor. The rheostat is set at $R_1 = 431\,\Omega$ and $R_1 = 569$ Ω. The simulation is done using the electronic circuit simulator hosted by [1]. The first step of the simulation consists of charging the capacitors, in order to obtain the initial values for the electric charges. For charging the capacitors, switches S_1, S_2 and S_4 must be connected. After this step, the power supply is disconnected and the circuit is closed, meaning that switches S_1 and S_2 must be disconnected and switch S_3 must be connected. Switch S_4 is Alice's switch. Based on the values that were set as input, we measured the voltage drop V_d on each capacitor and obtained the initial electric charges $q_A = 899.09$ nC ($V_{d_A} = 89.909$ mV) and $q_B = 910.091$ nC ($V_{d_B} = 910.091$ mV). After re-distributing charges (*i.e.* when Alice connects the circuit) the charges become $Q_A = 10$ nC ($V_{d_A} = 1$ mV) and $Q_B = 1$ nC ($V_{d_B} = 1$ mV). In the final step of the protocol, Bob computes Alice's electric charge:

$$q_A = Q_B \cdot (1 + \frac{c_A}{c_B}) - q_B$$

$$= 10 \cdot 10^{-9} \cdot (1 + \frac{10 \cdot 10^{-6}}{10^{-6}}) - 910.091 \cdot 10^{-9}$$

$$= -899.091 \cdot 10^{-9} \; C$$

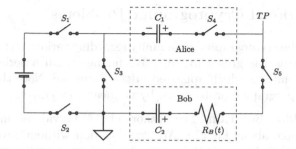

Fig. 3. Attack scenario "capacitors" solution

In [6], Courtois presents a rather intrusive attack in which Eve inserts a switch between Alice and Bob and measures the voltage (see Fig. 3). In this case, switches S_1 and S_2 are disconnected. Switch S_3 is connected, Alice's switch is S_4 and Eve's switch is S_5. S_4 and S_5 are disconnected. Eve measures the voltage between Alice and Bob, right after Alice connects her switch. After the measurement, Eve connects her switch too. This is a very simple way to determine V_{d_A}. Since Alice's capacitance is a public parameter, Eve just computes:

$$q_A = c_A \cdot V_{d_A}$$
$$= 10 \cdot 10^{-6} \cdot 89.909 \cdot 10^{-3}$$
$$= 899.09 \cdot 10^{-9} \ C$$

After running the simulation, we observed that the attack scenario is a plausible one. Note that the detection of Eve's attack depends on the quality of the equipment that she possesses.

Initially, for protecting the circuit we thought of adding a plus of security by connecting each capacitor to a different power supply. It turned out this is not enough, since Eve can measure the circuit in any point which surrounds each Alice's and Bob's private space. Thus, we dropped the idea and choose the simpler version of the two.

5   Conclusions

We recalled various physical cryptographic solutions and discussed their security in the "honest but curious" model. Thus, we provided the reader with different attacks scenarios against a set of schemes solving Yao's millionaires' problem, a number of protocols for comparing information without revealing it as well as a a public key cryptosystem based on physical properties of systems.

Acknowledgments. The authors would like to thank Valentin Petre for his helpful comments on the "Communicating Vessels" solution.

A   Recreational Cryptographic Problems

The interest of the cryptographic community regarding various recreational cryptography problems has grown in time. We further recall a series of physical cryptographic solutions which appeared in the literature. Note that our list of recreational cryptographic problems is, by no means, extensive.

"Finding Waldo" Solution. The authors of [17] provide an insight on how to convince people about knowing Waldo's location without revealing it. We initially assume that Alice and Bob have a large piece of cardboard[18]. As a first step, Alice cuts a Waldo shaped hole in the middle of the cardboard. To prove that she knows where Waldo is, Alice puts the shape precisely on top of Waldo while Bob is not looking and then calls Bob to check. Given the previous steps of the protocol, Bob learns nothing about the location of Waldo. Next, Alice must prove that she has the correct Waldo picture. Therefore, she must pull the book beneath the cardboard in front of Bob's eyes without revealing information about the place from which she is pulling the book[19].

"Ali Baba Cave" Solution. A well known story for explaining the intuition behind zero knowledge protocols is presented in [19]. The story is about a magical cave shaped like a ring with an entrance on one side as well as a magical door blocking the opposite side. We assume that Alice discovers the secret magical word that opens the door and wants to prove to Bob that she knows the secret without revealing it. Thus, they agree to label the left and right paths from the entrance `head` and `tail`. The protocol proceeds as follows. Bob waits outside the cave as Alice goes in. Then, Alice flips a coin to determine the path she follows. Note that Bob is not allowed to see which path she takes. Bob enters the cave, flips a coin and shouts the outcome. If Alice knows the magical word she opens the door, if necessary, and returns along the path chosen by Bob. If she lied about knowing it, then she has a 50% chance of returning through the correct path (*i.e.* by guessing Bob's outcome). If they repeat this protocol multiple times, the chance of Alice tricking Bob decreases. Thus, if Alice always exits through the right path, Bob can conclude that Alice really knows the secret word.

"Locked Boxes" Solution. A classical method for explaining symmetric encryption is through the use of "impenetrable" locked boxes (see [4,5]). More precisely, Alice and Bob both have a copy of the key that opens a chest. To exchange messages, Alice simply puts her letter in the box, locks it and sends it to Bob. Since Bob has an identical copy of the key, he opens the chest and reads the letter. Another protocol that can be explained using locked boxes is Shamir's three-pass protocol [14]. First, Alice puts her message in a box, locks it with her private padlock and sends it to Bob. Then, Bob places his private padlock on the box and sends it back to Alice. Once she receives the box, she removes her padlock and sends the box to Bob. Finally, Bob removes his padlock and

---

[18] at least twice as large as the picture in each dimension.

[19] At least the hole should be covered while the book is pulled out.

reads Alice's message. In order to popularize cryptography to non-specialized audiences, the authors of [4] used a toolbox or a loose chain to implement the previous physical example of Shamir's protocol. The authors point out it is easy to prove[20] to audiences that a persistent code-breaker could always dismantle a padlock, or X-ray it, and hence crack the code (*i.e.* knowing the inside of the lock is isomorphic to knowing the key). Thus, we have to employ other techniques than the secrecy of the encryption method.

By relaxing the security requirements from an "impenetrable" box to a tamper-evident box (*i.e.* the receiver can detect if someone managed to open the box) the authors of [15, 16] devise a series of secure protocols.

Ciphers Based on a Deck of Cards. Schneier designed the "Solitaire" cipher [20] for the book "Cryptonomicon" [23][21]. Solitaire was intended to be the first truly secure "pen and paper" cipher. It requires only a pack of cards both for encryption and decryption. A similar example is the "Mirdek" cipher [7].

"PEZ Dispenser" Solution. In [3] the authors present a solution for voting using a PEZ dispenser. Consider a group of kids wishing to vote between two candidates without revealing anything except the final outcome. Assume that they have a PEZ dispenser, which may be previously loaded with some publicly known sequence of red and yellow candies. The kids take turns. Each one decides how many candies to pop out of the dispenser according to his vote. Note that no other kid can see the number or the colors of these candies. Also, it is forbidden for the participants to weight the dispenser and, thus, deduce the number of remaining candies. When this process ends, the color of the candy on top has to correspond to the correct majority vote. The voting process is completed when one of the kids pops an additional candy and announces its color.

"Phonebook" Solution. Khovanova recalls on her blog [13] that, for explaining one-way functions, Micali used the following example of encryption. We start by assuming that Alice and Bob obtain the same edition of the white pages book for a particular town. For each letter Alice wants to encrypt, she finds a person in the book whose last name starts with this letter and uses his/her phone number as the encrypted version of that letter. To decrypt the message Bob has to read through the whole book to find all the numbers. The decryption will take a lot more time than the encryption. Unfortunately, the technology changes and the example is not up to date anymore: reverse look-up is always possible in a digital world. Furthermore, regarding the security of the scheme, an 8th grader said: "If I were Bob, I would just call all the phone numbers and ask their last names." A similar example may be found in [4]. Such examples are very good for teaching one-way functions to non-mathematicians.

"Colors" Solution. The Diffie-Hellman protocol can be depicted using colors as further presented. An illustration using common paint may be found in [2]. The idea, first proposed by Simon Singh [22], relies on two properties of colors:

---

[20] *e.g.* by showing a sawn up padlock.
[21] entitled "Pontifex" in the book.

① it is easy to mix two colors and ② given a color that was obtained by mixing two other colors, it is difficult to reverse the process[22]. As a specific example, we may assume that yellow ▪ is a public color. Let us further consider that Alice's secret color is blue ▪ and that Bob's secret color is red ▪. The parties wish to agree on a new shared secret color. In the first step, Alice sends green ▪ to Bob (*i.e.* the result of yellow ▪ mixed with blue ▪). Then, Bob sends orange ▪ to Alice (*i.e.* the result of yellow ▪ mixed with red ▪). By mixing the received color with the secret color, each party obtains the common secret brown ▪ (*i.e.* Alice mixes orange ▪ with her blue ▪ and Bob mixes green ▪ with red ▪).

Although insecure[23], the digital version of the above protocol is a good teaching tool *e.g.* when trying to explain beginners how to use colors in the case of programming languages used in web development.

B   Physical Public Key Encryption

We further present a generic protocol based on the protocols described in [11]. Alice and Bob have access to a physical medium characterized by a parameter $p(t)$, such that $p(t)$ has two components $p = p_a(t) \circ p_b(t)$, where $\circ$ is a group law and $p_a(t)$, $p_b(t)$ can randomly be changed by varying t. In her private spaces U and V, Alice and Bob secretly vary $p_a(t)$ and, respectively, $p_b(t)$. Note that Eve only has access to $p(t)$. First Alice and Bob randomly vary $p_a(t)$ and $p_b(t)$. When they agree to synchronize[24], Alice and Bob stabilize their parameters $p_a(t') = a$ and $p_b(t') = b$. Bob can measure $p(t') = a \circ b$ and deduce Alice's value a. Similarly, Alice can compute b.

Example. We consider the setup from Sect. 2.3. Thus, the components that Alice and Bob vary are their corresponding speeds values a and b. Once the system is stabilized Bob can deduce a using the attack we described in Sect. 2.3, but Eve can only deduce $b - a$.

References

1. Falstad Electronic Circuit. https://www.falstad.com
2. The Diffie-Hellman Key Exchange Using Paint. https://www.youtube.com/watch?v=3QnD2c4Xovk
3. Balogh, J., Csirik, J.A., Ishai, Y., Kushilevitz, E.: Private computation using a PEZ dispenser. Theor. Comput. Sci. **306**(1–3), 69–84 (2003)
4. Bell, T., Thimbleby, H., Fellows, M., Witten, I., Koblitz, N., Powell, M.: Explaining cryptographic systems. Comput. Educ. **40**(3), 199–215 (2003)
5. Bultel, X., Dreier, J., Lafourcade, P., More, M.: How to explain modern security concepts to your children. Cryptologia **41**(5), 422–447 (2017)

---

[22] And obtain the initial colors.

[23] When mixing two colors which can be described in the RGB (Red-Green-Blue) color model one can revert the process due to the uniqueness of each color. Note that such a phenomenon does not happen when working with paint.

[24] Through the use of an authenticated channel.

6. Courtois, N.T.: Cryptanalysis of Grigoriev-Shpilrain Physical Asymmetric Scheme With Capacitors. IACR Cryptology ePrint Archive (2013). http://eprint.iacr.org/2013/302
7. Crowley, P.: Mirdek: a card cipher inspired by "Solitaire". http://www.ciphergoth.org/crypto/mirdek/
8. Fagin, R., Naor, M., Winkler, P.: Comparing information without leaking it. Commun. ACM **39**(5), 77–85 (1996)
9. Grigoriev, D., Kish, L.B., Shpilrain, V.: Yao's Millionaires' problem and public-key encryption without computational assumptions. Int. J. Found. Comput. Sci. **28**(4), 379–390 (2017)
10. Grigoriev, D., Shpilrain, V.: Secure information transmission based on physical principles. In: Mauri, G., Dennunzio, A., Manzoni, L., Porreca, A.E. (eds.) UCNC 2013. LNCS, vol. 7956, pp. 113–124. Springer, Heidelberg (2013). https://doi.org/10.1007/978-3-642-39074-6_12
11. Grigoriev, D., Shpilrain, V.: Yao's millionaires' problem and decoy-based public key encryption by classical physics. Int. J. Found. Comput. Sci. **25**(4), 409–418 (2014)
12. Halliday, D., Resnick, R., Walker, J.: Fundamentals of Physics. Wiley, Hoboken (2010)
13. Khovanova, T.: One-Way Functions. https://blog.tanyakhovanova.com/2010/11/one-way-functions/
14. Menezes, A.J., Van Oorschot, P.C., Vanstone, S.A.: Handbook of Applied Cryptography. CRC Press, Boca Raton (1996)
15. Moran, T., Naor, M.: Polling with physical envelopes: a rigorous analysis of a human-centric protocol. In: Vaudenay, S. (ed.) EUROCRYPT 2006. LNCS, vol. 4004, pp. 88–108. Springer, Heidelberg (2006). https://doi.org/10.1007/11761679_7
16. Moran, T., Naor, M.: Basing cryptographic protocols on tamper-evident seals. Theor. Comput. Sci. **411**(10), 1283–1310 (2010)
17. Naor, M., Naor, Y., Reingold, O.: Applied kid cryptography or how to convince your children you are not cheating. http://www.wisdom.weizmann.ac.il/~naor/PAPERS/waldo.pdf
18. Nishigami, K., Iwamura, K.: Geometric pairwise key-sharing scheme. In: Lanet, J.-L., Toma, C. (eds.) SECITC 2018. LNCS, vol. 11359, pp. 518–528. Springer, Cham (2019). https://doi.org/10.1007/978-3-030-12942-2_38
19. Quisquater, J.-J., et al.: How to explain zero-knowledge protocols to your children. In: Brassard, G. (ed.) CRYPTO 1989. LNCS, vol. 435, pp. 628–631. Springer, New York (1990). https://doi.org/10.1007/0-387-34805-0_60
20. Schneier, B.: The Solitaire Encryption Algorithm. https://www.schneier.com/academic/solitaire/
21. Shpilrain, V.: Groups Complexity Cryptology. Decoy-Based Inf. Secur. **6**(2), 149–155 (2014)
22. Singh, S.: The Code Book: The Science of Secrecy from Ancient Egypt to Quantum Cryptography. Anchor, New York City (2000)
23. Stephenson, N.: Cryptonomicon. Arrow (2000)
24. Yao, A.C.: Protocols for secure computations. In: SFCS 1982, pp. 160–164. IEEE Computer Society (1982)

Logic Locking of Boolean Circuits: Provable Hardware-Based Obfuscation from a Tamper-Proof Memory

Giovanni Di Crescenzo[1(✉)], Abhrajit Sengupta[2], Ozgur Sinanoglu[3], and Muhammad Yasin[2]

[1] Perspecta Labs, Basking Ridge, NJ, USA
gdicrescenzo@perspectalabs.com
[2] New York University, New York, NY, USA
{as9397,yasin}@nyu.edu
[3] New York University, Abu Dhabi, UAE
os22@nyu.edu

Abstract. Today's integrated circuits are subject to a variety of attacks. Logic Locking is an area of hardware security that attempts to prevent reverse-engineering of integrated circuits based on a tamper-resistant memory. Despite significant attention from the research literature, no rigorous cryptographic modeling of logic locking and associated provable secure solutions have been proposed.

Based on the observation that logic locking can be seen as a special case of hardware-based cryptographic program obfuscation, we propose rigorous definitions, borrowing approaches from modern cryptography (and, specifically, cryptographic program obfuscation), for both tamper-proof memories and logic locking of boolean circuits. We then prove two positive results: (1) the existence of a circuit computationally indistinguishable from a random oracle, assuming the existence of a pseudo-random function and of a tamper-proof memory, and (2) logic locking of general polynomial-size boolean circuits, assuming the existence of a pseudo-random generator and a tamper-proof memory.

Our paper shows the possibility of provably boosting the capability of constructing a physical memory with a suitable tamper-resistant property into hardware-based obfuscation of any boolean circuit, as well as a practical hardware-based realization of a random oracle.

Keywords: Logic locking · Program obfuscation · Tamper-proof memory

The first author's work was supported by the Defense Advanced Research Projects Agency (DARPA) via U.S. Army Research Office (ARO), contract number W911NF-15-C-0233. The U.S. Government is authorized to reproduce and distribute reprints for Governmental purposes notwithstanding any copyright annotation hereon. Disclaimer: The views and conclusions contained herein are those of the authors and should not be interpreted as necessarily representing the official policies or endorsements, either expressed or implied, of DARPA, ARO or the U.S. Government.

© Springer Nature Switzerland AG 2020
E. Simion and R. Géraud-Stewart (Eds.): SecITC 2019, LNCS 12001, pp. 172–192, 2020.
https://doi.org/10.1007/978-3-030-41025-4_12

1   Introduction

In the past few decades, the semiconductor industry has seen a gradual shift from the vertical to the horizontal model, where many companies nowadays operate completely fabless. Though economically beneficial, it has lead to several security threats in the integrated circuit (IC) supply chain. The design companies are forced to share their valuable intellectual property (IP) with off-shore *untrusted* foundries, who can easily reverse-engineer the design with malicious intent. Given the inadequate state-of-the-art hardware protection techniques, these threats are becoming an increasing concern for commercial/government organizations. It has been estimated that out of all the "spare and replacement" semiconductors bought by the Pentagon, 15% are counterfeit [3].

To counter such threats at the silicon layer, logic locking was presented [23]. The idea is to insert additional circuitry in the design that expects a *secret* key for proper functioning of the IC. Without this secret key, the output of a locked IC is corrupted, thereby rendering a it completely useless. Usually, the secret key is assumed to be stored on chip in a *tamper-proof* memory [29]. The threat model involves an attacker having following capabilities: (1) access to complete reverse-engineered locked netlist, without the secret key; and (2) running a working chip with the correct key embedded into its memory, choosing input patterns and observing corresponding outputs to recover the key.

Motivated by recently increasing piracy concerns as well as recent interesting research in the logic locking area, we start a comprehensive and rigorous approach to the study of (provably secure) logic locking. To specifically target provable security, we leverage modeling and research approaches in the modern cryptography, where cryptosystems are proved secure under a widely accepted intractability assumption. In particular, our security modeling is inspired by research in cryptographic program obfuscation [5], where the most typical security requirement says that white-box attacks to a program are not significantly better than black-box attacks to an oracle that computes the program's function.

Prior Work. Roy et al. first presented the concept of logic locking in their pioneering work in [23]. Later, to improve output corruption a fault analysis-based technique was presented in [22]. However, both [22,23] were shown to be vulnerable against sensitization of individual key bits at the output ports of the IC [38]. Thus, to preclude such scenario, a clique-based approach was presented [38]. Nevertheless, a Boolean satisfiability (SAT)-based attack completely undermined the security of locking by breaking all the then-existing techniques [27]. This forced the community to develop SAT-resilient locking techniques such as SARLock [37], Anti-SAT [34], SFLL [34], CycLock [24], and Delay-Lock [35]. However, none of these techniques has been formally proved secure, and most of them suffer from structural flaws, which were eventually exploited to break these schemes [25,36,40]. Furthermore, other advanced variants of the SAT attack was presented that broke the remaining techniques [4,9,41]. For a comprehensive summary on logic locking, we refer the reader to [39].

In program obfuscation, the goal is to modify source or machine code into functionally equivalent code that is hard to understand to a human or another program. Early obfuscation techniques included heuristic code transformations; however, many of these techniques were found to be ineffective against sufficiently motivated adversaries. In the more recent area of cryptographic program obfuscation, researchers target the design of program obfuscators that are provably hiding the original program under a widely accepted intractability assumption, following the standard of modern cryptography solutions. An early negative result from [5] showed that most likely no software-only cryptographic program obfuscator can be given for any arbitrary polynomial-size program. Later, positive results showed software-only cryptographic program obfuscations of specific classes of polynomial-size programs (e.g., point functions of fixed [31] and arbitrary length [11], short-distance matching functions [13], monotone formulae over point functions [10], and compute-and-compare programs [32]). There are also results on hardware-based cryptographic program obfuscation (starting with encryptions and signatures [14]), which however do require a trusted physical module to perform actual computations.

Our Contribution. Based on our characterization of logic locking as a special case of hardware-based cryptographic program obfuscation, we use ideas from this latter area to propose a rigorous cryptographic model both for a tamper-proof memory and for logic locking (based on a tamper-proof memory). Briefly speaking, a logic locking scheme will be defined as a method to transform the *original circuit c* into a *locked circuit c'* made of two parts: a tamper-proof memory tpM containing a string k, and an *unlocked circuit* $c'(k, \cdot)$. This transformation will have to at least satisfy the following two properties: (a) the output of a locked circuit is (almost) always the same as that of the original circuit; and (b) even given oracle access to the locked circuit and read access to the unlocked circuit, an adversary cannot guess the original circuit better than an efficient algorithm which is given oracle access to the original circuit. Using modeling ideas from program obfuscation already proved useful in formulating the first rigorous model of circuit camouflaging [12].

Our first result is the *first provably secure logic locking* result. Assuming tamper-proof memories and the existence of families of pseudo-random functions (a standard assumption in modern cryptography), we prove security of logic locking of any pseudo-random function (key included). The provability of this result validates our formal definitions of tamper-proof memory and secure logic locking. Moreover, it results in a provable hardware-based implementation of a pseudo-random oracle only based on a tamper-proof memory (and a pseudo-random function). Finding conditions for provable realizations of random oracles has been an open problem for many years. On one hand, random oracles have been used to enable several cryptographic constructions; on the other hand a software-only provable implementation of random oracles was proved to be (almost certainly) impossible (see [8], as well as [19] for a survey of the area).

A previous hardware-based provable design of random oracles was presented in [12], assuming different physical techniques of gate camouflaging.

Our second provably secure logic locking result is a general-purpose result, saying that using pseudo-random generators and universal circuits, we can achieve logic locking of *any arbitrary* polynomial-size circuit. In this construction, the output of the pseudo-random generator is used as a pad that encrypts/decrypts the original circuit into/from a locked circuit, and only the generator's seed is stored onto the tamper-proof memory. To the best of our knowledge, this is the *first* logic locking result for the class of all polynomial-size circuits provably secure in a cryptographic model, and the *first* provably secure hardware-based obfuscation of any arbitrary polynomial-size circuit from a tamper-proof memory (previous hardware-based obfuscation results required the tamper-proof device to perform actual computation). This should be contrasted with positive results in cryptographic program obfuscation, where, using software-only techniques, obfuscators have been designed only for a handful of simple functions or specific classes of functions (see, e.g., [6,13,20,31,32]).

2   Models and Definitions

Basic Definitions. By $|x|$ we denote the length of x if x is a string, the size of x if x is a set, the number of gates of x if x is a circuit. By σ we denote the security parameter, available in unary notation (i.e., 1^σ) to all algorithms (and thus often omitted among algorithm inputs in the rest of the paper). A function ϵ over the set of natural numbers is *negligible* in parameter n if for any constant c, there exists an integer n_0 such that for all $n \geq n_0$, it holds that $\epsilon(n) \leq 1/n^c$. Unless otherwise specified, we will use functions that are negligible in the security parameter σ.

Given a (discrete) probability distribution D, the notation $x \leftarrow D$ is used to denote the random process of independently drawing a sample x according to D. Similarly, the notation $y \leftarrow A(x)$, where A is an algorithm, denotes the random process of obtaining y when running algorithm A on input x, where the probability space is given by the random coins (if any) of algorithm A. By $\text{Prob}[R_1; \ldots; R_n : E]$ we denote the probability of event E, after the sequential execution of random processes $R_1, \ldots, R_n$.

We assume the reader is familiar with the conventional notion of a *boolean circuit*. On input an n-bit string x, a circuit c returns an output $c(x)$. A circuit with two input strings, of which the first one has been set to a value s, is also denoted as $c(s, \cdot)$. We also fix a conventional encoding of a boolean circuit c into a binary string, denoted as $b(c)$. Such encodings are often used in the literature in constructions where a circuit takes as input (the binary encoding of) another circuit. For modeling purposes, we consider function computation as implemented on hardware via a generic, but also conventional, notion of *physical boolean circuit*. As algorithmic computation is defined over digital strings, and we would like to produce algorithm computation reasonings, we now define a suitable abstraction of physical boolean circuits into digital strings. More formally, we define the *logical abstraction of a physical boolean circuit c* as the above conventional encoding $b(c)$ of c as a binary string.

A Cryptographic Model for Tamper-Proof Memories. We consider a tamper-proof memory as a hardware-implemented *physical memory* containing a (typically, randomly chosen) binary string, also called the *key*. As algorithmic computation is defined over digital strings, we need to define logical abstractions of a physical memory into a digital string.

We formally define a *logical abstraction of a physical memory* as a map associating a physical memory to the binary string stored on it (i.e., the key). A *conventional logical abstraction* entails mapping a physical memory to its digital content, which can be set at startup time and then updated according to some distribution. In this paper, for simplicity, and without loss of generality, we focus on a single epoch, by considering physical memories whose content is set once according to a given distribution (typically, the uniform distribution over strings of a known length) and then left unchanged for the rest of the computation. Then, the logical abstraction of such physical memories is, to an honest user, a binary string of known length (but whose value is only known to the entity that had set it at startup time). We stress, however, that an adversary does not need to generate this same logical abstraction. Thus, in our formal definitions below, we target security even against adversaries maliciously generating logical abstractions of physical memories.

To formalize the *adversary's resources*, we consider adversaries as algorithms that run in time polynomial (in security parameter σ), where the size (i.e., number of gates) of circuit c, denoted as $|c|$, is also polynomial in σ. In terms of *resource access*, we consider adversaries with both read and oracle access to resources related to physical circuits. An efficient algorithm Adv has *read access* to a physical resource if it can generate a logical abstraction of the physical resource. We consider adversaries that have read access to two physical resources: the tamper-proof memory tpM and a circuit c. We note that although there is a conventional logical abstraction of the tamper-proof memory tpM (i.e., an unknown binary string of a known length), and of circuit c (i.e., the digital encoding of the same boolean circuit), the adversary is not restricted to use those logical abstractions. Moreover, we consider adversaries with oracle access to functions, meaning that they can return an output after multiple adaptive queries to the oracle. More formally, we say that an efficient algorithm Adv has *oracle access* to function O if it can run the following attack experiment, briefly denoted as '$out \leftarrow Adv^O(1^\sigma)$', for some m polynomial in σ:

1. for $i = 1, \ldots, m$,
   on input $x_1, y_1, \ldots, x_{i-1}, y_{i-1}$, compute x_i;
   call oracle O on input x_i; and
   set y_i be the response obtained from O on input x_i.
2. on input $x_1, y_1, \ldots, x_m, y_m$, return: *out*

We say that *Adv* is an *oracle adversary* if it is given oracle access to function *O*. In our model, the adversary has oracle access to the locked circuit (whose computation depends on the content of the tamper-proof memory).

We now define a tamper-proof memory as a physical object on which two operations are possible, which satisfy requirements on memory correctness, efficiency of runtime and memory size, and tamper-proof security, which are informally described as follows. The two possible operations consist of (a) storing a binary string of a given length (not larger than a parameter value), and (b) retrieving a binary string. The memory correctness requirement says that the retrieve operation always returns the binary string stored at the latest store operation. The efficient runtime and memory size naturally say that it is desirable to have computationally fast store and retrieve operation and a small-size memory. The tamper-proof security requirement is defined relatively to computation of the locked circuit and says that, for any circuit and any efficient adversary, the adversary's physical access to the tamper-proof memory is not significantly more useful in computing the original circuit than the length of the binary string stored on the memory. The formal definition of tamper-proof memories is split into two parts for better clarity. First, we define a (not necessarily secure) memory as a physical object with associated store and retrieve operations.

Definition 1. Let *tpM* denote a (physical) computer memory. We say that *tpM* is a (t, λ)-*memory* if there exists a pair of algorithms (tpMStore, tpMRetrieve) with the following syntax:

1. On input a length parameter 1^λ and a string r, and given store access to *tpM*, algorithm tpMStore returns either a failure output 0 (indicating that the storage operation somehow failed, possibly because r is too long) or a success output 1 (indicating that r is the next string to be stored on the tamper-proof memory *tpM*)
2. On input length parameter 1^λ, and given retrieve access from *tpM*, algorithm tpMRetrieve returns a string s (indicating that s is the string that is currently stored on the tamper-proof memory *tpM*).

which satisfies the following properties:

1. (Memory correctness): For any sequence of executions of algorithms tpMStore and tpMRetrieve, for any execution of tpMRetrieve in this sequence, the string s output by this execution is equal to the string r used as input in the most recent execution of tpMStore that returned 1.
2. (t-efficient runtime): Algorithms tpMStore, tpMRetrieve run in time $\leq t$
3. (λ-efficient memory size): Algorithms tpMStore, tpMRetrieve operate on memory *tpM* using a length parameter $\leq \lambda$.

Although for modeling purposes, we abstract both tpMStore and tpMRetrieve operations as algorithms, we note that in practice they might just be realized using minimal or no circuit logic. For instance, the tpMRetrieve operation could be realized by circuit wires exiting the memory, and the tpMStore operation is typically only used during the deployment phase, and is thus not part of the locked circuit.

We now formally define our notion of a tamper-proof property for a memory tpM from Definition 1, relatively to computation of circuits in a class $\mathcal{C}$. This property is defined to hold in the presence of an adversary who has oracle access to the locked circuit $c'(s, \cdot)$ corresponding to any circuit $c \in \mathcal{C}$, and tries to guess c after generating its own logical abstraction of memory tpM.

Definition 2. Let tpM denote a (t, λ)-memory, and let (tpMStore, tpMRetrieve) be the pair of algorithms associated with it. Also, let $\mathcal{C}$ be a family of boolean circuits. We say that tpM is ϵ-*tamper-proof with respect to computation of circuits in* $\mathcal{C}$ (briefly, ϵ-*tamper-proof*) if for any (original) circuit $c \in \mathcal{C}$, any string s returned by tpMRetrieve and any (unlocked) circuit c' such that $c'(s, x) = c(x)$ for all x, and for any efficient algorithm Adv, and any logical abstraction L, it holds that $|p_0 - p_1| \leq \epsilon$, where

$$p_0 = \mathrm{Prob}\left[c'' \leftarrow Adv^{c'(s, \cdot)}(c', L(tpM)) : c'' = c \right] \text{ and}$$

$$p_1 = \mathrm{Prob}\left[c'' \leftarrow Adv^{c'(s, \cdot)}(c', 1^\lambda) : c'' = c \right],$$

for some $\epsilon > 0$ (intended to be a known very small quantity or negligible as a function of security parameter σ). Finally, we define an (ϵ, t, λ)-*tamper-proof memory* as a (t, λ)-memory that is also ϵ-tamper-proof.

Remark: Average-Case Tamper-Proof Security. The above security property can be considered a worst-case variant, in that it holds for any arbitrary circuit from the circuit family $\mathcal{C}$. Also of interest is the *average-case* variant of this *tamper-proof security* property, which is formulated almost in the same way, but with respect to a randomly chosen circuit from its class. This variant's formalization is simply obtained by replacing the quantification 'For any circuit $c \in \mathcal{C}$' with the random process 'For any circuit c randomly chosen from $\mathcal{C}$', and c's random choice is also part of the probability space in which p_0, p_1 are computed.

Remark: Proofs vs Conjectures. Note that for any given physical realization of a tamper-proof memory, the memory correctness, efficient runtime and efficient memory size can be verified, while the security property can at best be conjectured to hold (as typically done for any security property assumed for these and similar physical devices in the literature).

Remark: Tamper-Resistance Approaches. A practical implementation of *read-proof* hardware was presented in [29], combining protective coating that contains much randomness, and fuzzy extractors. In the literature, tamper resistance is often categorized into these 4 categories: (1) tamper prevention, (2) tamper detection, (3) tamper response, and (4) tamper evidence. Tamper prevention against invasive and non-invasive attacks includes several approaches such as encapsulation/coating [17], security fuses [28], and/or layout and data bus scrambling [33]. Means to target tamper detection include anti-tamper switches, anti-tamper sensors, and anti-tamper circuits [2]. Tamper response is a type of technique that employs certain action upon detection of tampering with a device. Possible set of responses include disabling the device, erasing critical part of the memory [26], and complete destruction of the device [1]. Finally, tamper evidence techniques include ensuring visible footprint on the device if tampering occurs.

A Cryptographic Model for Logic Locking. We define a secure logic locking scheme as a pair of algorithms, satisfying requirements on lock correctness, security and efficiency of circuit expansion and memory size, informally described as follows. The algorithms consist of (a) generating a binary string of a given length (not larger than a parameter value), intended to be stored on the tamper-proof memory, and (b) generating a locked circuit to be used in conjunction with the tamper-proof memory content, and intended to produce an equivalent computation. The lock correctness requirement says that the computation performed by the combined locked circuit and tamper-proof memory content, is equivalent to the original circuit's computation, in the sense that no efficient algorithm can find an input on which the two differ with more than negligible probability.

The security requirement (relative to locked-circuit computation) says that, for any circuit and any efficient adversary, the adversary's read access to the locked circuit, physical access to the tamper-proof memory, and oracle access to the combined circuit are not significantly more useful in computing an expression for the original circuit than trying to compute such an expression only based on oracle access to the original circuit itself. The efficient circuit expansion and memory size naturally say that it is desirable to have computationally fast locked circuits and a small-size tamper-proof memory. A formal definition follows.

Definition 3. Let $\mathcal{C}$ be a class of boolean circuits, let tpM denote the physical object representing a tamper-proof memory, and let (tpMStore, tpMRetrieve) denote the pair of algorithms associated to it. We define an (ϵ, t, λ)-*secure logic locking scheme* for $\mathcal{C}$ as a pair of algorithms (KeyGen, LockGen) with the following syntax:

1. On input a length parameter 1^λ and a security parameter 1^σ, the *key generation* algorithm KeyGen returns a λ-bit key k.
2. On input a length parameter 1^λ, and a security parameter 1^σ, key k and circuit $c \in \mathcal{C}$, the *lock generation* algorithm LockGen returns the *unlocked circuit* c'. This implicitly defines the *locked circuit* $c'(k, \cdot)$, which is intended to be (almost) equivalent to the original circuit c.

and the following properties:

1. (Computation correctness): For any n-input circuit $c \in \mathcal{C}$, and all n-bit strings x, for any efficient algorithm Adv, the probability that $c'(k, x) \neq c(x)$ is negligible in σ, where k, c', x are generated as follows:

- $k \leftarrow \text{KeyGen}(1^\lambda)$;
- $c' \leftarrow \text{LockGen}(c, k)$;
- $x \leftarrow Adv^{c'(k, \cdot)}(1^\lambda, 1^\sigma, c', LogAbs(tpM))$

2. (lock ϵ-security, with respect to circuit computation, worst-case variant): For any circuit $c \in \mathcal{C}$, any efficient algorithm Adv, and any logical abstraction $LogAbs$, there exists an efficient algorithm Sim such that $|\text{Prob}[c_{adv} = c] - \text{Prob}[c_{sim} = c]| \leq \epsilon$, where ϵ is negligible as a function of σ, c_{sim} is generated as $c_{sim} \leftarrow Sim^{c(\cdot)}(1^\lambda, 1^\sigma)$ and c_{adv} is generated as follows:
   - $k \leftarrow \text{KeyGen}(1^\lambda, 1^\sigma)$;
   - $b \leftarrow \text{tpMStore}(1^\lambda, k; tpM)$
   - $c' \leftarrow \text{LockGen}(1^\lambda, 1^\sigma, c, k)$;
   - $c_{adv} \leftarrow Adv^{c'(k, \cdot)}(1^\lambda, 1^\sigma, c', LogAbs(tpM))$.

3. (t-efficient circuit expansion): The size of circuit c' is $\leq t$.
4. (λ-efficient memory size): The size of memory tpM is $\leq \lambda$.

Remark: Two Variants and One More Security Property. One can strengthen the above security property to a *no-oracle* version where Sim does *not* have oracle access to the original circuit. Our first construction satisfies this stronger version. Similarly as for tamper-proof memories, even the above security property can be considered a worst-case variant, in that it holds for any arbitrary circuit from the circuit family $\mathcal{C}$, and it is of interest to consider the *average-case* variant, formulated with respect to a randomly chosen circuit from its class. As before, in this variant the quantification 'For any circuit $c \in \mathcal{C}$' is replaced with the random process 'For any circuit c randomly chosen from $\mathcal{C}$', and c's random choice is also part of the probability space in which $\text{Prob}[c_{adv} = c]$ and $\text{Prob}[c_{sim} = c]$ are computed. Our main constructions will also directly achieve security against an attacker capable of reading the content of the tamper-proof memory before the latter is deployed in connection with a circuit. Informally, this *intrusion-resilience* property says that the content of the tamper-proof memory does not leak any information about the circuit or the circuit's sensitive information. Details of a formal treatment for this definition and proof are omitted in this version.

3   A Pseudo-random Oracle Construction

In this section we consider a rather natural logic locking scheme based on tamper-proof memories, and show a proof that it satisfies lock security (in the sense of the average-case variant of Definition 3) assuming the memory is tamper-proof (in the sense of the average-case variant of Definitions 1 and 2). This gives evidence that definitions from Sect. 2 meet intuitive notions of secure tamper-proof memories and secure logic locking schemes. Our construction is very natural: the unlocked circuit computes a pseudo-random function taking as input a random key locked in the tamper-proof memory. This gives a construction of a pseudo-random oracle under the existence of pseudo-random functions and rigorously specified hardware assumptions (i.e., the tamper-proof properties from Definitions 1 and 2). Formally, we obtain the following

Theorem 1. Let $\mathcal{C}$ be the family of all n-bit input and m-bit output circuits. If there exists

1. an $(\epsilon_{tpm}, t_{tpm}, \lambda)$-tamper-proof, in the average-case sense, memory tpM,
2. a family prF of ϵ_{prf}-pseudo-random functions with κ-bit keys, n-bit inputs and m-bit outputs, computable by circuits of size t_{prf},

where $\lambda \geq \kappa$, then there exists (constructively) a logic locking scheme for $\mathcal{C}$ that is $(\epsilon', t', \lambda')$-secure in the average-case sense, where $t' = O(t_{prf} + t_{tpm} + \lambda)$, $\epsilon' \leq \epsilon_{prf} + \epsilon_{tpm}$ is negligible in σ, and $\lambda' = \lambda$.

Note that a random oracle with n-bit inputs and m-bit outputs can be equivalently defined as a function randomly chosen in the family $\mathcal{C}$ used in Theorem 1. In the rest of this section we describe the logic locking scheme satisfying the theorem. The formal definition of pseudo-random functions is recalled in Appendix A.

The Logic Locking Scheme. On input an (original) circuit randomly chosen from the class of all polynomial-size circuits, this construction of a logic locking scheme first randomly chooses a key k and stores it into the tamper-proof memory tpM. Then, it returns an unlocked circuit computing a pseudo-random function $prF_{n,m}$ taking as input the key retrieved from the tamper-proof memory and the n-bit input string and returning an m-bit output. Finally, the locked circuit is implicitly defined as the direct combination of the tamper-proof memory and the unlocked circuit; i.e., the locked circuit performs the unlocked circuit's computation based on the key stored on the tamper-proof memory. Now, we proceed more formally.

Let 1^σ be a security parameter, let tpM be a tamper-proof memory with memory size $\lambda \geq \kappa$, and let (tpMStore, tpMRetrieve) be the pair of algorithms associated with it. We define logic locking scheme for the family $\mathcal{C}$ of all polynomial-size circuits with n-bit inputs and m-bit outputs as the following pair of algorithms (KeyGen1, LockGen1).

Input to KeyGen1: length parameter 1^λ

Instructions for KeyGen1:

1. $k \leftarrow \{0,1\}^\kappa$
2. $b \leftarrow \text{tpMStore}(1^\lambda, k; tpM)$
3. if $b = 1$ then return: k else return: $\perp$.

Input to LockGen1: length parameter 1^λ, key $k \in \{0,1\}^\kappa$, original circuit $c \in \mathcal{C}$

Instructions for LockGen1:

1. let $k = \text{tpMRetrieve}(1^\lambda; tpM)$
2. let n and m denote the input and output length, respectively, for c
3. let c' be the unlocked circuit computing $prF_{n,m}(k, \cdot)$ this implicitly defines locked circuit $c'(k, \cdot)$
4. return: c'.

The proof that scheme (KeyGen1, LockGen1) satisfies Theorem 1 is in Appendix C. Here, we give some intuitions behind the proof for the lock security requirement. We prove the (stronger) no-oracle variant of the lock security property by a hybrid argument [16], where, informally speaking, we evaluate and compare the success probability of adversary Adv in guessing the original circuit c in 4 different worlds. First, we use the tamper-proof security property of tpM to show that Adv's success probability p_0 in guessing c when given oracle access to the locked circuit and read access to the unlocked circuit and tamper-proof memory is only negligibly different than Adv's success probability p_0' in guessing c when given oracle access to the locked circuit and read access to the unlocked circuit and the length parameter for tpM. Next, we use the pseudo-randomness of $prF_{n,m}$ to show that p_0' is only negligibly different than Adv's success probability p_1' in guessing c when given oracle access to a random circuit and read access to the unlocked circuit and the length parameter for tpM. Finally, we use a simulation argument to show that p_1' is only negligibly different than an efficient algorithm's success probability p_1 in guessing c when given read access to the unlocked circuit and the length parameter for tpM. This proves the (no-oracle, average-case) version of the lock security definition.

4   A Provable General-Purpose Construction

In this section we show a logic locking construction that is general-purpose (i.e., it applies to any polynomial-size original circuit, thus being secure in the sense of the worst-case variant of Definition 3), and it satisfies some non-trivial efficiency properties (e.g., it uses a tamper-proof memory of size independent on the original circuit's size). Our scheme combines a tamper-proof memory with universal circuits and pseudo-random generators. Formally, we obtain the following

Theorem 2. Let C be the family of all ℓ_x-bit input and 1-bit output circuits. If there exist

1. a $(\epsilon_{tpm}, t_{tpm}, \lambda)$-secure, in the worst-case sense, tamper-proof memory tpM
2. a family prG of ϵ_{prg}-pseudo-random generators with σ-bit seeds, computable by circuits of size t_{prg},

where $\lambda \geq \sigma$, then there exists (constructively) a logic locking scheme for C that is $(\epsilon', t', \lambda')$-secure in the worst-case sense, where $t' = O(t_{prg} + t_{tpm} + \lambda)$, $\epsilon' \leq \epsilon_{prg} + \epsilon_{tpm}$ is negligible in σ, and $\lambda' = \lambda$.

We note that an arbitrary polynomial-size circuit with n-bit inputs can be defined as circuits arbitrarily chosen in the family C used in Theorem 2, and thus the theorem shows logic locking of any arbitrary polynomial-size circuit. In the rest of this section we describe the logic locking scheme satisfying the theorem. Definition and properties of universal circuits are recalled in Appendix B.

The Logic Locking Scheme. On input an arbitrary original circuit c with n-bit inputs and m-bit outputs, and size polynomial in n, our construction of a logic locking scheme goes as follows. As before a key k is randomly chosen and stored into the tamper-proof memory tpM. The lock generation algorithm returns an unlocked circuit composing a hardwired string, a circuit for a pseudo-random generator prG and a universal circuit, as follows: first, the hardwired string is defined as the xor between $prG(k)$ and a conventional binary encoding $b(c)$ of the original circuit c; then, the circuit for the pseudo-random generator prG computes $prG(k)$, where k is the string retrieved from the tamper-proof memory tpM; finally, the output of the circuit for prG and the hardwired string are xored, and the resulting string is the binary encoding of the circuit that is evaluated by the universal circuit. As before, the locked circuit is then implicitly defined as the natural combination of the unlocked circuit and the tamper-proof memory. Note that the hardwired string is distributed as a pseudo-random string (with its seed being hidden by the tamper-proof memory) and the remaining part of the unlocked circuit only uses xor, and the universal circuit. Thus, the entire unlocked circuit does not leak anything about the original circuit c, other than its size parameters. Now, we proceed more formally.

Let tpM be a tamper-proof memory, and let (tpMStore, tpMRetrieve) be the pair of algorithms associated with it. We define logic locking scheme for the family $\mathcal{C}$ of all circuits of size bounded by a polynomial in the number of inputs, as the following pair of algorithms (KeyGen2, LockGen2).

Input to KeyGen2: length parameter 1^λ

Instructions for KeyGen2:

1. $k \leftarrow \{0,1\}^\sigma$
2. $b \leftarrow \text{tpMStore}(1^\lambda, k; tpM)$
3. if $b = 1$ then return: k.

Input to LockGen2: length parameter 1^λ, polynomial bound parameter q, key $k \in \{0,1\}^\sigma$, circuit $c \in \mathcal{C}$ over ℓ_x-bit inputs with binary encoding length $\leq \ell_c$

Instructions for LockGen2:

1. let $k = \text{tpMRetrieve}(1^\lambda; tpM)$
2. let c_u be the universal circuit for circuits with binary encoding length $\leq \ell_c$ and taking ℓ_x-bit inputs
3. let $b(c)$ denote the binary string encoding circuit c
4. set $y = prG_{\sigma,m}(k)$ xor $b(c)$, where $m = \ell_c$
5. define circuit c'_y as follows:
   c'_y has string y hardwired
   c'_y takes 2 inputs:
     an ℓ_x-bit string x
     the string k previously retrieved from tpM
   c'_y computes $w = y$ xor $prG_{\sigma,m}(k)$, where $m = \ell_c$
   c'_y computes $c_u(w,x)$ and returns its output
   this implicitly defines locked circuit $c'_y(k, \cdot)$
6. return: c'_y.

The proof that scheme (KeyGen2, LockGen2) satisfies Theorem 2 is in Appendix D. Here, we give some intuitions behind the proof for the lock security requirement, which is proved by a hybrid argument [16], where, informally speaking, we evaluate and compare the success probability of adversary Adv in guessing the original circuit c in 4 different worlds. First, we use the tamper-proof security property of tpM to show that Adv's success probability $p_{adv,1}$ in guessing c when given oracle access to the locked circuit and read access to the unlocked circuit (with pseudo-random string y hardwired) and tamper-proof memory tpM, is only negligibly different than Adv's success probability $p_{adv,2}$ in guessing c when given oracle access to the locked circuit and read access to the unlocked circuit and the length parameter for tpM. Next, we use the pseudo-randomness of prG to show that $p_{adv,2}$ is only negligibly different than Adv's success probability $p_{adv,3}$ in guessing c when given oracle access to the locked circuit and read access to the unlocked circuit (with a random string z hardwired instead of y) and the length parameter for tpM. Finally, we use the simulatability property of the universal circuit to show that $p_{adv,3}$ is equal to an efficient algorithm's success probability $p_{adv,4}$ in guessing c when given oracle access to the locked circuit. This proves the (worst-case) version of the lock security definition.

5   Conclusions

Recent positive results in logic locking and hardware-based program obfuscation seem to suggest the possibility for protection of integrated circuits against various attacks (e.g., reverse-engineering). However, logic locking results were not accompanied by proofs in a rigorous cryptographic model, and hardware-based program obfuscation results were still based on strong assumptions, such as devices that perform trusted computations.

In this paper we started our investigation by observing similarities between the two areas of logic locking and hardware-based cryptographic program obfuscation. Most notably, a provable logic locking scheme for a given circuit implies provable hardware-based cryptographic program obfuscation of the same circuit, where the trusted device only needs to store and retrieve a random string (and perform no additional computation). We then proposed a formal model for the design and analysis of provable logic locking schemes, inspired by the formal model in [5] for cryptographic program obfuscation. In the proposed formal model, we show two constructions that validate our formal models and give us one practical hardware-based realization of a random oracle (which was proved to be very unlikely to exist without hardware [8]), and a hardware-based obfuscation of any arbitrary polynomial-time circuit, under widely believed hardness assumptions and much reduced trust assumptions (previously, trust assumptions included the existence of devices that already perform trusted computation).

A   Pseudo-random Generators and Functions

We recall the formal notions of pseudo-random generators and functions used in the cryptography literature.

Pseudo-random generators are stretching functions whose output is computationally indistinguishable from a random string of the same length. A function $prG_{\sigma,m} : \{0,1\}^\sigma \rightarrow \{0,1\}^m$, is a *stretching function* if $m > \sigma$. Let ϵ_{prg} be a function negligible in the security parameter σ. We say that a family of functions $prG = \{prG_{\sigma,m} : \sigma \in \mathcal{N}\}$ is a *family of ϵ_{prg}-pseudo-random generators* if each $prG_{\sigma,m}$ is a stretching function and if for any efficient adversary Adv, the difference $|p_r - p_{prG}|$ is smaller than $\epsilon_{prg}(\sigma)$, where

1. $p_r = \{r \leftarrow \{0,1\}^m : Adv(r) = 1\}$; and
2. $p_{prg} = \{s \leftarrow \{0,1\}^\sigma; z \leftarrow prG_{\sigma,m}(s) : Adv(z) = 1\}$.

Families of ϵ_{prg}-pseudo-random generators, for negligible functions ϵ_{prg}, have been constructed from any family of one-way functions [18], from any of a number of number-theoretic hard problems (e.g., [7]), as well as through more practical heuristic constructions (e.g., [21]).

We say that a function $R_{n,m} : \{0,1\}^n \rightarrow \{0,1\}^m$ is a *random function (over n-bit inputs and with m-bit outputs)* if it is randomly chosen among all functions with n-bit inputs and m-bit outputs. In a random function $R_{n,m}$, for any input string $x \in \{0,1\}^n$, the output string $R_{n,m}(x) \in \{0,1\}^m$ is uniformly and independently distributed. We say that a family of functions $\{R_{n,m} : n, m \in \mathcal{N}\}$ is a *family of random functions* if each function $R_{n,m}$ is a random function over n-bit inputs and with m-bit outputs. As a consequence, an adversary querying R_n on several input strings and obtaining the corresponding output strings still cannot predict the output string $R_{n,m}(x)$ corresponding to a new input string x, better than by randomly choosing a string of the same length. As any logical description of a random function over $\{0,1\}^n$ inputs requires $\Omega(2^n)$ space, families of random functions cannot be efficiently represented as a circuit (unless n is small). Pseudo-random functions [15] are widely used to approximate the properties of random functions. Their evaluation only requires a short random key, and their pseudo-randomness property holds as long as the key is kept secret.

A function $prF_{n,m} : \{0,1\}^\kappa \times \{0,1\}^n \rightarrow \{0,1\}^m$ is a *keyed function (over n-bit inputs and with m-bit outputs)* if for each $k \in \{0,1\}^\kappa$, the function $prF_{n,m}(k, \cdot)$, also denoted $prF_k(\cdot)$, is a function with n-bit inputs and m-bit outputs.

For any $n, m \in \mathcal{N}$, let $Rand_{n,m}$ be the set of all functions $R_{n,m} : \{0,1\}^n \rightarrow \{0,1\}^m$ and let $prF_k : \{0,1\}^n \rightarrow \{0,1\}^m$ be a keyed function. Consider the following probabilistic experiment $Init$:

1. Uniformly choose R_n from $Rand_{n,m}$; and
2. uniformly choose k from $\{0,1\}^\kappa$.

Let ϵ_{prf} be a function negligible in the security parameter. We say that a family of functions $prF = \{prF_{n,m} : n \in \mathcal{N}\}$ is a *family of ϵ_{prf}-pseudo-random functions* if for any efficient oracle adversary Adv, the difference $|p_R - p_{prF}|$ is smaller than ϵ_{prf}, where

1. $p_R = \{Init; O(\cdot) \leftarrow R_{n,m}(\cdot); A^O(1^n) = 1\}$; and
2. $p_{prF} = \{Init; O(\cdot) \leftarrow prF_{n,m}(k, \cdot); A^O(1^n) = 1\}$.

In other words, pseudo-random functions are computationally indistinguishable from random functions with the same input and output lengths.

B   Universal Circuits

In [30] it was proved that there exists a universal circuit c_u that can compute the output of any input circuit c on its input string x. Since circuit c is encoded as a binary string before being given as input to c_u, we re-state below this property of universal circuits with a natural constraint on the size of the input circuit c, which, in turn, implies a constraint on the length of the (conventional) binary encoding of c.

First, let $\mathcal{C}_{\ell_x,g}$ be the class of circuits that take as input an ℓ_x-bit input string x, have size at most $g(\ell_x)$ gates, for some polynomial g, and return a 1-bit output. Also, fix a conventional encoding of a circuit c from $\mathcal{C}_{\ell_x,g}$ as a binary string, and assume that any such circuit c is encoded into a string, denoted as $b(c)$, of length at most ℓ_c. Then, the *universal circuit* c_u *for circuits in* $\mathcal{C}_{\ell_x,g}$ is formally defined as a circuit with the following properties:

1. it takes as input an ℓ_x-bit string x and a ℓ_c string $b(c)$
2. $b(c)$ is the binary encoding of a boolean circuit c with at most $g(\ell_x)$ gates and ℓ_x-bit inputs
3. $c_u(b(c), x) = c(x)$ for all possible inputs c, x.

The result in [30] can be restated as follows:

Theorem 3. [30] Let g be a polynomial. There exists (constructively) an universal circuit c_u for circuits in $\mathcal{C}_{\ell_x,g}$ with size $O((\ell_c + \ell_x) \log(\ell_c + \ell_x))$.

We note that in principle the description of a universal circuit c_u might leak some information about the original circuit c, such as, for instance, the polynomial g used to describe the number of gates in c. For instance, a universal circuit for circuits in $\mathcal{C}_{\ell_x,g}$ with $g_1(\ell_x)$ gates might be easily distinguishable from a universal circuit for circuits in $\mathcal{C}_{\ell_x,g}$ with $g_2(\ell_x)$ gates, if polynomials g_1, g_2 are different, while satisfying $g_i(\ell_x) \leq g(\ell_x)$, for $i = 1, 2$. Since our goal is to design a logic locking scheme for all circuits in the class $\mathcal{C}_{\ell_x,g}$, we will need the following *size indistinguishability* property of universal circuits for circuits in $\mathcal{C}_{\ell_x,g}$: for any two pairs (ℓ_1, g_1) and (ℓ_2, g_2) such that $\ell_i \leq \ell_x$ and $g_i \leq g$, for $i = 1, 2$, it holds that the universal circuit generated for circuits in the subclass $\mathcal{C}_{\ell_1,g_1}$ and the universal circuit generated for circuits in the subclass $\mathcal{C}_{\ell_2,g_2}$ are equal.

We note that simple padding techniques can be used to transform any universal circuit into one that satisfies size indistinguishability. For instance, a circuit with $\ell_1 \leq \ell$ inputs and $g_1 \leq g$ gates might be padded with inputs and gates (that do not change the computation) so to have exactly ℓ inputs and g gates before generating the universal circuit. In the rest of the paper, we will assume such a procedure and therefore that all universal circuits satisfy size indistinguishability. Moreover, we will also assume that given a universal circuit for circuits in class $\mathcal{C}_{\ell_x,g}$, it is possible to derive the length ℓ_c of the binary representation $b(c)$ of the original circuit c from the class.

C   Proof that (KeyGen1, LockGen1) Satisfies Theorem 1

We prove that our logic locking scheme (KeyGen1, LockGen1) from Sect. 3 satisfies Theorem 1 by proving that it satisfies the 4 properties of Definition 3: computation correctness, lock security, efficient circuit and memory size.

Computation Correctness and Efficiency Properties. The correctness of the computation is a direct consequence of the definition of pseudo-random functions. That is, an adversary finding, with non-negligible probability, an x such that $prF_{n,m}(x) \neq c(x)$ can be used to distinguish pseudo-random functions from random functions. With respect to circuit size, we observe that the locked circuit contains the circuit for the pseudo-random function prF and the circuit for retrieval from tpM, and therefore the logic locking scheme satisfies t'-efficient circuit size, for $t' \leq O(t_{prf} + t_{tpm} + \lambda)$. With respect to memory size, we observe that the locked circuit only stores the key length for pseudo-random function $prF_{n,m}$ on the tamper-proof memory and therefore the logic locking scheme satisfies λ'-efficient memory size, for $\lambda' \geq \kappa$.

Lock Security. Let c be a Boolean circuit. If rP is a random process, we let $Pr_{lock}[rP]$ denote the probability that $c_{adv} = c$ after a sequential execution of the following 3 processes:

- $k \leftarrow \text{KeyGen}(1^\lambda)$,
- $b \leftarrow \text{tpMStore}(1^\lambda, k; tpM)$,
- rP.

We prove the lock security property by a hybrid argument [16], where, informally speaking, we evaluate and compare the success probability of adversary *Adv* or a related algorithm *Adv'* in guessing circuit c in the following 4 "worlds", where L denotes a logical abstraction function:

1. *Adv* has read access to $c', L(tpM)$ and oracle access to $c'(k, \cdot)$;
2. *Adv* has read access to $c', 1^\lambda$ and oracle access to $c'(k, \cdot)$;
3. *Adv* has read access to $c', 1^\lambda$ and oracle access to a random oracle $R_{n,m}$; and
4. *Adv'*, an efficient algorithm depending on *Adv*, has read access to $c', 1^\lambda$.

More formally, we first define the following random processes:

$$rP_1 = \text{``}c_{adv} \leftarrow Adv^{c'(k,\cdot)}(c', L(tpM))\text{''},$$
$$rP_2 = \text{``}c_{adv} \leftarrow Adv^{c'(k,\cdot)}(c', 1^\lambda)\text{''},$$
$$rP_3 = \text{``}c_{adv} \leftarrow Adv^{R_{n,m}}(c', 1^\lambda)\text{''},$$
$$rP_4 = \text{``}c_{adv} \leftarrow Adv'(c', 1^\lambda)\text{''}.$$

Then we obtain the following lemmas.

Lemma 1. $p_0 = Pr_{lock}[rP_1]$ and $p_1 = Pr_{lock}[rP_4]$

Proof. The first equality directly follows from definitions of p_0 and rP_1. The second equality directly follows from definitions of p_1 and rP_4, and by setting the simulator algorithm Sim as equal to Adv'. ∎

Lemma 2. $|Pr_{lock}[rP_1] - Pr_{lock}[rP_2]| \leq \epsilon_{tpm}$, for some ϵ_{tpm} negligible in σ.

Proof. Let p_0, p_1 be the probability quantities defined in Definition 2. By the definitions of rP_1, rP_2, we observe that $Pr_{lock}[rP_1] = p_0$ and $Pr_{lock}[rP_1] = p_1$. Then the lemma follows as a direct application of Definition 2 for the tamper-proof security of tpM. ∎

Lemma 3. $|Pr_{lock}[rP_2] - Pr_{lock}[rP_3]| \leq \epsilon_{prf}$, for some ϵ_{prf} negligible in σ.

Proof. We first observe that the difference between rP_2 and rP_3 only consists of the oracle to which Adv has oracle access. Specifically, in rP_2, Adv has access to locked circuit $c'(k, \cdot)$, an oracle that evaluates the circuit c' for pseudo-random function prF with key k, while in rP_3, Adv has access to a random oracle $R_{n,m}$. Moreover, in both rP_2 and rP_3, Adv has read access to unlocked circuit c' and 1^λ. Then we can directly apply the pseudo-randomness property of prF, and obtain that Adv can only distinguish the two worlds with at most negligible probability ϵ_{prf}. ∎

Lemma 4. For any efficient algorithm Adv, there exists an efficient algorithm Adv' such that $Pr_{lock}[rP_4] = Pr_{lock}[rP_3]$.

Proof. Consider algorithm Adv in random process rP_3. Then, define algorithm Adv' as the algorithm that runs Adv and, in this execution, simulates the answers to Adv's queries to the random oracle as random strings (for new queries) or previously generated random strings (for repeated queries); finally, Adv' returns the same output as Adv. Since the simulation performed by Adv' of the random oracle answers is perfect, we have that Adv' guesses the original circuit c in rP_4 with the same probability that Adv guesses the original circuit c in rP_3, and thus $Pr_{lock}[rP_4] = Pr_{lock}[rP_3]$, from which the lemma follows. ∎

Finally, we use these lemmas to conclude the proof that the logic locking scheme satisfies Definition 3. Specifically, we have that

$$|p_0 - p_1| = |Pr_{lock}[rP_1] - Pr_{lock}[rP_4]|$$
$$\leq \sum_{i=1}^{3} |Pr_{lock}[rP_i] - Pr_{lock}[rP_{i+1}]|$$
$$\leq \epsilon_{tpm} + |Pr_{lock}[rP_2] - Pr_{lock}[rP_3]| + |Pr_{lock}[rP_3] - Pr_{lock}[rP_4]|$$
$$\leq \epsilon_{tpm} + \epsilon_{prf} + |Pr_{lock}[rP_3] - Pr_{lock}[rP_4]|$$
$$\leq \epsilon_{tpm} + \epsilon_{prf} \leq \text{a function negligible in } \sigma,$$

where the first equality follows from Lemma 1, the first inequality follows by applying the triangle inequality, the second inequality follows from Lemma 2, the third inequality follows from Lemma 3, the fourth inequality follows from Lemma 4, and the fifth inequality follows from assumptions on $\epsilon_{tpm}, \epsilon_{prf}$.

D   Proof that (KeyGen2, LockGen2) Satisfies Theorem 2

The proof that our logic locking scheme (KeyGen2, LockGen2) satisfies Theorem 2 follows the same structure as the proof of Theorem 1. Specifically, we prove that it satisfies the 4 properties of Definition 3: computation correctness, lock security, efficient circuit size and efficient memory size.

Computation Correctness. The correctness of the computation of the locked circuit follows directly from the definition and properties of universal circuits.

Efficiency Properties. With respect to circuit size, we observe that the locked circuit contains the circuit for the pseudo-random generator prG, the circuit for retrieval from tpM, and circuit gates for computing the xor between two strings of length ℓ_c, and therefore the logic locking scheme satisfies t'-efficient circuit size, for $t' = O(t_{prg} + t_u + t_{tpm} + \lambda)$. With respect to memory size, we observe that the locked circuit only stores the key length for pseudo-random generator $prG_{\sigma,m}$ on the tamper-proof memory and therefore the logic locking scheme satisfies λ'-efficient memory size, for $\lambda' \geq \sigma$.

Lock Security. The proof for this property is structured very similarly as in the proof for Theorem 1. Thus, it suffices to discuss the differences, which are mainly in the definitions for the worlds and relative random processes used in the proof's hybrid argument. The main technical difference in the proof is in the simulation argument, as described in the proof of Lemma 7. As before, we evaluate and compare the success probability of adversary Adv or a related efficient algorithm Adv' in guessing circuit c in the following 4 "worlds":

1. Adv has read access to $c'_y, L(tpM)$ and oracle access to $c'_y(k, \cdot)$;
2. Adv has read access to $c'_y, 1^\lambda$ and oracle access to $c'_y(k, \cdot)$;
3. Adv has read access to $c'_z, 1^\lambda$, for some random ℓ_c-bit string z, and oracle access to $c'_y(k, \cdot)$; and
4. Adv', an efficient algorithm depending on Adv, has oracle access to $c'_y(k, \cdot)$.

Denote as $p_{adv,i}$ the probability that Adv correctly guesses c in world i, for $i = 1, 2, 3, 4$, after the same random processes used in Definition 3. We note that $p_{adv,1} = p_0$, by definition. Then, the proof is obtained by combining, similarly as in the proof for Theorem 1, the following lemmas.

Lemma 5. $|p_{adv,1} - p_{adv,2}| \leq \epsilon_{tpm}$, for some function ϵ_{tpm} negligible in σ.

Proof. This follows by Definition 2 since tpM is ϵ_{tpm}-secure. ∎

Lemma 6. $|p_{adv,2} - p_{adv,3}| \leq \epsilon_{prg}$, for some function ϵ_{prg} negligible in σ.

Proof. This follows by observing that c'_z is computationally indistinguishable from c'_y since z is random and y is pseudorandom, by the pseudo-randomness of prG. ∎

Lemma 7. $|p_{adv,3} - p_{adv,4}| = 0$.

Proof. This follows from the simulatability property of the universal circuit. Specifically, we observe that for any efficient adversary Adv, who is given the length of the (unknown) original circuit c, we can construct an efficient adversary Adv' that simulates c'_z as follows:

- derive length ℓ_c of the binary representation $b(c)$ of circuit c
- randomly choose $z \in \{0,1\}^{\ell_c}$
- define c'_z as the circuit that has string z hardwired and, on input x, k:
    computes $w = z$ xor $prG_{\sigma,m}(k)$
    computes and outputs $c_u(w, x)$.
- return: c'_z

By code inspection, we note that the simulation is perfect, in the sense that the distribution of circuit c'_z returned by Adv' in world 4 is identical to the distribution of c'_z returned by Adv in world 3. The lemma follows. ∎

Lemma 8. $p_{adv,4} = \text{Prob}\left[\,c_{sim} = c\,\right]$.

Proof. This follows directly from the above definition of $p_{adv,4}$ and of $\text{Prob}\left[\,c_{sim} = c\,\right]$ in Definition 3, and by setting the simulator algorithm Sim as equal to algorithm Adv' in the proof of Lemma 7. ∎

Finally, we use these lemmas to conclude the proof that the logic locking scheme satisfies Definition 3, similarly as done for the scheme underlying Theorem 1. Specifically, we have that

$$
\begin{aligned}
|p_0 - p_1| &= |p_{adv,1} - p_{adv,4}| \\
&\leq |p_{adv,1} - p_{adv,2}| + |p_{adv,2} - p_{adv,3}| + |p_{adv,3} - p_{adv,4}| \\
&\leq \epsilon_{tpm} + |p_{adv,2} - p_{adv,3}| + |p_{adv,3} - p_{adv,4}| \\
&\leq \epsilon_{tpm} + \epsilon_{prg} + |p_{adv,3} - p_{adv,4}| \\
&\leq \epsilon_{tpm} + \epsilon_{prg} \leq \text{a function negligible in } \sigma,
\end{aligned}
$$

where the first equality follows from Lemma 8, the first inequality follows by applying the triangle inequality, the second inequality follows from Lemma 5, the third inequality follows from Lemma 6, the fourth inequality follows from Lemma 7, and the fifth inequality follows from assumptions on $\epsilon_{tpm}, \epsilon_{prg}$.

References

1. http://securedrives.co.uk/
2. https://www.bunniestudios.com/blog/?page_id=40 (2012)
3. Detecting and Removing Counterfeit Semiconductors in the U.S. Supply Chain (2013)
4. Azar, K.Z., Kamali, H.M., Homayoun, H., Sasan, A.: SMT attack: next generation attack on obfuscated circuits with capabilities and performance beyond the SAT attacks. IACR Trans. Cryptogr. Hardw. Embedded Syst. **19**, 97–122 (2019)
5. Barak, B., et al.: On the (im)possibility of obfuscating programs. J. ACM **59**(2), 6 (2012)
6. Bellare, M., Stepanovs, I.: Point-function obfuscation: a framework and generic constructions. In: Kushilevitz, E., Malkin, T. (eds.) TCC 2016. LNCS, vol. 9563, pp. 565–594. Springer, Heidelberg (2016). https://doi.org/10.1007/978-3-662-49099-0_21
7. Blum, M., Micali, S.: How to generate cryptographically strong sequences of pseudo-random bits. SIAM J. Comput. **13**(4), 850–864 (1984)
8. Canetti, R., Goldreich, O., Halevi, S.: The random oracle methodology, revisited. J. ACM **51**(4), 557–594 (2004)
9. Chakraborty, A., Liu, Y., Srivastava, A.: TimingSAT: timing profile embedded SAT attack, pp. 6:1–6:6 (2018)
10. Crescenzo, G.: Cryptographic formula obfuscation. In: Zincir-Heywood, N., Bonfante, G., Debbabi, M., Garcia-Alfaro, J. (eds.) FPS 2018. LNCS, vol. 11358, pp. 208–224. Springer, Cham (2019). https://doi.org/10.1007/978-3-030-18419-3_14
11. Di Crescenzo, G., Bahler, L., Coan, B.: Cryptographic password obfuscation. In: Naccache, D., et al. (eds.) ICICS 2018. LNCS, vol. 11149, pp. 497–512. Springer, Cham (2018). https://doi.org/10.1007/978-3-030-01950-1_29
12. Di Crescenzo, G., Rajendran, J., Karri, R., Memon, N.D.: Boolean circuit camouflage: cryptographic models, limitations, provable results and a random oracle realization. In: Proceedings of the 2017 Workshop on Attacks and Solutions in Hardware Security, ASHES@CCS 2017 (2017)
13. Dodis, Y., Smith, A.D.: Correcting errors without leaking partial information. In: Proceedings of the 37th Annual ACM Symposium on Theory of Computing, pp. 654–663 (2005)
14. Gennaro, R., Lysyanskaya, A., Malkin, T., Micali, S., Rabin, T.: Algorithmic Tamper-Proof (ATP) Security: theoretical foundations for security against hardware tampering. In: Naor, M. (ed.) TCC 2004. LNCS, vol. 2951, pp. 258–277. Springer, Heidelberg (2004). https://doi.org/10.1007/978-3-540-24638-1_15
15. Goldreich, O., Goldwasser, S., Micali, S.: How to construct random functions. J. ACM **33**(4), 792–807 (1986)
16. Goldwasser, S., Micali, S.: Probabilistic encryption. J. Comput. Syst. Sci. **28**(2), 270–299 (1984)
17. Hanau, A., Hanson, E., Hughes, E.: Enabling IPX level 7-8 PCB waterproof protection. Printed Circuit Design and Fab (2018)
18. Håstad, J., Impagliazzo, R., Levin, L.A., Luby, M.: A pseudorandom generator from any one-way function. SIAM J. Comput. **28**(4), 1364–1396 (1999)
19. Koblitz, N., Menezes, A.J.: The random oracle model: a twenty-year retrospective. Des. Codes Cryptogr. **77**(2–3), 587–610 (2015)
20. Lynn, B., Prabhakaran, M., Sahai, A.: Positive results and techniques for obfuscation. In: Cachin, C., Camenisch, J.L. (eds.) EUROCRYPT 2004. LNCS, vol. 3027,

pp. 20–39. Springer, Heidelberg (2004). https://doi.org/10.1007/978-3-540-24676-3_2

21. Matsumoto, M., Nishimura, T.: Mersenne twister: a 623-dimensionally equidistributed uniform pseudo-random number generator. ACM Trans. Model. Comput. Simul. **8**(1), 3–30 (1998)

22. Rajendran, J., et al.: Fault analysis-based logic encryption. TCOMP **64**(2), 410–424 (2015)

23. Roy, J.A., Koushanfar, F., Markov, I.L.: Ending piracy of integrated circuits. IEEE Comput. **43**(10), 30–38 (2010)

24. Shamsi, K., Li, M., Meade, T., Zhao, Z., Pan, D.Z., Jin, Y.: Cyclic obfuscation for creating SAT-unresolvable circuits, pp. 173–178 (2017)

25. Sirone, D., Subramanyan, P.: Functional analysis attacks on logic locking. In: DATE (2018)

26. Skorobogatov, S.: Data remanence in flash memory devices. In: Rao, J.R., Sunar, B. (eds.) CHES 2005. LNCS, vol. 3659, pp. 339–353. Springer, Heidelberg (2005). https://doi.org/10.1007/11545262_25

27. Subramanyan, P., Ray, S., Malik, S.: Evaluating the security of logic encryption algorithms, pp. 137–143 (2015)

28. Tao, S., Dubrova, E.: Ultra-energy-efficient temperature-stable physical unclonable function in 65 nm CMOS. Electron. Lett. **52**(10), 805–806 (2016)

29. Tuyls, P., Schrijen, G.-J., Škorić, B., van Geloven, J., Verhaegh, N., Wolters, R.: Read-proof hardware from protective coatings. In: Goubin, L., Matsui, M. (eds.) CHES 2006. LNCS, vol. 4249, pp. 369–383. Springer, Heidelberg (2006). https://doi.org/10.1007/11894063_29

30. Valiant, L.G.: Universal circuits (preliminary report). In: Proceedings of the 8th Annual ACM Symposium on Theory of Computing, 3–5 May 1976, Hershey, Pennsylvania, USA, pp. 196–203 (1976)

31. Wee, H.: On obfuscating point functions. In: Proceedings of 37th ACM STOC, 2005, pp. 523–532 (2005)

32. Wichs, D., Zirdelis, G.: Obfuscating compute-and-compare programs under LWE. In: Proceedings of 58th IEEE FOCS 2017, pp. 600–611 (2017)

33. Worthman, E.: Chaologix: Integrated Security (2015)

34. Xie, Y., Srivastava, A.: Mitigating SAT attack on logic locking. In: CHES, no. 590 (2016)

35. Xie, Y., Srivastava, A.: Delay locking: security enhancement of logic locking against IC counterfeiting and overproduction, pp. 9:1–9:6 (2017)

36. Yang, F., Tang, M., Sinanoglu, O.: Stripped functionality logic locking with hamming distance based restore unit (SFLL-hd)-unlocked. In: TIFS (2019)

37. Yasin, M., Mazumdar, B., Rajendran, J.J.V., Sinanoglu, O.: SARLock: SAT attack resistant logic locking, pp. 236–241 (2016)

38. Yasin, M., Rajendran, J.J., Sinanoglu, O., Karri, R.: On improving the security of logic locking. TCAD **35**(9), 1411–1424 (2016)

39. Yasin, M., Mazumdar, B., Rajendran, J., Sinanoglu, O.: Hardware security and trust: logic locking as a design-for-trust solution. In: Elfadel, I.A.M., Ismail, M. (eds.) The IoT Physical Layer, pp. 353–373. Springer, Cham (2019). https://doi.org/10.1007/978-3-319-93100-5_20

40. Yasin, M., Mazumdar, B., Sinanoglu, O., Rajendran, J.: Security analysis of anti-SAT (2017)

41. Zhou, H., Jiang, R., Kong, S.: CycSAT: SAT-based attack on cyclic logic encryptions, pp. 49–56 (2017)

Speeding up OMD Instantiations in Hardware

Diana Maimuț[1](✉) ⓘ and Ștefan Alexandru Mega[1,2] ⓘ

[1] Advanced Technologies Institute, 10 Dinu Vintilă, Bucharest, Romania
{diana.maimut,ati}@dcti.ro
[2] Politehnica University of Bucharest, Bucharest, Romania
megastefanalexandru@gmail.com

Abstract. Particular instantiations of the Offset Merkle Damgård authenticated encryption scheme (OMD) represent highly secure alternatives for AES-GCM. It is already a fact that OMD can be efficiently implemented in software. Given this, in our paper we focus on speeding-up OMD in hardware, more precisely on FPGA platforms. Thus, we propose a new OMD instantiation based on the compression function of BLAKE2b. Moreover, to the best of our knowledge, we present the first FPGA implementation results for the SHA-512 instantiation of OMD as well as the first architecture of an online authenticated encryption system based on OMD.

Keywords: Authenticated encryption · Pseudorandom function · Compression function · Provable security · FPGA · Hardware optimization · Nonce respecting adversaries

1 Introduction

Authenticated encryption (AE) primitives ensure both message confidentiality and authenticity. Initially, AE algorithms achieved confidentiality and integrity by combining two distinct cryptographic primitives (one for each of the two goals). Around two decades ago the perspective of having a unique primitive for confidentiality and integrity started to appear. Rogaway [16] extended AE schemes by adding a new type of input for associated data (AD) and, thus, AEAD (authenticated encryption with associated data) was the next step. Such a model is helpful in real world scenario in which part of the message (*e.g.* a header) needs only to be authenticated. We do not recall the technical aspects of AEAD schemes as it is outside the scope of our paper. We refer the reader to [12,16,17] for a detailed description regarding the previously mentioned topic.

The *Competition for Authenticated Encryption: Security, Applicability, and Robustness* (CAESAR) started in early 2014 and finished in 2018 [1]. The *Offset Merkle-Damgård* (OMD) authenticated encryption scheme [2,11] was one of the CAESAR submissions. OMD is, in fact, an authenticated encryption mode of operation for keyed compression functions. The OMD instantiations presented in

© Springer Nature Switzerland AG 2020
E. Simion and R. Géraud-Stewart (Eds.): SecITC 2019, LNCS 12001, pp. 193–212, 2020.
https://doi.org/10.1007/978-3-030-41025-4_13

the original paper are based on the compression functions of two hash functions which are part of the SHA-2 family: SHA-256 and SHA-512.

OMD was accepted as a valid CAESAR submission for CAESAR and, thus, a process of public analysis from the community naturally followed. Given its characteristics which proved to be in accordance to the CAESAR requirements especially from the security point of view, OMD was further accepted as a second round candidate[1].

As stated in [2,7], in the case of the original scheme's software implementations the speed can be considerably increased due to, *e.g.*, the performance acceleration instructions of INTEL's architecture processors. Thus, the implementation efficiency of the two OMD original instantiations becomes comparable with the AES-GCM one in software.

Given that from the security point of view OMD has more secure versions than AES-GCM and its software implementations are highly efficient [10], we believe that due to the lack of a competitive hardware implementation OMD did not make it until the third CAESAR round [9].

Therefore, especially in view of the diversity of secure authenticated encryption schemes we have to focus on providing practical implementations for them.

We pay particular attention to using the compression functions of SHA-512 and BLAKE2b both for a higher security level and a more hardware friendly word dimension.

Prior Work. A rather unoptimized hardware implementation of the original OMD scheme was submitted to CAESAR. Thus, considering the initial metrics, OMD seemed quite unattractive as compared to AES-GCM. Later on, in 2017, the authors of [8] presented their results regarding selected hardware implementations of CAESAR round 2 candidates. We aim at improving the previous results, providing the reader with better hardware implementation metrics of various OMD instantiations. The OMD implementation discussed in [8] is the primary recommendation submitted to CAESAR, *i.e.* using the compression function of SHA-256. Thus, to the best of our knowledge, we present the first FPGA implementation results for the SHA-512 instantiation of OMD.

Motivation. Our motivation for choosing OMD among all the CAESAR submissions is at least threefold. ① OMD's design is an exotic one. The scheme represents the only CAESAR proposal based on a compression function. ② When it comes to real world cryptographic applications and systems there may perfectly be some use cases in which security requirements are way higher than usual and the physical resources of an implementation platform are abundant. Nevertheless, our results become meaningful either in the case of an enhanced security context (*e.g.* secure government applications). ③ In [8] it is reported that "OMD ends up near the bottom of Tp/A^2 ratios for all CAESAR Round

---

[1] All the withdrawn schemes are listed on the competition's website. Almost all the withdrawn submissions are due to attacks reported by the community. It can easily be observed that for OMD no attack was presented.

[2] Throughput to Area ratio.

Two candidates". The explanation pointed out by the authors focuses on the big number of rounds of SHA-256 and, thus, the limited throughput. Our results show that we can obtain superior implementation metrics, especially considering our new OMD instantiation with the compression function of BLAKE2b.

Structure of the Paper. In Sect. 2 we introduce notations, recall the OMD authenticated encryption scheme and shortly describe basic facts regarding the hash functions SHA-512 and BLAKE2b. We propose a new instantiation of OMD and provide the reader with a short discussion regarding the security of the new instantiation in Sect. 3. In Sect. 4 we present the architecture of an online authenticated encryption system based on OMD as well as the results of our optimized implementations in hardware. Finally, we conclude in Sect. 5 and discuss future work ideas. We recall the pseudocode of OMD in Appendix A. The description of the compression functions of SHA-512 and BLAKE2b are given in Appendix B. We plot specific metrics of our implementations in Appendix C.

2 Preliminaries

Notations. During the following, $\|$ denotes string concatenation, $\oplus$ expresses the XOR operation and the notation 0^x refers to a string of x bits of zero. We denote by $x \leftarrow y$ the assignment of the value y to the variable x.

2.1 Offset Merkle DamgåRd

For recalling the main technical details of OMD we follow the descriptions of [2,7].

From a Compression Function to a Keyed Compression Function. Let function $F' : \{0,1\}^n \times \{0,1\}^b \to \{0,1\}^n$ be a compression function. F' can be turned into a *keyed compression function* F by using k bits of its b-bit input. More precisely, we may define $F_K(H, M) = F'(H, K\|M)$.

Specific Notations. Let function $F : \mathcal{K} \times (\{0,1\}^n \times \{0,1\}^m) \to \{0,1\}^n$ be a keyed compression function with $\mathcal{K} = \{0,1\}^k$ and $m \leq n$. The encryption tag will be denoted by Tag_e while the authentication tag is referred to as Tag_a. The final tag is denoted by Tag. We consider the length of Tag as being $\tau \in \{0,1,\cdots,n\}$. Algorithms $\mathcal{E}$ (encryption) and $\mathcal{D}$ (decryption) can be called with arguments $K \in \mathcal{K}$, $N \in \{0,1\}^{\leq n-1}$ and $A, M, C \in \{0,1\}^*$, where A represents an associated data, M a message and C a ciphertext.

In the following, all OMD multiplications are performed in $\mathrm{GF}(2^n)$ and $\mathtt{ntz}(i)$ denotes the number of trailing zeros (*i.e.* the number of rightmost bits that are zero) in the binary representation of a positive integer i. Let N be the corresponding notation of a nonce[3]. We further denote by $\Delta_{N,i,j}$ and $\bar{\Delta}_{i,j}$ the masking

---

[3] Number used only once.

values used in the OMD scheme (for processing the message and, respectively, the associated data). Let L_i be a sequence of additional values and ℓ_{max} be the bound on the maximum number of m-bit blocks in any message that can be encrypted or decrypted.

Remark 1. The authors of [2,7] used the technique proposed in [10] to compute the masking values for assessing the security and efficiency requirements.

Initialization of OMD.

$$\begin{cases} \Delta_{N,0,0} \leftarrow F_K(N||10^{n-1-|N|}, 0^m) \\ \bar{\Delta}_{0,0} \leftarrow 0^n \\ L_* \leftarrow F_K(0^n, 0^m) \\ L[0] \leftarrow 4L_* \\ L[i] \leftarrow 2L[i-1] \text{ for } i \geq 1 \end{cases}$$

Remark 2. For a more efficient implementation, the values $L[i]$ can be preprocessed and stored in a table for $0 \leq i \leq \lceil \log_2(\ell_{max}) \rceil$. The values $L[i]$ can also be computed on-the-fly for $i \geq 1$ in case of memory restrictions.

Masking Sequences for Processing the Message Equation (1) *and the Associated Data Equation* (2). For $i \geq 1$ we have that:

$$\begin{cases} \Delta_{N,i,0} \leftarrow \Delta_{N,i-1,0} \oplus L[\mathtt{ntz}(i)] \\ \Delta_{N,i,1} \leftarrow \Delta_{N,i,0} \oplus 2L_* \\ \Delta_{N,i,2} \leftarrow \Delta_{N,i,0} \oplus 3L_* \end{cases} \tag{1}$$

$$\begin{cases} \bar{\Delta}_{i,0} \leftarrow \bar{\Delta}_{i-1,0} \oplus L[\mathtt{ntz}(i)] \text{ for } i \geq 1 \\ \bar{\Delta}_{i,1} \leftarrow \bar{\Delta}_{i,0} \oplus L_* \text{ for } i \geq 0 \end{cases} \tag{2}$$

The OMD encryption algorithm generically instantiated with the compression function F keyed with K is presented in Fig. 1. Note that for simplicity we depicted only the case of a message whose length is a multiple of the block length and an associated data whose length is a multiple of the input length. The cases in which padding is needed (both for messages and AD) are tackled in the pseudocode presented in Appendix A.

We recall the pseudocode of the four OMD sub-algorithms (*i.e.* INITIALIZE (K), HASH$_K(A)$, $\mathcal{E}_K(N, A, M)$ and $\mathcal{D}_K(N, A, C)$) in Appendix A.

Nonces. The security proofs of OMD hold as long as the principle of non-repeating nonces is respected (uniqueness criterion). In standard encryption applications the nonce is usually a counter sent over the communication channel along with the authenticated and encrypted message. In practice, the nonce has to be unique during an encryption session (*i.e* during the lifetime of a session key). The nonce is needed both for encryption and decryption and can be communicated in clear between the two corresponding parties. The uniqueness criterion is encryption related in the sense that the user wishing to transmit a message to another user is responsible of generating suitable[4] nonces.

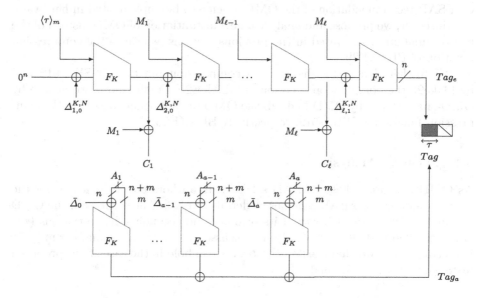

Fig. 1. OMD in the case of a message whose length is a multiple of the block length and an associated data whose length is a multiple of the input length.

2.2 The Hash Functions SHA-512 and BLAKE2b

The SHA-2 family of hash functions [13] is still one of the *de facto* standards when it comes to hash functions. Even though SHA-3 is the latest member of the SHA (Secure Hash Family) family of functions, SHA-2 still stands from the security point of view.

The hash function BLAKE2 [6] is a modified version of BLAKE [6] which is a finalist of the SHA-3 cryptographic competition. BLAKE2 was constructed to supersede BLAKE's efficiency (*i.e.* optimize it for modern applications). As BLAKE2 is really appealing developers it has already been used in several projects, including the widely adopted WinRAR archiving utility and the memory hard key derivation function Argon2 (the winner of the Password Hashing Competition [3]).

We provide the reader with technical details of sha-512 and blake2b which are relevant for our paper in Appendix B.

---

[4] From a security perspective.

3   A New OMD Instantiation. Security Aspects

As already mentioned, OMD is an authenticated encryption scheme based on compression functions. For the purpose of our paper we selected the secondary CAESAR recommendation of the OMD scheme to be implemented in hardware.

Moreover, we propose and analyze a new instantiation of OMD instead of the two original ones. As stated in the previous sections, we chose the compression function of BLAKE2b.

We further denote by sha-512 the compression function of SHA-512 and by blake2b the compression function of BLAKE2b. Furthermore, we denote by OMD-sha-512 and by OMD-blake2b the OMD instantiations based on the compression functions of SHA-512, respectively BLAKE2b.

3.1   Security Analysis

As OMD is a nonce-based AEAD scheme, its authors aimed at achieving the security notions for AEAD schemes as detailed in [16]. The security of the OMD scheme as well as the security of its primary and secondary instantiations (*i.e.* OMD-sha-256 and OMD-sha-512) are discussed in an extensive manner in [2,7]. It is straightforward that the security proofs still hold in the case of our proposed instantiation, *i.e.* OMD-blake2b.

4   Speeding-Up OMD in Hardware. Implementation Trade-Offs

In this section we present the architecture of an online authenticated encryption system based on specific OMD instantiations, while our main focus is on speeding-up OMD in hardware. We start by giving the general architecture and continue with implementation details of OMD and particular instantiations of it in Sect. 4.1 (OMD-sha-512 and OMD-blake2b). In order to underline our speed-ups, we provide the reader with comparison results between our implementations and other related works in Sect. 4.2.

Target FPGA Platform. The hardware implementation of the OMD scheme was realized using register transfer-level (RTL) design methodology. We adopted the VHDL as our preferred hardware description language (HDL) in order to implement the necessary hardware components for the FPGA circuit design. We opted for Virtex UltraScale+ VCU118[5] which is an effective platform from the point of view of its resources (I/O pins, QSFP28 Interfaces, high on-chip memory density, etc.). Thus, the platform we chose is a very good option for the future development of an online system.

All the development was done using the Xilinx Vivado Design Suite 2019.1 and it involved the following steps:

---

[5] xcvu9p-flga2104-2L-e.

1. Designing the top view architecture of the whole system and defining the input/output ports of the main modules;
2. Writing the VHDL code for the previous specified modules;
3. Writing simulation testbenches in order to validate the functionality of the modules;
4. Synthesizing the design and checking for any possible errors;
5. Implementing the design;
6. Analyzing the timing requirements and the resources.

4.1   The Architecture of a Real World Authenticated Encryption System

The design of our proposed system is composed of a Top Module (shown in Fig. 2) that contains all the components of the circuit which is described as:

- **PTXT IF:** this block represents the plaintext interface and it is used to receive and send data packets in the trusted area of a network;
- **Receive:** transfers the data from the receive PTXT IF to the FIFO PTXT block;
- **FIFO PTXT:** implements a FIFO module for plaintext packets storage; it is also used for Clock Domain Crossing (CDC);
- **PUT to ENC:** reads the data from FIFO PTXT and prepare the packets for the encryption block;
- **ENCRYPT:** encrypts the data using the OMD scheme depicted in Fig. 3;
- **GET from ENC:** takes the encrypted blocks and creates the encrypted packet which is then written in the FIFO ENC;
- **FIFO ENC:** implements a FIFO module for ciphertext packets storage; it is also used for Clock Domain Crossing (CDC);
- **Send:** transfers the data from the FIFO ENC block to the transmit CTXT IF;
- **CTXT IF:** this block represents the ciphertext interface and it is used to receive and send data packets in the untrusted area of a network;
- **KS GEN:** this block is used to generate a common session key between two communicating parties; it also computes the L and Tag_a values which are used by the ENCRYPT/DECRYPT blocks;
- **NONCE GEN:** this block is used to generate nonces which are unique per session;
- **DECRYPT:** this block is identical to ENCRYPT, except an additional tag verification that is done at the decryption of the message;
- the rest of the blocks complete the scheme in a symmetric manner, offering similar functionalities as the already described ones;

We continue to focus on the main blocks of the system (ENCRYPT and DECRYPT) which includes the OMD algorithm. The block diagram illustrated in Fig. 3 consists of modules which are further categorized as Datapath or Controller modules. Datapath describes how the data moves through the system at register level, leveraging the parallel nature of the FPGA circuits. The Controller consists of a Finite State Machine (FSM) which runs sequentially providing the decision logic of the system. In order to simplify the illustrated design, we presented in Fig. 3 only the Datapath logic.

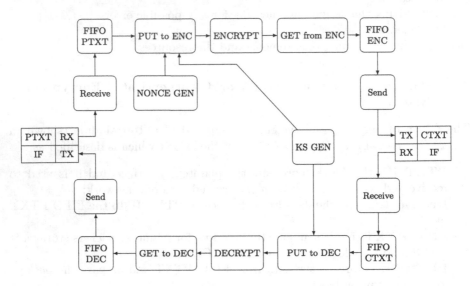

Fig. 2. A general architecture of an online system using OMD

In the case of the OMD algorithm the encryption of the current block is dependent on the previous one (*i.e.* the scheme is sequential), thus we can only use an iterative implementation. In this case, the pipelined implementation is not feasible. The original OMD scheme is reduced to a single F_k block where the inputs and outputs are managed by the controller in the following way: the inputs are multiplexed with different data paths and the outputs are used to compute the ciphertext and Tag_e or to be fed back into the F_k block. In Fig. 3, the Datapath is described in a simplified diagram which has the following main parts: ① data multiplexing modules (for changing the datapath to the inputs of the F_k block), ② registers (for storing temporary data) and ③ RAM memory (for storing the computed values).

The input of the ENCRYPT block consists of:

- Message M (divided into blocks of length 512 bits);
- Secret key K (of length 512 bits);
- Nonce N (of length 256 bits which are provided by the nonce generator and are unique per session);
- Two precomputed values L and Tag_a (calculated using the KS GEN block).

We chose to calculate Tag_a and L only once per session as they do not depend on the message or on the nonce. This fact is reflected in the number of LUTs and the TP/A values presented in Table 1. Thus, the values written inside the parentheses denote the number of LUTs and the TP/A values without the need of calculating Tag_a and L.

The output of the DECRYPT block consists of ciphertext C (divided into blocks of 512 bits) and Tag (of length 512 bits).

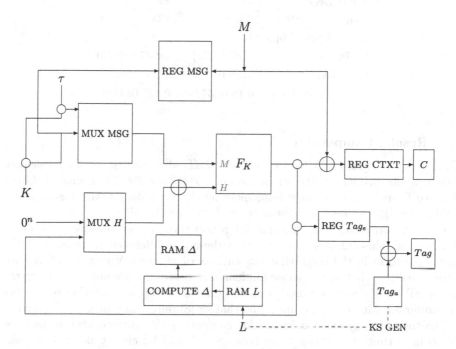

Fig. 3. OMD Encrypt Block Diagram.

The results of the OMD RTL implementations are described next. Implementation statistics in the Virtex UltraScale+ are shown in Table 1. We provide metrics regarding Throughput, Area and Throughput-to-Area (TP/A) ratio, LUTs, LUT RAM and Frequency. Throughput is defined in terms of 10^9 bits/second (Gbps) and area is defined in terms of LUTs (LookUp Tables). We also show the number of clock cycles used to calculate the throughput for long messages. The encryption process of OMD is splitted in three phases in the case of our hardware implementation: ① Setup (the initialization phase), ② Message (the processing time of all the n blocks of the message) and ③ Tag (the final phase in which the tag is computed).

Open Source Implementation. The VHDL source code of our OMD optimized implementations may be found at [4].

Table 1. Implementation Metrics for OMD-sha-512 and OMD-blake2b.

Metric	OMD-sha-512	OMD-blake2b
Setup (CLK)	116	48
Message (CLK)	$93 \cdot n$	$25 \cdot n$
Tag (CLK)	91	23
Frequency (MHz)	250	125
Throughput (Gbps)	1.3	2.56
LUTs	7187 (3451)	18907 (14875)
LUT RAM	3736 (0)	3736 (296)
Throughput/Area	0.18 (0.3736)	0.125 (0.159)

4.2   Results Comparison

Comparison Between OMD-sha-256 and OMD-sha-512. In [8] an implementation of the primary OMD instantiation (OMD-sha-256) is discussed. Given that we focused on efficiently implementing the secondary OMD instantiation (OMD-sha-512) we need to abstractly scale the results of [8] for a fair comparison taking into account the natural differences that appear because we replaced sha-256 with sha-512. Also, we note that there is a difference in terms of FPGA target platform in the sense that the authors of [8] use a Virtex 7 FPGA platform. We stress that our superior implementation results are not only due to the newer FPGA platform we used, but also due to the implementation techniques we employed. Moreover, we underline that in [8] only "long messages" (according to the authors) are considered for computing the implementation metrics. We believe that the notion "long message" should be clearly defined in order to obtain accurate results. All in all, we report the next differences between the two previously mentioned implementations:

- In terms of Throughput we obtained 1.3 Gbps as opposed to 1.071 Gbps;
- In terms of Throughput-to-Area we obtained 0.18 (0.3736) as opposed to 0.228;
- In terms of Frequency we obtained 250 MHz as opposed to 276 MHz;
- In terms of LUTs we obtained 7187 (3451) as opposed to 4701.

As a conclusion, even though OMD-sha-512's security is higher than OMD-sha-256's and we used a key length of 512 bits as opposed to a key length of 128 bits, our throughput supersedes the throughput reported in [8]. This is an important feature in real world applications which need to transfer data at a high rate. Although the parameters we used for implementing OMD-sha-512 are at least double as compared to the ones used in [8], the TP/A, the Frequency and the number of LUTs are way smaller than the double of the values reported in [8]. We also have to mention the fact that even though we used more LUTs, we utilized at most 3% of the platform's available resources. Furthermore, the authors of [8] do not implement a mechanism similar to ours for computing Tag_a and L only once per session.

Comparison Between OMD-sha-512 and OMD-blake2b. We report the next differences between our implementations of OMD-sha-512 and OMD-blake2b:

- In terms of Setup we obtained 116 clock cycles as opposed to 48;
- In terms of Message we obtained $93 \cdot n$ clock cycles as opposed to $25 \cdot n$;
- In terms of Tag we obtained 91 clock cycles as opposed 23;
- In terms of Throughput we obtained 1.3 Gbps as opposed to 2.56 Gbps;
- In terms of Throughput-to-Area we obtained 0.18 (0.3736) as opposed to 0.125 (0.159);
- In terms of Frequency we obtained 250 MHz as opposed to 125 MHz;
- In terms of LUTs we obtained 7187 (3451) as opposed to 18907 (14875).

As a conclusion, the Throughput of OMD-blake2b is higher than OMD-sha-512 due to the following facts: ① the blake2b compression function has only 12 rounds as opposed to sha-512 which has 80 rounds and ② each round of both blake2b and sha-512 compression functions takes only one clock cycle. Concerning the number of LUTs we have to mention that OMD-sha-512 is a better option for Area constrained platforms, while OMD-blake2b is a better option for real world applications which need to transfer data at a high rate. We also have to point out the differences between the frequency values in OMD-sha-512 (250 MHz) and OMD-blake2b (125 MHz), which are due to the more complex structure of the blake2b compression function.

5   Conclusions and Future Work

We proposed a new OMD instantiation (OMD-blake2b) and showed how to use it as the main cryptographic primitive of a real world authenticated encryption system. We presented the results of our optimized implementations in hardware and provided the reader with a security analysis of our proposed instantiation.

Future Work. After the original OMD scheme was submitted to CAESAR, different flavours of it were proposed in the literature: two nonce misuse-resistant variants [14] and pure OMD (p-OMD) [15], a more efficient OMD version (*i.e.* the associated data is processed almost for free). Besides inheriting all the security features of OMD, the authors claim authenticity against nonce-misusing adversaries. Note that an important update regarding the security of p-OMD is presented in [5]: it is shown that p-OMD does not actually achieve authenticity against misuse-resistant adversaries. The attack is strictly specific to p-OMD and does not invalidate its main result on nonce-respecting adversaries[6]. Thus, from both the diversity and efficiency points of view, we believe that a straightforward future approach is to provide hardware implementation metrics for all previously mentioned OMD variants.

---

[6] Moreover, the attack does not apply to the OMD CAESAR submission and to the misuse-resistant variants of [14].

Another interesting research direction would be to analyze the security of our proposed OMD optimized implementations against physical attacks. Additionally, suitable countermeasures against such attacks are to be considered as future work (*e.g.* masking techniques).

Acknowledgments. The authors would like to thank Traian Neacşa and George Teşeleanu for their helpful comments.

A   OMD Pseudocode

Algorithm 1. INITIALIZE (K)

1 $L_* \leftarrow F_K(0^n, 0^m)$
2 $L[0] \leftarrow 4.L_*$ $\triangleright$ $2.(2.L_*)$, doubling in GF(2^n)
3 **for** $i \leftarrow 1$ to $\lceil \log_2(\ell_{\max}) \rceil$ **do**
4 $\quad |\quad L[i] = 2.L[i-1]$ $\triangleright$ doubling in GF(2^n)
5 **end**
6 **return**

Algorithm 2. HASH$_K(A)$

1 $b \leftarrow n + m$
2 $A_1 || A_2 || \cdots || A_{\ell-1} || A_\ell \overset{b}{\leftarrow} A$, where $|A_i| = b$ for $1 \le i \le \ell - 1$ and $|A_\ell| \le b$
3 $\text{Tag}_a \leftarrow 0^n$
4 $\Delta \leftarrow 0^n$
5 **for** $i \leftarrow 1$ to $\ell - 1$ **do**
6 $\quad |\quad \Delta \leftarrow \Delta \oplus L[\text{ntz}(i)]$
7 $\quad |\quad$ Left $\leftarrow A_i[b-1, \cdots, m]$
8 $\quad |\quad$ Right $\leftarrow A_i[m-1, \cdots, 0]$
9 $\quad |\quad \text{Tag}_a \leftarrow \text{Tag}_a \oplus F_K(\text{Left} \oplus \Delta, \text{Right})$
10 **end**
11 **if** $|A_\ell| = b$ **then**
12 $\quad |\quad \Delta \leftarrow \Delta \oplus L[\text{ntz}(\ell)]$
13 $\quad |\quad$ Left $\leftarrow A_\ell[b-1, \cdots, m]$
14 $\quad |\quad$ Right $\leftarrow A_\ell[m-1, \cdots, 0]$
15 $\quad |\quad \text{Tag}_a \leftarrow \text{Tag}_a \oplus F_K(\text{Left} \oplus \Delta, \text{Right})$
16 **end**
17 **else**
18 $\quad |\quad \Delta \leftarrow \Delta \oplus L_*$
19 $\quad |\quad$ Left $\leftarrow A_\ell || 10^{b-|A_\ell|-1}[b-1, \cdots, m]$
20 $\quad |\quad$ Right $\leftarrow A_\ell || 10^{b-|A_\ell|-1}[m-1, \cdots, 0]$
21 $\quad |\quad \text{Tag}_a \leftarrow \text{Tag}_a \oplus F_K(\text{Left} \oplus \Delta, \text{Right})$
22 **end**
23 **return** Tag_a

Algorithm 3. $\mathcal{E}_K(N, A, M)$

1   **if** $|N| > n - 1$ **then**
2 | **return**
3   **end**
4   $\perp M_1 \| M_2 \| \cdots \| M_{\ell-1} \| M_\ell \xleftarrow{m} M$, where $|M_i| = m$ for $1 \leq i \leq \ell - 1$ and $|M_\ell| \leq m$
5   $\Delta \leftarrow F_K(N \| 10^{n-1-|N|}, 0^m)$ $\triangleright$ initialize $\Delta_{N,0,0}$
6   $H \leftarrow 0^n$
7   $\Delta \leftarrow \Delta \oplus L[0]$ $\triangleright$ compute $\Delta_{N,1,0}$
8   $H \leftarrow F_K(H \oplus \Delta, \langle \tau \rangle_m)$
9   **for** $i \leftarrow 1$ **to** $\ell - 1$ **do**
10 | $C_i \leftarrow H \oplus M_i$
11 | $\Delta \leftarrow \Delta \oplus L[\mathbf{ntz}(i+1)]$
12 | $H \leftarrow F_K(H \oplus \Delta, M_i)$
13   **end**
14   $C_\ell \leftarrow H \oplus M_\ell$ **if** $|M_\ell| = m$ **then**
15 | $\Delta \leftarrow \Delta \oplus 2.L_*$
16 | $\text{Tag}_e \leftarrow F_K(H \oplus \Delta, M_\ell)$
17   **end**
18   **else**
19 | **if** $|M_\ell| \neq 0$ **then**
20 | | $\Delta \leftarrow \Delta \oplus 3.L_*$
21 | | $\text{Tag}_e \leftarrow F_K(H \oplus \Delta, M_\ell \| 10^{m-|M_\ell|-1})$
22 | **end**
23   **end**
24   **else**
25 | $\text{Tag}_e \leftarrow H$
26   **end**
27   $\text{Tag}_a \leftarrow \text{HASH}_K(A)$
28   $\text{Tag} \leftarrow (\text{Tag}_e \oplus \text{Tag}_a)[n-1, \cdots, n-\tau]$
29   $C \leftarrow C_1 \| C_2 \| \cdots \| C_\ell \| \text{Tag}$ **return** C

Algorithm 4. $\mathcal{D}_K(N, A, \mathbb{C})$

1 **if** $|N| > n - 1$ or $|C| < \tau$ **then**
2 | **return** $\perp$
3 **end**

4 $C_1||C_2||\cdots||C_{\ell-1}||C_\ell||\mathsf{Tag} \xleftarrow{m} C$, where $|C_i| = m$ for $1 \le i \le \ell - 1$, $|C_\ell| \le m$ and $|\mathsf{Tag}| = \tau$

5 $\Delta \leftarrow F_K(N||10^{n-1-|N|}, 0^m)$ ▷ initialize $\Delta_{N,0,0}$

6 $H \leftarrow 0^n$

7 $\Delta \leftarrow \Delta \oplus L[0]$ ▷ compute $\Delta_{N,1,0}$

8 $H \leftarrow F_K(H \oplus \Delta, \langle \tau \rangle_m)$

9 **for** $i \leftarrow 1$ to $\ell - 1$ **do**
10 | $M_i \leftarrow H \oplus C_i$
11 | $\Delta \leftarrow \Delta \oplus L[\mathbf{ntz}(i + 1)]$
12 | $H \leftarrow F_K(H \oplus \Delta, M_i)$
13 **end**

14 $M_\ell \leftarrow H \oplus C_\ell$

15 **if** $|C_\ell| = m$ **then**
16 | $\Delta \leftarrow \Delta \oplus 2.L_*$
17 | $\mathsf{Tag}_e \leftarrow F_K(H \oplus \Delta, M_\ell)$
18 **end**

19 **else**
20 | **if** $|C_\ell| \neq 0$ **then**
21 | | $\Delta \leftarrow \Delta \oplus 3.L_*$
22 | | $\mathsf{Tag}_e \leftarrow F_K(H \oplus \Delta, M_\ell||10^{m-|M_\ell|-1})$
23 | **end**
24 **end**

25 **else**
26 | $\mathsf{Tag}_e \leftarrow H$
27 **end**

28 $\mathsf{Tag}_a \leftarrow \mathrm{HASH}_K(A)$
29 $\mathsf{Tag}' \leftarrow (\mathsf{Tag}_e \oplus \mathsf{Tag}_a)[n - 1, \cdots, n - \tau]$
30 **if** $\mathsf{Tag}' = \mathsf{Tag}$ **then**
31 | **return** $M \leftarrow M_1||M_2||\cdots||M_\ell$
32 **end**

33 **else**
34 | **return** $\perp$
35 **end**

B   The sha-512 and blake2b Compression Functions

B.1   Preliminaries

In the following, by "word" we mean a group of $w = 64$ bits. Namely, in sha-512 each word is a 64-bit string.

$ROTR^n(x)$ and $SHR^n(x)$: Let x be a w-bit word and n an integer with $0 \le n < w$. The *rotate right* (circular right shift) operation is defined by $ROTR^n(x) = (x \gg n) \vee (x \ll w - n)$. The *right shift* operation is defined by $SHR^n(x) = (x \gg n)$.

Choice and Majority Functions. The *choice function* and *majority function* (also called the median operator) functions can be defined as follows:

$$Ch : \left| \begin{array}{l} \{0,1\}^m \times \{0,1\}^m \times \{0,1\}^m \longrightarrow \{0,1\}^m \\ x,y,z \longmapsto (x \wedge y) \oplus (\neg x \wedge z) \end{array} \right.$$

$$Maj : \left| \begin{array}{l} \{0,1\}^m \times \{0,1\}^m \times \{0,1\}^m \longrightarrow \{0,1\}^m \\ x,y,z \longmapsto (x \wedge y) \oplus (x \wedge z) \oplus (y \wedge z) \end{array} \right.$$

B.2   The sha-512 Compression Function

Sigma Functions. The functions $\Sigma_0^{\{512\}}$ and $\Sigma_1^{\{512\}}$ are defined as follows:

$$\Sigma_0^{\{512\}} \left| \begin{array}{l} \{0,1\}^{64} \longrightarrow \{0,1\}^{64} \\ x \longmapsto ROTR^{28}(x) \oplus ROTR^{34}(x) \oplus ROTR^{39}(x) \end{array} \right.$$

$$\Sigma_1^{\{512\}} \left| \begin{array}{l} \{0,1\}^{64} \longrightarrow \{0,1\}^{64} \\ x \longmapsto ROTR^{14}(x) \oplus ROTR^{18}(x) \oplus ROTR^{41}(x) \end{array} \right.$$

The $\sigma_0^{\{512\}}$ and $\sigma_1^{\{512\}}$ functions are defined as follows:

$$\sigma_0^{\{512\}} \left| \begin{array}{l} \{0,1\}^{64} \longrightarrow \{0,1\}^{64} \\ x \longmapsto ROTR^{1}(x) \oplus ROTR^{8}(x) \oplus SHR^{7}(x) \end{array} \right.$$

$$\sigma_0^{\{512\}} \left| \begin{array}{l} \{0,1\}^{64} \longrightarrow \{0,1\}^{64} \\ x \longmapsto SHR^{19}(x) \oplus SHR^{61}(x) \oplus SHR^{6}(x) \end{array} \right.$$

The Process. The sha-512 compression function is defined as:

$$sha - 512 \left| \begin{array}{l} \{0,1\}^{512} \times \{0,1\}^{1024} \longrightarrow \{0,1\}^{512} \\ H, M \longmapsto D \end{array} \right.$$

Let M be the 1024-bit *message input* and H the 512-bit *hash input* (chaining input). These two inputs are represented respectively by an array of 16 64-bit words $M_0 \| \cdots \| M_{15}$, and an array of 8 64-bit words $H_0 \| \cdots \| H_7$. The 512-bit output value C is also represented as an array of 8 64-bit words $D_0 \| \cdots \| D_7$.

Table 2. sha-512 initial values

$$H_0 = \text{6a09e667f3bcc908}$$
$$H_1 = \text{bb67ae8584caa73b}$$
$$H_2 = \text{3c6ef372fe94f82b}$$
$$H_3 = \text{a54ff53a5f1d36f1}$$
$$H_4 = \text{510e527fade682d1}$$
$$H_5 = \text{9b05688c2b3e6c1f}$$
$$H_6 = \text{1f83d9abfb41bd6b}$$
$$H_7 = \text{5be0cd19137e2179}$$

Let H be the 512-bit *hash input* (chaining input) and M be the 1024-bit *message input*. These two inputs are represented respectively by an array of 8 64-bit words $H_0 \| \cdots \| H_7$ (see Table 2) and an array of 16 64-bit words $M_0 \| \cdots \| M_{15}$. The 512-bit output value D is also represented as an array of 8 64-bit words $D_0 \| \cdots \| D_7$.

During the process of compression, a sequence of 80 constant 64-bit words $K_0^{\{512\}}, ..., K_{79}^{\{512\}}$ is used. These 64-bit words represent the first 64 bits of the fractional parts of the cube roots of the first 80 prime numbers. In hex, these constant words are given in Table 3 (from left to right).

We further provide the reader with the description of the sha-512 compression function. The addition $(+)$ is performed modulo 2^{64}.

1. Preparing the message schedule, $\{W_t\}$:

$$W_t = \begin{cases} M_t, & 0 \le t \le 15 \\ \sigma_1^{\{512\}}(W_{t-2}) + W_{t-7} + \sigma_0^{\{512\}}(W_{t-15}) + W_{t-16}, & 16 \le t \le 79 \end{cases}$$

2. Initialize the eight working variables, a, b, c, d, e, f, g and h with the hash input value H:

$a = H_0 \qquad b = H_1 \qquad c = H_2 \qquad d = H_3$
$e = H_4 \qquad f = H_5 \qquad g = H_6 \qquad h = H_7$

2. For $t = 0$ to 79, do:
   {
   $$T_1 = h + \Sigma_1^{\{512\}}(e) + Ch(e, f, g) + K_t^{\{512\}} + W_t$$
   $$T_2 = \Sigma_0^{\{512\}}(a) + Maj(a, b, c)$$
   $h = g \qquad g = f \qquad f = e \qquad e = d + T_1$
   $d = c \qquad c = b \qquad b = a \qquad a = T_1 + T_2$
   }

3. Computing the 512-bit output (hash) value $C = C_0 \cdots C_7$ as:
   $C_0 = a + H_0 \qquad C_1 = b + H_1 \qquad C_2 = c + H_2 \qquad C_3 = d + H_3$
   $C_4 = e + H_4 \qquad C_5 = f + H_5 \qquad C_6 = g + H_6 \qquad C_7 = h + H_7$

Table 3. sha-512 constants

428a2f98d728ae22	7137449123ef65cd	b5c0fbcfec4d3b2f	e9b5dba58189dbbc
3956c25bf348b538	59f111f1b605d019	923f82a4af194f9b	ab1c5ed5da6d8118
d807aa98a3030242	12835b0145706fbe	243185be4ee4b28c	550c7dc3d5ffb4e2
72be5d74f27b896f	80deb1fe3b1696b1	9bdc06a725c71235	c19bf174cf692694
e49b69c19ef14ad2	efbe4786384f25e3	0fc19dc68b8cd5b5	240ca1cc77ac9c65
2de92c6f592b0275	4a7484aa6ea6e483	5cb0a9dcbd41fbd4	76f988da831153b5
983e5152ee66dfab	a831c66d2db43210	b00327c898fb213f	bf597fc7beef0ee4
c6e00bf33da88fc2	d5a79147930aa725	06ca6351e003826f	142929670a0e6e70
27b70a8546d22ffc	2e1b21385c26c926	4d2c6dfc5ac42aed	53380d139d95b3df
650a73548baf63de	766a0abb3c77b2a8	81c2c92e47edaee6	92722c851482353b
a2bfe8a14cf10364	a81a664bbc423001	c24b8b70d0f89791	c76c51a30654be30
d192e819d6ef5218	d69906245565a910	f40e35855771202a	106aa07032bbd1b8
19a4c116b8d2d0c8	1e376c085141ab53	2748774cdf8eeb99	34b0bcb5e19b48a8
391c0cb3c5c95a63	4ed8aa4ae3418acb	5b9cca4f7763e373	682e6ff3d6b2b8a3
748f82ee5defb2fc	78a5636f43172f60	84c87814a1f0ab72	8cc702081a6439ec
90befffa23631e28	a4506cebde82bde9	bef9a3f7b2c67915	c67178f2e372532b
ca273eceea26619c	d186b8c721c0c207	eada7dd6cde0eb1e	f57d4f7fee6ed178
06f067aa72176fba	0a637dc5a2c898a6	113f9804bef90dae	1b710b35131c471b
28db77f523047d84	32caab7b40c72493	3c9ebe0a15c9bebc	431d67c49c100d4c
4cc5d4becb3e42b6	597f299cfc657e2a	5fcb6fab3ad6faec	6c44198c4a475817

B.3   The blake2b Compression Function

The initial values H of blake2b was chosen precisely as the ones for SHA-512 (given in Table 2). These values "were obtained by taking the first sixty-four bits of the fractional parts of the square roots of the first eight prime numbers", according to [13].

Thus, the compression function blake2b takes as input:

$H = H_0\|H_1\|\dots\|H_7$ (of length 512 bits)
$M = M_0\|M_1\|\dots\|M_7$ (of length 1024 bits)
$T = T_0\|T_1$ (of length 128 bits)
$F = F_0\|F_1$ (of length 128 bits)

$$\begin{pmatrix} \nu_0 & \nu_1 & \nu_2 & \nu_3 \\ \nu_4 & \nu_5 & \nu_6 & \nu_7 \\ \nu_8 & \nu_9 & \nu_{10} & \nu_{11} \\ \nu_{12} & \nu_{13} & \nu_{14} & \nu_{15} \end{pmatrix} := \begin{pmatrix} h_0 & h_1 & h_2 & h_3 \\ h_4 & h_5 & h_6 & h_7 \\ H_0 & H_1 & H_2 & H_3 \\ T_0 \oplus H_4 & T_1 \oplus H_5 & F_0 \oplus H_6 & F_1 \oplus H_7 \end{pmatrix}$$

Let the round permutations σ_r be in accordance with Table 4, where $r = \overline{0,9}$. Note that for rounds $r \geq 10$ the permutation used is $\sigma_{r \bmod 10}$. The core function G of blake2b is defined as follows:

Table 4. Permutations of blake2b

$$\sigma_0 : [\ \ 0,\ \ 1,\ \ 2,\ \ 3,\ \ 4,\ \ 5,\ \ 6,\ \ 7,\ \ 8,\ \ 9,\ 10,\ 11,\ 12,\ 13,\ 14,\ 15]$$
$$\sigma_1 : [\ 14,\ 10,\ \ 4,\ \ 8,\ \ 9,\ 15,\ 13,\ \ 6,\ \ 1,\ 12,\ \ 0,\ \ 2,\ 11,\ \ 7,\ \ 5,\ \ 3]$$
$$\sigma_2 : [\ 11,\ \ 8,\ 12,\ \ 0,\ \ 5,\ \ 2,\ 15,\ 13,\ 10,\ 14,\ \ 3,\ \ 6,\ \ 7,\ \ 1,\ \ 9,\ \ 4]$$
$$\sigma_3 : [\ \ 7,\ \ 9,\ \ 3,\ \ 1,\ 13,\ 12,\ 11,\ 14,\ \ 2,\ \ 6,\ \ 5,\ 10,\ \ 4,\ \ 0,\ 15,\ \ 8]$$
$$\sigma_4 : [\ \ 9,\ \ 0,\ \ 5,\ \ 7,\ \ 2,\ \ 4,\ 10,\ 15,\ 14,\ \ 1,\ 11,\ 12,\ \ 6,\ \ 8,\ \ 3,\ 13]$$
$$\sigma_5 : [\ \ 2,\ 12,\ \ 6,\ 10,\ \ 0,\ 11,\ \ 8,\ \ 3,\ \ 4,\ 13,\ \ 7,\ \ 5,\ 15,\ 14,\ \ 1,\ \ 9]$$
$$\sigma_6 : [\ 12,\ \ 5,\ \ 1,\ 15,\ 14,\ 13,\ \ 4,\ 10,\ \ 0,\ \ 7,\ \ 6,\ \ 3,\ \ 9,\ \ 2,\ \ 8,\ 11]$$
$$\sigma_7 : [\ 13,\ 11,\ \ 7,\ 14,\ 12,\ \ 1,\ \ 3,\ \ 9,\ \ 5,\ \ 0,\ 15,\ \ 4,\ \ 8,\ \ 6,\ \ 2,\ 10]$$
$$\sigma_8 : [\ \ 6,\ 15,\ 14,\ \ 9,\ 11,\ \ 3,\ \ 0,\ \ 8,\ 12,\ \ 2,\ 13,\ \ 7,\ \ 1,\ \ 4,\ 10,\ \ 5]$$
$$\sigma_9 : [\ 10,\ \ 2,\ \ 8,\ \ 4,\ \ 7,\ \ 6,\ \ 1,\ \ 5,\ 15,\ 11,\ \ 9,\ 14,\ \ 3,\ 12,\ 13,\ \ 0]$$

$$a := a + b + m_{\sigma_r(2i)} \quad d := ROTR^{32}(d \oplus a) \quad c := c + d \quad b := ROTR^{24}(b \oplus c)$$
$$a := a + b + m_{\sigma_r(2i+1)} \quad d := ROTR^{16}(d \oplus a) \quad c := c + d \quad b := ROTR^{63}(b \oplus c)$$

C   Explicit Performance Metrics

The main performance metrics which are used in our work are throughput, area and throughput to area ratio (Tp/A). They are presented in Figs. 4, 5 and 6 in comparison with the block size of a message (which is represented on the x axis in all plots). The block size n goes from 64 bytes to 9600 bytes (we chose these values in order to meet the requirements of an online system). Both OMD-sha-512 and OMD-blake2b instantiations are taken into consideration.

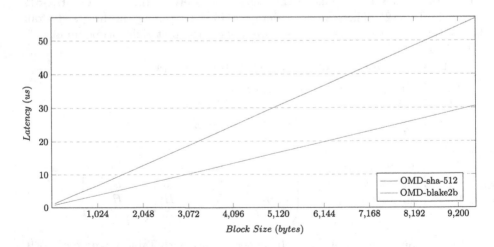

Fig. 4. Latency vs. block size

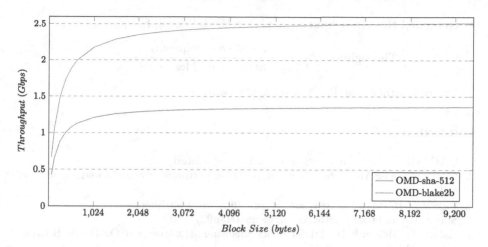

Fig. 5. Throughput vs. block size

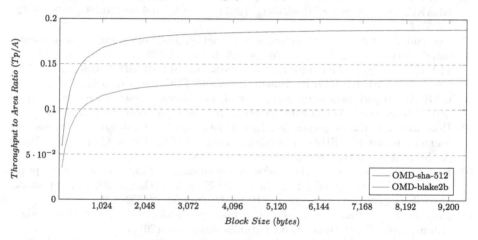

Fig. 6. Throughput to area ratio (Tp/A) vs. block size

All formulas used to generate the plots are based on the metrics described in Table 1. We recall that, during the following, ① *Setup* represents the number of clock cycles necessary in the initialization phase, ② *Message* refers to the number of clock cycles necessary to process a message composed of n blocks, ③ *Tag* represents the number of clock cycles necessary to calculate *Tag* and ④ *Frequency* refers to the frequency of the FPGA circuit.

In Fig. 4 we use latency as the parameter represented by the y axis. We computed latency by the following formula:

$$\text{Latency} = \text{CLK} \cdot (\text{Setup} + n \cdot \text{Message} + \text{Tag}) \cdot 1/\text{Frequency}.$$

We computed the throughput by applying the following formula:

$$\text{Throughput} = \frac{n \cdot 64 \cdot 8 \cdot \text{Frequency}}{\text{CLK} \cdot (\text{Setup} + n \cdot \text{Message} + \text{Tag})}.$$

The computation of Tp/A is straightforward.

References

1. CAESAR. https://competitions.cr.yp.to/caesar.html
2. OMDv2 CAESAR Submission. https://competitions.cr.yp.to/round2/omdv20c.pdf
3. Password Hashing Competition. https://password-hashing.net
4. Source Code. https://github.com/megastefan22/OMD
5. Ashur, T., Mennink, B.: Trivial Nonce-misusing attack on pure OMD. IACR Cryptology ePrint Archive (2015)
6. Aumasson, J.-P., Meier, W., Phan, R.C.-W., Henzen, L.: The Hash Function BLAKE. ISC. Springer, Heidelberg (2014). https://doi.org/10.1007/978-3-662-44757-4
7. Cogliani, S., et al.: OMD: a compression function mode of operation for authenticated encryption. In: Joux, A., Youssef, A. (eds.) SAC 2014. LNCS, vol. 8781, pp. 112–128. Springer, Cham (2014). https://doi.org/10.1007/978-3-319-13051-4_7
8. Diehl, W., Gaj, K.: RTL implementations and FPGA benchmarking of selected CAESAR round two authenticated ciphers. Microprocess. Microsyst. (2017). https://www.sciencedirect.com/science/article/abs/pii/S0141933117300352
9. Homsirikamol, E., Rogawski, M., Gaj, K.: Comparing hardware performance of fourteen round two SHA-3 candidates using FPGAs. IACR Cryptology ePrint Archive (2010). http://eprint.iacr.org/2010/445
10. Krovetz, T., Rogaway, P.: The software performance of authenticated-encryption modes. In: Joux, A. (ed.) FSE 2011. LNCS, vol. 6733, pp. 306–327. Springer, Heidelberg (2011). https://doi.org/10.1007/978-3-642-21702-9_18
11. Maimuț, D.: Authentication and encryption protocols: design, attacks and algorithmic tools. Ph.D. thesis, École normale supérieure (2015)
12. Maimuț, D., Reyhanitabar, R.: Authenticated encryption: toward next-generation algorithms. IEEE Secur. Privacy 12(2), 70–72 (2014)
13. National Institute of Standards and Technology: FIPS PUB 180–4: Secure Hash Standard. NIST, August 2015
14. Reyhanitabar, R., Vaudenay, S., Vizár, D.: Misuse-resistant variants of the OMD authenticated encryption mode. In: Chow, S.S.M., Liu, J.K., Hui, L.C.K., Yiu, S.M. (eds.) ProvSec 2014. LNCS, vol. 8782, pp. 55–70. Springer, Cham (2014). https://doi.org/10.1007/978-3-319-12475-9_5
15. Reyhanitabar, R., Vaudenay, S., Vizár, D.: Boosting OMD for almost free authentication of associated data. In: Leander, G. (ed.) FSE 2015. LNCS, vol. 9054, pp. 411–427. Springer, Heidelberg (2015). https://doi.org/10.1007/978-3-662-48116-5_20
16. Rogaway, P.: Authenticated-encryption with associated-data. In: CCS 2002, pp. 98–107. ACM (2002)
17. Rogaway, P.: Nonce-based symmetric encryption. In: Roy, B., Meier, W. (eds.) FSE 2004. LNCS, vol. 3017, pp. 348–358. Springer, Heidelberg (2004). https://doi.org/10.1007/978-3-540-25937-4_22

Reputation-Based Security Framework for Internet of Things

Ion Bica[✉] ⓘ, Bogdan-Cosmin Chifor ⓘ, Ştefan-Ciprian Arseni ⓘ,
and Ioana Matei ⓘ

Faculty of Information Systems and Cybersecurity,
"Ferdinand I" Military Technical Academy, 050141 Bucharest, Romania
{ion.bica, bogdan.chifor, stefan.arseni,
ioana.matei}@mta.ro

Abstract. Mobile crowdsensing has emerged as a new paradigm in the IoT world, exploiting users' mobility in conjunction with advanced capabilities and proliferation of mobile devices. Smartphones, tablets and smartwatches are now typically equipped with sensing and wireless capabilities, enabling them to produce and upload data for different IoT applications. The mobile crowdsensing approach has the advantage of being cost-effective, while also providing real-time data. However, a number of challenges should be addressed in order for mobile crowdsensing to reach its full potential. Security, privacy and reliability of the data provided by mobile devices are the most important ones. In this paper, we propose a security framework with a multi-layer architecture that addresses the trust evaluation of sensing devices based on reputation scores calculated using a naive Bayes algorithm.

Keywords: Mobile crowdsensing · Security framework · Trust management

1 Introduction

The Internet of Things (IoT) refers to a network of interconnected "smart objects" that have incorporated the technology needed to detect and communicate data about their internal state, as well as interacting with the external environment. One direction of development in IoT is currently represented by mobile crowdsensing. The devices that we carry with us every day (such as smartphones, tablets, smartwatches) are equipped with several physical and virtual sensors that may collect and share information about the surrounding environment for different purposes.

Mobile crowdsourcing has attracted the attention of researchers with applications designed for air quality monitoring [1], traffic monitoring [2] or intelligent parking [3, 4]. The idea behind mobile crowdsensing applications is to reduce costs by replacing or complementing traditional wireless sensor networks. A conventional sensors network in IoT is usually intended for a specific application, but mobile crowdsensing is trying to reuse data for multiple purposes [5]. There are a series of researches regarding the definition of frameworks for mobile crowdsourcing [6, 7], as well as specific implementations [8, 9] that allow the development of applications by reusing the data from multiple sensors.

© Springer Nature Switzerland AG 2020
E. Simion and R. Géraud-Stewart (Eds.): SecITC 2019, LNCS 12001, pp. 213–226, 2020.
https://doi.org/10.1007/978-3-030-41025-4_14

The main drawback of mobile crowdsensing is finding out a method of establishing the degree of trust of the sensing nodes within the network, because they may affect the quality of services provided. In crowdsensing applications, devices involved in the sensing process are vulnerable and they can insert erroneous data into the system either intentionally (attacks of malicious people) or unintentional (environmental disturbances). Consequently, it is challenging to ascertain the correctness of the collected data and is difficult to establish the reliability of it without knowing whether the data is valid or not.

This paper proposes a security framework with a multi-layer architecture that addresses the trust evaluation of sensing devices based on reputation scores calculated using a naive Bayes algorithm. The proposed framework consists of interconnected modules that are integrated at each of the main layers of an IoT system: Cloud, gateway, and device. The framework is built on a customized decentralized architecture, empowering middle-layer devices, such as gateways, while having a central point of management through a Cloud platform. Following the gateway-centric model, our framework moves the main part of the security logic at the gateway layer, where we integrate the core of the reputation-based trust management system.

The framework's key components are presented in the remaining sections of the paper, which has the following structure. Section 2 presents the related work being done in this domain. Section 3 describes the architecture of the proposed framework, followed by Sect. 4, in which the tests and analyses are presented. Section 5 ends the paper with conclusions and future research directions.

2 Related Work

In distributed and collaborative systems, trust management plays a significant role. Ensuring a high degree of trust and security is a critical issue that must be considered when designing a mobile crowdsensing application. Reputation is a concept closely related to establishing a trust relationship between participants. Based on previous experiences and the reference information already collected, a degree of trust or mistrust can be assigned to each participant. Recent studies present an overview of trust management in IoT, explaining its usefulness in a security framework and how it should be exploited. In [10], the security objectives of a trust management system are presented and a review of the current research that deals with the subject of trust in IoT systems is made. It also presents a conceptual model for a holistic framework that contains elements of trust management at each layer and cross-layers. Another detailed study of trust management techniques is described in [11], where a series of frameworks that are based on node reputation are presented: AETS (Adaptive Trust Estimation Scheme), ATBP (Adaption Trust-Based Protocol), TDFDS (Trust-based Development Framework for distributed systems), CTMS-SIOT (Context-based trust management system for the social Internet of Things), etc. The last one is presented in the context of dynamic systems that want to maintain a realistic approach. Regardless of the nature of the architecture (centralized or decentralized), CTMS-SIOT depends on both the past interaction and future prediction and is based on two modules: one for storing contextual trust and one for calculating reputation.

A trust management system based on reputation can defend a network against attacks at nodes level because it facilitates the detection of untrustworthy entities, thus contributing to the decision-making process. Today, there are several proposals and algorithms for computing reputation based on K-Nearest Neighbors, naive Bayes Case-Based Reasoning (CBR) [12] or Fuzzy logic [13]. In [14], the author uses Bayesian inference and self-observation to evaluate trust based on feedback received from neighboring nodes. The proposed model updates the confidence level of the nodes in real-time in order to prevent opportunistic attacks. A different approach to trust calculation is provided in [13] using Fuzzy logic. The system allows the nodes to interact with each other, recording all transactions, then evaluates the performance of each node based on the package delivery ratio (PDR).

A security framework that relies on the trust management module can bring improvements to an IoT architecture in terms of detecting abnormal node behaviors and isolating them. An approach to such a security framework for IoT is presented in [15, 16]. They address the possibility of building services only on the basis of information received from trusted nodes. The information is actually the feedback sent by the neighboring nodes or from the gateway. A slightly different approach is presented in [17, 18] which implements an identity-based key agreement framework to prevent attacks outside the network and to recognize malicious nodes.

To address the problems that appear at all layers in an IoT architecture, we have defined a modularized security framework that allows a decision to be made in accordance with the reliable information collected from the devices that can be used in crowdsensing architectures. Compared to the above-mentioned frameworks, the reputation module is deployed at the gateway layer so that the gateway can select the devices that contribute to data in the mobile crowdsensing architecture.

3 Proposed Architecture Design

The security framework, detailed in the following subsections, makes use of the advantages that reputation-based trust management has, for enforcing the distribution of valid data throughout the system and mitigating different types of attacks. Following the gateway-centric approach that many IoT systems are based upon, we propose a security framework that empowers the gateway as its central element. In this scenario, the Cloud component plays a secondary role, ensuring the communication between the gateway and crowdsensing devices, data consumers or static nodes.

The system architecture contains the following modules: the IoT end-points, the gateway, and the Cloud. The IoT layer comprises devices that produce aggregated data using the on-board sensors and the most trusted crowdsensing information. The gateway layer is the most critical part of our system, being the element that computes the IoT device's reputation and acts as a communication bridge for the local IoT data flow and for uploading the local computed IoT data to an upstream application. The Cloud layer is used to manage local gateways, along with establishing the trust relations between them, and acts as a passive repository for storing the IoT generated data. This architecture is based on a mobile crowdsensing model that enables a collaboratory IoT data delivery application. Thus, the core element of this system is a local network of static IoT devices that generates and aggregates data. These local IoT modules are either low-cost devices or devices which need data generated by other mobile devices located in the environment. The mobile crowdsensing model reduces the cost of the static IoT group deployment by allowing an IoT device with a small number of on-board sensors (simple hardware design) to virtually extend it's sensor capabilities. This mechanism also improves the IoT static group flexibility, by handling other types of sensor data without having to re-deploy the entire sensor fleet. The system architecture is depicted in Fig. 1.

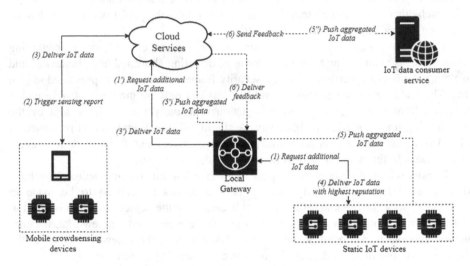

Fig. 1. The architecture of the system

As it can be observed, the static group of IoT devices is extending it's sensor capabilities with the aid of the mobile crowdsensing IoT devices. Thus, when a static IoT device needs additional data, it chooses the information published by the most trusted mobile crowdsensing module (the device with the highest reputation within a certain data category). For instance, if a static device is not equipped with a temperature sensor, it may choose to query the gateway, which in turn delivers the most trusted information provided by a mobile crowdsensing device. By using this approach, the static device can aggregate data from various sources (on-board and participatory sensors), and deliver the information to an upstream application. The upstream application consumes the static IoT delivered data and provides feedback based on the information quality/relevance. If it receives positive feedback, the static device rewards the mobile crowdsourcing module which contributed to the delivered information.

3.1   IoT Device Layer

As mentioned before, the IoT device layer comprises two groups: mobile crowdsensing and the static IoT group which communicate through the Cloud services and the local gateway. The mobile crowdsensing IoT device group is composed of sensors that sample data from the environment and voluntarily submit it to a local gateway. The information submit process is orchestrated through a smartphone application that acquires data from two sources: on-board (local) smartphone sensors and wearables. The smartphone application acts as a data aggregator and submits the information to a local gateway, through the Cloud module, following the mobile crowdsensing paradigm. The controller application acquires sensor data using the following mechanisms:

- it uses the smartphone operating system API's to sample data using the on-board sensors (e.g. use the Android API to query the barometer sensor in order to detect changes in air pressure).
- it uses a low energy connection (e.g. BLE) with wearables in order to extract the sensor data. The controller smartphone application uses the management API exposed by the wearables (e.g. smart-watch, smart-bracelet).

The wearables along with the smartphone onboard sensors share the same trust domain or use an already existing security link (e.g. authentication between the smartphone and the wearable), thus an additional security mechanism is not required. The user device-generated data is relevant only for a certain geographical area, thus the data sampling process is triggered by the smartphone controller, only when the user is located within the local gateway's area of interest. Taking into consideration that the mobile crowdsensing data is consumed based on the reputation value, the controller application generates an identity and uses that identity every time a sensor data is submitted to the gateway. The controller's identity consists of a pair of asymmetric cryptographic keys, each mobile crowdsensing report being signed with the controller's private key. The application controller communicates with the gateway through a data submission protocol, which consists of the following steps:

1. at start-up, the controller application generates an asymmetric key pair and submits to the Cloud service, the public key along with a pseudonym. This tuple represents the application controller's identity.
2. the gateway initiates a report submission session, by sending a request to the Cloud service, which in turn relays the request to all the devices within a geographical area. The session metadata consists of a unique session identifier (randomly generated) and a data category (e.g. temperature, noise).
3. if applicable, the controller application acquires data from the local smartphone and from the connected wearables, aggregates the data in a report, appends the session metadata and signs the report with his private key.

After a member of the mobile crowdsensing IoT group submits a sensing report to the local gateway, the information is stored on the gateway side for a period of time. The mobile device does not have a direct communication link with the gateway, the communication being established by means of the Cloud platform. The mobile device to gateway communication consists of the following steps:

1. the gateway triggers a data sensing query by sending a request to the Cloud platform. The request contains the gateway GPS location, taking into consideration that the mobile crowdsensing data is relevant only for the gateway's proximity.

2. the Cloud platform relays the sensing request to all mobile crowdsensing applications which are located in the gateway's proximity.
3. the targeted mobile application controllers trigger a data sampling process.
4. after the controller mobile application acquires the data, it sends the response to the Cloud platform, which in turn relays it to the gateway.

The Cloud-based communication between the mobile application and the gateway requires only a data connection on the user's smartphone. Although the gateway has communication capabilities (acting as a hotspot or as a base station for the static IoT devices), scanning and subscribing to different networks is a battery intensive task for a smartphone. This is an import factor, taking into consideration that the mobile crowdsensing is not the primary task of a smartphone, and such a solution must be non-intrusive from the performance and user-experience perspectives.

During this time interval, the data is eligible for being consumed by a member of the static IoT group, if the data producer's reputation is the highest within a category. The reputation of the mobile IoT device is computed locally, but it can be transferred from a gateway domain to another, thus the device must use the same identity in order to preserve the reputation value. If a member of the static group needs additional sensor data, it executes a sensor query and the gateway returns the most trusted data within the requested category. After computing the aggregated data with the aid of a mobile device, the static device publishes the information (through the gateway) to a higher layer application that consumes the information. This can be either a smartphone application or a web application that delivers data to end-users or to another IoT device. The gateway exposes an API that allows the data consumer (e.g. end-user smartphone application or web service) to provide feedback for the delivered data. In accordance with the feedback, the gateway increases or decreases the reputation of the participatory sensing device. The transaction is asynchronous because the mobile sensing data can be queried by a static device anytime during the data time-to-live interval, with the gateway acting as a buffer for storing the most recent published information. The gateway publishes the information received from the static IoT devices to the Cloud platform, which in turn relays it to the consumer applications. The data is delivered to the consumer application through a TLS channel, each consumer application having an identity registered on the Cloud platform. The feedback is also delivered to the gateway via the trusted Cloud communication channel, thus the feedback cannot be altered or submitted multiple times.

3.2   Gateway Layer

The gateway module is responsible for computing the reputation of the mobile crowdsensing devices that contribute with sensor data to the static IoT modules. The crowdsensing devices do not share a trust relationship with the gateway, these contributing with information in an ad-hoc manner. By using a reputation algorithm, the gateway delivers to the static IoT device the most trusted information within a category. If a device contributes with relevant information constantly, its' reputation value will be increased, otherwise, the reputation level will decrease if a transaction is considered failed. For computing the reputation level, a naive Bayes algorithm is used. This algorithm was chosen because it does not require high computational resources, being adequate for resource-constrained gateways. In an IoT network, the number of deployed gateways is high, given that these are part of the leaf network segment. Taking this into consideration, low cost gateways are critical in the cost-effectiveness of an IoT application. Thus, a lightweight algorithm like naive Bayes can be executed on general purpose gateways that do not have security as a primary task.

The gateway maintains a repository with the reputation level for each mobile crowdsensing device that submits a sensing report. This repository can be modified only by the naive Bayes algorithm and the reputation value can be transferred to another gateway domain. Taking into consideration that the crowdsensing devices are mobile, there is a low probability for the same device to submit data to the same gateway multiple times, thus the reputation must be transferred from one gateway to another. Given the trust relationship between the gateways, when a new device submits data into a zone, the gateway sends a broadcast request to all gateways in order to find a baseline reputation score. The communication between the gateways is achieved by means of the Cloud platform, which relays the messages. The gateway that executes the query chooses the minimum reputation score received from other gateways and uses this value as the baseline reputation level for the newly registered crowdsensing device.

As stressed before, the naive Bayes method was chosen due to its simplicity, which assumes that an agent can deliver information with the characteristic that one delivered feature is independent of the others. For instance, in our crowdsensing IoT scenario, the naive Bayes paradigm is translated into the characteristic that a mobile user can deliver a trustworthy temperature value without influencing the trustworthiness of the delivered air pressure value. In Fig. 2 is depicted the structure of the proposed naive Bayes network. The purpose of our naive Bayes algorithm is to predict the probability of a mobile device to deliver trustworthy information, based on the previously delivered data.

As presented in Fig. 2, the root node of the naive Bayes network indicates if the mobile agent is trustworthy and the leaves contain the sensor data features. The features are represented by the agent delivered data type (e.g. temperature, CO2) and by meta-information generated by the gateway (e.g. how fast and how often a mobile agent uploads a sensing report).

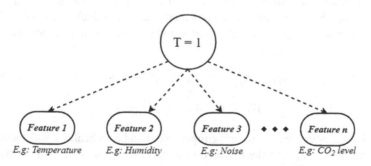

Fig. 2. The naive Bayes network

The local gateway maintains a naive Bayes network for every mobile crowdsensing agent. In order to increase the reputation value, each transaction must be evaluated and classified as satisfying or unsatisfying (Formula 1).

$$p(T = 1) = \frac{\# \, of \, successful \, transactions}{\# \, of \, total \, transactions} \tag{1}$$

In order to compute the Bayes probability, given any set of features as input, the gateway maintains a conditional probability table (CPT) as presented in Table 1.

Table 1. Example of a conditional probability table

	T = 1	T = 0
F_1	$p(FT = F_1\|T = 1)$	$p(FT = F_1\|T = 0)$
F_2	$p(FT = F_2\|T = 1)$	$p(FT = F_2\|T = 0)$
F_3	$p(FT = F_3\|T = 1)$	$p(FT = F_3\|T = 0)$

Each entry from Table 1 indicates the conditional probability of a mobile agent to deliver a sensing report which contains data with a given feature (e.g. temperature data), given a trustworthy transaction. According to Bayes formula, the entry from CPT can be computed following Formula 2:

$$p(FT = F_1|T = 1) = \frac{p(FT = F_1, T = 1)}{P(T = 1)}, \text{ where} \tag{2}$$

$$p(FT = F_1, T = 1) = \frac{\# \, of \, successful \, transactions \, with \, F_1}{\# \, of \, total \, transactions} \tag{3}$$

A transaction is classified as successful if its' degree of satisfaction passes a given threshold. This process is executed on the consumer application side by an evaluator agent that can contain a customized method of evaluation chosen by the user, thus it is considered out of the scope of this paper. For a static IoT device, a certain feature may be more important than others (e.g. receiving a high-quality temperature value may be more important than receiving an accurate air pressure value), thus the satisfaction degree formula allows assigning different weights to the evaluated features (as presented in Formula 4):

$$s = W_{F_1} \times S_{F_1} + W_{F_2} \times S_{F_2} + \ldots + W_{F_n} \times S_{F_n} \tag{4}$$

$$W_{F_1} + W_{F_2} + \ldots + W_{F_n} = 1 \tag{5}$$

where W indicates the feature weight (importance) and S indicates a satisfaction value for a feature. If $S > S_t$ then the transaction is successful, otherwise it is unsuccessful.

Using Bayes theorem, the probability of a given mobile crowding IoT device to deliver a satisfying transaction that involves a feature set F is predicted.

$$p(T = 1|F) = \frac{p(F|T = 1) \times p(T = 1)}{p(F)} \qquad (6)$$

When feature set F is expanded to features $F_1, F_2, \ldots, F_n$, the Formula 6 becomes:

$$p(T = 1, F_1, F_2, \ldots, F_n) = p(T = 1) \times PROD\left(\frac{p\ (F_i, T = 1)}{p\ (T = 1)}\right) \qquad (7)$$

The naive Bayes algorithm implemented in the proposed framework provides a compact method of determining the reputation of data collected from crowdsensing devices, eliminating the risk of allowing nodes to inject malicious data into the IoT system.

3.3   Cloud Layer

In the proposed framework, the central position of the Cloud module empowers it to act as a management module and data relay for the entire IoT system. Considering the data relay role, the main task of the Cloud module is to relay sensing data requests coming from gateways. In order to do this, the request is first parsed and specific fields are extracted so that the request can be forwarded to a certain group of mobile crowd-sensing IoT devices located in the proximity of the gateway that made the request. This is achieved by using the GPS location field found in the data sensing request. Furthermore, from this request the Cloud module will also filter the type of data the gateway requires, thus limiting the resources consumption from both implied parties (the crowdsensing IoT devices and the gateway).

Given that the mobile crowdsensing devices notify the Cloud module only when they connect to the network, it is difficult for it to have a real-time updated map of the entire network, but rather one that has the last status of each device. Therefore, several requests can be rejected, if the devices are not located in the targeted area, or discarded if the devices are not active anymore. In the first case, the crowdsensing devices send a message to notify the Cloud that their location has changed, while in the second case the Cloud module retries, for a customizable number of times, to send the request and, if no reply is received, it will mark the crowdsensing devices as inactive and remove them from further queries, until a reconnect message is received. Also, taking into consideration that these crowdsensing devices are mobile, some of them can move between areas of interest. In this case, the Cloud module will extend the area where the requests will be forwarded, so that any possible device that is currently active in the area of interest will be notified. Each communication link is secured using a symmetric key, randomly chosen by the Cloud module and specific for each crowdsensing device. For secretly sharing these symmetric keys with the corresponding crowdsensing devices, the Cloud module encrypts them with the public key of the crowdsensing devices.

Data gathered from the crowdsensing IoT devices groups, as producers, and used by the static IoT devices groups, as consumers, is trusted by the consumers in accordance with the reputation that the producers have. This level of reputation can fluctuate during the entire lifecycle of a producer and it can be used to detect malicious devices. Gateways can send reputation queries between them to see if a producer that crossed between areas covered by different gateways has been already assessed by the previous gateway and what is its level of reputation, or if it needs to be considered as a freshly registered producer and begin the reputation assessment process. Since gateways are manually registered by the administrator on the Cloud module, the setting of a trust relationship between different gateways is done automatically.

4 Implementation and Analysis

For the system implementation, we used Qemu for emulating the gateway and the static IoT devices, along with an Android application for the mobile crowdsensing. The static IoT devices logic was implemented as a Linux process that acts as an MQTT-SN client and communicates with the gateway for requesting data with the highest reputation. The aggregated data is published by the static IoT device to the gateway using MQTT-SN, the latter transporting the information to the consumer application through HTTPs (web service). For the mobile crowdsensing, we implemented a proof-of-concept Android application that communicates with the Cloud platform through Firebase messages (real-time push notifications). For the initial implementation we used only the smartphone onboard sensors along with software simulated sensors. We implemented a sensor abstraction layer to integrate the Android application with the simulated sensors, this abstraction layer allowing a rapid integration with a third-party wearable API.

For testing the naive Bayes reputation algorithm, we designed a custom Python simulator. The simulator allows declaring IoT nodes and associates different sensor types with the IoT node (e.g. an IoT node can deliver temperature and noise values). For each sensor type, a target value and a deviation interval were declared, this tuple being used to model the IoT node's behavior in a stochastic manner. For each sensor type we defined an evaluator model which gives a score (between 0 and 1) to each delivered data: if the data is accurate (close to the target value) the score is high. The evaluator model transmits the score to the naive Bayes engine that updates the reputation value on each simulation step. The goal of this experiment is to observe that an IoT node's reputation history is updated correctly by the naive Bayes engine based on the delivered data quality. In this experiment we used 3 sensors that deliver one or more data types. In the first test scenario, the sensors deliver temperature and humidity values: sensor 1 delivers the best values, followed by sensor 2 and sensor 3, as reflected in Fig. 3.

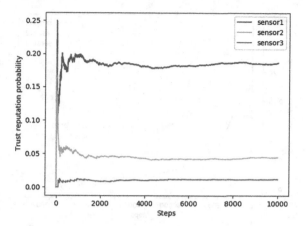

Fig. 3. First test scenario

In the second test case, the sensors deliver also temperature and humidity values: sensor 1 delivers the best temperature value and the second best humidity value, sensor 2 delivers the best humidity value and the second best temperature value, sensor 3 delivers the worst values. In this scenario, the humidity has a bigger weight (it is more important than the temperature value), as presented in Fig. 4.

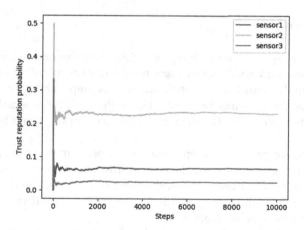

Fig. 4. Second test scenario

In the third test case, the sensors deliver temperature, humidity, and CO_2 values: sensor 1 delivers the best values, followed by sensor 2 and sensor 3 for the first part of the simulation. For the second part of the simulation, sensor 3 delivers the best values, followed by sensor 2 and sensor 1, as presented in Fig. 5. This last test case simulates a data manipulation attack, where an IoT node achieves a high reputation score and then tries to manipulate the system by injecting false data.

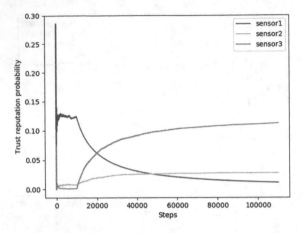

Fig. 5. Third test scenario

As the results for these three scenarios show, the reputation-based trust management system is able to adapt to changes and responds adequately to malicious intentions of pushing erroneous data into the IoT system. Also, as presented in the second scenario, if a weighted method of calculating reputation is chosen, the framework can cope with these changes and correctly assess the reputation of each node.

5   Conclusions

Mobile crowdsensing is trying to bring new data collection techniques into IoT by exploiting the sensing capabilities of users mobile devices to collect and share data. A major problem that arises in such applications is the impossibility of guaranteeing a suitable behavior for each mobile device. Hence the need for a security framework based on reputation, so that mobile device intervention with suspicious behavior can be minimized.

In this paper, we presented an approach to this problem by proposing a modular security framework able to compute the level of trust of a mobile device based on the feedback received from the consumer. A drawback of the model used in the decision-making process in the reputation system is that we use a threshold value that has to be set according to each type of application.

Regarding our future work, to prevent the aforementioned drawback, we plan to implement and test several reputation calculation algorithms in order to offer a trade-off between the algorithm accuracy and the required computing resources. By implementing a suite of algorithms either using Fuzzy logic, Case-Based Reasoning, or even naive Bayes, we can approach distinct IoT interaction models so that we can choose the right method of calculating reputation depending on the type of application. Another direction that we will focus on consists of improving the mechanism that ensures the anonymity of the crowdsensing devices while maintaining the system's responsiveness in the event of the occurrence of untrustworthy actions.

Acknowledgments. This work was supported by a grant of the Romanian Ministry of Research and Innovation, CCCDI – UEFISCDI, project number PN-III-P1-1.2-PCCDI-2017-0272/Avant-garde Technology Hub for Advanced Security (ATLAS), within PNCDI III.

References

1. Leonardi, C., Cappellotto, A., Caraviello, M., Lepri, B., Antonelli, F.: SecondNose: an air quality mobile crowdsensing system. In: Proceedings of the 8th Nordic Conference on Human-Computer Interaction, Helsinki, Finland, pp. 1051–1054 (2014)
2. Pan, B., Zheng, Y., Wilkie, D., Shahabi, C.: Crowd sensing of traffic anomalies based on human mobility and social media. In: Proceedings of the 21st ACM SIGSPATIAL International Conference on Advances in Geographic Information Systems, Orlando, FL, USA, pp. 344–353 (2013)
3. Coric, V., Gruteser, M.: Crowdsensing maps of on-street parking spaces. In: Proceedings of the 9th IEEE International Conference on Distributed Computing in Sensor Systems, Cambridge, MA, USA, pp. 115–122 (2013)
4. Salpietro, R., Bedogni, L., Di Felice, M., Bononi, L.: Park Here! a smart parking system based on smartphones' embedded sensors and short range Communication Technologies. In: Proceedings of the 2015 IEEE 2nd World Forum on Internet of Things, Milan, Italy, pp. 18–23 (2015)
5. Ganti, R., Ye, F., Lei, H.: Mobile crowdsensing: current state and future challenges. IEEE Commun. Mag. **49**(11), 32–39 (2011)
6. Guo, B., Yu, Z., Zhang, D., Zhou, X.: From participatory sensing to mobile crowd sensing. In: Proceedings of the 12th IEEE International Conference on Pervasive Computing and Communications Workshops (PERCOM Workshop), Budapest, Hungary, pp. 593–598 (2014)
7. Giannetsos, T., Gisdakis, S., Papadimitratos, P.: Trustworthy people-centric sensing: privacy, security and user incentives road-map. In: Proceedings of the 13th Annual Mediterranean Workshop on Ad Hoc Networking, Piran, Slovenia, pp. 39–46 (2014)
8. Gunasekaran, S., Rathnamala, J.: Review on various architectural models in mobile crowdsensing (2015)
9. Montori, F., Bedogni, L., Di Chiappari, A., Bononi, L.: SenSquare: a mobile crowdsensing architecture for smart cities. In: 2016 IEEE 3rd World Forum on Internet of Things (WF-IoT), Reston, VA, pp. 536–541 (2016)
10. Zheng, Y., Peng, Z., Athanasios, V.: A survey on trust management for Internet of Things. J. Netw. Comput. Appl. **42**, 120–134 (2014)
11. Ud Din, I., Guizani, M., Kim, B.-S., Hassan, S., Khan, K.: Trust management techniques for the Internet of Things: a survey. IEEE Access **7**, 29763–29787 (2018)
12. Chettri, R., Pradhan, S., Chettri, L.: Internet of Things: comparative study on classification algorithms (K-NN, naive Bayes and case based reasoning). Int. J. Comput. Appl. **130**, 7–9 (2015)
13. Chen, D., Chang, G., Sun, D., Li, J., Jia, J., Wang, X.: TRM-IoT: a trust management model based on fuzzy reputation for Internet of Things. Comput. Sci. Inf. Syst. **8**, 1207–1228 (2011)
14. Chen, I.R., Guo, J., Bao, F.: Trust management for SOA-based IoT and its application to service composition. IEEE Trans. Serv. Comput. **9**(3), 482–495 (2016)

15. Bao, F., Chen, I.: Trust management for the Internet of Things and its application to service composition. In: 13th IEEE International Symposium on a World of Wireless, Mobile and Multimedia Networks, San Francisco, CA, United States, pp. 1–6 (2012)
16. Nitti, M., Giran, R., Atzori, L., Iera, A., Morabito, G.: A subjective model for trustworthiness evaluation in the social Internet of Things. In: 2012 IEEE 23rd International Symposium on Personal Indoor and Mobile Radio Communication, Sydney, Australia, pp. 18–23 (2012)
17. Liu, T., Guan, Y., Yan, Y., Liu, L., Deng, Q.: A WSN-oriented key agreement protocol in Internet of Things. In: 3rd International Conference on Frontiers of Manufacturing Science and Measuring Technology, LiJiang, China, pp. 1792–1795 (2013)
18. Martinez-Julia, P., Skarmeta, A.F.: Beyond the separation of identifier and locator: building an identity-based overlay network architecture for the Future Internet. Comput. Netw. **57**(10), 2280–2300 (2013)

Learned Lessons from Implementing an Android Client for the Cloud Signature Consortium API

Iulian Aciobanitei(✉), Paul-Danut Urian, and Mihai-Lica Pura

Military Technical Academy, 050141 Bucharest, Romania
`aciobanitei.iulian@gmail.com`

Abstract. Advanced electronic signatures are the main security mechanism used for assuring authentication, integrity and non-repudiation of electronic documents. Digitization on a large scale requires secure and flexible electronic signature systems. In E.U., the use of remote qualified electronic signatures has considerably increased after the adoption of the Regulation (EU) No 910/2014 ("eIDAS"). Thanks to the new legislative measures, owning a physical device to create a qualified electronic signature in no longer mandatory, so the user experience has been considerably improved. However, the full potential of remote qualified electronic signatures has not been reached yet. Our work supports the adoption of the remote digital signature in various fields by implementing an Android application that can apply qualified electronic signatures. To assure interoperability, the client-server communication follows a standard protocol: the Cloud Signature Consortium API. The main advantage of our approach is that the Android application is able to sign using certificates issued by different Trust Service Providers. This paper will analyze the current situation and will present the main challenges encountered when designing and developing a digital signature application that uses remote qualified digital certificates as well as the learned lessons that could be of tremendous help for others activating in this field.

Keywords: Remote qualified electronic signature · Cloud Signature Consortium API · Android

1 Introduction

The main goal of digitization and use of digital signatures is the simplification of the administrative procedures and the stimulation of a competitive market in the field of service provision. Advanced electronic signature is supported by a strong set of standards and laws in order to be globally recognized. At European level, laws and regulations ensure that the qualified electronic signatures can be legally equated to the handwritten signatures. Standards are referred to in the legislation in order to achieve interoperability between the technical systems of the Member States and efficiency in creating such systems.

E. Simion and R. Géraud-Stewart (Eds.): SecITC 2019, LNCS 12001, pp. 227–240, 2020.
https://doi.org/10.1007/978-3-030-41025-4_15

The main law regarding electronic signatures in the E.U. is Regulation (EU) No 910/2014 [1], also known as the eIDAS Regulation. eIDAS recognises for the first time the possibility of creating qualified electronic signatures (QES) using private keys stored on remote servers, managed by the Qualified Trust Service Providers (QTSP).

This paper presents the design and implementation of an Android application for remote electronic signature of PDF documents using the remote qualified digital certificates issued by Trans Sped. The Android application is designed and implemented considering that it have to assure, with a high level of confidence, the sole control of the user over the private keys. Besides its main functionality (computing signatures), the application is able to display the certificates available for the authenticated user and signatures applied on PDF documents. The remote electronic signature is computed through the signature web API exposed by Trans Sped, compliant with the remote signature protocol specification proposed by the Cloud Signature Consortium (CSC) version 0.1.7.9 and standardized by ETSI [2]. Besides the ETSI standard regarding the communication between the client application(SCA) and the remote Trust Service Provider (TSP), CEN standards [3,4] enforce a set of security requirements on every component of the system, including the implemented client application.

Given that the working legislation and standards in this area are relatively new, the industry has not yet matured in providing products that exploit the possibilities of remote qualified electronic signature. The main goal of the paper is to support remote QES adoption, by helping the community to develop signature applications compliant with working standards. The main advantage of our implemented application is the interoperability with the TSPs that expose standard interfaces for computing electronic signatures.

The presented application presented uses Trans Sped's solution for remote electronic signature. Trans Sped is a QTSP certified against the eIDAS Regulation, located in Romania. The main particularity of the Trans Sped's remote signature solution is the fact that the OTP is sent to the user via SMS.

With the support of current electronic signature legislation, many remote signature solutions were proposed and developed, like [5–7] and [8]. As presented in [9], back in 2014 there were already a significant number of private companies to provide remote signature solutions: Adobe EchoSign, Amazon CloudHSM, Austrian MObile Phone Signature, DocuSign and Intesi Time4Mind.

The remainder of the paper is organized as follows. The second section presents the main aspects of legislation and standards related to remote electronic signatures and a comparison between local and remote signatures. The third section presents the Cloud Signature Consortium API, the remote signature protocol used for implementing the digital signature application. The fourth section describes the architecture of the implemented application. Section number five depicts the main points to consider when implementing a digital signature application that uses remote qualified digital certificates. The last section concludes the paper and enumerates future work directions.

2   Remote Electronic Signatures

Remote electronic signatures, also called server-side, mobile or cloud signatures, are created by generating, storing and using the private key of an user on a remote electronic signature creation device. The key point of such electronic signature creation environments is to assure the sole control of the owners over the private keys.

2.1   Legislation on Qualified Electronic Signatures

The E.U. legislation regarding electronic signature was adopted for the first time in 1999 and it evolved to these days. The first major step for legalization of electronic signatures was the adoption of 1999/93/CE Directive [10], since the electronic signature was legally equated with a handwritten signature for the first time. Until 2014 it was changed and completed by different Decisions of the European Commission. The second main step in the evolution of the use of electronic signatures was the 910/2014 Regulation (which revoked the 1999/93/CE Directive). The eIDAS regulation is the core of the whole European electronic signature ecosystem. For example, eIDAS defines three different types of signatures: electronic, advanced and qualified. The latter is an advanced signature based on a qualified certificate for electronic signatures and is created using a qualified electronic signature creation device[1]. An advanced electronic signature is implemented based on asymmetric cryptography, is created on a electronic signature creation device under the sole control of the signer[2]. The electronic signature as defined by eIDAS is a more general type of signature, that is not necessarily based on public key cryptography[3]. Still, eIDAS Regulation does not define only signature types, but it covers all the components involved in the electronic signature ecosystem, like: electronic identification, trust lists, signature creation devices, electronic seals, qualified electronic services, supervisory bodies, electronic time-stamps, etc.

2.2   Standards Regarding Remote Electronic Signatures

The core of the remote signature standards are the CEN EN 419 241 series - Trustworthy Systems Supporting Server Signing (T4WS). The main aspect that needs to be solved when designing and developing a remote signature solution is the user's exclusive control over the signature creation material - namely, his private key. Two levels of user's exclusive control over its own private key are

---

[1] REGULATION (EU) No 910/2014 OF THE EUROPEAN PARLIAMENT AND OF THE COUNCIL, Art.3, Definition of "qualified electronic signature".
[2] REGULATION (EU) No 910/2014 OF THE EUROPEAN PARLIAMENT AND OF THE COUNCIL, Art.26.
[3] REGULATION (EU) No 910/2014 OF THE EUROPEAN PARLIAMENT AND OF THE COUNCIL, Art.3, Definition of "electronic signature".

defined[4]: low (SCAL1) and high (SCAL2), where SCAL stands for Sole Control Assurance Level. SCAL2 have to be used for QES.

The CEN standard defines three different environment types in which system components are placed, as follows:

1. **Tamper protected environment** - operates in the protected environment of the trust service provider (TSP), has no direct access to the Internet, assures integrity of the executed code and protects the signing keys. The environment varies depending on sole control assurance level:
   - SCAL1 - It is recommended that private/secret keys generation and usage to be performed in this environment.
   - SCAL2 - Private/secret keys MUST be generated and used in the tamper protected environment. Also, the Signature Activation Module (SAM) component MUST be placed here.
2. **TSP protected environment** - Assures protection against Internet attacks and may keep a protected form of the signing keys or links between keys and signers. It contains the SSA, which is the main component outside the tamper protected environment [4].
3. **Signer environment** - Mainly contains the SCA. For SCAL2, the Signer Interaction Component (SIC) is used in order to achieve two factor authentication. The protection of this environment is a responsibility of the user.

According to [3,4] and [11] the components of a remote signature solution are the following:

1. **SCA** *(Signature Application)* - is located in the user environment. It has three main roles:
   - Document processing - obtaining the Data To Be Signed Representation (DTBSR).
   - Obtaining the signature from the SSA - in our case, by using CSC API.
   - Signature processing - for example, integration in a PDF file.
2. **SSA** *(Server Signing Application)* - Internet exposed component of the TSP. Interacts with the SCA and with the tamper protected components.
3. **SCDev** *(Signature Creation Device)* - Located in the tamper protected environment, it is responsible with key generation, key protection and actual signature computation. This component is materialized by an Hardware Security Module (HSM), that must be FIPS 140-2 level 3 or EAL4 compliant [12]. Signature creation material might be stored outside this component if it is properly protected.
4. **SIC** *(Signer Interaction Module)* - Specific for SCAL2 solutions, it is situated in the user's environment [4]. It participates in user authentication and Signature Activation Data (SAD) creation. SIC assures two factor authentication and might be materialized by a software application, a SIM card, a cryptographic device own by the signer or other similar means.

---

[4] CEN EN 419 241-1. "Trustworthy Systems Supporting Server Signing Part 1: General System Security Requirements", Section 5.4.

5. **SAM** *(Signature Activation Module)* - Specific for SCAL2 solutions, it is protected by the tamper protected environment. The SAM is responsible for SAD validation and authorization of the access to the private key of the authenticated user.

ETSI also published three standards for remote signature systems, as follows:

1. **ETSI TS 119 432** - Defines available protocols between SCA and SSA used for obtaining an electronic signature [2].
2. **ETSI TS 119 431-1** - Completes eIDAS Regulation by defining the policy and security requirements for TSPs which offer remote QES [11].
3. **ETSI TS 119 431-2** - Guides the creation remote Advanced Electronic Signatures (AdES) [13].

Communication between the SCA and the SSA is standardized by ETSI in the technical standard regarding remote signature creation protocols [2]. This protocol is the main component for assuring interoperability between SAs and different TSPs. This protocol permits authentication using username and password, but also supports authorization using an OAuth 2.0 server. In the process of writing the technical specifications of this protocol, ETSI took into consideration both CSC [14] and OASIS - DSS [15] protocols. This way, the actual implementation of the protocol might use JSON or XML syntax.

2.3 The Advantages of Remote Electronic Signatures

eIDAS aimed to improve the user experience and the usability of digital signatures by adopting remote electronic signatures. The Regulation came with the change of criteria to decide the qualified status of a signature. The main change consists in the fact that obtaining a qualified electronic signature (QES) is possible without the user physically owning a Signature Creation Device (SCDev). QES is an advanced electronic signature (AdES) based on a qualified certificate (see footnote 1). For advanced electronic signature creation, owning a physical device is not needed, but the signature creation data (e.g. private key) must be used by the signatory, with a high level of confidence, use under his sole control[5].

Obtaining a qualified electronic signature without having to own a hardware device came with a numerous set of advantages, as follows:

o **Mobility** - Qualified electronic signatures can now be created on smartphones. When the 93/1999 Directive was in force, achieving this goal did not worth the price. Mainly, the restrictions are technical in nature, as mobile devices cannot connect to a cryptographic token in a simple manner, and from the best of our knowledge, there is no cryptographic token provider to offer middleware suitable for mobile device operation systems(namely Android and iOS).

---

[5] REGULATION (EU) No 910/2014 OF THE EUROPEAN PARLIAMENT AND OF THE COUNCIL, Art.26 (c).

o **No Additional Hardware** - Owning a hardware device for creating an electronic signature considerably lowered the user experience, because the physical device might get lost or broke. Also, users might encounter problems with device versions not matching installed driver versions. On short, it is another devices that the user must take care of.

o **No Additional Software** - One of the main problems encountered by the users when creating electronic signatures, was the need of installing different drivers and middleware for assuring the right communication between the signature application and the hardware signature creation device.

o **Reduced costs** - Using a centralized approach, the overall costs for administration and operating get lower for the TSP. The user can optimize costs depending on the business model (taxing only the issuance of the certificate or taxing by computed signature). In some cases, where one signs lots of documents, the cost efficient decision would be to use a personal cryptographic token for signing.

o **Interoperability** - Thanks to the standardized protocols between the SCA and SSA, interoperability between the two components became an achievable goal. For example, a SCA might change the TSP by simply changing the base URL of the exposed CSC API. SCA can be implemented as a web application, which means that creation of qualified signatures is now possible using any device that is able to run a web browser.

It is worth mentioning that the main disadvantage of remote electronic signatures is the fact that, by their nature, they cannot be created without an Internet connection.

2.4   SCA Security Requirements

The main standards regarding remote signature services offered by TSPs, do not target the user environment and the SCA. From the best of our knowledge, all the security requirements for the SCA are the following:

o **ETSI TS 119 432** - specifies the protocol to be respected for communication between SCA/SIC and SSA/SAM. Since the ETSI standard also includes the CSC proposed API, it is enough to be compliant with the CSC protocol.

o **CEN EN 419 241-2** - requires secure manipulation of the SAD and SAP. At the implementation level, sensitive information, like the SAD, shall be stored as char array, not as a string. After finishing the usage of the data, the memory where it was stored should be wiped.

o **ETSI TS 119 431-2**
  o SCA shall process the Signature creation policy (OID)
  o SCA signature shall protect the signing certificate. This requirement is inherited from CAdES specification (ETSI TS 101 733, clause 5.6)

o **ETSI TS 119 101, clause 5.2**
  o **General Requirements**: SCA is well tested; user uses up-to-date security fixes and anti-virus if possible.

o **Application environment**: SCA uses established cryptographic libraries, code is digitally signed, maintains integrity and confidentiality of all info supplied, securely deletes authentication data after the end of the session, and securely manages multiple users using the same application.

3   Cloud Signature Consortium API

Cloud Signature Consortium (CSC) is a private consortium, Adobe being the founding member. The consortium proposed one of the two standards for creation of remote electronic signatures. The CSC maintains a close connection with the ETSI ESI (Electronic Signatures and Infrastructures) working group. Until the writing of this paper, three versions of the standard have been published: 0.1.7.9, 1.0.3.0 and 1.0.4.0.

CSC defines an API for the protocol used between the Signature Application (SCA) and Server Signing Application (SSA). The protocol uses POST HTTP requests. The information transmitted to the server and the responses are transmitted in JSON format. All sent and received parameters are Base64 encoded. To access the API, the client has to use a base URI of the remote signature service, and add the specific string for each available method.

The way to use the CSC protocol to create a signature depends on the chosen mode of authentication and authorization. User experience may also vary depending on this factor. OAuth2.0 authorization is suitable for web applications, since using an OAuth2.0 authorization server inherently involves a number of redirects between the signing application and the authorization server.

An user may access its private key by authentication directly in the SCA or by authentication to the OAuth2.0 authorization server. The main difference between the two models of access to resources is that in the first scenario the user enters information such as username, password, PIN and OTP in the SCA. Even without malicious intentions, but for improving user experience, the signing application could store this sensitive information, which can lead to critical security issues. In case of compromise of the device that stores these pieces of information, the only element that can still ensure the exclusive control of the user at the credentials is the OTP. Therefore, CSC recommends using signature flows with OAuth2.0 authorization.

Presenting the full specification of CSC remote signature API is out of the scope of this paper. The interested readers may find it in the corresponding CSC documents[6].

The CSC proposed protocol has two different levels of authorization: to access the API and to access the private cryptographic material. Access to the API gives the SCA the right to call methods like credentials/list, credentials/info or credentials/sendOTP.

---

[6] https://cloudsignatureconsortium.org/resources/download-api-specifications/.

4   Proposed Digital Signature Application

The digital signature application designed and developed in the work presented in this paper (named Cloud Signer) is intended for devices running Android operating system and aims at offering a solution for signing PDF documents with remote qualified digital certificates issued by any qualified trust service provider exposing a remote signature web API compliant to the CSC specification.

4.1   Architecture

The architecture of the solution (including the parts operated by the TSP) consists of the following components: SCA - Android Client Application, namely Cloud Signer (which also includes a component for signature integration in PDF files based on SecureBlackBox library), the SSA (Remote Signing Service), the SCDev (namely, an HSM), the Certificate Authority and the authorization component (OAuth2 server). Communication between the SCA and the SSA in realized over the Internet. Figure 1 offers an overview of how this solution works.

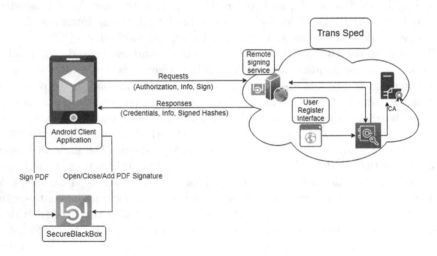

Fig. 1. Architecture of the remote signing solution

The SCA, written in Java and intended for the Android operating system, is an application for creating QES upon PDF documents through a remote signing service compliant with the CSC API exposed by the TSP (in our case Trans Sped). Communication between SCA and SSA is achieved by using asynchronous methods which transmit requests and receive responses from the server as JSON class objects. For integrating the raw digital signatures into the PDF documents, SecureBlackBox library was used.

4.2   Android Activities

The client application has a multi-window architecture. Within the Android operating system, these windows are called activities. Figure 2 highlights the main components of the application and the connections between them. Within the developed application the following activities are used:

○ **Open Activity** - Includes a login page to the SSA.
○ **Sign Activity** - Used by the user to actually perform a signature.
○ **Config Activity** - Allows users to set different parameters.
○ **View Signatures** - Allows authenticated users to view signatures applied on a document.
○ **View Document** - Displays the selected PDF document and navigates through its content.

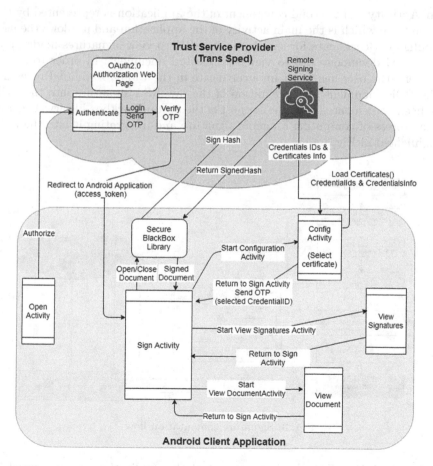

Fig. 2. Android activities

Open Activity. The first used component of the application is *Open Activity*. When the user selects a PDF document, a list of available applications associated with this type of documents is displayed, Cloud Signer included. In order to sign the given PDF document, the user chooses Cloud Signer. When opening the application, it will request for storage, Internet and SMS permissions, which are mandatory for the proper functioning of the application.

Open Activity also includes a component for client authorization to the SSA. The authorization is based on the OAuth2.0 protocol. After successful authentication to the OAuth2.0 server, the SCA obtains an authorization token that is further used for authorizing the access to the CSC API. After obtaining the authorization code, the user is redirected to the client application (through a redirect URI registered at the service provider). Any request to the SSA without using the access token will receive an access denied response.

Sign Activity. The second component of the application is represented by the *Sign Activity* which is the main activity of the application and it allows the user to configure a certificate for signing documents, to view signatures made upon the selected document and to view the selected document. In order to sign a document, the user has to set up a certificate in the *Config Activity*. Processing of the PDF document and integration of the raw RSA signature into the PDF have been implemented with the support of the SecureBlackbox library. The flow of the process of computing a remote signature and integrating it into the PDF is highlighted in Fig. 3.

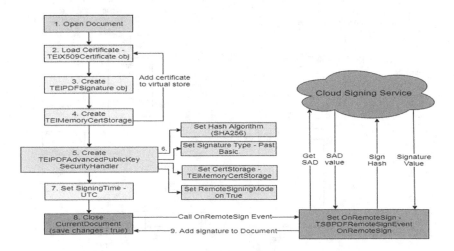

Fig. 3. Signature computation flow

Config Activity. The third component of the application is represented by the *Config Activity*, which allows the user to view a list with their own remote certificates. It also allows the user to select a certificate from that list in order to use it for signing the document with its corresponding private key. When opening the *Config Activity*, several operations are performed in the background, in order to populate the list of available user certificates (Fig. 4) from Annex A:

1. The authorization token is sent from the *Sign Activity* to the *Config Activity* via an object of the Intent class.
2. SCA calls *credentials/list* CSC method via *getCredentialIds*, which gets as input parameter the access token and returns the list of credential ids corresponding to the certificates of the user certificates.
3. For each credential id previously received, the SCA calls *credentials/info* CSC method which is the method used to obtain additional information about the credentials, such as the actual X.509 v3 certificate, data about supported algorithms, authentication mode and used SCAL level.

View Signatures. Another component is the *View Signatures* activity. This component is accessible only to authenticated users and only if the selected document has been previously signed or only after the user has signed the document. For each signature the user can see several details like: signature type, signer's full name, issuer of the signing certificate, serial number of the signing certificate, signing time, timestamp and validity.

View Document. The last component of the application is represented by the *View Document* activity, which uses PDFView to display the selected PDF document and navigates through its content.

4.3   Key Elements of the Implementation

This section presents the key elements of the implementation and the key aspects that one has to take into consideration when developing a client application for computing remote QES. The elements noticed are related to development, security and user experience:

1. **SecureBlackBox** - SCA has the responsibility to process the document to be signed in order obtain DTBSR and then to incorporate the received raw signature from the remote service. To accomplish this, SecureBlackBox library was used.
2. **OAuth 2.0 parameters** - SCA has to be registered in advance to the QTSP. Each application will have a different pair of client_id and client_secret parameters and a set of redirect_uris, as mentioned by the CSC API specification.
3. **Certificate validation** - SCA receives from SSA the list of certificates by using *credentials/list* and *credentials/info* CSC API methods. It is a good practice to check validity of the certificates and filter them accordingly. Remote signatures cannot be performed with expired or revoked certificates.

4. **Assuring SCAL2** - The main requirement for assuring SCAL2 is that the sole control over the signing key must be enforced by the SAM (see footnote 4). The SAD is obtained using the SIC and sent to the SAM via SAP (Signature Activation Protocol). Specifically, our application is performing 2 factor authentication using the SIM card, which is the actual materialization of the SIC.

5. **User experience** - Usability is very important when developing the user interface of an application. The following aspects were considered:

    o *Default certificate* - typically, users own only one credential or tend to use the same credential most of the times, therefore the ability to set a default certificate might prove to be very handy.
    o *OTP processing* - OTP is sent by SMS, therefore using a broadcast receiver could further improve user experience by automatically reading the OTP and then send it to the SSA. The annoying operation of switching between two Android applications is no longer needed.

5   Conclusions and Future Work

This paper presents the key points of the legislation and standards related to remote qualified electronic signatures and the learned lessons from the process of designing and implementing an Android digital signature application for creating remote qualified electronic signatures using CSC API service exposed by a qualified trust service provider. The implemented Android application uses the CSC API in order to obtain a QES from the SSA. Compared to the approach introduced by Theuermann et al. in [16], we decided to stick with the standard CSC protocol in order to achieve interoperability from one QTSP to another. One important advantage of the proposed solution consists in the fact that the remote QES is obtained by using a single mobile device. The paper also presents the main aspects to be taken into consideration when developing an eIDAS compliant application for computing remote qualified electronic signatures. For further research and development, we take into account the following: (1) implement the designed application for iOS devices too and (2) improving user experience by exploiting secure hardware mechanisms available on nowadays mobile devices and new authentication methods like fingerprints or face recognition would also contribute to a higher adoption rate of the remote QES.

Acknowledgment. This work was supported by a grant of the Romanian Ministry of Research and Innovation, CCCDI - UEFISCDI, project number PN-III-P1-1.2-PCCDI-2017-0272/Avant-garde Technology Hub for Advanced Security (ATLAS), within PNCDI III.

Annex A

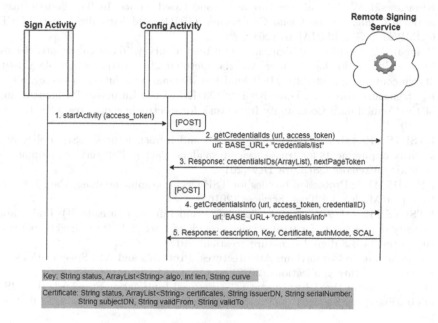

Fig. 4. Remote signing certificate retrieval

References

1. European Commission, Regulation (EU) No 910/2014 of the European Parliament and of the council on electronic identification and trust services for electronic transactions in the internal market and repealing Directive 1999/93/EC. Off. J. Eur. Union, July 2014. https://doi.org/10.1145/1219092.1219093
2. ETSI TS 119 432: Electronic Signatures and Infrastructures (ESI); Protocols for remote digital signature creation (2019)
3. CEN EN 419 241-1: Trustworthy Systems Supporting Server Signing Part 1: General System Security Requirements (2016)
4. CEN EN 419 241-2: Trustworthy Systems Supporting Server Signing. Part 2: Protection Profile for QSCD for Server Signing (2018)
5. Orthacker, C., Centner, M., Kittl, C.: Qualified mobile server signature. In: Rannenberg, K., Varadharajan, V., Weber, C. (eds.) SEC 2010. IAICT, vol. 330, pp. 103–111. Springer, Heidelberg (2010). https://doi.org/10.1007/978-3-642-15257-3_10
6. Rath, C., Roth, S., Bratko, H., Zefferer, T.: Encryption-based second authentication factor solutions for qualified server-side signature creation. In: Kő, A., Francesconi, E. (eds.) EGOVIS 2015. LNCS, vol. 9265, pp. 71–85. Springer, Cham (2015). https://doi.org/10.1007/978-3-319-22389-6_6

7. Rath, C., Roth, S., Schallar, M., Zefferer, T.: Design and application of a secure and flexible server-based mobile eID and e-Signature solution. Int. J. Adv. Secur **7**(3&4), 50–130 (2014)

8. Kinastowski, W.: Digital signature as a cloud-based service. In: The Fourth International Conference on Cloud Computing, GRIDs, and Virtualization (CLOUD COMPUTING 2013). IARIA (2013)

9. Reimair, F.: Cloud-based signature solutions: a survey. Technical report, Secure Information Technology Center Austria, October 2014. https://technology.a-sit.at/wp-content/uploads/2014/10/Cloud-based-signature-solutions-a-survey.pdf

10. EU Signature Directive: Directive 1999/93/EC of the European Parliament and of the Council on a Community framework for electronic signatures. Off. J. L 13 (1999)

11. ETSI TS 119 431–1: Electronic Signatures and Infrastructures (ESI); Policy and security requirements for trust service providers; Part 1: TSP service components operating a remote QSCD/SCDev (2018)

12. CEN 419241–5: Protection profiles for TSP Cryptographic modules. Part 5: Cryptographic Module for Trust Services (2016)

13. ETSI TS 119 431–2: Electronic Signatures and Infrastructures (ESI); Policy and security requirements for trust service providers; Part 2: TSP service components supporting AdES digital signature creation (2018)

14. Cloud Signature Consortium: Architectures, Protocols and API Specifications for Remote Signature applications (2017)

15. Organization for the Advancement of Structured Information Standards (OASIS): Digital Signature Service Core Protocols, Elements, and Bindings Version 1.0, April 2007

16. Theuermann, K., Tauber, A., Lenz, T.: Mobile-only solution for server-based qualified electronic signatures. In: 2019 IEEE International Conference on Communications (ICC 2019). IEEE (2019)

Integrating Adversary Models
and Intrusion Detection Systems
for In-vehicle Networks in CANoe

Camil Jichici[✉], Bogdan Groza, and Pal-Stefan Murvay

Faculty of Automatics and Computers,
Politehnica University of Timisoara, Timişoara, Romania
`jichicicamil93@gmail.com`
{`bogdan.groza,pal-stefan.murvay`}`@aut.upt.ro`

Abstract. In-vehicle buses and the Controller Area Network (CAN) in particular have been shown to be vulnerable to adversarial actions. We embed adversary models and intrusion detection systems (IDS) inside a CANoe based application. Based on real-world CAN traces collected from several vehicles we build attack traces that are subject to intrusion detection algorithms. We also take benefit from existing machine-learning support in MATLAB that is ported via C++ code in CANoe in order to integrate intrusion detection functionality. A unified framework for attacks and intrusion detection has the benefit of providing a testbed for various intrusion detection algorithms. CANoe integration makes the use of these functionalities ready for realistic testing as CANoe is an industry-standard tool in the automotive domain.

Keywords: CAN bus · Vehicle security · Intrusion detection

1 Introduction and Related Work

Contemporary vehicles incorporate dozens of Electronic Control Units (ECUs), sensor networks and actuators interconnected through in-vehicle networks such as: Local Interconnect Network (LIN), Controller Area Network (CAN), FlexRay, etc. Access to these in-vehicle networks is mediated by several interfaces, more commonly the On-Board Diagnostic (OBD) port which is used by our work as well (more details in a later section). However, the high complexity and connectivity of modern vehicles leads to cyber security risks which might undermine the privacy of the vehicle and endanger the life of passengers. This was well proved by a strong body of research in [3,13]. Recent advances regarding autonomous driving, enhanced technologies for infotainment systems and vehicle-to vehicle communications (V2V) will transform vehicles into devices that interact with each other over the Internet and can be remotely controlled. This trend opens even more attack surfaces that were well exploited by recent works [10,18].

© Springer Nature Switzerland AG 2020
E. Simion and R. Géraud-Stewart (Eds.): SecITC 2019, LNCS 12001, pp. 241–256, 2020.
https://doi.org/10.1007/978-3-030-41025-4_16

Most of the reported attacks on in-vehicle communication employ the CAN protocol. This is natural as CAN is the most widely used bus in the automotive domain and is often exposed through the diagnostic port. Details on the CAN bus topology, bit rates and the frame format are deferred to Appendix 1.

As vulnerabilities on the CAN bus are easy exploitable by adversaries, the development of intrusion detection systems (IDS) is an immediate necessity in order to quickly detect such attacks. A comprehensive survey on IDSs for in-vehicle buses can be found in [1]. The authors in [1] provide a hierarchical and structured picture of IDS proposed in the literature for passenger cars. There are many relevant proposals, we outline some of them next. Binary distance, i.e., Hamming distance, is proposed in [19]. Their approach includes two stages: a preliminary stage and a detection phase. In the first stage, for each CAN ID the authors calculate the Hamming distances between consecutive CAN frames on 20% of the trace and build message validity ranges bounded by the minimum and maximum distance computed for each ID. The rest of the frames (80% of the recorded trace) are used in the detection phase. An anomaly is detected when the Hamming distance is outside the validity range. In a similar vein, entropy has also been used to detect intrusions in [12] and [15]. Groza et al. proposed an IDSs based on Bloom filtering in [7]. Their detection mechanism filters the transmission frequency and the data field of the frames for each identifier in order to detect replay and modification attacks and takes advantage regarding low consumption of resources which are compulsory in deployment of a real-world IDS.

On the other hand, there are several machine learning and statistic based approaches for in-vehicle networks intrusion detection. Narayanan *et al.* create a Hidden Markov Model based on CAN data collected through the OBD port in order to detect intrusion on CAN bus in [16]. Their model describes vehicle states and possible transitions between them. The intrusion is detected when an unexpected transition occurs. Support vector machine and k-Nearest Neighbor (k-NN) classifier were proposed in [2]. The authors from [2] build a classifier model that is not able to detect replay attacks since they do not use the frequency of the messages in the training phase. In our work, we also use the periodicity of messages to enable identifying replay attacks since, in such attacks, the timestamp of the CAN messages is the single attack indicator. Another proposed approach [9] is the use of deep neural networks. The result of this work is not based on a real-world CAN traffic, instead the authors use CAN traffic generated by a software tool OCTANE [6]. The authors of [9] do not account for message transmission frequency in the training phase which leads to the inability to detect replay attacks. Decisions tree having as inputs entropy-based characteristics extracted from CAN IDs and timestamps were used in [21].

The idea of using CANoe (i.e. an industry-standard tool in the automotive domain), for evaluating security is not new and has been explored by previous works. Some of the first simulation-based attacks on the CAN [8] and FlexRay [17] examine vulnerabilities of simulated in-vehicle networks based on the CAN and FlexRay protocol respectively to spoofing and replay attacks.

We complement these ideas by integrating intrusion detection along with the adversarial model in CANoe. Thus, our work aims to provide a more complex framework based on the support from two widely-used tools in the automotive-industry, CANoe and Matlab, in order to simulate adversarial actions and detect them in real-world scenarios.

2 Data Collection and Experimental Setup

In this section we first discuss how data collection was performed and then how we use it in CANoe simulation.

2.1 Data Extraction from OBD

In order to develop an intrusion detection mechanism based on real-world CAN traces, we first collect data from the CAN bus via the OBD port of several cars. The OBD port aims to collect diagnostic data from all ECUs. Consequently, in most cases, it is connected directly to the main CAN bus of the vehicle. For enhancing the in-vehicle security, the OBD port should be directly connected only to an ECU gateway which then collects the diagnostic information from all other ECUs in order. In such case, only diagnostic messages corresponding to request-response protocol would be visible through the OBD port. However, in order to reduce costs, many vehicles do not have such a gateway ECU and the OBD port is connected to the main CAN bus. For the cars employed in our experiments we determined that in-vehicle traffic is indeed exposed over the OBD port.

As a first step, to enable data collection, we determined if there is any traffic exposed to the CAN pins of the OBD port and what is the employed bit rate. We achieved this with the help of an oscilloscope revealing that CAN traffic is indeed available and that one of the vehicles uses a baud rate of 250 Kbit/s while the other uses 500 Kbit/s. Then, we proceeded to logging the traffic from CAN bus for about 20 min with the car stationary and 20 min with the car in motion. During this interval, several driver-specific actions were performed, e.g., toggling low beam and long beam, sudden accelerations and brakes, etc. This was done for both the cars that we used, a sedan and an SUV.

Figure 1 depicts our experimental setup based on the Vector VN1630 USB-to-CAN interface, the OBD plug, the CAN cable and an application based on the Vector XL Driver Library running on the laptop. The VN1630 device is a part of the VN1600 family developed by Vector, a provider of solutions for auto-motive networking development. Support for the VN1630 exists in a number of software tools such as CANoe and CANape along with support for building dedicated applications through the XL Driver Library. The XL Driver Library is an Application Programming Interface (API) compatible with Vector's devices. The library provides access to device functionalities (e.g., message reception and transmission, various configuration settings) and handles interfacing with protocols such as CAN, CAN-FD, LIN, FlexRay, etc. An example of messages intercepted from the vehicle CAN bus (via the OBD port) with a small application using this library is shown in Fig. 2. Each message consists of the VN1630 channel number on which the message is received, the timestamp (in nanoseconds), the message identifier, the length (in bytes) of the data field and the actual data field. In our work, we run an application that only receives messages from the vehicles and did not try to inject frames in the car to avoid potential damage to the vehicle. Consequently, the injections will be performed in the CANoe simulation.

Fig. 1. Setup for data collection inside car

```
RX_MSG c=2, t=1548288, id=01A5 l=8, AFFF012000000080 tid=00
RX_MSG c=2, t=8593408, id=0161 l=5, 3225600010 tid=00
RX_MSG c=2, t=8790016, id=01F9 l=6, 201E18F4F8FF tid=00
RX_MSG c=2, t=9027584, id=0181 l=8, 18F4331032213F4E tid=00
RX_MSG c=2, t=10485760, id=0284 l=8, 0000000000000000 tid=00
RX_MSG c=2, t=10739712, id=0285 l=8, 0000000000000000 tid=00
RX_MSG c=2, t=12304384, id=01A5 l=8, BFFF012000000080 tid=00
RX_MSG c=2, t=18096128, id=0161 l=5, 3225600010 tid=00
RX_MSG c=2, t=18300928, id=01F9 l=6, 201E18F4F8FF tid=00
RX_MSG c=2, t=18530304, id=0181 l=8, 18F4331032213F4E tid=00
RX_MSG c=2, t=20520960, id=0244 l=7, FEFE00000000FE tid=00
RX_MSG c=2, t=21536768, id=01A5 l=8, CFFF012000000080 tid=00
RX_MSG c=2, t=28196864, id=0161 l=5, 3225600010 tid=00
RX_MSG c=2, t=28393472, id=01F9 l=6, 201E18F4F8FF tid=00
RX_MSG c=2, t=28622848, id=0181 l=8, 18F4331032213F4E tid=00
RX_MSG c=2, t=30498816, id=0284 l=8, 0000000000000000 tid=00
RX_MSG c=2, t=30752768, id=0285 l=8, 0000000000000000 tid=00
RX_MSG c=2, t=32309248, id=01A5 l=8, DFFF012000000080 tid=00
RX_MSG c=2, t=38305792, id=0161 l=5, 3225600010 tid=00
RX_MSG c=2, t=38535168, id=0551 l=8, 776D6488FF7A0070 tid=00
RX_MSG c=2, t=38731776, id=01F9 l=6, 201E18F4F8FF tid=00
RX_MSG c=2, t=38961152, id=0181 l=8, 18F4331032213F4E tid=00
RX_MSG c=2, t=39198720, id=0511 l=7, 0000000000000000 tid=00
```

Fig. 2. Recorded CAN messages

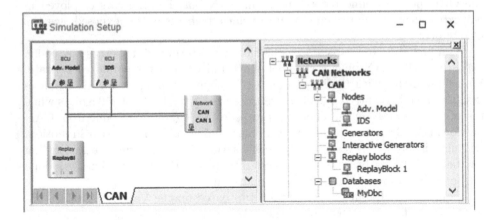

Fig. 3. CAN network architecture

2.2   CANoe Environment

We integrate the attacker model and intrusion detection capabilities in a CANoe simulation. CANoe is an unified integrated software used for designing, simulating, testing and analyzing real-time communication between ECUs. In the automotive domain, CANoe is the most wide-spread tool used by automotive manufacturers in the development process of in-vehicle networks.

CANoe provides us with all the building blocks for simulating and detecting real-world attacks on the CAN bus. The designed CAN analysis network from CANoe is depicted in Fig. 3. This structure includes three blocks: a *replay node*, an *adversary model node* and the *IDS node*. The real traffic recorded from the vehicles is replayed in the simulation through a specialized type of node called a Replay block. For on-line attacks and analysis of vehicle traffic, the replay block can be simply disabled while connecting the CANoe simulated bus to the in-vehicle bus through a VN interfacing device. The adversary model node is implemented as a CAPL (CAN Application Programming Language) network node that mimics the behaviour of a real-world adversary. CAPL is a C-based language and provides additional CANoe specific functionalities, e.g., events, system variables, message structures and message databases. Finally, the overall traffic will be evaluated by an IDS node that is also programmed through CAPL.

3 Adversary Models

In this section we discuss the adversarial model that we account for and give a brief overview of its integration in CANoe.

3.1 Types of Attacks

In general, adversary models are based on the Dolev-Yao adversary which has full control over the network [5]. That is, the adversary can record, block, replay, modify or inject messages in the network. If any security mechanisms are in place, they are considered to be secure and the adversary can manipulate them only if he has the corresponding keys. In our work, we do not address security mechanisms since these are generally absent on the CAN traffic that we recorded and even if they are present we would not have access to manufacturer specifications (e.g., in case of authentication protocols over the CAN bus) since these are in general considered confidential information.

Our adversary has access to the entire traffic that was logged inside the vehicle. Based on existing literature on adversarial models for the CAN bus, our work considers the following types of attacks which we also integrate in the CANoe application:

1. **Replay of regular CAN frames** is the attack in which the adversary intercepts genuine frames and then replays them on the CAN bus. In this case the malicious frames are identical to genuine frames having the same identifier and data field. The only indicator for this type of attack is the frequency of the CAN messages (i.e., more frames with the same ID will be visible on the bus). The identifier of the attacked frame and the delay at which the attack frame is sent can be configured from the interface. The replay attacks can increase the busload which delays other frames or even aborts their transmission.

2. **Injection attacks** which consist in the insertion of adversarial frames on the bus and which we refine across the following lines:

   - **Injection of random data**, also referred in other works as fuzzy attacks [11], is an attack in which the adversary intercepts genuine frames and then injects the malicious frames on the CAN bus at a chosen delay after interception. The malicious frames have the same identifier as a genuine frame, but the data field is randomly generated. The delay is the time measured from the interception of the genuine frame event to triggering injection event of the attack frame. As in the previously described attack, our graphical user interface (GUI) allows for selecting the identifier of the targeted message. The transmission delay can be configured within 1 µs increments.

   - **Injection with scalar addition/multiplication of the datafield** - the data retrieved from in-vehicle sensors, e.g., speed sensor, engine temperature, steering angle, fuel pressure, brake pressure, are transmitted by network nodes via the CAN bus. Since sensors may have a linear transfer function, the slope of the function is a constant. This leads to attacks in which bytes of the CAN frames are incremented or multiplied by some constant values. Delays to the injected frames can be added as well.

   - **Arbitrary injections** is the case in which the adversary can inject frames at will with the specified data or randomly generated data field and ID. In contrast to the previously defined attacks, the transmission of the injected frame will be done cyclically according to the configured cycle time.

Other attacks have been also considered in the literature but are not included in our interface. In what follows, we explain why, at least for the moment, we did not considered them.

DoS attacks are trivial to mount on the CAN bus. Since the CAN ID is used in the arbitration mechanism to provide collision avoidance, continuously injecting messages with the highest priority ID, i.e., 0x000, leads to unavailability of the bus and the genuine frames are unable to transmit due to the loaded bus. However, detecting such an attack in which the ID 0x000 is sent in order to lock the bus would be trivial. For this, one can simply look for the consecutive occurrence of messages with this ID which does not show up in regular traces. A more sophisticated variant would be to send a low priority ID which is not null, but still has higher priority than regular IDs. This again can be detected trivially since the values of the genuine IDs are known by the manufacturer. Such attacks are accessible from the interface that we designed as *arbitrary injections* which allows to edit both the ID and data field but we do not view them separately as DoS attacks (which may be a consequence). The attack can be detected by the IDS, but the problem still remains since such attacks cannot be circumvented as high-priority IDs will win the bus anyway.

Bus off attacks are the adversarial action after which genuine nodes are placed in bus-off state. This can be done due to the error management system of CAN and such attacks are proved to be feasible by the works in [4] and [14]. Modeling such attacks may be of interest but our network is simulated based on

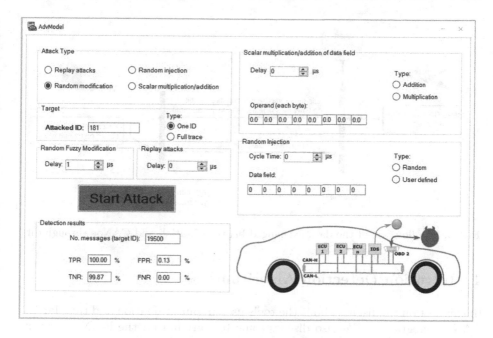

Fig. 4. Graphical interface for the designed application

existing traces and we don't have the specific behavior of the ECU implemented in the model. Moreover, such attacks can be circumvented only by modifying the error-handling mechanisms of CAN which is out of scope for the current work.

3.2 Application Interface

The application interface implemented in CANoe for allowing the configuration of the adversary node and IDS node is shown in Fig. 4. We employ common controls, e.g., radio buttons, combo box, to provide an user friendly interface. The relationship between the graphical interface and CAPL is made through system variables since they can be retrieved by specific CAPL functions and events. Consequently, our adversary model has the benefit of providing various types of attacks and can perform the following actions: read, modify and replay messages. In the first step, the user must select the type of attack that will be used. Another option allows the user to select if the attack should target a single specified ID or all messages in the trace. For each type of attack, specific parameters can be configured. On the other hand, during the simulation run, the detection algorithm is running on the IDS node to classify frames. The indicator led will switch to either green or red depending on genuine or malicious received frame. Moreover, at the end of the simulation the results of the detection rates and the number of the targeted messages are presented.

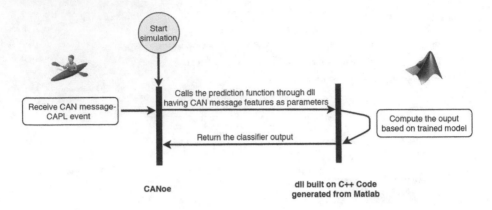

Fig. 5. The flowcart of the data exchanged between Matlab and CANoe through dll

4   Intrusion Detection Algorithms

In this section we discuss about the tools used in our evaluation and the Matlab-CANoe integration. We also discuss some background on the k-NN algorithm which we use for intrusion detection.

4.1   Statistics and Machine Learning Toolbox

For implementing the intrusion detection mechanism we employ Matlab, namely, the *statistics and machine learning toolbox* made available by the framework. This toolbox provides a range of machine learning algorithms for solving regression or classification problems. These algorithms are based on either supervised or unsupervised learning and we choose k-NN since it is a commonly employed solution when little is known about the input data. Indeed, in our case the data comes from traces that were logged inside vehicles and we don't have any access to the manufacturer's requirements. Consequently, there is no prior knowledge on the data, but we can label the malicious CAN frames that we inject for the training trace. In the training phase, the supervised learning (employed also by the k-NN algorithm) has as observation samples, a collection of n pairs $\{(i_0, o_0), (i_1, o_1), \ldots (i_{n-1}, o_{n-1})\}$, which consists of the inputs and the desired outputs. The output of the training phase is a model (a trained function) responsible for predictions over new data that will be given in the test phase.

We also took advantage of Matlab's capability to generate C/C++ code with the trained model and prediction function. We build a dynamic library (dll) based on this code and integrate the functionality in CANoe through CAPL code. The integration of a custom library into CANoe provides the advantage of accessing system resources, e.g, CPU, memory [22], which are otherwise not directly available in CANoe. Figure 5 illustrates the interaction between CANoe and the Matlab-based library for analyzing CAN messages.

4.2 k-NN Algorithm

We use the k-NN algorithm as a basis for our evaluation. This algorithm is commonly employed in classification problems and even in network IDS [20]. The k-NN uses a distance metric, e.g., the Euclidean, Hamming, Minkowski, Jaccard distances, etc. For most of our analysis we choose the Euclidean distance but it is easy to switch to any of the previously mentioned.

In general, a machine-learning algorithm has two stages: the training stage and the testing stage. Consequently, we split the CAN trace into a training and a testing part. In our experiments, the first stage is performed offline with the purpose of training the classifier based on inputs-output pairs. In this stage, each input is mapped to the true class c (genuine or malicious frame). The end of this stage outputs the k-NN model. The second stage is the real-time detection based on the trained model. In this stage, each input is mapped to the predicted class $\hat{c}$ based on the decision rule. The decision rule depends on the number of neighbors k as follows:

1. Decision rule when $k = 1$: let m_t be a test frame and m_i a training frame, then m_n is nearest neighbor to m_t if and only if the Euclidean distance: $d_e(m_t, m_n) = min_i\{d_e(m_t, m_i)\}$, where i covers the range of training frames. The predicted response of $\hat{c}$ from the trained model will be equal with the true class c of the m_i which has the minimum Euclidean distance to m_t.
2. Decision rule when $k > 1$: The predicted response $\hat{c}$ of the m_t from the trained model will be equal with the most encountered c, through the k nearest training messages.

The k-NN input observation is a vector that accounts for the data field and the delay between consecutive timestamps of the same ID. In such case, the input sample $I \in \{0,1\}^9$ is described mathematically as follows: $I = \{i_0, i_1, i_2, ..., i_8\}$, where i_0 represents the delay and $i_1...i_8$ represent each byte from the data field. We choose an odd number of neighbors (e.g. 1, 3, 15) in order to avoid an equal number of votes and select a majority.

5 Experimental Results

We first discuss the metrics employed for evaluating the intrusion detection algorithms, then we proceed to presenting the experimental results.

5.1 Metrics for Evaluating the Performance of the IDS

Since our evaluation performs a binary classification of the CAN frames, we measure the performance of the IDS based on the most commonly four metrics:

1. the sensitivity or the true positive rate - measures the percentage of the CAN frames that are correctly classified as malicious, i.e., $TPR = TP/(TP+FN)$.

2. the false negative rate- measures the percentage of the CAN frames that are reported as genuine frames but are actually malicious frames, i.e., $FNR = FN/(FN + TP)$.
3. the specificity or the true negative rate - measures the percentage of the CAN frames that are correctly classified as genuine, i.e., $TNR = TN/(TN + FP)$.
4. fall-out or the false positive rate - measures the percentage of the CAN frames that are reported as malicious, but the true class of the frames is genuine, i.e., $FPR = FP/(FP + TN)$.

Table 1. Detection rates for various types of attacks

No.	Att. type	Operand	Delay ms	training	testing	No. neigh.	Distance	TNR	TPR	FPR	FNR
1.	r	n/a	9.750	500	19500	1	Euclidean	99.00%	99.65%	1.00%	0.35%
2.	r	n/a	0.001	500	19500	1	Euclidean	100%	100%	0%	0%
3.	r	n/a	0.001	500	19500	1	Euclidean	88.86%	100%	11.14%	0%
4.	r	n/a	5	500	19500	1	Euclidean	88.88%	100%	11.12%	0%
5.	r	n/a	9	500	19500	1	Euclidean	90.33%	83.47%	9.67%	16.53%
6.	r	n/a	9.750	500	19500	1	Euclidean	87.98%	51.88%	12.02%	48.12%
7.	r	n/a	50	500	19500	1	Euclidean	88.31%	84.66%	11.69%	15.34%
8.	ir	n/a	0.001	500	19500	1	Euclidean	99.87%	100%	0.13%	0%
9.	ir	n/a	9.750	500	19500	1	Euclidean	99.87%	100%	0.13%	0%
10.	isa	$\alpha = 2$	0.001	500	19500	1	Euclidean	89.63%	100%	10.37%	0%
11.	isa	$\alpha = 2$	9.750	500	19500	1	Euclidean	91.34%	53.98%	8.66%	46.02%
12.	ism	$\alpha = 2$	0.001	500	19500	1	Euclidean	89.65%	100%	10.35%	0%
13.	ism	$\alpha = 2$	9.750	500	19500	1	Euclidean	91.38%	67.74%	8.62%	32.26%
14.	isa	$\alpha = 2$	9.750	500	19500	1	$E(\Delta t)$, H(data)	90.72%	100%	9.28%	0%
15.	ism	$\alpha = 2$	9.750	500	19500	1	$E(\Delta t)$, H(data)	90.75%	85.87%	9.25%	14.13%
16.	r	n/a	0.001	5000	45000	1	Euclidean	95.21%	100%	4.79%	0%
17.	r	n/a	5	5000	45000	1	Euclidean	95.45%	100%	4.55%	0%
18.	r	n/a	9.750	5000	45000	1	Euclidean	95.23%	66.58%	4.77%	33.42%
19.	r	n/a	$\{9.75, 19.75, 39.75, 99.75\}$	5000	45000	1	Euclidean	94.76%	50.06%	5.24%	49.94%
20.	ir	n/a	0.001	5000	45000	1	Euclidean	99.53%	100%	0.47%	0%
21.	ir	n/a	5	5000	45000	1	Euclidean	99.40%	100%	0.6%	0%
22.	ir	n/a	9.750	5000	45000	1	Euclidean	99.57%	91.52%	0.43%	8.48%

5.2 Results on Detection Accuracy

We devise our experiments to cover the previously defined adversarial models. For each type of attack, we have different scenarios depending on the delay of the attack frame. Multiplication or addition coefficients may be also applied to the data field. Since the traces we obtained from vehicles that did not contain extended frames, we experiment only with standard frames. We build our datasets using the CANoe simulation by injecting malicious frames on a single targeted CAN ID or over the full trace, i.e., all CAN IDs. The results obtained for detecting attacks on a single CAN ID are based on portions of traces containing 500 frames used for training and 19500 frames for the actual tests. We choose only a small percent for training to cover the more realistic scenario where the IDS is trained for a limited time, e.g., during production, and then runs for a longer period. In the current experiments (on a single CAN ID) we have only attacked frames that have a cycle time of 10 ms since this is a very common periodicity, but similar results will be likely obtained for other delays. For the full trace attacks we employ 5000 training frames and 45000 test frames.

We now discuss the results on replay attacks which are presented in Table 1. Extended results for this scenario are deferred to Table 2 from Appendix 2. In this case the training phase was performed on traces that contain regular frames and replay attack frames sent at a 9.750 ms (row 1 from Table 1, rows 1–2 from Table 2) and 0.001 ms (row 2 from Table 1, rows 3–4 from Table 2) delay after the genuine frame. The first delay is chosen specifically for the attack frame to arrive just before the genuine frame on the bus (the genuine frame will arrive periodically at 10 ms and ≈250 μs is the physical time of the frame on the bus) while the second is to assure that the attack frame arrives immediately after the genuine frame. We use both the content of the datafield and the delay between consecutive timestamps of the targeted CAN ID (Δt) as inputs for the training phase. The detection rates were 100% in case of 0.001 ms delay and around 99% in case of 9.750 ms while the false positive rate is 0% in the first scenario and around 1% in the second. There is a slight increase of false positive rate in the first scenario since in case of the 9.750 ms delay, the injected frames are sent very close to the transmission time of genuine frames. Consequently, in some cases the legit frame is mismatched for the attack frame. The good detection result is also due to the less realistic assumption that an attacker will send all its frames with the fixed delay that was used in the training phase.

Thus the next step in our evaluation, was to train the classifier based on one delay, i.e., 9.750 ms while the evaluation frames were built with other delay, i.e., 9 ms. As expected, the detection rate drops under 20%. Consequently, to overcome this problem, we chose to train the classifier based on traces built with replay injections at a random delay covering the whole range between 0 and the cycle time of the frame, since the IDS must be able to detect attacks frames sent with any delay. All the results that follow are based on such randomized delays. We present the results for this scenario in Table 1 (rows 3–7) and their extension is deferred to Table 2 (rows 5–14) from Appendix 2. In case of 0.001 ms and 5 ms delays, the true positive rate is close to 100% while the false positive rate is around 10%. The false positive rates are caused by the identical data field of regular and injected frames.

In the next two attack scenarios (rows 5–6 from Table 1, rows 9–12 from Table 2) the adversarial actions are more refined and well thought out. These actions are designed so that the injected message is sent on the bus shortly before, i.e., 9 ms delay, or even close enough to overlap with the genuine message in some cases, i.e., 9.750 ms delay. The detection rate degrades to the point that the TPR drops to below 80% for the first case and around 50% for the second. What can also be observed, from the majority of the results, is that with the growth in the number of neighbors comes a slight increase in specificity and a decrease in sensitivity, which is sometimes more pronounced, i.e., from 83% (row 5 from Table 1) to 52% (row 9 from Table 2).

The results obtained on injections with random data are shown in Table 1 (rows 8–9) while the extension of the results is presented in Table 2 (rows 15–18) from Appendix 2. In this case we obtained detection rates close to 100% percents for both of the tested delay scenarios. We also observe a negligible amount of false positives. The high detection rate is justified by the high entropy of the injected frames data field that differs from the authentic messages. In general, this type of attacks is much easier to detect than replay attacks.

As expected, results for injection attacks using scalar addition or multiplication, presented in Table 1 (rows 10–15) and the extension in Table 2 from Appendix 2 (rows 19–30), exhibit a lower detection rate especially as we used a very low value for the scalar (thus modifications of the datafield are small). At a first view, the results are very similar to those obtained for replay attacks for the same delays: 0.001 ms (row 3 from Table 1 and rows 5–6 from Table 2) and 9.750 ms (row 6 from Table 1 and rows 11–12 from Table 2). This can be explained by the message periodicity having a greater influence on the result of the prediction function than the data field. This happens since the operation of adding $\alpha = 2$ to each byte of the data field does not have a considerable effect on the Euclidean distance. We chose $\alpha = 2$ to assure only a small change in the message (obviously, a larger α will lead to more modifications and will be easier to detect). In case of scalar multiplication the detection rate increases to around 67% (row 13 from the Table 1) since the operation of scalar multiplication with $\alpha = 2$ has a greater impact on the resulting Euclidean distance.

A better approach to improve the detection results, is the use of two trained models: the first trained with Δt based on the Euclidean distance and the second trained based on the data field using the Hamming distance. In this case, each model classifier predicts a class for each message. Denoting the predicted class for the first model as $\hat{c}_1$ and the second one as $\hat{c}_2$, the final predicted class $\hat{c}$ is : $\hat{c} \in \hat{c}_1 \vee \hat{c}_2$. This approach improves the sensitivity to 100% in case of scalar addition and at 85% in case of multiplication while the false positive rate remains around the 10% level as can be seen in Table 1 (rows 14–15). By E(Δt) and H(data) we denote the Euclidean and Hamming distances on the delay and data respectively.

The next step in improving detection capabilities consists in covering the full trace since monitoring a single ID would involve one trained model for each CAN ID and leads to the need for large computational/memory resources which may not be available. The full trace contains frames having 10 ms, 20 ms, 40 ms, and 100 ms cycle times. The full attack trace was build as following. We define the attack probability for each frame as a constant $P_r(A)$. A variable $\epsilon \in [0, 100]$ is randomly generated and if ϵ is less than or equal to $P_r(A)$, then the frame is attacked otherwise it is left unaltered. For our experiments we configured $P_r(A) = 30$. Therefore, the input in our classifier accounts for the CAN ID before the Δt and data field.

The results over the full trace for replay attacks, are presented in Table 1 (rows 16–19), Table 2 from Appendix 2 (rows 31–38), and rows 20–22 from Table 1, rows 39–44 from Table 2, for fuzzy attacks. Even if for an extended evaluation, with a single trained model, the results remain satisfactory. In case of replay attacks, the detection rates are similar (for 0.001 ms and 5 ms delays) or even better (for 9.750 ms delays) than those obtained for a single ID. This happens since the attack frame that has 9.750 ms delay is sent on the bus ahead or even overlaps with the authentic frame just in case of 10 ms cycle, while the full trace contains more cycle times values for which the attack frame is even more conspicuous. A cleverer adversary may of course choose delays that are closer to the cycle time of each frame. This scenario is presented in the row 18 of Table 1 and rows 37–38 of Table 2. The detection rate is approximately two percents lower than monitoring for a single ID in case of the directed replay attacks (around 50%). For random attacks, the sensitivity is most of the part close to 100%, except for the 9.750 ms delay, where it drops to around to 90% in case of using one neighbor and to 60% when more neighbors are employed.

6   Conclusion

Our work explores the integration of adversary models and intrusion detection systems in CANoe. Since adversarial actions are modeled over real-world in-vehicle traces, the results offer a more realistic testbed for in-vehicle network attacks. As future work it would be of interest to allocate specific parts of the traffic to a particular ECU which would allow targeted attacks toward specific ECUs. A complete simulation for the behavior of each ECU is a more complex goal but perhaps achievable in the future. Adversarial actions are easier to test inside a simulation environment and the risk for damaging the actual car is removed. Adding MATLAB functionalities for machine-learning in order to classify CAN packets is a convenient way for designing and testing such an IDS due to the rich machine learning toolset offered by MATLAB. Adding other algorithms for intrusion detection is an immediate goal for extending our framework.

Acknowledgement. This work was supported by a grant of the Romanian Ministry of Research and Innovation, CNCS - UEFISCDI, project number PN-III-P1-1.1-PD-2016-1198, within PNCDI III.

Appendix 1 - Brief Description of the CAN bus

CAN provides bit rates of up to 125 kbit/s for low-speed CAN and up to 1 Mbit/s on high-speed CAN while carrying up to 8 bytes of payload. Increased communication speeds and payloads of up to 64 bytes are possible by using the CAN-FD (CAN- Flexible Data) protocol extension.

At the physical layer, CAN is implemented as a two wire (CAN-high and CAN-low) differential bus. A common CAN network topology is shown in Fig. 6(a). The main communication element used by CAN is the data frame with a structure as presented in Fig. 6(b). The data frame is received by all ECUs but it is only used by ECUs interested in its content for processing purposes. This frame filtering is usually done based on the CAN ID (identifier). The ID also serves for assuring packet arbitration as part of the collision avoidance mechanism which gives higher priority to frames with lower ID values in the case two frames are simultaneously transmitted. The CAN ID can be either 11 bits long (in standard frames), or 29 bits (in extended format).

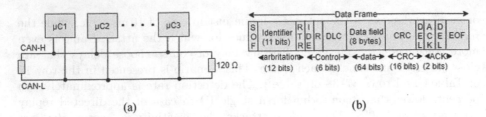

Fig. 6. CAN network topology (a) and data frame format (b)

Appendix 2 - Results for Various Number of Neighbors over a Single ID and over Full Trace

Table 2. Detection rates for various types of attacks (k-NN with 3 or 15 neighbors)

		Attack params.		No. messages		k-NN Parameters		Detection rates			
No.	Att. type	Operand	Delay ms	training	testing	No. neigh.	Distance	TNR	TPR	FPR	FNR
1.	r	n/a	9.750	500	19500	3	Euclidean	98.55%	99.31%	1.45%	0.69%
2.	r	n/a	9.750	500	19500	15	Euclidean	97.55%	97.83%	2.45%	2.17%
3.	r	n/a	0.001	500	19500	3	Euclidean	100%	100%	0%	0%
4.	r	n/a	0.001	500	19500	15	Euclidean	100%	100%	0%	0%
5.	r	n/a	0.001	500	19500	3	Euclidean	90.02%	100%	9.98%	0%
6.	r	n/a	0.001	500	19500	15	Euclidean	91.32%	100%	8.68%	0%
7.	r	n/a	5	500	19500	3	Euclidean	89.99%	100%	10.01%	0%
8.	r	n/a	5	500	19500	15	Euclidean	91.30%	100%	8.70%	0%
9.	r	n/a	9	500	19500	3	Euclidean	91.61%	52.53%	8.39%	47.47%
10.	r	n/a	9	500	19500	15	Euclidean	91.33%	31.11%	8.67%	68.89%
11.	r	n/a	9.750	500	19500	3	Euclidean	89.33%	50.67%	10.67%	49.33%
12.	r	n/a	9.750	500	19500	15	Euclidean	91.26%	50.67%	8.74%	49.33%
13.	r	n/a	50	500	19500	3	Euclidean	89.96%	83.75%	10.04%	16.25%
14.	r	n/a	50	500	19500	15	Euclidean	91.40%	83.75%	8.60%	16.25%
15.	ir	n/a	0.001	500	19500	3	Euclidean	99.70%	100%	0.30%	0%
16.	ir	n/a	0.001	500	19500	15	Euclidean	98.63%	100%	1.37%	0%
17.	ir	n/a	9.750	500	19500	3	Euclidean	99.70%	100%	0.30%	0%
18.	ir	n/a	9.750	500	19500	15	Euclidean	98.63%	100%	1.37%	0%
19.	isa	$\alpha = 2$	0.001	500	19500	3	Euclidean	91.37%	100%	8.63%	0%
20.	isa	$\alpha = 2$	0.001	500	19500	15	Euclidean	91.13%	100%	8.87%	0%
21.	isa	$\alpha = 2$	9.750	500	19500	3	Euclidean	92.15%	51.01%	7.85%	48.99%
22.	isa	$\alpha = 2$	9.750	500	19500	15	Euclidean	91.09%	50.40%	8.91%	46.60%
23.	ism	$\alpha = 2$	0.001	500	19500	3	Euclidean	91.39%	100%	8.61%	0%
24.	ism	$\alpha = 2$	0.001	500	19500	15	Euclidean	91.12%	100%	8.88%	0%
25.	ism	$\alpha = 2$	9.750	500	19500	3	Euclidean	92.16%	60.70%	7.84%	39.30%
26.	ism	$\alpha = 2$	9.750	500	19500	15	Euclidean	91.11%	50.59%	8.89%	49.41%
27.	isa	$\alpha = 2$	9.750	500	19500	3	$E(\Delta t)$, H(data)	91.07%	100%	8.93%	0%
28.	isa	$\alpha = 2$	9.750	500	19500	15	$E(\Delta t)$, H(data)	91.06%	100%	8.94%	0%
29.	ism	$\alpha = 2$	9.750	500	19500	3	$E(\Delta t)$, H(data)	91.06%	85.52%	8.94%	14.48%
30.	ism	$\alpha = 2$	9.750	500	19500	15	$E(\Delta t)$, H(data)	91.09%	85.17%	8.91%	14.83%
31.	r	n/a	0.001	5000	45000	3	Euclidean	96.74%	100%	3.26%	0%
32.	r	n/a	0.001	5000	45000	15	Euclidean	98.77%	100%	1.23%	0%
33.	r	n/a	5	5000	45000	3	Euclidean	96.75%	100%	3.25%	0%
34.	r	n/a	5	5000	45000	15	Euclidean	98.70%	100%	1.30%	0%
35.	r	n/a	9.750	5000	45000	3	Euclidean	96.79%	65.33%	3.21%	34.67%
36.	r	n/a	9.750	5000	45000	15	Euclidean	98.83%	35.95%	1.17%	64.05%
37.	r	n/a	{9.75, 19.75, 39.75, 99.75}	5000	45000	3	Euclidean	96.40%	48.94%	3.60%	51.06%
38.	r	n/a	{9.75, 19.75, 39.75, 99.75}	5000	45000	15	Euclidean	98.68%	47.41%	1.32%	52.59%
39.	ir	n/a	0.001	5000	45000	3	Euclidean	99.47%	100%	0.53%	0%
40.	ir	n/a	0.001	5000	45000	15	Euclidean	99.57%	100%	0.43%	0%
41.	ir	n/a	5	5000	45000	3	Euclidean	99.31%	100%	0.69%	0%
42.	ir	n/a	5	5000	45000	15	Euclidean	99.49%	100%	0.51%	0%
43.	ir	n/a	9.750	5000	45000	3	Euclidean	99.53%	86.46%	0.47%	13.54%
44.	ir	n/a	9.750	5000	45000	15	Euclidean	99.63%	60.97%	0.37%	39.03%

References

1. Al-Jarrah, O.Y., Maple, C., Dianati, M., Oxtoby, D., Mouzakitis, A.: Intrusion detection systems for intra-vehicle networks: a review. IEEE Access **7**, 21266–21289 (2019)
2. Alshammari, A., Zohdy, M.A., Debnath, D., Corser, G.: Classification approach for intrusion detection in vehicle systems. Wirel. Eng. Technol. **9**(4), 79–94 (2018)
3. Checkoway, S., et al.: Comprehensive experimental analyses of automotive attack surfaces. In: USENIX Security Symposium, vol. 4, pp. 447–462, San Francisco (2011)
4. Cho, K.-T., Shin, K.G.: Error handling of in-vehicle networks makes them vulnerable. In: Proceedings of the 2016 ACM SIGSAC Conference on Computer and Communications Security, pp. 1044–1055. ACM (2016)
5. Dolev, D., Yao, A.: On the security of public key protocols. IEEE Trans. Inf. Theory **29**(2), 198–208 (1983)
6. Everett, C.E., McCoy, D.: {OCTANE} (open car testbed and network experiments): bringing cyber-physical security research to researchers and students. Presented as Part of the 6th Workshop on Cyber Security Experimentation and Test (2013)
7. Groza, B., Murvay, P.-S.: Efficient intrusion detection with bloom filtering in controller area networks. IEEE Trans. Inf. Forensics Secur. **14**(4), 1037–1051 (2019)
8. Hoppe, T., Kiltz, S., Dittmann, J.: Security threats to automotive CAN networks-practical examples and selected short-term countermeasures. Reliab. Eng. Syst. Saf. **96**(1), 11–25 (2011)
9. Kang, M.-J., Kang, J.-W.: Intrusion detection system using deep neural network for in-vehicle network security. PloS One **11**(6), e0155781 (2016)
10. Kleberger, P., Olovsson, T., Jonsson, E.: Security aspects of the in-vehicle network in the connected car. In: 2011 IEEE Intelligent Vehicles Symposium (IV), pp. 528–533. IEEE (2011)
11. Lee, H., Jeong, S.H., Kim, H.K.: OTIDS: a novel intrusion detection system for in-vehicle network by using remote frame. In: 2017 Privacy, Security and Trust (PST) (2017)
12. Marchetti, M., Stabili, D., Guido, A., Colajanni, M.: Evaluation of anomaly detection for in-vehicle networks through information-theoretic algorithms. In: Research and Technologies for Society and Industry Leveraging a Better Tomorrow (RTSI), pp. 1–6. IEEE (2016)
13. Miller, C., Valasek, C.: Adventures in automotive networks and control units. Def. Con. **21**, 260–264 (2013)
14. Murvay, P.-S., Groza, B.: DoS attacks on controller area networks by fault injections from the software layer. In: Proceedings of the 12th International Conference on Availability, Reliability and Security, ARES 2017, pp. 71:1–71:10 (2017)
15. Müter, M., Asaj, N.: Entropy-based anomaly detection for in-vehicle networks. In: 2011 IEEE Intelligent Vehicles Symposium (IV), pp. 1110–1115. IEEE (2011)
16. Narayanan, S.N., Mittal, S., Joshi, A.: OBD_SecureAlert: an anomaly detection system for vehicles. In: 2016 IEEE International Conference on Smart Computing (SMARTCOMP), pp. 1–6. IEEE (2016)
17. Nilsson, D.K., Larson, U.E., Picasso, F., Jonsson, E.: A first simulation of attacks in the automotive network communications protocol FlexRay. In: Proceedings of the International Workshop on Computational Intelligence in Security for Information

Systems, CISIS 2008, pp. 84–91. Springer (2009). https://doi.org/10.1007/978-3-540-88181-0_11

18. Petit, J., Shladover, S.E.: Potential cyberattacks on automated vehicles. IEEE Trans. Intell. Transp. Syst. **16**(2), 546–556 (2014)
19. Stabili, D., Marchetti, M., Colajanni, M.: Detecting attacks to internal vehicle networks through Hamming distance. In: 2017 AEIT International Annual Conference, pp. 1–6. IEEE (2017)
20. Su, M.-Y.: Real-time anomaly detection systems for denial-of-service attacks by weighted k-nearest-neighbor classifiers. Expert Syst. Appl. **38**(4), 3492–3498 (2011)
21. Tian, D., et al.: An intrusion detection system based on machine learning for CAN-bus. In: Chen, Y., Duong, T.Q. (eds.) INISCOM 2017. LNICST, vol. 221, pp. 285–294. Springer, Cham (2018). https://doi.org/10.1007/978-3-319-74176-5_25
22. Vector: CAPL DLL Description (2007)

Author Index

Printed in the United States
By Bookmasters